# An Advocacy Primer

## 4th Edition

D1273928

Lee Stuesser

B.A. (Hons.), B.Ed., M.A., LL.B., LL.M.

**CARSWELL**®

© 2015 Thomson Canada Limited

NOTICE AND DISCLAIMER: All rights reserved. No part of this publication may be reproduced, stored in a retrieval system, or transmitted, in any form or by any means, electronic, mechanical, photocopying, recording or otherwise, without prior written consent of the publisher (Carswell).

Carswell and all persons involved in the preparation and sale of this publication disclaim any warranty as to accuracy or currency of the publication. This publication is provided on the understanding and basis that none of Carswell, the author/s or other persons involved in the creation of this publication shall be responsible for the accuracy or currency of the contents, or for the results of any action taken on the basis of the information contained in this publication, or for any errors or omissions contained herein.

No one involved in this publication is attempting herein to render legal, accounting or other professional advice. If legal advice or other expert assistance is required, the services of a competent professional should be sought. The analysis contained herein should in no way be construed as being either official or unofficial policy of any governmental body.

**A cataloguing record for this publication is available from Library and Archives Canada.**

ISBN 978-0-7798-6716-5

Composition: Computer Composition of Canada

Printed in Canada by Thomson Reuters.

**TELL US HOW WE'RE DOING**
Scan the QR code to the right with your smartphone to send your comments regarding our products and services.
Free QR Code Readers are available from your mobile device app store.
You can also email us at carswell.feedback@thomsonreuters.com

**THOMSON REUTERS**

**CARSWELL, A DIVISION OF THOMSON REUTERS CANADA LIMITED**

| | |
|---|---|
| One Corporate Plaza | Customer Relations |
| 2075 Kennedy Road | Toronto 1-416-609-3800 |
| Toronto, Ontario | Elsewhere in Canada/U.S. 1-800-387-5164 |
| M1T 3V4 | Fax 1-416-298-5082 |
| | www.carswell.com |
| | E-mail: www.carswell.com/email |

*To my family, Linda, Kelly, Jenny, Brett and Jessie;*
*to my mother, Doreen;*
*and in memory of my father, Arno — a great motivator in my life.*

# PREFACE

The focus of this fourth edition remains unchanged from the first: it is intended as a starter reference on how properly to prepare and present a case for trial and, if necessary, for appeal. It is an introductory text for the beginner or occasional advocate.

The text is guided by four fundamental points of reference. First, the text strives to provide a framework of principles on how to litigate a case from start to finish. The conduct of a trial is placed within the context of a complete litigation strategy. In this way, a new advocate has a reference text on how to handle a matter from the initial interview, through the discovery process, on to trial and, if necessary, on to appeal.

Second, the emphasis of the text is on basics. A well-presented trial is built upon a solid understanding of trial procedure, court practice, evidence fundamentals and trial techniques and tactics.

Third, this is a text on trials before judge alone. The reality in my home province of Manitoba and throughout Canada is that jury trials are rare, and certainly are not conducted by new counsel. Most advocacy texts concentrate on jury trials. While it is true that many of the principles of advocacy are the same for jury and non-jury trials, it is also true that there are important differences. The opening and closing addresses are different; raising, arguing and ruling on objections are different; and, in many instances, the examination of witnesses is handled differently.

Fourth, throughout the text, a point is made to discuss the professional responsibilities of counsel. One cannot overemphasize the importance of counsel acting in a professionally responsible manner towards the court, fellow lawyers, clients and witnesses.

The first edition of this text was written in 1990. Times have changed. The most telling change in the last 25 years has been the continued demise of civil trials. Unfortunately, the civil litigation bar and civil courts have created too cumbersome and too expensive a process for the average Canadian. Disputes do not go to trial; they settle. Therefore, new counsel will gain their litigation experience in the criminal courts. Given this reality, this text now tries to provide a foundation in the conduct of both civil and criminal trials.

Principles of advocacy are generic. Accordingly advocacy — the art of effective and persuasive communication — will assist you wherever you argue a case; whether it is an appeal hearing before the Court of Appeal, civil and criminal trials in the Superior Courts, summary conviction trials, small claim actions, provincial offence trials, to motions and arbitrations.

Although the text has expanded in size and content, I do hope that the text remains an "easy read." Why? Because a basic principle of good advocacy is to maintain interest. I hope that what is written in the pages that follow is both informative and interesting.

*Lee Stuesser*
Thunder Bay, Ontario
July, 2015

# CONTENTS

# 1

# DEVELOPING A TRIAL PLAN

- **A Theory and Theme for Your Case**

- **Garnering the Facts**

- **Researching the Law**

- **Putting Facts into Evidence**

- **Assess the Opposing Case**

- **A Case Study**

The conduct of any trial, in any forum, from a small claims action to a full jury trial, is a formidable challenge and requires the highest order of legal skill. Consider all that is required in order to be successful in trial work.

*First*, you must know the substantive law. This means that you know the legal elements of the case that need to be proven, any potential defences, and are able to apply that law to the given facts. Your challenge is to identify and address the correct legal issues.

*Second*, you must master the rules of trial practice. A trial is a process — there is formality and procedure. You are entering an adversarial contest and you need to know the rules.

*Third*, you must have an understanding of the rules of evidence. Evidence comes to life at trial. The information you have in your case file will do you no good unless you can get it admitted into evidence at trial.

*Fourth*, you must have skill and tact in dealing with witnesses. Trials rely upon the testimony of witnesses and your objective as counsel is to direct, focus, highlight and, if need be, challenge that testimony. Wisdom, as well as understanding of people and of human nature, is essential.

*Fifth*, you must convey your trial message to a judge, who knows nothing about the facts of your case, and who may not know the applicable law. Do not assume that judges are masters of all known law in the universe. Your task is to inform the judge of the facts and law in short order. Your message, therefore, needs to be communicated clearly and concisely.

The *sixth*, and perhaps most stressful point, is that throughout the entire trial you will be watched. Your trial work is subject to public display. Your client, witnesses, court officers and the judge are watching. Most importantly, opposing counsel is watching too, waiting to pounce on any errors that you make. In other words, waiting for you to screw up!

So how do you avoid screwing up? For new counsel the key is preparation. The litigator *prepares* and *presents* cases for trial. Although these two aspects of litigation are distinct in the sense of the mechanics involved, they are inextricably connected. The trial lawyer presents what has been prepared and, the better the preparation, the better the presentation. Of the two, preparation is far more important, in that proper preparation gives substance to what transpires in court. This is especially true for the beginner litigator, where meticulous preparation can make up for courtroom inexperience.

New counsel need to compensate for their trial inexperience through thorough preparation of their case. This is not to say that experienced counsel need not prepare. On the contrary, preparation is always of prime importance. Rather, the truth is that, as one gains experience, the time it takes to prepare diminishes because the body of known law and procedure increases with experience. For example, the experienced counsel who anticipates a *voir dire* on the voluntariness of a confession already knows the formalities of the process, burden of proof and applicable case law. That particular counsel only needs to hone up on the facts. On the other hand, for new counsel everything is new.

Now, it does help to be a "performer," but that standing alone is not enough. Just as good acting cannot, in the end, salvage a poor script, so too a good trial presence cannot save a poorly prepared case. Imagine a performance by a theatre company that has not rehearsed, or a professional golfer who has not practised, or a champion boxer who has not trained.

In contrast, thorough preparation can overcome inadequacies in performance. If the right facts and the right law are presented to the court, rarely will a judge or jury be deceived by theatrics. Substance will prevail over form, but it is best to have both.

## 1. A THEORY AND THEME FOR YOUR CASE

Preparation for trial begins early. It is not left to the eve of trial. Why? Because you need to control and dictate the conduct of the trial. Do not wait for the trial, uncontrollably and unexpectedly, to direct you. You mould the trial.

Yogi Berra is credited with saying, "If you don't know where you are going, when you get there you are sure to be lost." Heed this advice. You need to know where you are going in a trial. Everything you do in the trial should be planned. Therefore, you need a trial plan, which will give your case focus and order. Never proceed to trial without a plan.

In developing a trial plan, start with your closing submission and work backwards. Think about what you will say in closing about the evidence, the credibility of witnesses and the law. Everything you then do at trial should be geared towards what you will say in closing. That is why I suggest that you start your trial preparation by preparing your closing first. Everything else follows. Constantly ask yourself, "How will I use this in closing?"

Your trial plan may well include your theory of the case. A theory of the case is your explanation for what has occurred. It should be simple. Capture in one paragraph what your case is all about. In turn, your theory may well be put in headline form, which becomes your case "theme." A case theme captures in a phrase or sentence the essence of your case. It is a sound bite that reinforces your theory of the case.[1]

An excellent example of a case theory and theme is found in *R. v. Khan*.[2] Khan was charged with first degree murder in the death of his sister,

---

[1] Wendy Matheson, "Keys to successful oral advocacy: One view from the bar" (2007) 26 Advocates' Soc. J. 9 at para. 37.

[2] *R. v. Khan* (1996), 108 C.C.C. (3d) 108 (Man. C.A.). The *Khan* case has a lengthy history. Khan was convicted of two counts of first degree murder in the deaths of his sister and wife. The Court of Appeal overturned the convictions and ordered that the counts be severed. Khan was then tried for the murder of his sister and was convicted. On appeal the conviction was overturned and a new trial ordered (1998), 126 C.C.C. (3d) 353 (Man. C.A.). Meanwhile, Khan was put on trial for the murder of his wife. He was convicted and this time the conviction was upheld

Bibi, and a few years later in that of his wife, Sureta. In 1990, Bibi was found dead in a freezer in the accused's home. There was no sign of injury. Her cause of death was consistent with asphyxia. The police investigated, but no charges were laid and the proceeds of a life insurance policy were paid out to Khan. In 1994, Sureta was found dead in a bathtub in the accused's home. Once again, there was no sign of injury and her death was consistent with asphyxia. One "natural" death might well be an accident, but two "natural" deaths, according to the Crown, was murder. Both were living with the accused in his home. Both had ingested therapeutic or sub-therapeutic levels of drugs. Both victims were discovered by the accused. The home was locked both times and there were no signs of forced entry. Both victims were heavily insured and in each case the accused was the beneficiary of the proceeds of the insurance. The Crown's theory was that Khan heavily insured both women. He then killed them in such a way as to make it look natural in order to recover the life insurance proceeds. The Crown's theory was captured in the phrase, "This is a case of murder for profit." Khan's motive turned the case from accident to murder.

Motive, as a general proposition, is not an essential element of a crime but it is always relevant. Proof of motive goes to confirm the case against the accused and the reverse is true for proved absence of motive.[3] Consider the role that motive could well play in a case like *R. v. Lamb*.[4] Lamb was fooling around with a revolver. Two bullets were in the chambers. Lamb looked and saw that neither bullet was aligned with the barrel, so he thought it safe to pull the trigger. He pointed the revolver at a friend and pulled the trigger. He shot his friend dead. Lamb said that he never realized that when the trigger was pulled the chambers rotated into the firing position. He thought that revolvers work by revolving after the bullet is fired. He was wrong. They revolve before the bullet is fired. Lamb was convicted of manslaughter, but the conviction was overturned on appeal. Arguably he never intended to kill his friend. He had no reason to do so. However, if the person killed was not his friend, but a person Lamb hated, say his former girlfriend's new boyfriend, then you might view the shooting very differently. Motive can make all the difference.

---

(1999), 136 C.C.C. (3d) 391; affirmed by Supreme Court of Canada (2001), 160 C.C.C. (3d) 1. The Crown then decided not to put Khan on trial a third time for the death of his sister.

[3] See *R. v. Lewis* (1979), 98 D.L.R. (3d) 111 (S.C.C.).

[4] *R. v. Lamb* [1967] 2 Q.B. 981.

## 1.1    Alternative Theories

Presenting one theory of the case is the most consistent and understandable way of presenting it to a judge or jury. The danger is that you may be wrong and there will be no alternative available for the trier of fact to find in your favour. The "one shot" approach is for the confident, and, hopefully, wise counsel. More insecure counsel use the "shotgun" approach and barrage the court with a number of options in the hope that one of them will be accepted. The danger of this strategy is that a valid theory can get lost in the confusion.

Although running with one theory keeps things simple and consistent, one can present alternative theories. Irving Younger is credited with the following wonderful parody on alternative theories:[5]

> . . . at common law you are entitled to reply to a plaintiff who claims his cabbages were eaten by your goat:
>
> You did not have any cabbages.
> If you did, they were not eaten.
> If they were eaten by a goat, it was not my goat.
> And if it was my goat, he was insane.

*R. v. Thatcher* is an example of an alternative theory case. Colin Thatcher, a well known Saskatchewan politician, was charged with the murder of his former wife, JoAnn Wilson.[6] The two had been involved in a bitter divorce and custody battle over their children. In fact, a year and a half prior to her death, JoAnn was shot and wounded while in the kitchen of her home. After this attack, she gave up custody of her son and accepted a much reduced matrimonial settlement from Thatcher. Subsequently, JoAnn was savagely beaten and shot to death in the garage of her Regina home. The Crown's theories were:

1) Colin Thatcher killed JoAnn himself, or

2) he had someone kill her.

It did not matter which theory the jury accepted and they did not need to be unanimous in their choice of theories. Under either theory, Colin Thatcher was guilty of murder.

---

[5] As quoted in J. McElheney, *Trial Notebook* (1981), American Bar Association, at p. 4.
[6] *R. v. Thatcher* (1987), 32 C.C.C. (3d) 481 (S.C.C.).

## 1.2   Conflicting Theories

The danger with alternative theories is that they may conflict with one another, undermining your credibility with the court. You must consider how various theories will impact upon one another. Certain theories may simply provide different legal avenues available to arrive at a result, for example, finding an insurance agent liable to a customer based on tort, contract or breach of a fiduciary duty. Other theories complement one another, as is the norm in most negligence actions, where numerous allegations of negligence are pleaded and cumulatively paint a powerful picture of negligence. Other theories, however, conflict. Beware.

A tragic example of conflicting theories is *R. v. Gauthier.*[7] The accused was charged with the murder of her three young children; they had been poisoned. The Crown theory was that the accused along with her husband had planned a murder-suicide pact. The husband died but the accused, whose wrist was slit, lived. At trial the accused's primary defence was that she was in a dissociative state and had no intention to be part of any pact to kill her children. However, she wanted the trial judge to put forth the alternative theory to the jury of abandonment arguing that it was open to the jury to find that she withdrew from the pact. The two theories are incompatible with one another. On the one hand she is denying the very existence of a pact, while on the other hand claiming that she withdrew from a plan she denied ever existed. The Supreme Court of Canada recognized that in theory it is open to an accused to put forth any defence that meets the air of reality test and that there is no cardinal rule against putting forth incompatible theories. However, the wisdom of so doing is quite another matter. The accused was convicted of first degree murder of her three children.

A professor of mine used to put it in these terms, "You can't suck and blow at the same time."[8]

## 1.3   You May Not Need a Theory

Certain cases have no theory or theme and this is especially true in criminal cases. Many crimes require no explanation. For example, in a shoplift situation there is no need for the Crown to theorize as to why the accused took the stolen property. People shoplift for all kinds of reasons: greed, need, excitement, compulsion, or simple opportunity. The same holds

---

[7] *R. c. Gauthier,* 2013 SCC 32 (S.C.C.).
[8] For a noteworthy discussion on conflicting theories, see R. Keeton, *Trial Tactics and Methods,* 2nd ed. (1973), at pp. 280-285.

true for many sexual assault cases. The Crown need not explain why the accused attacked the woman. On the other hand, the defence, if alleging that the complainant did consent and is actually lying on the stand, will present a far more plausible case if an explanation can be provided as to why she is lying.

The defence at times also requires no theory. Their trial plan is simple. Make the Crown prove the case beyond a reasonable doubt. The defence will then test the evidence throughout in the hope that the Crown drops the ball. The defence is simply saying, "Prove it."

## 2.   GARNERING THE FACTS

Developing a theory of the case involves four parts:

1)   garnering the facts;

2)   finding the applicable law;

3)   considering how to get the necessary facts into evidence; and,

4)   assessing the opponent's theory of the case.

Each of these components is intertwined. New facts give rise to new questions of law. In turn, the law determines which facts are relevant and may direct further inquiries. Finally, you must also relay the law and facts into evidence. The process is then repeated as you assess the facts, law and evidence available to the opposing side.

Fact gathering begins in the initial interview. Fleshing out the facts should quickly follow. Concentrate on gathering information first. Thorough research on the law, in most cases, can wait. The reason is simple. The law, unlike your client and witnesses, does not suffer from a faulty memory. Therefore, begin your fact investigation early, conduct a detailed interview with your client, interview witnesses, photograph the scene and gather documentary evidence.[9]

The informal gathering of facts has taken on increased importance in that courts are moving towards the restriction of the formal, but costly, discovery process in certain cases. Simplified, speedy trial procedures have

---

[9] For a more complete list of investigatory hints, see Keeton, *ibid.*, at pp. 307-319.

been mandated for cases involving claims of under $100,000 in Ontario and Manitoba.[10]

As a preliminary matter, consider using a professional investigator. Most lawyers have neither the time nor the experience to properly investigate a case and it is very expensive to have the lawyer chase down witnesses and take statements. Therefore, find a good, trustworthy investigator and leave the fact gathering to the professionals. You are admonished to direct the investigation; don't do it yourself.[11] Whether or not you heed this advice, there are a number of basic points about fact gathering to be aware of.

The first rule of fact gathering is to interview all potential witnesses. Keep in mind that witnesses may be reluctant to talk to you, and are under no obligation to do so. Simply put, you may want to speak with them, but they may not want to speak with you.

There is no property in witnesses. For example, in a criminal case, it is open to the defence to interview the complainant if need be. But be wary. These witnesses may be all too ready to misconstrue your contact as a form of harassment. Prudence dictates that you need to protect yourself against any such allegations by having another person with you when communicating with a complainant or another potentially adverse witness.

There are also certain other provisos. First, you should disclose your interest. Second, it is improper to contact witnesses who are parties and are represented by counsel. In this situation, the lawyer should only deal with the opposite party through his or her counsel.[12]

Employees of corporations constitute a grey area. If you bring an action against a corporation, are you precluded from contacting the employees of that corporate party? Are the employees parties to the action or witnesses? The suggested test is: "Is he likely to be involved in the decision-making process of the party, or does he merely carry out the directions of others?"[13]

---

[10] *Ontario Rules of Civil Procedure*, R.R.O. 1990, Reg. 194, as amended, Rule 76 and *Manitoba Court of Queen's Bench Rules*, Man. Reg. 553/ 88, as amended, Rule 20A. For example, under both the Ontario and Manitoba rules limits are placed on examinations for discovery.

[11] John A. DeMay, *The Plaintiff's Personal Injury Case: Its Preparation, Trial and Settlement* (1977), p. 31.

[12] See, e.g., The Law Society of Upper Canada, Rules of Professional Conduct, Rule 7.2-6.

[13] *MacMillan Bloedel Ltd. v. Freeman & Co.*, [1992] B.C.J. No. 2815 (S.C.).

The Law Society of Alberta, under its Code of Conduct, provides this additional clarification:[14]

> Generally, all directors and officers, as well as management-level personnel with decision-making authority, have sufficient identity with the corporation to be considered equivalent to the client for the purposes of this rule.

In Ontario, however, the Law Society of Upper Canada is more restrictive in allowing access to employees of corporations and organizations. Under the Ontario rules, a lawyer acting in a suit brought against a corporation is not to approach the employees or agents of the corporation directly responsible for the conduct giving rise to the cause of action.[15] For example, counsel for the plaintiff would not be able to talk to the driver of the semi-truck that struck and injured his client. Counsel would be able to talk to other employees of the truck corporation, just not the driver. The Ontario rule is regrettable and, hopefully, will not be followed elsewhere in Canada. The fundamental principle ought to be that there is no property in a witness and, unless the truck driver in our example is a party to the action, he should be treated as a "witness." Whether the truck driver agrees to talk with opposing counsel is another matter, but preventing counsel from even approaching the potential witness is too restrictive. This is especially true in civil cases where we do not readily allow for examinations for discovery of non-parties.

The mere obtaining of information is not sufficient. Your task is to gather, protect and preserve the evidence for trial. Many counsel find that their case investigation consists of notes jotted down in the file of conversations with witnesses. Where is the proof of these conversations? What happens if the witness forgets or suddenly remembers a completely different story? It is wise to preserve this evidence by way of written and signed statements, taken down by someone other than yourself who can, if need be, testify as to what the witness said and as to the taking of the statement. You should not take or witness the statement. As counsel conducting the trial, you cannot take the stand and testify as to what the witness said; if you do, you must pass the conduct of the trial on to other counsel.[16] The preferred route, therefore, is to leave the taking of statements to professional

---

[14] The Law Society of Alberta, Code of Conduct, 2013 v2, Rule 4.03, commentary b.

[15] The Law Society of Upper Canada, Rules of Professional Conduct, Rule 7.2-8 (c). See also Paul Perell, "The Effects of Professional Conduct Rules that Impose Restrictions on Interviewing Witnesses" (2002) 26 Advocates Quarterly 203.

[16] See, e.g., The Law Society of Upper Canada, Rules of Professional Conduct, Rule 5.2-1.

investigators. Should that not be possible, then, at the very least, have another member of your firm present to witness the interview.[17]

There are some who suggest that written statements should *not* be taken. F. Lee Bailey, for one, is of the view that witnesses will be more likely to talk and tell more if not faced with having a statement taken in writing.[18] This is true. A suggested compromise approach then is to interview witnesses by talking with them and having them tell what they know. Then, at the end of the interview, when a degree of trust and rapport has been established, a request to have the statement put into writing can be made. Expect the friendly witness to agree, the adverse witness to refuse and the disinterested witness to go either way.

There are a number of reasons why it is prudent to obtain written statements from all witnesses. First, the statement will help the witness in preparing to give evidence if called to testify at trial months or years after the event. Secondly, the statement is available to refresh the witness's memory in court. Thirdly, should the witness die, disappear, or otherwise become unavailable, the written statement, in certain circumstances, may be admitted into evidence.[19] Fourthly, should the witness testify to a different version of events from that contained in the statement, you can cross-examine the witness on the prior inconsistent statement.[20] If you called the witness, this may require that the witness be found adverse.[21]

For witnesses who balk at signing a statement it is absolutely imperative that the investigator takes clear and complete notes of what was said. The investigator may even read back to the witness or have the witness read

---

[17] See Paul Lisnek, *Lawyer's Handbook For Interviewing and Counseling* (1991), West Publishing Co., ch. 7, for a discussion on how to interview witnesses.

[18] F. Lee Bailey, *To Be a Trial Lawyer*, 2nd ed., (1994), p. 89.

[19] The *Manitoba Evidence Act*, R.S.M. 1987, c. E-150, s. 58, allows for the admission of "any statement made by a person in a document" when the maker of the statement had personal knowledge of the matters dealt with in the statement and the maker is dead or otherwise unavailable to testify. The statement may also be admissible as a hearsay exception resting upon the principles of reliability and necessity as outlined by the Supreme court of Canada in *R. v. Khan* (1990), 79 C.R. (3d) 1 (S.C.C.) and *R. v. Smith* (1992), 15 C.R. (4th) 133 (S.C.C.).

[20] See, e.g., *Canada Evidence Act*, R.S.C. 1985, c. C-15, s. 10; Ontario, *Evidence Act*, R.S.O. 1990, c. E.23, s. 20; *Manitoba Evidence Act*, R.S.M. 1987, c. E-150, s. 20.

[21] See, e.g., Ontario, *Evidence Act*, R.S.O. 1990, c. E.23, s. 23; *Manitoba Evidence Act*, R.S.M. 1987, c. E-150, s. 19. The *Canada Evidence Act*, R.S.C. 1985, c. C-15, ss. 9(2) provides for the cross-examination of one's own witness on a prior inconsistent statement *in writing* without a preliminary finding of adversity.

what he has written to confirm that it is accurate. If this is done, the investigator may put a notation at the bottom of the statement: "I have read the above statement to Mr. Jones and he acknowledges that it is true but prefers not to sign it."[22] In this situation, the witness can still be impeached at trial using the prior inconsistent "oral" statement.[23] Moreover, since the statement was confirmed by the witness to be accurate at the time, it may well be used to refresh the witness's memory at trial.

Witnesses may also have much to tell or nothing to tell. In the latter case it is wise to obtain a "negative" statement.[24] Such a statement merely confirms that the witness has no evidence to offer. For example, the eyewitness who did not actually see the accident, but merely turned when hearing the impact. Get this statement in writing and you will be protected against witnesses whose memory does improve with time.

Consider the audiotaping of statements. There is considerable efficiency in taking a taped statement and many witnesses do not mind. Of concern is preserving the integrity of the tape. To that end, have the investigator dictate the date, time and place of taping at the beginning; have the witness confirm that he is aware of and consents to the taping; should there be an interruption in the tape, have the witness confirm what occurred and that nothing was said during the interruption; and finally, have the witness confirm when the interview has come an end, and the investigator indicate the time on the tape.

Obtain all documents you can. Increasingly, cases are won or lost based on a trail of paper. You, not your client, should keep the paper. Also have your client sign authorizations to obtain necessary documents from hospitals, banks or government agencies.

Preserve the physical evidence. In a personal injury case what comes to mind is the photographing of the accident scene, photographing of the injuries, preserving of the damaged goods. These things need to be done immediately or else this evidence will be lost.

As a final point, visit the scene. There is no substitute for being there. Photographs or diagrams simply cannot accurately capture the true essence of a place.

---

[22] Joseph Kelner and Francis McGovern, *Successful Litigation Techniques*, student ed. (1981), pp. 4-7.

[23] See, e.g., *Canada Evidence Act*, R.S.C. 1985, c. C-15, s. 11; Ontario, *Evidence Act*, R.S.O. 1990, c. E.23, s. 21; *Manitoba Evidence Act*, R.S.M. 1987, c. E-150, s. 21.

[24] See John Olah, *The Art and Science of Advocacy* (1991), p. 2-9.

Most valuable are "incontestable" facts that bolster your case. For example:

- in a car/pedestrian negligence case — the fact that at the time of the accident it was raining heavily;

- in a contract case — the fact that the opposite party signed the contract;

- in a break and enter case — the fact that the accused's fingerprints were found at the point of entry.

An "incontestable" fact will place the opposite side on the defensive. The more "incontestable" facts you build upon, the stronger your case.

## 3.   RESEARCHING THE LAW

Legal research complements the fact gathering process. As I mentioned earlier, in most cases the law can wait — but not for too long. In certain cases, however, following the initial interview, you may be required to do a memorandum on the law to save the client the time and expense of needless investigation. For example, there may be a question whether a cause of action exists, or whether the potential cause of action is a novel one.

The law provides a context for the facts. Research into the law will expose new factual areas to explore and, in this way, direct the fact gathering process. It is important, therefore, to complete the legal research early.

A general research strategy is outlined below. It proceeds from *general* to *specific*.[25] If a client comes to you with a problem in a new area of law for you, which in your early years of practice covers most cases, you need to get a general understanding of the area before turning your mind to the special facts of your specific case. I suggest that you browse first, then focus on specifics.

---

[25] This outline is provided by Professor John Eaton, Head Librarian at the Robson Hall Library.

# RESEARCH STRATEGY

## STEP I: ISSUE IDENTIFICATION

### Start broad and then refine

Begin your research by looking at your topic broadly. It is important that you understand fully the context in which your issues arise.

### Begin with secondary sources

Secondary sources (texts, articles, commentaries) are a tremendous starting point because they do much of the intellectual "grunt" work for you. To begin by reading a parade of cases is neither productive nor efficient. Most secondary sources will streamline your research by directing you to authoritative and instructive primary sources.[26] Secondary sources include:

- Subject textbooks

- Legal encyclopedias (Canadian Encyclopedic Digest)

- Looseleaf current awareness services

- Journal literature

- Annotated statutes

- Online books, netletters, newsletters, and commentaries

## STEP II: SPECIFIC SEARCH

### Move to primary sources

Once you have the "lay of the land" from your reading of secondary sources, you can begin reading pertinent cases and statutory provisions. You will find many of the most important cases and statutes in the secondary materials you have read and also in sources such as:

- Digests (e.g., Canadian Abridgment – Canadian Case Digests)

---

[26] An excellent starting point on secondary sources is found in John Eaton and Denis Le May, *Essential Sources of Canadian Law* (2009).

- Index to relevant report series (e.g. topical, jurisdictional)

- Online databases of cases and statutes

**Facts are important too**

Do not forget about the facts of the situation that give rise to the dispute. The facts will help to refine your search.

**STEP III: FOLLOW-UP**

It is absolutely imperative that you check that the cases and statutes you rely upon are still good law and have not been overturned. This process of "noting up" both your case and statute law is a key step in the research process. It will also enable you to find more potentially relevant cases in that you will encounter other cases, which have considered the cases and statutes you rely upon. There are a variety of sources for noting up cases and statutes:

**Cases:**

- Canadian Abridgment – Canadian Case Citations

- QuickCite (online case citatory on Quicklaw)

- KeyCite (online citatory on WestlaweCarswell)

- Indexes to relevant law reporters

**Statutes:**

- Canadian Abridgment – Canadian Statute Citations

- Canadian Abridgment – Legislation

- Canada Statute Citator

- Indexes to relevant law reporters

- KeyCite (online citatory on WestlaweCarswell)

Once the initial research is complete, it is equally important to organize the research into a legal brief. The brief summarizes the law and highlights the legal issues. It serves as an invaluable reference for the lawyer as the matter ponderously proceeds to trial.

## 4.  PUTTING FACTS INTO EVIDENCE

The law will tell you what facts you need. These facts will do you little good, however, unless you can get them admitted into evidence at trial. In other words, you must consider how to *prove* the facts. One method is to maintain an evidence chart that will list the law, the facts and the means of getting these facts into evidence. A sample evidence chart is provided below.

| **CONTRACT DISPUTE** **(Party alleges contract entered into by mistake)** | | |
| --- | --- | --- |
| *Law* | *Facts* | *Evidence* |
| • A person who signs a contract, in the absence of fraud, deceit or incapacity, is bound by its terms. | • Signature of party on contract | • Document into evidence through the defendant who was present when signed or • By consent • Witness X present at signing |

A review of the evidence will reveal gaps that need filling and highlight any problem areas that deserve greater attention and preparation. These are critical moments in a trial. Evidentiary questions are often made in relative haste by judges. If an evidentiary issue is critical, you have identified it and are in a position to persuade. I refer you to the message contained in the parting comment made by Madam Justice Southin of the British Columbia Court of Appeal in *Olynyk v. Yeo*, a case where the Court of Appeal ordered a new trial because certain critical documents were admitted and ought not to have been:[27]

> Finally, I make this comment: A new trial, especially in a civil case, is regrettable. Had this question of admissibility been argued before the learned trial judge as it was argued before us, I do not think that this unfortunate result would have been necessary. For that, counsel for the appellant below (who, of course, was not counsel before us) must take the blame.

---

[27] *Olynyk v. Yeo*, [1988] B.C.J. No. 2289 at 23 (C.A.).

Do not let this happen to you.

One suggestion is an "evidentiary brief." The brief succinctly summarizes the law of evidence on the issue contested and shows how your interpretation or application of that law is the correct one. More and more, evidentiary briefs are included as part of the pre-trial materials. The brief can then be referred to by the judge or provide the basis for your oral argument.[28] Such a brief assists the judge and at the same time stamps your preparedness for trial. But keep the brief *brief*; one page is preferred. Your purpose is to assist the court and not to deluge it with the law. Consider the scenario below, where the defence is seeking to exclude evidence under section 24(2) of the Charter. You are prepared.

> Your Honour, we seek to exclude the drugs seized from the locker under section 24(2) of the Charter. To assist you I have prepared a brief that summarizes the law from the Supreme Court of Canada's decision in *R. v. Buhay* (2003), 174 C.C.C. (3d) 97 (S.C.C.). *Buhay* is a decision right on point and it is found at tab 1 in the materials that I provided to Your Honour at the start of trial. My learned friend [*who has no brief*] has a copy. . .

You may not win your argument, but you were prepared to be persuasive.

## 5.    ASSESS THE OPPOSING CASE

You must give your opposing counsel credit and assume that they too have a theory of the case. Like a chess match, you must concentrate on both your own moves and the moves of your opponent. The task is to make your theory the more plausible one.

Facing incontestable facts is difficult. For example, in the case where your client has signed the contract, a denial of the signing is futile and will only cost you credibility with the court (see the diagram in section 4 of this chapter). Far better for you to accept the signing, but raise "undue influence;" after all, the defendant was present when the contract was signed. Rather than a stubborn, ineffective frontal attack on the objective fact, you finesse it by admitting the fact and then explaining it away in a reasonable fashion.

---

[28] For an excellent example by eminent counsel of an evidentiary brief presented orally, see: John Sopinka, *The Trial of an Action* (1981), at pp. 197-200.

Consider the law, facts and evidence that the other side must rely upon and you can plan to meet their case. Evidentiary points may present themselves which will allow you to block evidence they need to adduce. Thus, preparation entails not only preparation of your case, but also preparation for your opponent's case.

This is especially true in criminal cases when you act for the defence. The prosecution is required to present its case beyond a reasonable doubt and in many cases your task as defence counsel is not to present an affirmative defence, but merely to challenge the prosecution's case.

Having gone through the above preparation for trial, you are now in a position to truly assess the wisdom of so doing. The outcome of any trial is an uncertainty. The greater the number of uncertainties that you have in your case, be it in the law, facts or evidence, the greater the chance of an adverse judgment. The option is always there to settle the case and now, because you have a real appreciation of your own case and of your opponent's case, you are in a better position to negotiate. Settlement is not a sign of weakness, rather, in most instances, it is a sign of wisdom. Trial is a last resort.

A trial is often referred to as a "war" or "battle." The analogy is apt. Just as countries prepare for war in the hope that war never comes, so too should the wise litigator prepare for trial in the hope that the matter never goes to trial.

## 6.    A CASE STUDY

To illustrate the various aspects of developing a trial plan outlined in this chapter, I will be referring to the case of *R. v. Vandergraaf*.[29] It is a wonderful little case that could well fall into the lap of junior counsel.

On November 5, 1993 the Winnipeg Jets were playing a home game against the Ottawa Senators. At that time, the Senators were an expansion team and they were awful. The Jets had a half decent team, but you would not know it on that night. The Jets blew an early lead and lost to the Senators in overtime. It was an ugly loss and the fans were not happy. It just so happened that it was "Kraft Peanut Butter Night" and, at the start of the game, thousands of fans received a free jar of Kraft peanut butter. After the game was over, the jars of peanut butter became lethal projectiles as unhappy fans threw them onto the ice. Unfortunately, the complainant, who was

---

[29] *R. v. Vandergraaf* (1994), 93 C.C.C. (3d) 286 (Man. C.A.).

standing in the front row at ice level, was struck and injured by a flying jar of peanut butter. Mr. Vandergraaf was charged with assault with weapon, to wit, a jar of peanut butter.

The information would have read:

That Marc Vandergraaf on November 5, 1993 at the city of Winnipeg in the Province of Manitoba did in committing an assault on Jane Doe use a weapon, to wit a jar of peanut butter, contrary to s. 267(1)(a) of the Criminal Code.

Imagine that you have been handed the *Vandergraaf* file.

## 6.1    Start with the Charge

Where do you begin? The charge is the starting point for both Crown and defence counsel, even though they approach the case from different perspectives. Crown counsel are builders. They bear the burden of proof. They are asserting that the accused committed an offence. Therefore, they are called upon to garner the evidence and mold it into a legal case. The charge is the legal foundation for the case and it is incumbent upon the Crown to see that all the essential elements of the charge are proven. In contrast, defence counsel are wreckers. Their task is to inspect each and every element of the Crown's case and ensure that the case is sound. If not, the case fails. Only if the Crown's case is sound, does the defence need to present an affirmative defence.

Let us start by breaking the charge into its component parts, as outlined in the case checklist below. The checklist helps to identify potential issues. First, identification certainly seems to be an issue. How do we know that Mr. Vandergraaf threw a jar of peanut butter and that that jar struck the complainant? After all, thousands of jars were handed out and many were thrown. Second, is a jar of peanut butter a weapon? Further research will be needed on this point. Third, how do we know that Mr. Vandergraaf intended to strike the complainant and, if he did not intend to hit her, what did he intend?

You are now in a position to read the file. On the issue of identification, presumably the complainant did not see the jar coming and did not see the thrower. However, are there eyewitnesses? How many? Where were they? How were they able to see that Mr. Vandergraaf threw the specific jar that struck the complainant? Was Mr. Vandergraaf arrested at the scene? Did he admit to throwing the jar that struck the complainant? If so, is this statement admissible into evidence? On the issue of intention, is there any evidence that he was intending to throw the jar at the complainant? Did he know the complainant? If not, was he throwing the jar at players on the ice, or at the referees? If so, can we transfer the intent to assault them to the assault upon the complainant? What does Mr. Vandergraaf say about his intent?

| CASE CHECKLIST | |
|---|---|
| **File Number:** 93 - 00976<br>**Name:** R. v. Marc Vandergraaf<br>**Charge:** Assault with Weapon | |
| **NEED TO PROVE** | **CHECK** |
| **Identification**: Marc Vandergraaf<br>**Jurisdiction**:<br>  - Time: November 5, 1993 in PM<br>  - Place: Winnipeg Arena, Winnipeg<br><br>**Elements of Charge**:<br><br>  *Actus Reus*:<br><br>  1) **Committing an assault, s. 265:** applies force intentionally to that other person, directly or indirectly;<br><br>  2) **"Uses a weapon"**: Is a jar of Kraft peanut butter a weapon?<br><br>  *Mens Rea*:<br><br>  1) "Intentional use of force" —> requires intention<br><br>**Defences**: ??? | |

On the issue of the "weapon," your research directs you to s. 2 of the *Criminal Code*, which reads, in part:

> Weapon means any thing used, designed to be used or intended for use a) in causing death or injury to any person.

Did Mr. Vandergraaf intend to use the jar to injure any person? We are back to the issue of intention.

A careful reading of the charge now focuses the case to two key issues: identification and intention. Even if the Crown can prove that Mr. Vandergraaf was the thrower, there is a real problem with intention. There is precedent to transfer intention where a wrongdoer intended to assault one person and by mistake struck another.[30] However, what if Mr. Vandergraaf was merely intending to throw his jar of peanut butter onto the ice? You need more information. Where was Mr. Vandergraaf when he threw the jar? Was it even possible for him to reach the ice surface? When did Mr. Vandergraaf throw the jar? Were the players and game officials still on the ice? If so, were they in the vicinity where Mr. Vandergraaf was throwing?

## 6.2   Planning to Get Your Facts into Evidence

As the trial nears, you need to plan on how you are going to get your facts into evidence. What you are really doing is turning your mind towards the organization of your case. You draft a witness list of all the potential witnesses and the evidence you anticipate each will give. Evidence issues are identified and a response prepared.

The *Vandergraaf* file includes witness statements from the complainant, a husband and wife who were seated behind Mr. Vandergraaf and who saw him throw the jar of peanut butter, and a police officer who was called, arrested Mr. Vandergraaf and took his statement.

The witness list for the *Vandergraaf* case is provided below and can help to focus your examinations. For example, the complainant cannot identify who threw the jar, but she can set the scene of the incident and is needed to establish the assault. The impression that the Crown would like to convey is that this was a completely innocent person, who was struck by the jar and injured. The husband and wife are the key identification witnesses. Counsel will need to concentrate on the accuracy of their observation in seeing Mr. Vandergraaf throw the jar and also seeing it strike the complainant. The police officer is called with respect to the statement and it will be a decision for Crown counsel as to whether the statement made by Mr. Vandergraaf is introduced into evidence. Let us assume that Mr. Vandergraaf said something like, "I threw the jar. I was aiming for the ice, but hit the woman. I'm sorry." The statement is both incriminating and exculpatory. He admits being the "thrower" and hitting the woman, but denies intention. If Crown counsel decides to admit the statement, it will have to be admitted in its entirety. A *voir dire* is necessary and counsel will have to prepare for such, unless waived by the defence.

---

[30]  *R. v. Deakin* (1974), 16 C.C.C. (2d) 1 (Man. C.A.).

## WITNESS LIST

**Case:** *R. v. Vandergraaf*

| WITNESS | EVIDENCE | LAW |
|---|---|---|
| Complainant<br>Name<br>Address<br>Occupation | - Background: set the scene<br>- Establish assault:<br>Struck by jar of peanut butter<br>- Where standing<br>- Injury | - Jurisdiction<br>- Assault |
| Husband<br>Name<br>Address<br>Occupation | - Know Vandergraaf?<br>- Seated behind Vandergraaf<br>- Saw him throw jar<br>- Saw jar strike complainant<br>- Detained Vandergraaf | - Identify Vandergraaf as person who assaulted the complainant |
| Wife<br>Name<br>Address<br>Occupation | - Identify Vandergraaf<br>- Seated behind Vandergraaf<br>- Saw him throw jar<br>- Saw jar strike complainant<br>- Went to get police | - Identify Vandergraaf as person who assaulted the complainant |
| Police Officer | - Arrested Vandergraaf<br>- Statement taken<br>- Vandergraaf admits throwing jar. Says slipped when throwing. No intention to hit complainant. | - Tender statement as admission? If so: require *voir dire* on statement<br>- Ensure rights read / no breach of Charter |

## 6.3    Tie Your Theory to Objective Facts

In developing your trial plan, concentrate on "objective" facts. In *Vandergraaf*, there are certain objective facts consistent with the defence's contention that Mr. Vandergraaf was intending to throw the jar onto the ice and was not intending to hit anyone:

- The complainant was standing next to the ice;

- He threw the jar from the 12th row—in other words, the throw was very doable;

- The players had left the ice;

- The officials had left the ice;

- He had no reason to hit the complainant or any other fan.

It is one thing for Mr. Vandergraaf, or any other witness, to testify as to a particular state of mind. It is far more powerful to show how that person's intent reasonably coincides with the objective facts.

## 6.4    Formulating Your Trial Plan

Defence counsel's plan, after talking to her client, is to concentrate on lack of intention. The defence theory is that the accused threw the jar of peanut butter out of frustration over the Jets' loss. He intended to throw the jar onto the ice. The players and officials had left the ice and so he was not aiming at any person. He was not thinking and, when he threw the jar, he slipped. The jar then did not make it to the ice and struck the complainant. The defence theme is "He did not mean to hit anyone." With this theory in hand, defence counsel can now concentrate on the examination of the various Crown witnesses. The examination of each might well focus on the following points:

| Complainant: | She was standing in the first row, which is right beside the ice. When struck by the jar the players were already off the ice. The officials also had left the ice. She does not know Mr. Vandergraaf [no motive for him to hurt her.] |
|---|---|
| Husband and Wife: | Mr. Vandergraaf was standing in the 12th row. When he threw the jar the players had already left the ice. The officials had also left the ice. He slipped when he threw the jar. |
| Police Officer: | You may waive the *voir dire* and consent to the statement being admitted. After all it is consistent with your theory of the case. |

## 6.5 The Need for Flexibility

Having said that you have a trial plan, you also need the wisdom to abandon the plan when necessary. Flexibility is essential, especially in the Provincial Courts, where there may well be many surprises waiting, given the vicissitudes of heavy trial dockets. For example, in *Vandergraaf*, defence counsel's trial plan is to focus on lack of intention. She has researched the law and is ready to argue the point. She anticipates calling Mr. Vandergraaf to confirm what was in his mind at the time. Counsel assumes that the Crown will prove identification easily enough through the evidence of the husband and wife. However, the testimony of the husband and wife falls short. They both are not sure that the jar Mr. Vandergraaf threw actually was the one that hit the complainant. In cross-examination, defence counsel now quickly shifts direction and confirms with both of them that there were many jars thrown onto the ice. Identification is now very much in issue. As a result, defence counsel decides to contest the statement. If the statement is excluded, then the Crown's case on identification is weak, if not non-existent. Should the Crown fail to prove identification, there really is no need to call Mr. Vandergraaf to the stand. Your case may well be won by way of a no evidence motion and all of your in-depth legal research on transferred intention will have to wait for another trial. Such is the reality of criminal trial work.

In the actual case, Mr. Vandergraaf was convicted of assault with weapon at trial. He should not have been. On appeal, the conviction was set aside and an acquittal was entered. His target was the ice and not people. He threw the jar from the 12th row. The teams had left the ice. Mr. Vandergraaf was frustrated and his conduct, in the words of Justice Philp, "was foolhardy, perhaps negligent" but, absent an intention to apply force to another person, he was not guilty of assault with weapon.

# 2

# DRAFTING THE PLEADINGS

- **The Function of Pleadings**

- **The Rules of Pleading**

- **Specific Rules**

- **Drafting a Statement of Claim**

- **Drafting a Statement of Defence**

- **Sample Pleadings**

- **Drafting Problem**

Generally speaking, a civil action commences with the plaintiff filing a statement of claim and the defendant responding by way of statement of defence. The pleadings, if properly done, define the issues and, by so doing, direct the attention of both counsel and the Court to the real matters in dispute between the parties.[1] Shoddy pleadings invite confusion, interlocutory motions, delay, and unnecessary expense.

The drafting of pleadings is not a mere formality. The statement of claim and statement of defence are the first documents that a judge will look at. If well drafted, they will leave a good impression. The pleadings will also be your first opportunity to put forth your theory of the case and you should strive to persuade. You will do so by being *clear, brief* and *strong*. The authors of the leading English text on pleadings, *Bullen & Leake & Jacob's Precedents of Pleadings*, describe the place of pleadings as follows:[2]

---

[1] See, e.g., *Miller v. Jaguar Canada Inc.* (1997), 123 Man. R. (2d) 161 (C.A.).

[2] *Bullen & Leake & Jacob's Precedents of Pleadings*, I.H. Jacob (ed.), 12th ed. (1975), p. 17.

The drafting of a pleading is the equivalent of laying the foundation on which to build the claim or defence of a party, and as the foundation is laid, whether badly or well and truly, so will the claim or defence be weak and fall or be well sustained and upheld. Pleadings should therefore be drafted with all due care and circumspection, and they require the exercise of much skill and not a little art, to fulfil their whole function.

In the past, "form" seemed to dominate over "substance" in pleadings and pleadings were a breeding ground for legalese. Today courts take a more liberal view towards procedure and process. Refer to RR. 1.04 and 2.01 of the Ontario and Manitoba Rules of Court:

General Principle

1.04 (1) These rules shall be liberally construed to secure the just, most expeditious and least expensive determination of every civil proceeding on its merits.

EFFECT OF NON-COMPLIANCE

2.01 (1) A failure to comply with these rules is an irregularity and does not render a proceeding or a step, document or order in a proceeding a nullity, and the court,

(a) may grant all necessary amendments or other relief, on such terms as are just, to secure the just determination of the real matters in dispute; or

(b) only where and as necessary in the interest of justice, may set aside the proceeding or a step, document or order in the proceeding in whole or in part.

Poorly drafted pleadings can be amended but why give your opponent the opportunity to highlight your errors through a motion to strike the pleadings, which will only result in delay and cost to your client?[3] It is far better to start the litigation off correctly with correct pleadings.

## 1.   THE FUNCTION OF PLEADINGS

The function of pleadings is fourfold:[4]

1) To define with clarity and precision the question in controversy between litigants.

---

[3] See Manitoba and Ontario R. 26 regarding amending pleadings and R. 25.11 regarding motions to strike a pleading.

[4] W.B. Williston and R.J. Rolls, *The Law of Civil Procedure* (1970), p. 637.

2)  To give fair notice of the case which has to be met so that the opposing party may direct his evidence to the issues disclosed by them. A defendant is entitled to know what it is that the plaintiff asserts against him; the plaintiff is entitled to know the nature of the defence raised in answer to his claim.

3)  To assist the court in its investigation of the truth of the allegations made by the litigants.

4)  To constitute a record of the issues involved in the action so as to prevent future litigation upon the matter adjudicated between the parties.

The pleadings, therefore, set the court's agenda.[5] The issues are narrowed to allow each side to prepare its case adequately and specifically. The pleadings determine the relevant law and evidence and their purpose is to clarify the legal and factual issues that go to ensure a fair trial. The purpose of pleadings is *not* to confuse, deceive or hide issues. Our entire system of civil procedure is now geared towards the discovery and exposure of each side's case. The era of surprise or ambush justice is past. Pleadings are there for you to advance your theory of the case for the court and for the opposing party. A pleading is an opportunity to persuade.

On drafting a pleading, you should be concerned with "substantive adequacy" and "formal adequacy." "Substantive adequacy" refers to the need for a pleading to disclose a valid cause of action or valid defence. If a pleading is substantively defective, then the opposing party may move to strike the pleading or perhaps move for summary judgment.[6] "Formal adequacy" ensures compliance with the rules of the court and really provides the procedural framework for the substantive law to be stated. In the following, the formal pleading requirements will be outlined.

## 2.   THE RULES OF PLEADING

Manitoba and Ontario R. 25.06(1) sets out the fundamental rule of pleading:

> 25.06 (1) Every pleading shall contain a concise statement of the material facts on which the party relies for a [ [the] ] claim or defence, but not the evidence by which those facts are to be proved.

---

[5] *Bullen & Leake, supra,* note 2, at p. 9.

[6] An excellent reference text on the substantive requirement for various causes of action is *Bullen & Leake, supra,* note 2.

This general rule involves three specific demands:

(1)  be concise;

(2)  material facts only;

(3)  material facts and not evidence.

## 2.1   Be Concise

You are advised to be concise and to be precise:[7]

> Facts should be alleged as facts. Use terse, short, curt, blunt sentences, all in the indicative mood. Be positive. Do not beat about the bush. Go straight to the point. If you mean to allege a particular fact, state it boldly, plainly, clearly and concisely. . . A pleading is not the place for fine writing, but simply for hard, downright, business-like assertion . . .

> Then, again, it always conduces to clearness to observe the strict order of time. In any case not of the simplest, dates are of the greatest importance. The only way to tell a long or complicated story clearly and intelligently is to keep to strict chronological order. . .

> This, then, is the *first* essential of good pleading — to be *clear.* The next is to be *brief.* The Rules repeatedly insist on the necessity of brevity. . .

> A certain amount of detail is essential to ensure clearness and precision. "Although pleadings must now be concise, they must also be precise."

The problem is that most lawyers do not heed this advice. The pleadings are regarded as a "formal" court document with the result that they are often written in archaic legalese. Pleadings, as with any document prepared by a lawyer, should use plain language. Look through your pleading precedents. Are they clear and concise? I doubt it. Consider the following paragraph taken from a statement of claim in my own precedent file:

> On or about September 20th, 1992 A.D., at or about 1:00 in the forenoon a collision between the two above-described motor vehicles occurred in the South bound lane of the said highway at a point in time when the deceased was proceeding South bound and the defendant was proceeding North bound. As a result of the collision the deceased was killed, her passenger Belinda L., above-named, was injured and considerable property loss was effected to the motor vehicle above-described of which the deceased was driver.

---

[7] *Odgers Principles of Pleading and Practice*, 21st ed. (1975), pp. 99-102.

Is it not simpler, clearer and more powerful to say the following:

> On September 20, 1992 at 1:00 a.m. the deceased was driving her car
> south on highway 205. The defendant was driving his van north on that same
> highway. The defendant crossed the median into the oncoming south bound
> lane and struck the deceased's car. The collision was entirely the fault of the
> defendant in being on the wrong side of the highway.
>
> As a result of the collision the deceased was killed, her daughter, Belinda
> L., who was a passenger, was injured and the car was demolished.

## 2.2    Material Facts Only

A "fact" that is pleaded does not readily fit into our notion of a "fact."
Pleaded "facts" are assertions of what the party will prove at trial; they are
allegations stated as "facts." For example, in an automobile accident case,
the plaintiff pleads: "The defendant failed to stop, as required, at the posted
intersection." The plaintiff never saw the defendant until hit broadside. The
plaintiff, therefore, has no actual knowledge of the above fact, but two
witnesses will be called, who can testify that they saw the defendant go
through the stop sign. This then is pleaded as a "fact," a fact to be proven
at trial.

The requirement for "material facts" narrows the pleading in two
senses. First, only facts relevant to the claim, defence or issue of quantum
of damages ought to be pleaded. Second, argument, theories or conclusions
of law arising from the facts, as a general proposition, ought not be pleaded.
Also you must be careful to ensure the accuracy of the material facts. You
do not want to be placed in the position of presenting evidence contrary to
the facts pleaded.[8]

## 2.3    Plead Material Facts and Not Evidence

Do not expand upon the statement of fact by detailing the evidence
going to prove the fact. For example, in the stop sign allegation pleaded
above, you have two witnesses. Do not plead:

> The defendant was observed by a Mr. John Smith and a Mrs. Jane Doe to
> proceed through the intersection without stopping at a posted stop sign.

The testimony of the two witnesses is evidence — not fact.

---

[8] R. McNicol, "Pleadings and Particulars: The Process and the Practice," 1981 Isaac
Pitblado Lectures, p. 8.

The following examples further illustrate the difference between material facts and evidence:

**Material Fact:**    Defendant drove on the wrong side of the road and struck John Smith as he walked along the roadway.

**Evidence:**    Fred White saw the defendant drive onto the wrong side of the road.

**Material Fact:**    As a result of the accident John Smith lost the use of his right arm.

**Evidence:**    As a result of the accident John Smith was examined by Doctor H. Weisental, who has found that John Smith has lost 85% exterior rotation and 90% interior rotation of his right arm.

**Material Fact:**    At the time of the accident the defendant was intoxicated and his ability to drive was impaired by alcohol.

**Evidence:**    After having struck the plaintiff, the police were called and a blood sample was taken from the defendant. It showed that he had a blood alcohol reading of 180 milligrams of alcohol in 100 millilitres of blood.

## 3.  SPECIFIC RULES

### 3.1  Alternative Theories

If you have more than one theory of the case, these theories should be revealed in the pleadings together with the material facts in support of each separate and distinct claim or defence.[9] For example, in an action based on breach of contract and on tort, the material facts supporting each must be pleaded. The Rules allow for inconsistent pleadings so long as they are pleaded in the alternative. The introductory phrase "In the alternative . . . " clarifies for the reader that a new and distinct cause of action or defence is pleaded and the phrase should not be looked at as wasted verbiage.

---

[9]  See Manitoba R. 25.06(2) and 25.06(6) and Ontario R. 25.06(4).

## 3.2   Pleading Law

As a general rule, it is not necessary to plead specific causes of action.[10] The material facts are allowed to speak for themselves and from them the court will apply the appropriate cause of action or conclusion. However, I am of the view that it helps to clarify the issues if you do plead the legal conclusion to be reached from the facts stated and, as a matter of form, certain statements of law must be pleaded such as contributory negligence, foreign law, and estoppel, to name but a few.[11] Keep in mind the primary function of pleading is clarity, then if a conclusion on the law will help to state the issues clearly, include it. *What you must not do is to provide a legal conclusion without supporting facts.* For example:

**Yes** — The defendant did not keep a proper lookout and as a result negligently struck the plaintiff.

**No** — The defendant negligently struck the plaintiff.

Certain points of law are not to be pleaded, such as the burden of proof.[12] Nor do you anticipate defences. For example, in a statement of claim, the plaintiff does not plead, "And I was not contributorily negligent." Let the defendant raise the defence and, if necessary, you can respond through a reply. If you do not file a reply, the facts as alleged by the defendant are deemed to be denied by the plaintiff.[13]

Specific sections relied upon from a statute or regulation need to be pleaded along with the material facts that show how the statute is applicable to the action.[14] This is a practical requirement. Imagine if a party simply pleads the *Criminal Code* or the *Income Tax Act*. Where do you begin to look? The party, who has pleaded the statute, knows the section or sections being relied upon and is now bound to tell the court and opposing counsel.

## 3.3   Miscellaneous Rules

The following pleading rules are self-explanatory and are designed to assist in the drafting of succinct pleadings:

---

[10] See Manitoba R. 25.06(3) and Ontario R. 25.06(2).
[11] For a list of matters that must be pleaded, see D. Stockwood, *Civil Litigation*, 5th ed., (2004), at p. 177.
[12] See Manitoba R. 25.06(12).
[13] See Manitoba and Ontario R. 25.08(4).
[14] See Manitoba R. 25.06(4).

### Condition Precedent

Manitoba R. 25.06(5) [Ontario comparable R. 25.06(3)] Allegations of the performance or occurrence of all conditions precedent to the assertion of a claim or defence of a party are implied in the party's pleading and need not be set out, and where the opposite party intends to contest the performance or occurrence of a condition precedent, the pleadings of the opposite party shall specify the condition and its pleadings of non-performance or non-occurrence.

### Notice

Manitoba R. 25.06(8) [Ontario comparable R. 25.06(6)] Where notice to a person is alleged, it is sufficient to allege notice as a fact unless the form or a precise term of the notice is material.

### Documents or conversations

Manitoba R. 25.06(9) [Ontario comparable R. 25.06(7)] The effect of a document or the purport of a conversation, if material, shall be pleaded as briefly as possible, but the precise words of the document or conversation need not be pleaded unless those words are themselves material.

### Nature of act or condition of mind

Manitoba R. 25.06(11) [Ontario comparable R. 25.06(8)] Where fraud, misrepresentation or breach of trust is alleged, the pleading shall contain full particulars, but malice, intent or knowledge may be alleged as a fact without pleading the circumstances from which it is to be inferred.

## 4.   DRAFTING A STATEMENT OF CLAIM

The format for a statement of claim is dictated by the Rules of Court. Under the Manitoba and Ontario Rules, Form 4A sets out the "General Heading" and Form 14A sets out the actual format for the statement of claim:

MANITOBA

FORM 4A

GENERAL HEADING OF DOCUMENTS — ACTIONS

THE QUEEN'S BENCH

_____ Centre

BETWEEN:

(name)          plaintiff,

— and —

(name)          defendant

(Title of Document)

(Text of Document)

---

MANITOBA

FORM 14A

STATEMENT OF CLAIM

(General Heading — Form 4A)

(court seal)

STATEMENT OF CLAIM

• • •

CLAIM

1. The plaintiff claims (state the precise relief claimed)

(Then set out in separate, consecutively numbered paragraphs each allegation of material fact relied on to substantiate the claim and the precise relief claimed.)

(Date of Issue)

(name, address and telephone
number of lawyer or plaintiff)

The body of the statement of claim includes:

1) the claim for relief;

2) description of the parties;

3) material facts;

4) description of damages.

The statement of claim should set out the who, what, where, when, and why of your cause of action. Who are the parties? What is it they want? What is the cause of action? What happened to give rise to the cause of action? When did it occur? Where did it occur? Why is it a valid cause of action? What are the damages? The statement of claim begins with the claim for relief, in other words, with what the plaintiff wants.

## 4.1   The Claim for Relief

The claim for relief advises the court and the opposing side what it is that the plaintiff wants. The relief sought can be claimed simply or in the alternative.[15] The amount of special or calculable damages should be specified. Should further special damages arise, they can be included when known. General or incalculable damages need not be specified as to amount.

In Manitoba, R. 25.06(14) implies a claim for general relief in a pleading. This provision should do away with the "catchall" claim "and such further and other relief as this honourable court may deem just."

Besides damages, the claim for relief may also include any number of other remedies, such as an injunction, possession of land, an accounting, specific performance of a contract, or a declaration. Two items which you should include are a claim for prejudgment and/or postjudgment interest, where appropriate, and, in all actions, a claim for *costs*.

## 4.2   The Description of the Parties

This part of the statement of claim is intended to tell who the parties to the action are and their connection, if relevant, to one another. Where there are multiple parties, use a separate paragraph for each. Be brief, be simple and be clear. Here are some suggestions:

(a) Where there is only one plaintiff or one defendant use the term "plain-

---

[15] See Manitoba R. 25.06(13) and Ontario RR. 25.06(13), 25.06(9).

tiff" or "defendant." There is no need to say "the plaintiff Smith" or "the defendant Jones" — we know who they are.

(b)  Where there is more than one plaintiff or defendant, give each a separate designation and use that designation throughout: The defendant company — The defendant Jones.

(c)  It is advisable to be consistent with whatever term you use throughout the pleading. For example, if suing on a contract, do not, for the sake of style, use different terms for the contract, such as "the agreement" or "the document," as this only creates confusion. It is the "contract" or, and I suggest this reluctantly, it is the "said contract."

(d)  When giving the designation to a party, do not be long on the explanation. I see nothing wrong with the prudent use of brackets. The meaning is clear. For example:

The defendant Acme Consolidated Company of Canada ("Acme"). . .

instead of saying:

The defendant Acme Consolidated Company of Canada, hereinafter referred to as "Acme". . .

(e)  For corporations include which law they are incorporated under and, if relevant, where they carry on business in the province:

The defendant Acme Consolidated Company of Canada ("Acme") is a company incorporated under the laws of Manitoba which carries on business at 5008 Broadway Avenue in Winnipeg, Manitoba.

Note that the specific incorporating statute was not included. Most companies simply incorporate under either the provincial or federal Corporations Act and I would not refer to that statute. Where the corporation is incorporated under a special statute, I would include it. For example, the Workers Compensation Board is a commission constituted by the Workers Compensation Act of Manitoba.

For the address, include it if known, but in describing the locality do not say:

. . . in the city of Winnipeg in the province of Manitoba.

We know what *Winnipeg, Manitoba* means — two words are better than ten.

(f)  The occupation of the parties need not be included unless it is relevant. For example, in the sample statement of claim (found in section 6 of this chapter) the plaintiff's occupation as "broadcaster" is included. It is relevant because: 1) the plaintiff had to broadcast later that evening and one would not suppose that he would wish to get involved in a fight just prior to going on the air; and 2) his occupation is relevant to the issue of damages. The occupation of the defendant, in contrast, is not needed.

(g)  Special rules apply for "parties under disability" (R. 7), "partnerships and sole proprietorships" (R. 8), and "executors, administrators or trustees" (R. 9). For example, a minor must sue by way of a "litigation guardian" (R. 7). This would be reflected in the style of cause:

> JOHN ROBERT SMITH, a minor, who sues by way of his father and litigation guardian, THOMAS ALFRED SMITH, Plaintiff;

and, where his father also advances a claim:

> . . . and the said THOMAS ALFRED SMITH, Plaintiffs.

Note that in representing a minor or a person under a disability, an affidavit of consent and authority must be filed with the court (see R. 7). Using the litigation guardian example, the descriptive paragraph in the statement of claim would read:

> The Plaintiff is 6 years old and lives with his father, who is litigation guardian, and mother, Doris Smith, at 13 Elm Street in Winnipeg, Manitoba.

## 4.3   Material Facts

The general admonitions about pleading, already discussed in this chapter, pertain most directly to this portion of the statement of claim. Be concise, plead material facts only and do not plead evidence. One of the purposes of the statement of claim, besides outlining your theory of the case, is to obtain admissions from the opposite party. Short, specific paragraphs are recommended. They will contain fewer contentious allegations and are more likely to be admitted by the defendant. However, a series of one sentence paragraphs is not recommended. The statement of claim must still tell a story in narrative form and short statements make for a pleading that does not flow or read well.

The material fact portion of the claim usually begins with what happened. On a personal injury claim the accident is described. Next you tie the facts to the law. You may allege negligence, with particularization of the negligence. Or, if a statute is relied upon, this can be tied into the facts. For example, "in proceeding through the stop sign without stopping, the defendant was in breach of s. 89 of the Highway Traffic Act." If you are relying on a term in a contract or a statute, use the precise words of the contract or statute in your pleading. At the end of this portion of your statement of claim, check to confirm that you have established a viable cause of action.

### 4.4    Description of Damages

Particulars of damage or other claims for relief should be given to avoid surprise at trial and to give the defendant an opportunity to assess his case adequately and perhaps make a payment into court. Punitive or exemplary damages should be pleaded, and the material facts in support of such a claim should be outlined in the body of the claim. Damages which are more "indirect" certainly ought to be pleaded, such as loss of employment due to the accident or a psychological disorder attributable to the injuries sustained, and special damages should be expressly detailed. (See the sample statement of claim found in section 6 of this chapter.)

## 5.    DRAFTING A STATEMENT OF DEFENCE

Prior to drafting the statement of defence you should carefully review the statement of claim filed. Does it disclose a cause of action? Are there allegations that should be struck out? Do you require particulars? Allow for this period of reflection before taking pen in hand.

The format for the statement of defence is provided in Form 18A:

---

MANITOBA

FORM 18A

STATEMENT OF DEFENCE

(General Heading — Form 4A or 4B)

STATEMENT OF DEFENCE

1. The defendant admits the allegations contained in paragraphs ____ of the statement of claim.

2. The defendant denies the allegations contained in paragraphs ____ of the statement of claim.

3. The defendant has no knowledge in respect of the allegations contained in paragraphs _____ of the statement of claim.

4. (Set out in separate, consecutively numbered paragraphs each allegation of material fact relied on by way of defence).

(Date)                    (Name, address and telephone number of defendant's lawyer or defendant)

TO:  (Name and address of plaintiff's
      lawyer or plaintiff)

---

Allegations of fact in the statement of claim that are not denied in the defendant's statement of defence are deemed to be admitted:

### Denials

Manitoba R. 25.07(2) [Ontario Comparable R. 25.07(2)] Subject to subrule (6), all allegations of fact affecting a party that are not denied in that party's defence shall be deemed to be admitted unless the party pleads having no knowledge in respect of the fact.

One often sees a statement of defence begin with a general denial: "Save as hereinafter expressly admitted, the defendant denies each and every allegation contained in the statement of claim as though the same were herein set out and traversed *seriatim*." This is to be avoided. The phrase is archaic and, as one observer commented, "suggests that one is still copying precedents prepared before the First World War, if not before 1875."[16] It also offends the rule that denials must be *specific* to the allegations contained in the statement of claim.

The statement of defence should begin with the defendant admitting to any of the non-controversial facts alleged in the statement of claim as provided for in Form 18A and under R. 25.07(1). Usually reference is made to the specific paragraphs in the statement of claim, hence, to reiterate, the value of short paragraphs in the plaintiff's pleadings. Admissions are not a sign of weakness. The defendant should admit to those non-controversial facts which will help to narrow the issues and save time and expense at trial.

Allegations not admitted can be responded to in any of three ways:

1)    Deny the allegation (traverse);

2)    Confess or admit the allegation but assert new facts to avoid the legal consequences (confession and avoidance); or,

3)    Admit the facts as alleged but counter that they raise no cause of action against your client (demurrer).

## 5.1   The Denial

A defendant might be tempted to deny everything and simply make the plaintiff prove everything. Such is not permitted. The defendant is obligated to put forth his defence, his case. The defendant is required to outline to the court the different versions of the facts relied upon and any affirmative defences.[17]

The defendant may also plead "no knowledge of the fact alleged" (see Form 18A). Often the superfluous phrase "and puts the plaintiff to the strict proof thereof" is annexed to the plea of no knowledge. There is no need to do this. Once a fact is denied or stated as not known by the defendant, the plaintiff has the burden of proving the allegation. In certain instances you may only deny a portion of a paragraph in the statement of claim. If you do so, make certain that the denial is expressed in clear terms. The following example shows clearly what the defendant admits to and denies:[18]

---

[16] J.E. Cote, "Some Notes on Pleadings" (1974), 12 Alta. L. Rev. 535, at p. 539.

[17] See Manitoba R. 25.07(4) and 25.07(5) and Ontario Rr. 25.07(3), 25.07(4).

[18] *Bullen & Leake, supra,* note 2, at p. 80.

The defendant admits that he made to the plaintiff the representation set out in paragraph 3 of the statement of claim, but denies that he did so falsely or fraudulently or with any intention to mislead the plaintiff as alleged or at all.

Keep in mind that the statement of defence is more than a response to the plaintiff's claim. It is your argument and it should be presented in your way. There is a tendency to respond to the plaintiff's argument paragraph by paragraph, as set out in the statement of claim. In so doing, you follow the plaintiff's agenda and that order may not be well suited to your argument. Therefore, re-order your response where necessary. There is no need for you to argue on the plaintiff's terms. Certain paragraphs in the statement of claim may represent a convoluted mix of facts, some which you can admit and others which you cannot. Rather than answer with a convoluted reply, simply deny the entire paragraph and counter with an uncluttered version of the facts.

One of the purposes of the statement of defence is to tell your story, to put your theory of the case to the court. A statement of defence that is totally responsive to a claim in all likelihood tells a poor story. Deny what you need to deny or state no knowledge if not known, admit that which should be admitted, but then go on and clearly state your defence. Remember, you need to tell your story in the statement of defence.

## 5.2   Confession and Avoidance

Here you are prepared to admit to certain of the material facts alleged by the plaintiff, but you raise new facts to avoid the legal consequences. For example, in the sample pleading (section 6) the defendant admits to a fight with the plaintiff but alleges, in turn, that he fought in self-defence. The defendant must then plead the material facts necessary to support the "avoidance."

## 5.3   No Cause of Action

This is a simple form of plea. The facts are admitted, but you deny that they give rise to a legal claim. The "demurrer" may simply be stated: "The Statement of Claim discloses no right to the relief claimed."[19]

Although there is no need to respond to the damages claimed in relief, the material facts supporting the claim for damages must be addressed, either through a denial or statement of no knowledge.[20] Moreover, since the

---

[19] Cote, *supra*, note 16, at p. 540.
[20] See Manitoba R. 25.07(7) and Ontario R. 25.07(6).

pleadings are primarily concerned with allegations of fact, there is no need for the defendant to respond to specific points of law raised by the plaintiff.

Other pleadings are not outlined in these materials: set-off, counter-claim, reply. Nor are the areas of amendments and particulars developed. I recommend the references cited in this chapter for further information on these pleadings and processes.

## 6.    SAMPLE PLEADINGS

### 6.1    Statement of Facts

#### *Waite v. Stewart*

On 13th March 2015, Richard Waite approached James Stewart in the parking lot of the Highlander Sports Complex in Winnipeg. Waite was upset because Stewart had high-sticked him in the forehead during a recreational hockey game played at the sports complex. As a result, Waite was cut above his right eye.

Waite stayed behind for Stewart and confronted him in the parking lot. Stewart was loading his hockey gear into the trunk of his car. Waite was angry about the high-sticking and wanted to talk to Stewart. Stewart wanted nothing to do with Waite and endeavoured to get into his car. Waite then pulled Stewart by the arm and turned Stewart around to face him. Waite then flicked his glove into Stewart's face and pushed Stewart into a snow bank. At this point Stewart said something to the effect, "If it's a fight you want, then let's go."

Waite and Stewart squared off in the parking lot. Waite attempted to hit Stewart with a swing of his right arm. Stewart then kicked Waite in the abdomen, which knocked the wind out of Waite. Waite doubled over and while he was still doubled over Stewart kicked him a second time, this time in the head. Waite's lower jaw was fractured.

At the time of the incident, Stewart had a brown belt in karate. He had been studying karate for three years and had participated in various regional karate tournaments. Waite says that if he knew that Stewart was a "karate expert" he would never have fought him.

Waite worked as a broadcaster with CKBI-TV. Because of the injury to his jaw he was unable to work for two months. During this time he was reassigned to desk duties. His regular broadcast position was taken up by another, who stayed in this position even after Waite had recovered and was able to broadcast. Waite was a probationary employee and he was terminated from CKBI-TV on 30th June 2015. He immediately obtained a broadcast position with another city television station, but at a lesser salary and, in Waite's view, with fewer career opportunities.

The PLAINTIFF, RICHARD WAITE, brings an action in battery against the DEFENDANT, JAMES STEWART. Stewart defends on the basis of: self-defence, consent to fight and injury (Volenti), ex turpi causa non oritur actio (illegal acts of the plaintiff), and provocation is raised in mitigation of any damages.

THE QUEEN'S BENCH
WINNIPEG CENTRE

BETWEEN:                    RICHARD WAITE

                                                                    plaintiff,

                              -and-


                           JAMES STEWART

                                                                    defendant.

                        STATEMENT OF CLAIM

(court seal)

TO THE DEFENDANT

    A LEGAL PROCEEDING HAS BEEN COMMENCED
AGAINST YOU by the plaintiff. The claim made against you is set
out in the following pages.

    IF YOU WISH TO DEFEND THIS PROCEEDING, you or a
Manitoba lawyer acting for you must prepare a statement of defence
in Form 18A prescribed by the Queen's Bench Rules, serve it on the
plaintiff's lawyer or, where the plaintiff does not have a lawyer,
serve it on the plaintiff, and file it in this court office, WITHIN
TWENTY DAYS after this statement of claim is served on you, if
you are served in Manitoba.

    If you are served in another province or territory of Canada or
in the United States of America, the period for serving and filing
your statement of defence is forty days. If you are served outside
Canada and the United States of America, the period is sixty days.

    IF YOU FAIL TO DEFEND THIS PROCEEDING, JUDG-
MENT MAY BE GIVEN AGAINST YOU IN YOUR ABSENCE
AND WITHOUT FURTHER NOTICE TO YOU.

    September 19, 2015                    Issued by _____
                                         Registrar

TO:  JAMES STEWART 389 Beaverton Street,
     Winnipeg, Manitoba R3T 0P8

                                                    *(cont'd)*

**Claim**

1. The Plaintiff claims:

   (a) Special damages as follows:
   - Medication                                          $128.00
   - Travel to medical treatment                          $50.00
   - Medical report cost                                 $300.00
                                         TOTAL           $478.00

   (b) General damages for pain and suffering and for loss of employment income;

   (c) Punitive damages;

   (d) Interest on the damages awarded;

   (e) The costs of this action.

2. The Plaintiff is a television broadcaster and resides at 392 Morningside Drive in Winnipeg, Manitoba.

3. The Defendant is a university student and resides at 389 Beaverton Street in Winnipeg, Manitoba.

4. On or about 8:50 p.m. on 13th March 2015, in the parking lot of the Highlander Sports Complex on Ellice Avenue in Winnipeg, the Defendant challenged the Plaintiff to a fight. In the course of the fight the Defendant wilfully and maliciously kicked the Plaintiff in the stomach, which winded the Plaintiff, and while the Plaintiff was in this helpless state the Defendant then kicked the Plaintiff in the face.

5. At the time of the fight, the Defendant was trained and proficient in karate, a fact which was not disclosed to the Plaintiff and of which the Plaintiff was not aware.

*(cont'd)*

6. The Plaintiff suffered a fractured lower jaw as a result of the kick to the face and the fractured jaw had to be wired in place for two months. This injury caused the Plaintiff severe pain, suffering and discomfort.

7. Further, the Plaintiff was unable to continue his work as a television broadcaster for the two months when his jaw was wired and as a consequence lost his employment with CKBI-TV, 83 Portage Avenue, Winnipeg, Manitoba.

Filed this 20th day of September 2015 by Horace Zilch, c/o Zero, Zilch & Nothing, Barristers and Solicitors, 1900 TD Tower, 100 Portage Avenue, Winnipeg, Manitoba.

THE QUEEN'S BENCH
WINNIPEG CENTRE

BETWEEN:            RICHARD WAITE

plaintiff,

- and -

JAMES STEWART

defendant.

STATEMENT OF DEFENCE

1. The Defendant admits the allegations contained in paragraphs 2 and 3 of the Statement of Claim.

2. In reply to paragraph 4, the Defendant admits that a fight took place between the Plaintiff and the Defendant at the time and place indicated, but denies all other allegations contained in paragraph 4.

3. The Defendant claims that the fight was instigated and provoked by the Plaintiff, who confronted the Defendant in the parking lot and prevented the Defendant from leaving. The Plaintiff verbally abused the Defendant, pushed the Defendant and struck the Defendant and it was then that the Defendant agreed to fight the Plaintiff. The fight, therefore, was forced on the Defendant and willingly consented to by the Plaintiff.

4. The Defendant admits to kicking the Plaintiff in the fight but did so in self-defence against the assault by the Plaintiff.

5. In reply to paragraph 5 of the Statement of Claim, the Defendant has no knowledge as to what the Plaintiff may have known about the Defendant's karate training. The Defendant admits to having taken karate lessons, but claims that such training was confined to sport competitions. The Defendant further admits that he did not disclose his karate training to the Plaintiff, but states that there was no duty on him or opportunity for him to do so.

*(cont'd)*

6. In the alternative, the Defendant claims that the illegal conduct of the Plaintiff, namely the assault on the Defendant in a public place, precludes the award of any damages to the Plaintiff.

7. The Defendant pleads and relies upon s. 175 and s. 266 of the Criminal Code, R.S.C. 1985, c. C-46 and on the doctrine of ex turpi causa non oritur actio.

8. The Defendant has no knowledge as to the allegations contained in paragraphs 6 and 7 of the Statement of Claim.

9. The Defendant therefore submits that the Statement of Claim be dismissed with costs.

Filed this 30th day of September 2015 by O. Holmes, Barrister and Solicitor, 1900 Portage Avenue, Winnipeg, Manitoba (944-5777).

TO: Plaintiff's Solicitor
Mr. Horace Zilch,
c/o Zero, Zilch & Nothing,
Barristers and Solicitors,
1900 TD Tower,
100 Portage Avenue,
Winnipeg, Manitoba.

## 7.  PROBLEM — DRAFTING PLEADINGS

### 7.1  Pleadings Information

The purpose of this exercise is to give you practice at drafting a pleading. You need not know any more law than that provided, nor do you need any further facts. Prepare in rough:

(1)  a statement of claim given the information available to plaintiff counsel,

(2)  an outline of your strategy as defence counsel, and

(3)  a draft of a statement of defence to the statement of claim that you have drafted.

Compare your draft pleadings to the sample answers in Appendix 1.

### 7.2  Information Available to Plaintiff Counsel

**Client:**         Mary White     **Age:** 32

**Address:**        22 Wood Street
                    Smalltown, Province

**Marital Status:**  Married     3 children ages 6, 10 and 12

**Occupation:**     At home (Note: formerly a waitress at Mike's Restaurant, 35 Main Street, Smalltown, Province)

#### (a)  Notes from Interview with Client and Husband (Richard)

The client is very upset by the actions of a Mr. Wilber John (23 Maple Street, Smalltown), who works as an automobile salesman at Prairie Motor Sales, 3 Main Street, Smalltown. Mr. John is spreading a rumour that Mrs. White is a former prostitute.

She tearfully admits that in 1999-2000, when she was 16 years of age, she was a prostitute for a short period in Toronto. At the time she had run away from her home where her stepfather had abused her. With nowhere to go, she lived on the streets and came under the influence of a pimp. In the spring of 2000 she fled Toronto and took up employment as a waitress in Midtown, Ontario. There she met her husband and they were married in 2001. The client was embarrassed about her past and was terrified that if her husband found out he would leave her. Consequently she never revealed her past to anyone. Her fears about her husband appear to be unfounded as he seems to be very supportive.

She relates that she first heard the disclosure of her past when she went to a dance at the Legion with friends on 24th May 2015. As she entered the hall she was greeted by John's call, "There's the hooker housewife," which was followed by loud laughter from the group seated with John. She ignored the comment, but later in the evening a friend and neighbour approached her and asked whether it was true that she used to be a prostitute. The client left the dance in tears.

Subsequently, the client and her husband both recount numerous incidents where friends, neighbours and even strangers have made comments or inquiries about her past. The client described her mental anguish and embarrassment over the disclosure. Her children had come home crying because of the teasing at school about their "bad" mother. She has noted a coolness towards her by former acquaintances. A number of members of the community have voiced their personal contempt for her. The client was formerly actively involved in the community. Since the revelations she has resigned as a girl guide leader. Her church involvement, formerly extensive, is now limited to weekly service attendance. Now she rarely goes out socially, has stopped attending dances and quit curling. She and her husband have seriously considered moving to Bigtown from Smalltown, which has been their home for ten years. She quit her work as a waitress at Mike's Restaurant when a number of customers propositioned her and called her a "hooker."

Prior to the dance incident the client did not know John. She contacted him shortly after (June 2015), and asked him to stop spreading the "news" because it was hurting her deeply. He refused.

Names are provided of persons who have confronted her with the allegation.

**Note:**  Jack Morris, 38 Spring St., Smalltown — John told him about White in conversation at automobile dealership, when Morris was looking at an automobile.

Susan Morden, 72 Portage Ave., Smalltown — John told her about White in a conversation at the local shopping market.

Cecil Wright, 2 Singer Blvd., Smalltown — John told him at Smalltown Golf Club.

None of the above individuals was aware of client's past.

## 7.3    Information Available to Defence Counsel

**Client:**            Wilber John        **Age:** 38

**Address:**           23 Maple Street
                       Smalltown, Province

**Occupation:**        Automobile Salesman
                       Prairie Motor Sales
                       3 Main Street
                       Smalltown

### (a)    Interview with Client

The client is indignant that a "hooker" is suing him. [Note: The statement of claim was filed 13th September 2015 and served on same day.] He moved to Smalltown from Toronto in 2014. He saw White in a local shopping centre. He recognized her immediately. She used to be "stationed" outside a hamburger place he worked at in Toronto in 1999-2000. What bothers him is that White is actively involved in girl guides and with the local church. He commented, "Once a hooker always a hooker." It was apparent to him that the community did not know about Mrs. White. He decided to expose her for what she was and he makes no apologies for so doing. In his words, "I don't want her messing with the kids." He recalls that she phoned him in June-July 2015 and asked him to stop; he refused. "I got a right to speak out. And the people got a right to know." He did not make any written publication of the information, nor did he make any "formal" public pronouncement of the fact. He simply spread the word privately.

**Instructions:** To fight the matter as strongly as possible. Retainer received [$5000].

## 7.4    Summary of the Law

You will base your claim on the tort of Public Disclosure of a Private Fact. This tort is recognized in the United States, where there is extensive precedent:[21]

---

[21] Prosser and Keeton, *The Law of Torts*, 5th ed. (1984), pp. 809-811.

Public disclosure of a private fact is a "cause of action in publicity, of a highly objectionable kind, given to private information about the plaintiff, even though it is true and no action would lie for defamation."

You must have publicity of the matter and "The final limitation is that the matter made public must be one which would be offensive and objectionable to a reasonable man of ordinary sensibilities . . .

The law is not for the protection of the hypersensitive and all of us must, to some reasonable extent, lead lives exposed to the public gaze."

One who gives publicity to a matter concerning the private life of another is subject to liability to the other for invasion of his privacy, if the matter publicized is of a kind that

   (a)  would be highly offensive to a reasonable person, and

   (b)  is not of legitimate concern to the public . . .

When the matter to which publicity is given is true, it is not enough that the publicity would be highly offensive to a reasonable person. The common law has long recognized that the public has a proper interest in learning about many matters. When the subject-matter of the publicity is of legitimate public concern, there is no invasion of privacy.[22]

For a sample answer, see Appendix 1.

---

[22] The American Law Institute, *Restatement of the Law Second, Torts* (1977), Vol. 3, para. 652D.

# 3

# A CIVIL CASE:
# THE EXAMINATION
# FOR DISCOVERY

- **The Examination for Discovery**

- **Purposes of the Examination for Discovery**

- **Lawyer Preparation**

- **Client Preparation**

- **Conducting the Examination for Discovery**

- **Acting for the Party Being Examined**

The pre-trial process is the necessary precursor to a trial. Unfortunately, many impatient litigators view the pre-trial preliminaries as unnecessary tedium. These litigators are too anxious to get on with the trial and they fail to recognize that the pre-trial process prepares the evidentiary foundation for the trial. These counsel are also fodder for good litigators who are thoroughly familiar with the pre-trial tools at their disposal and have learned to use them to their advantage. Therefore, it is essential that a litigator know, and know how to use, the rules of pre-trial procedure. But this chapter is not about the rules or substantive law on pre-trial procedure. For that, you can refer to bar admission materials or texts on civil procedure. Rather, this chapter concentrates on *pre-trial advocacy*. There is a tendency to confine advocacy to the courtroom and to assume that everything else is incidental procedure. This view of advocacy is wrong. Successful pre-trial advocacy, in fact, renders many trials unnecessary. My focus in the civil area is on the preparation and presentation of an effective examination for discovery, an area where counsel can be most persuasive.

## 1.   THE EXAMINATION FOR DISCOVERY

Most law students leave law school with only a vague notion of what an examination for discovery entails. Their ignorance usually persists until the time they are literally thrown into one. It seems that they are expected simply to know how to conduct an examination for discovery. They are given little guidance, little preparation and have little idea of what they are expected to achieve. The examination for discovery deserves better. It is too important to be left to the uninitiated.

An examination for discovery or, as the Americans say, "a deposition," is where counsel for a party orally examines an adverse party, who is sworn and whose testimony is transcribed by a court reporter. In Manitoba, an examination for discovery may include written or oral questions and answers or both (R. 31.02). In Ontario, you cannot do both except with leave of the court (R. 31.02). Written "interrogatories" are not favoured in Canada. The reason is that you are not getting a direct response from the party. Opposing counsel answer the questions and as a result the client always comes across as a "Rhodes Scholar" and you rarely get a straight answer.[1]

The examination for discovery is not held in a courtroom. In some locales they are conducted at the offices of "special examiners" or they are held in one of the lawyer's boardrooms. Present are the court reporter, counsel for the parties and the parties themselves.

The examination for discovery is but one part of the discovery process. Full discovery includes:

*   discovery of documents (R. 30);

*   inspection of documents (R. 30.04);

*   oral examination for discovery (RR. 31 and 34);

*   written examinations for discovery (RR. 31 and 35);

*   inspection of property (R. 32); and,

---

[1] See the comments of Professor G. Dilts in "Examination For Discovery," papers and proceedings held by the Law Society of Manitoba, March 8, 1980, at p. 12.

- physical and mental examinations of parties (R. 33).

The examination for discovery should be conducted in conjunction with the other examination processes. To proceed to an oral examination of a party without first obtaining and inspecting all relevant documents is most unwise.

During discovery, unlike at trial, counsel are expected to assist one another in providing relevant information. The Rules of Court so demand. For example, with respect to the production of documents, the lawyers acting for the parties are to certify by affidavit that they have "explained to the deponent the necessity of making full disclosure of all relevant documents in issue in the action" (R. 30.03). Moreover, there is a continuing obligation on counsel to advise the other side of subsequently discovered relevant documents (R. 30.07). Similarly there is a subsequent duty on counsel to correct any incorrect or incomplete answer given in an examination for discovery (R. 31.09).

Today the courts recognize and encourage broad discovery to combat "trial by ambush." Surprises are to be minimized in favour of an informed trial on the known issues and facts. Still, the courts will not do your work for you. Counsel must be vigilant to ensure that they receive full disclosure. Opposing counsel are obliged to provide information *when asked*, but there is no duty on them to *volunteer* this information. It is incumbent upon counsel to ask all the right questions.

## 2. PURPOSES OF THE EXAMINATION FOR DISCOVERY

The examination for discovery serves five general purposes:

- to be informed as to the other party's case;

- to obtain admissions from the other party that will dispense with the need for proof and thereby save time and expense at trial;

- to obtain admissions aimed at destroying the other party's case;

- to provide an opportunity to assess the other party as a witness; and,

- to facilitate settlement.

The information purpose serves in "fleshing out" the pleadings.[2] The opponent is called upon to support the allegations made in the pleadings

---

[2] *Ibid.*, per K. Twaddle, Q.C. (as he then was), at p. 8.

and you are afforded a real opportunity to assess the strength of the opposing case. The issues are narrowed. Certain allegations will be seen to be without substance and the "true" issues will be identified.

You require both "defensive" and "offensive" admissions. "Defensive" admissions are those designed to help your case at trial, without necessarily weakening the other party's case. These admissions are most often sought with respect to documents. The opposite party is asked to identify and authenticate various documents and this dispenses with the need to do so at trial. The documents can be simply filed by consent at the start of the trial. In seeking "offensive" admissions, you attack. Damaging admissions are sought from the other party that will then be read in at trial as part of your evidence or used for impeachment, if at trial the other party strays from what was said at the examination for discovery. The obtaining of damaging admissions made by the defendant, for example, may be essential for the plaintiff to make his case and thereby force the defendant to take the stand to respond to the admissions. The use of the examination for discovery at trial will be dealt with in more detail in subsequent chapters.

Credibility is always a factor with the parties to an action. The examination for discovery gives you an opportunity to test the other party as a witness. Conversely, you are also given an opportunity to observe your client as a witness. The parties' respective performances help you to gauge the impression they will make as witnesses at trial.

The above factors serve dual purposes — to facilitate trial and to facilitate settlement. Following the examination for discovery of the parties, you have a far better idea of the strength or weakness of your opponent's case and they of yours. Counsel are in a far better position to assess the wisdom of trial or the wisdom of settlement and this is precisely what should be contemplated very seriously at the close of the discovery process.

These varied purposes translate into different approaches that require different techniques at the examination. Good examiners know beforehand what they want and tailor the examination accordingly. Poor examiners know not what they want and meander through a meaningless examination. Mr. Justice Middleton's observations made over 50 years ago in *Graydon v. Graydon* hold true:[3]

> Discovery is intended to be an engine to be prudently used for the extraction of truth, but it must not be made an instrument of torture, nor should it be regarded as a mere opportunity for solicitors to multiply irrelevant and im-

---

[3] *Graydon v. Graydon* (1921), 51 O.L.R. 301 at 304.

pertinent questions. Intelligently conducted, an examination should eliminate much waste of time at a hearing; unintelligently conducted and abused by being unduly read at a trial, it is a nuisance well-nigh past endurance.

It is true that the examination for discovery can become an instrument of abuse and cause unnecessary delay and expense. To prevent that from occurring, the best defence that counsel has is proper preparation and a proper understanding of the purposes and procedure of the examination.

## 3.  LAWYER PREPARATION

You must be prepared for the examination for discovery. The "grab the file, give it a glance and ask the question" approach does not work. Counsel who approach it in such a fashion have no appreciation of the importance of the examination for discovery. The need for preparation was masterfully described by Clare Choate, in the leading Canadian text on discovery, as follows:[4]

> The examination for discovery is a most important step in the course of an action. It has been described as a microscopic trial within a trial. The advisability of careful preparation for the examination cannot be given too much emphasis. Full preparation is imperative for there may be no second opportunity before trial. Read the file, the brief, and the pleadings, and review the law. At the outset of any litigation, counsel should plan an effective use of the various discovery and inspection procedures available. Such an initial discovery plan can be expanded or contracted as desired during the development of the case. This skeleton plan should be developed at the outset of the litigation for even then counsel should have some idea of the facts he needs to know or to have admitted. This will also be an important step in assisting counsel to think through his case, possibly putting him in a position to take advantage of early opportunities for settlement. The sooner that counsel has a fuller appreciation of his case, the sooner he may recognize the desirability of a settlement and be able to effect a good settlement to the advantage of his client.

You begin with a thorough review of the file. The pleadings are dissected. Specific allegations and issues are identified, each of which becomes a separate head of examination.

Review the law. The law and authorities dictate the relevance of evidence and facts and give you a focus as to what facts to pursue in the examination.

Review the evidence. If you act for the plaintiff, you must be concerned about establishing your cause of action. Critically examine the evidence

---

[4] C. Choate, *Discovery In Canada* (1977), p. 11.

that is needed to prove the case. Identify any gaps in evidence and ask, "Can these gaps be filled by obtaining admissions from the other side? What evidence does the other side have?" Under the new rules for discovery it is open to you to seek out evidence and to be informed of the names and addresses of witnesses (R. 31.06).

Review the documents. Obtain the documents prior to the examination for discovery and inspect them. Organize them for use at the examination. You may separate them into plaintiff or defendant documents or put them in chronological order. Identify the documents that you will have the opposite side authenticate.

Once your review is complete, turn to organizing your questions. An "outline," "checklist" or "game plan" is a must.[5] Whatever you call it, you need it.[6]

> The Boy Scouts and Girl Scouts have a sound motto: Be prepared. If there is one absolute rule that should be followed it is: Prepare a complete and detailed outline for the deposition. The degree of detail depends upon several factors, one of which is your level of experience. The more experience you have, the less exhaustive the outline need be. Maybe.

You have to structure your questioning. It is not necessary that you prepare each question. Rather, the outline guides you through the examination and acts as a checklist to ensure that you do not leave anything out.

Being organized will impress. It shows your preparation. It shows that you are a professional. It shows that you will be a force to be reckoned with at trial. In short, it strengthens your settlement position.

In Ontario counsel are to co-operate in formulating a discovery plan (R. 29.1).[7] "Discovery planning is intended to permit the parties to map out the most efficient and effective way to organize the production and discov-

---

[5] See R. Haydock and D. Herr, *Discovery Practice*, 2nd ed. (1988), p. 233; E. Haines, "Examinations For Discovery" in Special Lectures of the Law Society of Upper Canada 1955, p. 23, at pp. 35-41; R. Manes and V. Edwards, *Manes Organized Advocacy*, 2nd ed. (1988), p. 10-5.

[6] Haydock, *ibid.*, at p. 233.

[7] See S. Cronyn, "Formulating a discovery plan" (Spring 2010) 28 Advocates' J. No. 4, 9-10.

ery needs of the particular action having regard to the complexity of the records, the issues in dispute and the amounts at stake."[8]

Finally, your preparation concludes by reading the rules on examination for discovery. It is amazing what you learn by simply reading the rules. You need to be familiar with your rights on examination and the procedure for the examination. Knowing the rules will allow you to take full advantage of the examination and, at the same time, prevent your being taken advantage of by opposing counsel.

## 4.  CLIENT PREPARATION

You know what to expect on an examination for discovery. Your clients do not. What you take for granted is entirely foreign to the legally inexperienced client. You want your client to be a good witness. Then you must prepare your client to be good. Edson Haines provided this analogy:[9]

Let us say, for example, that next Monday morning you are going to have a slight surgical operation. You worry about it today, and on Saturday and on Sunday and finally by Monday morning even your wife hardly knows you. Without breakfast, you go down to the hospital, they give you a pill to quiet your nerves. They take your clothes off and put you in bed. You try not to act frightened. Finally they put you on a cart and take you up to the operating room and, as the doctor puts the mask over your face and gives you an anaesthetic, you are ready to die then and there. Why? Because you know nothing about the procedure of doctors and nurses. It is the great unknown. If you knew what was going on, the old heart would not be pounding and the knees would not be shaking quite so much.

Explain the examination for discovery to your clients. They will be better witnesses for it.

---

[8]  *Lecompte Electric Inc. v. Doran (Residential) Contractors Ltd.*, 2010 ONSC 6290 (Ont. Master) at para. 14. For an extensive discussion on discovery planning see *Teti v. Mueller Water Products Inc.*, 2015 ONSC 2289 (Ont. S.C.J.), additional reasons 2015 CarswellOnt 6689 (Ont. S.C.J.).

[9]  Haines, *supra*, note 5, at p. 26.

## Explain the Examination for Discovery

- Emphasize that the examination is designed to provide evidence *to the other side*.

- Warn that their testimony can come back to haunt them and they must be careful in what they say.

- What is said is under oath or affirmation and will be transcribed. This testimony can then be used *by the other side* at trial.

**(Explain where the examination will take place.)**

- Warn that although the examination does not take place in a courtroom, it is nonetheless a formal process conducted in an informal setting.

## Explain Who Will be Present

- Explain the function of the court reporter.

- Explain that counsel for the other side will be asking the questions, but that you will be present to object to any improper questions.

- Explain that the other party will also be present in most cases.

**(Explain how the examination is conducted.)**

- Questions will be put by the opposing lawyer and examinees are expected to answer as best they can.

- At the end of the examination you may re-examine.

You must also prepare your party as to the facts of the case. The examination for discovery is not confined to the personal observations of the party. Questions may be asked of the party based on "knowledge, information and belief" (R. 31.06). Hearsay evidence therefore is permitted. For example, in a common automobile personal injury claim, the plaintiff may have no recollection as to how the accident occurred. However, she is expected to become familiar with the evidence of witnesses that the plaintiff expects to call.

The client should be familiarized with the pleadings.[10]

> It is proper scope for Discovery, to refer to the pleadings and ask a witness what facts he relies on in support of the particular allegation, for example, where he has alleged without proper particulars that the accident was caused by the negligence of the defendant. One is entitled to ask him in what respect he alleges the negligence — what form it took — and, consequently, the client, who probably has never seen the pleading, and doesn't understand the "mumbo-jumbo" in which the lawyers put the case down on paper, may be hard-pressed to explain what he understands that the lawyer meant in the pleading. You are entitled to know what facts the lawyer is relying on in making certain allegations. There's nothing more embarrassing than having your client asked the facts that he relies on in support of an allegation, and he says "Oh, I don't know. My lawyer drew this up." And yet that so often happens. He should know.

The above illustration also highlights why superfluous allegations in the pleadings serve little purpose. They will quickly be seen to be a sham at the examination and, if not abandoned prior to the hearing, only provide grist for embarrassment of your client at the hearing.

Review any documents with your client. Make certain that he or she is familiar with them. Go over the circumstances of the making of the documents. Explain that the client may be asked to authenticate the documents.

Next, prepare your client to give testimony. Such preparation is similar to preparation of witnesses for giving evidence at trial. Your advice should include:[11]

---

[10] K. Twaddle, *supra*, note 1, at pp. 16-17.

[11] For checklists on advice to clients in giving evidence on discovery: see Manes, *supra*, note 5, at p. 10-15; P. Kolczynski, "Depositions as Evidence" (Winter 1983), 9 Litigation No. 2, at p. 25; W. Barthold, *Attorney's Guide to Effective Discovery Techniques* (1975), pp. 282-284.

- Tell the truth.

- Do not guess.

- Do not be afraid of saying you do not know.

- If you cannot remember, say so.

- If you do not understand a question, say so.

- Think before you answer. There is no rush.

- Do not volunteer information.

- Answer only what is asked.

- Do not lose your temper.

- Do not argue with counsel.

- If an objection is made, stop answering.

Your preparation should culminate with a mock run-through of an examination. Pose expected questions to the client. This is entirely proper preparation. You are not telling the client what to say. You are simply assisting the witness with how to tell her story.

## 5.   CONDUCTING THE EXAMINATION FOR DISCOVERY

### 5.1   Opening the Examination

Start the examination with proper identification. This confirms that the party being examined is one of the parties to the action.

For example:

**Q.1** Your name is Richard Waite?
**A.**   Yes.

**Q.2** And you are the plaintiff in an action against Mr. James Stewart, is that correct?

**A.** Yes.

**Counsel for Mr. Waite:** For the record this will confirm that Mr. Waite is the plaintiff in Queens Bench action 722/05.

For corporate parties it is important that you obtain confirmation that the person being examined is giving evidence on behalf of the corporation:

**Q.1** Mr. Smith, you are the executive officer of XYZ Corporation?
**A.** Yes.

**Q.2** You are testifying today on behalf of XYZ Corporation and your evidence is binding on that corporation?
**A.** I think so.

**Counsel for XYZ Corporation:** Mr. Smith is giving evidence on behalf of the corporate defendant and his evidence is binding on the corporate defendant.

Mark Dombroff provides a more elaborate opening series of questions, which is designed to fix the examinee's testimony and prevent any subsequent waffling:[12]

"Good morning, sir. My name is Mark Dombroff," (I suggest you not use my name, however). "I represent the defendant in this case, a civil case. Do you understand that?"

We'll assume a basically honest witness, "Yes, I do."

"And sir, you have filed a law suit against my client, have you not?"

"Yes, I have."

"And you understand, sir, don't you, that that makes you an adversary to my client?"

"Yes, I understand that."

"Now, sir, I am here to ask you some questions about what occurred that gave rise to your law suit. Have you been told that?"

"Yes, I have."

---

[12] M. Dombroff, "Dirty Tricks and Unfair Tactics," in The Seventh Annual Advocacy Symposium, presented by the Canadian Bar Association - Ontario and the Law Society of Upper Canada (6th and 7th May 1988), p. 149, at pp. 150-151.

"And, sir, if for any reason you don't understand one of my questions, will you tell me that? That you don't understand my question?"

"Yes, I will."

"And I'll rephrase my question. Is that agreeable to you?"

"Yes, it is."

"And, sir, if for any reason you don't hear one of my questions, will you tell me that?"

"Yes, I will."

"And I'll repeat the question. Is that agreeable with you? Is that fair."

"I think that's fair."

"And, sir, would I be correct in understanding, would I be fair in understanding that, if you don't tell me that you didn't understand my question, and you don't tell me that you didn't hear my question, that you heard and understood my question?"

"Yes, I think that's a fair understanding on your part."

"And that your answer is truthful to the very best of your knowledge and ability."

"Oh, absolutely. I would never tell a lie."

At trial, Mr. Dombroff impeaches the witness using the examination for discovery and the opening is resurrected.

"Sir, do you recall having your testimony taken prior to trial in this matter?"

"Yes, I do."

"And were you under oath?"

"Yes, I was."

"And did I tell you, sir, that if you didn't understand one of my questions that you should tell me that?"

"Yes, you did."

"And that I would rephrase or restate the question so you understood it. Did I tell you that?"

"Yes, you did."

"And did I tell you, if you didn't hear one of my questions, you should tell me that as well?"

"Yes, you did."

"And I would repeat the question."

"Yes, you told me that."

"And, sir, did you tell me that, if you didn't indicate a lack of understanding or a lack of hearing, you heard and understood the question?"

"Yes, I believe I did."

"Now, sir, would you turn to page, or referring to page, 32 of your examination prior to trial. Did you anywhere on that page, sir, say you didn't understand my question?"

"No."

"Did you anywhere on that page, sir, say you didn't hear my question?"

"No."

Mr. Dombroff's example is intended for a jury and is a bit too dramatic for a judge, who well knows the reality of an examination for discovery, but it does illustrate how the impeachment could be enhanced through such an opening to the examination.

## 5.2   Seeking Information

The examination of a party on discovery is not a cross-examination. There is no need for you to ask only narrow leading questions. There is no need to fear the examinee's responses. The examination for discovery is for you to use or not use at trial. Ask anything and everything. Do not be afraid of open-ended questions. Ask who, what, when, where, why and how questions.[13] Turn to the pleadings. Ask the party what evidence there is to support a particular allegation:

---

[13]  Haydock, *supra*, note 5, at p. 264.

**Q.** Mr. Waite, in paragraph seven of your statement of claim you say that as a consequence of your injury you lost your broadcast job at CKBI-TV. Why do you say that? [See Chapter 2.]

General questions will give you fertile ground to pursue more specific points.

**Q.** Mr. Waite, you were terminated by CKBI-TV on 30th June 2015, is that correct?
**A.** Yes.

**Q.** And was it not the case that 30th June 2015 was the end of your probationary period at CKBI-TV?
**A.** Yes.

**Q.** And by being on probation, you were subject to being fired without reasons. Is that not the case?
**A.** Yes.

Use *closing questions*. These questions are designed to prevent the party from adding to the examination testimony other evidence or information. It is important to ask these questions in order to activate directly R. 31.09(1), the duty to correct *answers*:

31.09 (1) Where a party has been examined for discovery or a person has been examined for discovery on behalf of, or in addition to the party, and the party subsequently discovers that the *answer to a question* on the examination,

(*a*) was incorrect or incomplete when made; or
(*b*) is no longer correct and complete,

the party shall forthwith provide the information in writing to every other party. [Emphasis added.]

Let us return to the case of Richard Waite:

**Q.** You received no further written reasons for your termination from CKBI-TV, other than the letter of 15th June 2015 from Mr. James Tickoff?
**A.** That's correct.

**Q.** Were you given any oral reasons for your firing?
**A.** No.

Subsequently Mr. Waite remembers that the station manager at CKBI-TV said to him:

We would have kept you on, if you hadn't been injured.

He is obliged to inform the defendant of this information. If Mr. Waite does not do so, he will be precluded from introducing the statement at trial, except with leave of the court.

The same applies for witnesses. Remember it is open to you to ask the party for the names and addresses of witnesses.

**Q.** Mr. Waite, who were your supervisors at CKBI-TV?
**A.** Mr. Robert Smith and Mr. James Tickoff.

**Q.** Would these individuals be the only persons at CKBI-TV familiar with the reasons for your firing?
**A.** Yes.

At trial, Mr. Waite seeks to call a Ms Susan Jones, an assistant to Mr. Tickoff, who was present when the decision to fire Mr. Waite was made. Once again, Mr. Waite runs afoul of R. 31.09.

Should the party not know the answer to your question, obtain an *undertaking* from the party to provide an answer.

**Q.** Mr. Waite, will you undertake to provide me with those salary receipts from CKBI-TV for January to June 2015?

**Counsel for Mr. Waite:** We will endeavour to do so.

Counsel should keep a list of all undertakings and follow the examination with a written request listing the undertakings. Should the party prove to be thoroughly unprepared to answer many questions, adjourn the examination rather than resort to undertakings upon undertakings, which effectively turn your oral examination into a written examination. Put on record the reason for so doing and arrange to reconvene when the party is properly prepared.[14]

## 5.3    Seeking Admissions

There are cases where plaintiff's counsel rises at the start of a trial and reads in a number of extracts from the examination for discovery of the defendant and concludes by saying, "That is the case for the plaintiff." Yes,

---

[14] Law Society of Manitoba, Bar Admission Materials for Civil Procedure (1989), p. 2-38.

the admissions you obtain on discovery can prove your case.[15] Admissions are extremely valuable. They may not always prove your case, but they certainly can help.

In obtaining admissions, you need to be specific. Ask a specific question seeking a specific answer. The questions should be simple. What you want is a clear, simply stated admission. You may have to pursue a matter with the party until you have your clear admission. Consider a car-pedestrian personal injury case. You are examining the defendant driver.

> **Q.** How fast were you driving down Elm Street, between 1st and 2nd Avenues?
> **A.** I was going around the speed limit.

> **Q.** When you say "speed limit," what is the speed you mean?
> **A.** 50 kilometres per hour.

> **Q.** You say that you were going "around" 50 km/h. Did you look at your speedometer at this time?
> **A.** No.

> **Q.** So would it be fair to say that you do not know your exact speed at this time?
> **A.** Yes.

> **Q.** So you could have been going faster than 50 km/h?
> **A.** Yes.

---

[The importance of this admission is that you have two witnesses and a police expert who put the defendant's speed at around 60 km/h. You have effectively removed the defendant as a witness who could challenge your evidence on this point.]

---

> **Q.** Mr. Roberts, how far is your home from the intersection of 1st Avenue and Elm Street?
> **A.** About three blocks.

> **Q.** You're familiar with that intersection then?
> **A.** Yes.

---

[15] Mr. Justice Hamilton was most impressed when this occurred in a case he was presiding over, *supra*, note 1, at p. 68.

**Q.** You know then that there is an elementary school on the northwest corner of 1st Avenue and Elm Street?

**A.** Yes, I am aware of that.

---

[You are building specific "fact" admissions against the defendant using the defendant's own evidence. He was aware of the school. The time was 4:30 p.m. Children could be expected. He was entering a school zone.]

---

The posing of admission questions is directed at their use at trial. Long and unwieldy questions and answers are not conducive to reading in, nor are they effective for impeachment. You want clear, crisp and concise statements that will stand on their own and stand out for the judge. Simple, specific questions are best.

## 5.4    Using Documents at the Examination

The method of introducing documents at an examination for discovery is different from that at trial. The question of admissibility does not arise. Counsel are free to introduce whatever documents they wish and the documents are tendered through counsel. The documents need not be tendered through the examinee. Nor is a foundation for the documents necessary. Counsel tenders the document, asks that it be marked for *identification*, then proceeds to question the party using the marked document. The examination record will then be clear. You are not referring to "that letter" or "this letter," you refer to the "letter marked as Exhibit 1."

**Counsel:** Could I have this "Repair Estimate", from Al's Automotive Repair, dated 13th October 2014 and signed by a Tom Bull, B-U-L-L, marked as plaintiff's Exhibit 1 for identification?

**Q.** Mr. Roberts, I show you Exhibit 1, a repair estimate from Al's Automotive Repair. Do you recognize this document?

**A.** Yes, I received it on 13th October 2014.

**Q.** And this repair estimate concerns your car?

**A.** Yes.

**Q.** The same car that you were driving at the time of the accident involving Jimmy Jones, is that correct?

**A.** Yes.

**Q.** Mr. Roberts, do you recall seeing written on the repair estimate the notation, "Front brakes extremely worn. Need replacement."?

**A.** Yes, I saw that.

*[One of your allegations is that the defendant was negligent in driving with defective brakes.]*

In the example above, you have established a sufficient foundation *possibly* to introduce the document into evidence at trial. If your purpose is to show that Mr. Roberts had *notice* that his brakes were defective, then the document can be admitted for that purpose — given Mr. Roberts' admissions made on discovery. The document is being tendered simply to show that the statement as to defective brakes was made. There is no hearsay problem. However, if your purpose is to introduce the document to show that the brakes *were defective*, the document is inadmissible. It is hearsay. You are tendering it as the "truth," that the brakes were defective. You would have to call Tom Bull. An admission identifying the document does not automatically translate into admissibility at trial.

### 5.5   Cross-examination

Cross-examination of the party is allowed in the examination for discovery. But it is not recommended. If you use a cross-examination mode, you are giving the witness an opportunity to educate himself on your approach. There is no need. A prime function of cross-examination is to discredit a witness. *But credibility is not a permitted area of questioning in an examination for discovery.* A less aggressive approach will be more successful. This is not to say that there will not be times when you will need to be forceful and assert control over an uncooperative witness, but this should not be the norm. You are seeking information, you are seeking admissions. This is not the time to attack the witness. This is the time to gather ammunition for your attack at trial.

## 5.6    Concluding the Examination

Before you conclude your examination for discovery, go through your checklist to ensure that you have covered everything. If there are undertakings, conclude the examination subject to obtaining the undertakings.

> **Counsel:** That concludes my examination subject to any questions possibly arising from the undertakings that you have entered into. Thank you, Mr. Waite.

# 6.    ACTING FOR THE PARTY BEING EXAMINED

During examinations for discovery counsel for the most part police themselves. There is no judge present to oversee conduct. The special examiner or court reporter has minimal influence over counsel. Counsel have a responsibility to act responsibly. Some counsel do not:[16]

> Unfortunately there are counsel who, far from seeking to avoid refusals to answer and infrequent resort to judicial intervention, appear to welcome, if not precipitate, such circumstances. Thinking such conduct to be good tactics, they disrupt the continuity of the examination with constant objections and refusals together with challenges to the examiner to take up the matter with the court. Either these tactics mask an insecurity based on ignorance of the rules or their purpose is to prevent or hinder discovery.

It is important that counsel understand the function of the examination for discovery. It is not intended to be an adversarial contest. Its prime purpose is the *exchange* of information. It is equally important, therefore, that counsel understand their role. They are both a *protector* of their client's interests and a *facilitator* of the discovery.

---

[16] J. Facher, "Taking Depositions", in J. Koeltl (ed.), *The Litigation Manual*, 2nd ed. (1989), p. 186, at p. 199.

There are a number of legitimate ways that you can assist your client:[17]

> • If you do not hear or understand a question, you can ask the court reporter to read the question back.
>
> • If the examining attorney hands your client a document and begins to ask questions, you can interrupt, peruse the document, and ask your client to read the entire document before answering any questions.
>
> • If your deponent appears fatigued, you can insist upon a recess.
>
> • If your client asks for some assistance or appears to be having some difficulty, you can confer with him or her.
>
> • If the deponent has made a misstatement, you may want to interrupt and ask the deponent whether he or she understood the question or even suggest that the witness may have misunderstood the question.
>
> • If the deponent has difficulty remembering a name, date, time, distance, or some other precise fact, and the fact is a minor consideration in the case, you can volunteer the answer.
>
> • If the deponent has difficulty with a response, and the answer appears in a document or other writing, you can offer that document or writing to the deponent.
>
> • If the deponent has answered a question and begins to ramble, you can interrupt and say, "Thank you, you have answered the question."

The line between assistance and obstruction, however, is a fine one. Counsel can abuse the informality of the examination setting through excessive interference. An occasional whispered conversation between counsel and client is usually tolerated. Constant communication is not. An occasional break at the request of counsel to calm an agitated client or to clarify obvious confusion is perfectly permissible. Repeated breaks to confer with the client are not. The examining counsel is entitled to an examination of the party — not the party's counsel. To defend against these tactics, examining counsel should have them put on the record:

---

[17] Haydock, *supra*, note 5, at p. 285.

**Counsel:** Let the record show that counsel for the plaintiff is conferring with
the plaintiff.

Let the record show that during the break counsel for the plaintiff
conferred with the plaintiff.

If the improper tactics continue, make your objections known and adjourn
the examination to seek a ruling on motion to the court.

The case of *McLeod v. Cdn. Newspapers Co.* provides a good example
of excessive interference. The master considered the rules of professional
conduct pertaining to communications between a lawyer and a witness and
he concluded:[18]

> . . . it seems to me that there is an analogy to be drawn between the conduct
> of a lawyer in communicating with his witness/client during an adjudicative
> proceeding on the one hand, and during a non-adjudicative proceeding such
> as an examination for discovery or cross-examination before a special exam-
> iner on the other. Particularly because there is no judge or master present to
> supervise the conduct of the lawyer and the witness, counsel should show
> great restraint and take care not to make unnecessary or inappropriate intru-
> sions into the discovery or cross-examination being conducted of his client so
> as to interfere with the rights of discovery or cross-examination by the opposite
> party . . .
>
> I therefore direct counsel for the plaintiffs not to communicate privately
> with either of the plaintiffs during the course of their being questioned on their
> examinations for discovery before the special examiner, either by the passing
> of notes or by consultations about the answer to be given, unless with the
> consent of defendant's counsel . . .

Objections at the examination should be few. Many of the rules of
evidence do not apply. Under the recent rule changes, the scope of possible
objections has been narrowed even further. Basically, counsel are confined
to objections concerning relevancy, credibility, improper opinion and improper phrasing where there is confusion or ambiguity. If an objection is
raised, the objecting counsel is called upon to provide brief reasons. This
preserves the record for any potential motion to the court to compel an
answer.

Counsel, as *facilitator*, can help to clarify the discovery. Earlier in this
chapter there were examples of where counsel for the party interjected to
admit identity or to admit that the person was giving evidence binding on

---

[18] *McLeod v. Cdn. Newspapers Co.* (1987), 15 C.P.C. (2d) 151 at 160 (Ont. Master).

the corporate party. These helpful interruptions make the record clear. Answers by counsel are binding on the party, unless the party repudiates counsel's answer (R. 31.08).

It is a wise tactic to be a facilitator. The examinations for discovery are a two-way street. If you obstruct the opposing counsel in the examination of your client, expect to be obstructed in turn. A degree of co-operation will make the entire discovery process easier for all concerned.

A final matter concerns the right of re-examination. Rarely is this done. The reason is that the examination is for the exclusive use of the opposite party and any damaging answers that you elicit can be used by the opposite party. Re-examination should be left to clarify simple, clear points. Otherwise, save your response for trial.

# 4

# A CRIMINAL CASE: CROWN DISCLOSURE

- **Crown Disclosure in Criminal Cases**

- **Disclosure of Information Held by Third Parties: The Common Law**

- **Disclosure of Third Party Records in Sexual Offences: The Statute Law**

## 1. CROWN DISCLOSURE IN CRIMINAL CASES

It is somewhat ironic that in criminal cases, where the liberty interest of a person is at stake, there is no elaborate statutory scheme for pre-trial discovery. Certainly the preliminary inquiry acts as a tool of discovery for the defence.[1] However beyond that, the Crown, under statute, is only obligated to provide the accused with minimal discovery.[2] The accused, in turn, need not disclose anything to the Crown — save for alibi and notice of defence experts.[3]

For far too long, what was relied upon was informal disclosure by the Crown. The result was that too much was left to the whim of the particular Crown attorney. Abuses arose. Injustices occurred. Donald Marshall's wrongful conviction in Nova Scotia is the most public example. Absent

---

[1] See *R. v. R. (L.)* (1995), 100 C.C.C. (3d) 329 (Ont. C.A.).
[2] See *Criminal Code of Canada*, s. 603.
[3] For a discussion on disclosure of alibi to the Crown, see *R. v. Cleghorn* (1995), 100 C.C.C. (3d) 393 (S.C.C.). Notice of experts is provided for in s. 657.3 of the *Criminal Code*.

legislative action, the Supreme Court of Canada undertook judicial reform of the law in *R. v. Stinchcombe*.[4]

*Stinchcombe* provides an excellent example of why reform was needed. Stinchcombe, a lawyer, was charged with numerous theft and breach of trust offences, all of which related to his dealings with a client. Stinchcombe's defence was that the client authorized him to use the funds under dispute as a part of a business arrangement. Stinchcombe's secretary ("L") was called at the preliminary hearing, her evidence was favourable to the defence. She gave a videotaped interview to the R.C.M.P. At trial the police reinterviewed the secretary and took a written statement. The defence was informed of the existence of these statements, but was not shown them. The Crown did not call the secretary at trial because she was, in their words, "Not worthy of credit." At trial, the defence made a motion to force the Crown to reveal the statements. The trial judge refused. The defence then sought to have the judge call the secretary. The judge refused. In the end, the defence chose not to call the secretary as a witness. Stinchcombe was convicted. The defence appealed, arguing that the accused had a right to receive the statements. The Supreme Court of Canada agreed and stated that the Crown is under a general duty to disclose all relevant information. The overriding concern was, and is, that failure to disclose impedes the ability of the accused to make full answer and defence.

The Court then went on to fashion a regime for disclosure by the Crown to the defence and it is absolutely essential that defence counsel familiarize themselves with the scope and dictates of *Stinchcombe*. The key principles taken from the case are summarized below:[5]

1) The fruits of the investigation which are *in the possession* of the Crown are not the property of the Crown for use in securing a conviction, but, rather, are the property of the public to ensure that justice is done.

2) The general principle is that *all relevant information must be disclosed*, whether or not the Crown intends to introduce it in evidence. The Crown must disclose all relevant information, whether it is inculpatory or exculpatory, and must produce information which may assist the accused. If the information is of no use, then it is irrelevant and will be excluded by Crown counsel in the exercise of the Crown's discretion, which is reviewable by the trial judge.

---

[4] *R. v. Stinchcombe* (1991), 8 C.R. (4th) 277 (S.C.C.).
[5] Taken from *Charge Screening, Disclosure, and Resolution Discussions*, Report of the Attorney General's Advisory Committee, the Honourable G. Arthur Martin, Chair (1993), at pp. 146-149.

3) Apart from practical advantages, the overriding concern is that failure to disclose impedes the ability to make full answer and defence, which is now enshrined in s. 7 of the *Charter*.

4) All statements obtained from persons who have provided relevant information to the authorities should be produced even though the Crown does not propose to call them. When statements are not in existence, other information, such as investigator's notes, must be produced; if there are no notes, then, in addition to the name, address, and occupation of the witness, *all information in the possession of the prosecution*, relating to any relevant evidence that the person could give, should be disclosed.

5) Crown counsel has a discretion, *reviewable by the trial judge*, with respect to the relevance of information. Although the Crown must err on the side of inclusion, it need not produce what is clearly irrelevant.

6) Crown counsel has a discretion, reviewable by the trial judge, to delay production of information in order to protect the identity of informers, the safety of witnesses or persons who have supplied information to the authorities, or to protect those persons from harassment. The Crown also has a discretion to delay disclosure in order to complete an investigation, but delays in disclosure on this ground should be rare. The absolute withholding of evidence relevant to the defence can only be justified, however, on the basis of the existence of a legal privilege which excludes the evidence from disclosure.

7) The trial judge, on a review, should be guided by the principle that information ought not to be withheld if there is a *reasonable possibility* that the withholding of information will impair the accused's right to make full answer and defence, unless the non-disclosure is justified by the law of privilege. The trial judge, in some circumstances, may conclude that the existing law of privilege does not constitute a reasonable limit on the accused's right to make full answer and defence, and, thus, require disclosure in spite of the law of privilege.

8) The denial of disclosure cannot be justified on the ground that the material disclosed will enable the defence to tailor its evidence, for example, to conform with a prior statement to the police. There is nothing wrong with a witness refreshing his or her memory from a previous statement. The witness may even change his or her evidence as a result. The cross-examiner may be deprived of a substantial advantage, but fairness to the witness may require that a trap not be laid, by allowing the witness to testify without the benefit of seeing contradic-

tory writings. The principle has been accepted that the search for truth is advanced rather than retarded by disclosure of all relevant material.

9) The obligation of the Crown to make disclosure where an accused is represented by counsel is *triggered by a request* by or on behalf of the accused.

10) In the rare case in which the accused is unrepresented by counsel, Crown counsel should advise the accused of his or her right to disclose, and a plea should not be taken unless the trial judge is satisfied that this has been done.

11) Disclosure should be made *before the accused is called upon to elect the mode of trial or to plead.* These are crucial decisions which the accused must make, that may affect his or her rights, and it will be of great assistance to know, before making these decisions, the strengths and weaknesses of the Crown's case. Provided the request for disclosure has been timely, it should be complied with so as to enable the accused, before plea or election, to consider the information disclosed.

12) The Crown's obligation to disclose is a *continuing one*, and disclosure must be made with respect to additional information when it is received.

13) Disputes over disclosure will arise infrequently when it is made clear that Crown counsel is under a general duty to disclose *all* relevant information. The tradition in Canada of Crown counsel carrying out their role as ministers of justice has generally been very high. Having regard to this fact, and to the obligation on defence counsel as officers of the court to act responsibly, disputes with respect to disclosure will usually be resolved without the intervention of the trial judge. But, when they cannot be resolved by counsel, the trial judge must resolve them. At trial, a *voir dire* can be a useful method of exploring and resolving outstanding disclosure issues.

14) Defence counsel has a duty to bring any non-disclosure to the attention of the trial judge as soon as he or she becomes aware of it.

15) The administration of justice will also benefit from early disclosure. There is compelling evidence that much time would be saved, and delays reduced by reason of guilty pleas, withdrawal of charges, and the shortening or waiver of preliminary hearings, by early disclosure.

The "duty to disclose all relevant information" has broad sweep. The word "information" is used. "Information" refers to the fruits of the investigation made available to the Crown. It includes both inculpatory and exculpatory information and information not intended to be used by the Crown at trial. Similarly, "relevant" has broad meaning. "Relevant," as applied in *Stinchcombe*, goes to *the ability* of the accused to make full answer and defence. In a subsequent decision, *R. v. Egger*, Mr. Justice Sopinka explained relevancy in terms of its use to the defence. He wrote:[6]

> One measure of the relevance of information in the Crown's hands is its usefulness to the defence: if it is of some use, it is relevant and should be disclosed [citing *Stinchcombe*]. This requires a determination by the reviewing judge that production of the information can reasonably be used by the accused either in meeting the case for the Crown, advancing a defence or otherwise in making a decision which may affect the conduct of the defence such as, for example, whether to call evidence.

The "relevant information" must, however, be in the Crown's "possession." The situation in *Stinchcombe* was straightforward in that the witness statements under dispute were in the actual possession of the Crown counsel. What of information not in the actual possession of Crown counsel? The courts have extended the duty to disclose to the police[7] and other investigative arms of the state involved in the particular prosecution.[8] But the duty to disclose does not extend to arms of government not involved in the investigation. In other words, the "Crown" is not indivisible and cannot be equated with "government."[9]

It is also the case that the Crown is under no obligation to disclose information in the possession of third persons. This was made quite clear in *R. v. Chaplin* where Mr. Justice Sopinka wrote:[10]

> This Court has clearly established that the Crown is under a general duty to disclose all information, whether inculpatory or exculpatory, *except evidence that is beyond the control of the prosecution*, clearly irrelevant, or privileged. [Emphasis added.]

The police, although separate and distinct in law from the Crown, have a corollary duty to disclose to the Crown all relevant information in their

---

[6] *R. v. Egger* (1993), 82 C.C.C. (3d) 193 at 204 (S.C.C.).
[7] *R. v. McNeil*, 2009 SCC 3 (S.C.C.) at para. 14. See also: *Charge Screening, Disclosure, and Resolution Discussions, supra*, note 5, at p. 199.
[8] See *R. v. Arsenault* (1994), 93 C.C.C. (3d) 111 (N.B. C.A.) and *R. v. Lenny* (1994), 155 A.R. 225 (C.A.).
[9] *R. v. McNeil, supra*, note 7 at para. 22.
[10] *R. v. Chaplin* (1994), 36 C.R. (4th) 201 at 209 (S.C.C.).

possession.[11] In *R. v. McNeil* the Supreme Court of Canada extended the reach of "first party" disclosure. McNeil was charged with drug offences. A key witness for the Crown was the arresting officer. The accused sought production of documents related to the misconduct of the arresting police officer, who himself was facing drug charges and internal discipline. The Court reasoned that where the Crown or the police are aware that relevant information exists, they should secure it as part of the investigation. There was a "duty to inquire." Where misconduct records of officers who play a material role in an investigation are either related to, or could reasonably impact on, the case against the accused, they should be retrieved and disclosed in accordance with the obligations under *Stinchcombe*.[12]

One area of uncertainty concerns the Crown counsel's own "work product" — notes, memoranda, research, observations and interview records prepared in anticipation of trial. For example, in *R. v. Bernardo*, the Crown was required to turn over to the defence information on the details and negotiations that took place between the Crown and its "crown" witness, Karla Homolka, which lead to her famous (or infamous) plea bargain and partial grant of immunity.[13] In determining what "work product" to disclose, one suggested approach is to differentiate between matters of opinion and matters of fact. Trial strategy, theories, conclusions are matters of opinion and should be exempt from disclosure. On the other hand, witness statements are matters of fact, which would need to be disclosed. Crown expert reports would also need to be disclosed in that they provide the factual basis for the expert's opinion.[14]

## 2.   DISCLOSURE OF INFORMATION HELD BY THIRD PARTIES: THE COMMON LAW

Pre-trial disclosure on the part of third parties has never been a part of our criminal process. Third parties were always regarded as strangers to the prosecution with no duty to disclose anything to the defence prior to trial. *Stinchcombe* was seized upon to change this state of affairs. Essentially the

---

[11] *R. v. McNeil, supra*, note 7 at para. 24.
[12] For a further discussion of the "duty to inquire" see *R. v. Darwish*, 2010 ONCA 124 (Ont. C.A.), leave to appeal refused 2010 CarswellOnt 8021 (S.C.C.). For a good example of a case applying and working with *McNeil* see *R. v. Borne*, 2011 ONSC 1662 (Ont. S.C.J.).
[13] *R. v. Bernardo* (May 10, 1994), Doc. 247/94, [1994] O.J. No. 1718 (Ont. Gen.Div.) per Lesage J.
[14] *Charge Screening, Disclosure, and Resolution Discussions, supra*, note 5 at p. 252. See also s. 657.3 of the *Criminal Code*.

courts were asked to move the law from "disclosure" by the Crown to the right of an accused to pre-trial "discovery" of any person.

The Supreme Court of Canada in *R. v. O'Connor* held that third parties may be called upon to disclose materials in their possession, so the Court fashioned a two-step procedure. In step 1, the accused must convince the trial judge that the information sought from the third party is "likely to be relevant." This threshold of proof was termed "significant" but not "onerous." "Likely relevant" means that there is a "reasonable possibility that the information is logically probative to an issue at trial or the competence of a witness to testify."[15] If this threshold is met, the information is provided to the judge for review. In step 2, upon the production of records to the court, the trial judge should examine the records to determine whether, and to what extent, they should be produced to the accused. In making this determination, the trial judge must balance competing interests: the accused's right to potentially relevant information against the third party's privacy interests.

The procedure in an *O'Connor* application is as follows:[16]

(1) The accused first obtains a *subpoena duces tecum* under ss. 698(1) and 700(1) of the Criminal Code and serves it on the third party record holder. The subpoena compels the person to whom it is directed to attend court with the targeted records or materials.

(2) The accused also brings an application, supported by appropriate affidavit evidence, showing that the records sought are likely to be relevant in his or her trial. Notice of the application is given to the prosecuting Crown, the person who is the subject of the records and any other person who may have a privacy interest in the records targeted for production.

(3) The *O'Connor* application is brought before the judge seized with the trial, although it may be heard before the trial commences. If production is unopposed, of course, the application for production becomes moot and there is no need for a hearing.

(4) If the record holder or some other interested person advances a well-founded claim that the targeted documents are privileged, in all but the rarest cases where the accused's innocence is at stake, the existence of

---

[15] *R. v. McNeil, supra,* note 7 at para. 33
[16] *R. v. McNeil, supra,* note 7 at para. 27.

privilege will effectively bar the accused's application for production of the targeted documents, regardless of their relevance. Issues of privilege are therefore best resolved at the outset of the *O'Connor* process.

(5) Where privilege is not in question, the judge determines whether production should be compelled in accordance with the two-step test established in *O'Connor*. At the first stage, if satisfied that the record is likely relevant to the proceeding against the accused, the judge may order production of the record for the court's inspection. At the next stage, with the records in hand, the judge determines whether, and to what extent, production should be ordered to the accused.

Interestingly, in *O'Connor*, the majority went on to find that documents or records provided to the Crown by complainants or other third parties lost any cloak of confidentiality or privilege. The material, once in the possession of the Crown, becomes "public property" and, under *Stinchcombe*, needs to be disclosed to the accused.

*O'Connor* sparked a legislative response. Parliament passed ss. 278.1 to 278.91 of the *Criminal Code*. These sections apply to sexual offence prosecutions and they modify *O'Connor*. *O'Connor*, however, remains good law in all criminal prosecutions not caught by s. 278.2, which lists the applicable sexual offences. In other words, we have two regimes for the disclosure of information from third parties:

1) the common law under *O'Connor* for non-sexual offences, and

2) the statute law for sexual offences.

## 3. DISCLOSURE OF THIRD PARTY RECORDS IN SEXUAL OFFENCES: THE STATUTE LAW[17]

As indicated, legislation soon followed in response to the Supreme Court's decision in *O'Connor*. On its face, this legislation, found in sections 278.1-278.91 of the *Criminal Code,* rejects the *O'Connor* test. However, the legislation was upheld by the Supreme Court in *R. v. Mills*.[18] Through creative interpretation, the Supreme Court managed to read down the legislation so that it could pass constitutional muster and not infringe the accused's right to make full answer and defence.

---

[17] This section is taken from David Paciocco and Lee Stuesser. *The Law of Evidence*, 3rd ed., (2002), pp. 213-217.

[18] (1999), 139 C.C.C. (3d) 321 (S.C.C.).

The legislation is broad in scope. It applies to both complainants and other witnesses in sexual offence prosecutions. "Record" is defined as including "any form of record that contains personal information for which there is a reasonable expectation of privacy" [see s. 278.1]. To address concerns that the legislation is overly broad, the Court in *Mills* emphasized that only records that "truly raise a legally recognized privacy interest are caught and protected."[19] Presumably records otherwise public in nature, such as public school or employment records, would not be caught.[20]

The legislation applies even though the witness or complainant may have turned over the records to the prosecution, *contra O'Connor*. In these situations, the Crown is under a duty to notify the accused that it has such a record in its possession, but it is not to disclose the record's contents unless the witness waives the protection or the court so orders [see s. 278.2].

The legislation adopts the two-step procedure from *O'Connor* in form, but appears to change it markedly in substance. The first step remains — the accused must convince the trial judge to review the record. The threshold appears to remain the same in that the accused must establish that the record "is likely relevant to an issue at trial or to the competence of a witness to testify." Section 278.3(4) then goes on to state that, "any one or more of the following assertions by the accused are not sufficient on their own to establish that the record is likely relevant. . ." The section lists eleven assertions, which cover virtually every conceivable relevancy for third party records and, if read literally, would block any review of the records. Keep in mind that defence counsel are arguing in the dark in that they have not seen the contents of the records, and that the objective is to have a judge inspect the records to see whether they do, indeed, contain important, relevant information.

The Court in *Mills* rejected the "plain reading" of this section. Instead, the Court chose the "constitutional reading" of the statute. The Court explained that s. 278.3(4) "does not entirely prevent an accused from relying on the factors listed, but simply prevents reliance on bare *"assertions"* of the listed matters, where there is no other evidence and they stand on their own." What the section requires is that the accused be able to point to "case-specific evidence or information" that shows the record is likely relevant to an issue at trial.[21] The accused must be able to point to something in the record that provides added information, which is not already available to

---

[19]  *Ibid.*, at 372.
[20]  *R. v. Regan* (1998), 174 N.S.R. (2d) 230 (N.S.S.C.), cited by the Court in *Mills*, *ibid.* at 372.
[21]  *Ibid.* at 380.

the defence, or some potential to impeach the credibility of the third party.[22] The mere assertion that a record is relevant to credibility is not enough.

It will not be easy to lay the proper foundation. The keepers of the record and those to whom it relates are not compellable witnesses at the hearing [see s. 278.4]. The Court in *Mills* is of the view that means are available through Crown disclosure; the statements of complainants and witnesses are not caught by the legislation [see s. 278.1] and will have to be disclosed to the defence. Furthermore, the defence can look to their own witnesses and the cross-examination of Crown witnesses, at both the pre-liminary and at trial. On this last point, it anticipates that the respective judges will allow the defence some latitude in exploring the records involved – without divulging their specific contents.[23]

The nature of the records in question will also often provide the trial judge with an important informational foundation. The privacy interest involved varies with the records. As the Court noted in *Mills*, the privacy interest in adoption or counseling records may be very different from school attendance records. Similarly, a consideration of the probative value of records can often be informed by the nature and purposes of the record, as well as the record-taking practices used to create it.[24] Thus, it is open to defence and Crown alike to argue inferences from the nature of the record – without necessarily providing a "case-specific" foundation.

Besides demonstrating that the information is "likely to be relevant" the accused must convince the trial judge that production of the record to the judge for inspection is "necessary in the interests of justice." This requires that the trial judge, without having seen the record, balance the accused's right to make full answer and defence against the right to privacy and equality of the complainant or witness. Under *O'Connor*, this balancing would only occur in step two, after the judge had decided to review the material.

The Court recognized that the balancing required under the section runs counter to *O'Connor*, but relied on judges to interpret and apply the section in a constitutional manner. Accordingly, the factors listed in s. 278.5(2) are not to be "conclusively assessed." The trial judge is directed merely to "consider" and "take into account" the factors listed. As a final protection for the accused, the trial judge is always free to make whatever

---

[22] *R. v. Batte* (2000), 145 C.C.C. (3d) 449 at 474 (Ont. C.A.).

[23] *R. v. M. (D.)* (2000), 37 C.R. (5th) 80 (Ont. S.C.).

[24] *R. v. Mills, supra*, note 18 at 387.

order is "necessary in the interests of justice."[25] If the application establishes likely relevance, but the judge is left uncertain as to whether its production is necessary to make full answer and defence, then the judge should rule in favour of inspecting the document. The Court's advice is, when in doubt—inspect.

Step two involves the review by the trial judge of the record and the determination as to whether or not the record, or part of the record, should be produced to the accused. In deciding whether or not to order production, the same balancing factors considered earlier are once again to be taken into account.

It has been suggested that *Mills*, through its interpretation of the new legislation, has essentially confirmed much of the law as found in the majority decision in *O'Connor*.[26] Certainly, this is true. However, it is also true that we have gone from the *O'Connor* standard of requiring an accused only to demonstrate likely relevance to a requirement of likely relevance, plus a demonstration that production is "necessary in the interests of justice." This is a stricter standard.[27]

## 3.1   The Procedure

The procedure to obtain production of third party records in a sexual offence case is outlined in s. 278.3. The accused must make application to the trial judge. The application must be made in writing and identify the record sought to be produced, the name of the person currently in possession of the record and the grounds relied upon by the accused to establish the likely relevancy of the record. Most importantly, the application is to be served on the prosecutor, possessor of the record, applicable complainant or witness, and any other person to whom the record relates and who is known to the accused. Service must take place seven days before the hearing. In addition, the possessor of the record is to be served with a subpoena that notifies the possessor that the applicable record may be required to be disclosed, but that the record need not be disclosed to anyone nor brought to the court until a judge makes an order for production.

The hearing is held *in camera*. The possessor of the record, complainant, witness, and any other person to whom the record relates are not compellable witnesses at the hearing for the accused, but they may appear

---

[25] *Ibid.*, at 387.

[26] For an excellent analysis of *Mills*, see Steve Coughlan, "Complainants' Records After *Mills*: Same As It Ever Was" (2000), 33 C.R. (5th) 300.

[27] See *R. v. Batte, supra*, note 22.

and make submissions. Obviously, it is open to the accused to testify and to call other witnesses in order to establish the relevancy of the record in dispute.

# 5

# MAKING SUBMISSIONS

- **Court Formalities**

- **Guiding Principles on Submissions**

- **Using Technology**

Effective communication lies at the heart of good advocacy and, quite frankly, we expect a lawyer to be a good communicator. The pressure is on and the expectations are there. Therefore, before we turn to examine specific types of submissions, namely opening and closing addresses, it is worth our while to pause and reflect on what makes for an effective presentation.

Although the focus in this chapter will be on "how" to make submissions, it should not be forgotten that the starting point for an effective submission is thorough preparation. Command of the law and of the facts in any case is absolutely critical. Saying things in the "right" way is not enough and is doomed to fail unless the content is "right." The bottom line is that substance usually prevails over form, but certainly it is preferable to have both. Another offshoot of solid preparation is that knowing the law and knowing the facts will give you greater confidence and control over your submissions.

## 1.   COURT FORMALITIES

There is a formality and decorum expected of counsel in the courtroom and it is important for new counsel to become comfortable with the court formalities. Much of this formality is designed to enhance the respect for, and the power of, the court. A lawyer is both an advocate and an officer of the court. The guiding principle, taken from the Law Society of Upper Canada's *Rules of Professional Conduct*, is that:[1]

> When acting as an advocate, a lawyer shall represent the client resolutely and honourably within the limits of the law while treating the tribunal with candour, fairness, courtesy, and respect.

Trial counsel, therefore, are to present their cases in a forceful and vigorous manner, but with respect – respect for the court, the litigants, the witnesses and opposing counsel. Such is not just good manners, but good advocacy.

Unfortunately, civility and respect in our courts seems to be on the decline.[2] Such is regrettable and wrong. The notion that aggressive, belligerent conduct is good advocacy is mistaken. The problem often arises when counsel do not like each other and things get personal. When matters "get personal," counsel can lose perspective. A sorry example is found in *Marchand (Litigation guardian of) v. Public General Hospital Society of Chatham*.[3] The case is a tragic one. The Marchands' baby boy was born profoundly disabled. The Marchands sued the hospital. The hospital was defended by senior counsel, whose conduct throughout the trial was deplorable (a term used by the Court of Appeal.) They verbally attacked plaintiff counsel's competency and integrity. They accused plaintiff counsel of "flatly lying," of "manipulating" the evidence and facts, of "trickery," of "sleight of hand," and more. The trial judge pleaded for professionalism. The verbal sniping continued. On appeal, the Court was of the opinion that the trial judge should have done more to control the trial, but that this failure did not give rise to a reasonable apprehension of bias. The Court, however, provided this reminder to counsel and trial judges:[4]

> Just as civility in the courtroom is very much the responsibility of counsel, it is also very much the responsibility of the trial judge. It is [a] shared responsibility of profound importance to the administration of justice and its standing in the eyes of the public it serves. Unfortunately, we have no doubt that the failure to satisfactorily discharge this responsibility in this case tarnished the reputation of the administration of justice. This case underlines the importance

---

[1] Law Society of Upper Canada, *Rules of Professional Conduct* (2014 as amended), 5.1-1.

[2] See Lauren Epstein, "Privilege and responsibility: Addressing rising levels of incivility among litigators" (summer 2013) 32 Adv J No. 1, 30-34.

[3] *Marchand (Litigation guardian of) v. Public General Hospital Society of Chatham* (2000), 51 O.R. (3d) 97 (C.A.); application for leave to appeal to the Supreme Court of Canada dismissed.

[4] *Ibid.*, at para. 148.

being given by leaders of the bench and bar to improving civility in the courtroom.

My advice to counsel is, "Keep it professional and not personal."

What is even more disturbing in *Marchand* is how defence counsel on occasion treated Mrs. Marchand. The record suggests that "defence counsel rolled their eyes, smiled and laughed out loud during parts of Mrs. Marchand's cross-examination."[5] No judge likes to see a nice witness needlessly abused by counsel. No witness deserves such abuse. A cross-examination may be vigorous and aggressive without disparaging comments or body language.

Finally, and perhaps most importantly, in a judge alone trial it is absolutely imperative that counsel treat the judge with respect. Look at it this way — even if you have complete contempt for the individual judge, have respect for the judicial office. At times a judge may be unfair, unreasonable, just plain wrong, abusive or rude — they are human. Stand strong. Present your argument. Make your case. Object, but do not respond in kind. Hold your tongue. A sharp retort may give immediate personal satisfaction, but it will also further antagonize the judge. More significantly, it mars the record. Let the transcript show a stoic counsel, who objected in a professional manner. Save your retort for appeal.

Justice Abella, writing for the Court in *Doré c. Québec,* which was a case that involved judge and counsel recriminations, put it well: counsel are to respond "with dignified restraint."[6]

## 1.1    Courtroom Courtesies

There are certain courtroom courtesies, which add to the dignity of the trial process and help to cultivate a respectful hearing. These courtesies are part of trial practice and are listed below:

* Provincial Court Judges are addressed as "Your Honour."

* In many Superior Courts, which include the Courts of Appeal, Supreme Courts and Courts of Queen's Bench, the justice is addressed as "My Lord (M'Lord)" or "My Lady (M'Lady)." Ontario, however, has expanded the use of "Your Honour" to its Superior Courts and uses

---

[5] *Ibid.,* at para. 152.
[6] *Doré c. Québec (Tribunal des professions),* 2012 SCC 12 (S.C.C.) at para. 68.

"Justice" in the Court of Appeal.[7] The Ontario move is to be applauded and hopefully other provinces will follow suit. "My Lord/My Lady" is an anachronism, not well suited to this day and age. Moreover, it is clumsy, especially when counsel is before a mixed gender panel on appeal. "Your Honour" and "Justice" are nicely gender neutral.

- Before the Supreme Court of Canada, counsel may use either "Justice," "Mr. Justice" or "Madam Justice" when addressing the members of the panel hearing the appeal.[8]

- In court, opposing counsel is often referred to by name, position ("counsel for the Crown"), "my friend" or "my learned friend," although certain jurisdictions shy away from using "learned." The key is to treat opposing counsel with courtesy.

- Counsel appearing with you is your "colleague."

- Witnesses, if adults, should be addressed by their last names, unless it seems more appropriate to use their first name, as in the case of a young adult witness and more mature counsel. Beware, some judges may insist upon the use of last names. Child witnesses merit the use of first names.

- Whenever you speak in court, stand. This practice is to be commended in that when you stand it automatically indicates to the judge that you wish to speak. Also standing allows you to better project your voice.

- Do not talk to opposing counsel directly. Speak through the judge.

---

**No**: Objection, you are leading the witness. **Reply**: I am not.

**Yes**: Objection, Your Honour. My friend is leading the witness.

---

Remember that both counsel should not be standing at the same time. Therefore, if opposing counsel rises to make an objection, unless her submissions are brief, you should sit down. Should you both be standing, the temptation arises to talk to one another, especially when you disagree over an objection. Communicating through the judge keeps

---

[7] *Courts of Justice Act*, R.S.O. 1990, s. 86. See also s. 86(2), where judges appointed prior to 1990 may elect to be addressed as My Lord or My Lady. See Practice Direction Concerning Civil Appeals in the Court of Appeal.
[8] Refer to the Supreme Court of Canada website found at *www.scc-csc.gc.ca*.

order. It makes for a clear transcript. Further, it acknowledges the authority of the judge to control the proceedings.

- Counsel should bow upon the entry and exit of the judge or if they enter a court when in session. "A court bow is a dignified nod."[9]

- Counsel should conduct their examinations and make submissions from the podium. The podium is your home. Generally stay put. Do not be misled by Hollywood trial theatrics, where counsel roam the courtroom and question witnesses from close quarters. Such would not be allowed in a Canadian courtroom. There are a number of practical reasons for this. First, most courtrooms now use electronic monitors and the microphones are stationed on the podiums. Second, speaking from the podium will force you to project your voice and thereby be heard. Should you move close to the witness, you will invariably strike up a conversation with the witness, which the judge may not hear. Third, it is intimidating to move into the witness's private space.

- Having said that you stay at the podium, this does not mean that you cannot approach witnesses to show them an exhibit. It is natural to do so. For example, you wish to have a police officer identify clothing found at the scene of a crime. You may retrieve the clothing from the witness table and take it to the officer on the stand. Furthermore, it may well be natural to ask the officer a number of questions about the clothing as you stand beside him. The clothing is then authenticated and you hand it to the clerk to be marked as an exhibit and return to the podium.

- In most jurisdictions, it is not necessary to ask the judge's permission to approach a witness with a document or other exhibit. However, this may not be the practice in your jurisdiction; it is best to check.

- If you wish to have a witness leave the witness box to give a demonstration or to mark a diagram, ask permission from the judge.

- Remember the judge controls the courtroom. Ask to have a document made an exhibit. Ask for a break or an adjournment. Let the judge make the "orders."

---

[9] Mr. Justice John deP. Wright, "The Bow," in the Ontario Justice Education Network found at *www.ojen.ca*.

## 2.   GUIDING PRINCIPLES ON SUBMISSIONS

In terms of "how" to make submissions, there are certain principles that apply for any and all oral presentations, whether it is a luncheon talk to the local community club or argument before the Supreme Court of Canada. Outlined below are certain touchstones for an effective oral presentation.

### 2.1   Know Your Audience

Different approaches are needed for different audiences. Beware — most books on trial advocacy concentrate on jury trials, yet submissions that may be suitable for a jury may well not be suitable for a judge sitting alone. Few judges, and for that matter few juries, will be swayed by the power of oratory. Stick to the law and the facts. A trial judge has a duty and responsibility to do justice in an individual case and your task is to help the judge find that justice. Adopt a "helping" approach. Point out how a case or statute will help the judge resolve the particular legal question, or how the evidence can be marshalled to assist the judge in making certain credibility findings. Note that with this approach the judge is not "told" what to do, rather the judge is assisted in determining the case. No one likes to be told what to do — especially judges.

Of course, the primary difference between a judge and jury is that trial judges are a knowledgeable audience. They know the process and, although they may not be familiar with the specific legal issue at hand, they know general legal principles. This means that you can dispense with many of the preliminaries and get right to the core issue. Your submissions can be focused and surgical. For example, over the years I have had students argue countless motions to exclude evidence under s. 24(2) of the *Charter*. Invariably, the students feel compelled to provide a lecture on the s. 24(2) test from the Supreme Court of Canada's decision in *R. v. Grant*.[10] I venture to say that most judges, with any criminal trial experience, know section 24(2) well. The law might be new and exciting to the students, but is old news for the judges. Move on. Focus your argument on the key concerns that you have under the test.

There is one further reality – you need to know your judge. Therefore, scout the judge out, do your homework. Use the court grapevine to find out what the judge is like and, more importantly, what he or she likes or dislikes. Some judges are fact driven and are impatient with legal argument. For these judges, where possible, concentrate on the facts. Other judges are

---

[10]   *R. v. Grant*, 2009 SCC 32 (S.C.C.).

more receptive to legal argument. Some judges are "Crown-oriented" and others are "defence-oriented;" you need to know that going into the trial. This is no reflection on the impartiality of judges, rather it is simply a fact of human nature and a trial reality.

## 2.2    Remember: Reason over Rhetoric

The second principle flows from the first. If we accept that a trial judge wants to come to a just decision, the task of counsel is to show the way. In any trial, counsel truly are the experts on the specific law and facts of the case. The challenge for counsel is to marshal the law and the facts and put them into a logical whole for the judge. The key is to reason with the judge and, better yet, invite the judge to reason with you.

Rhetoric is the art of persuasive speaking. Unfortunately, rhetoric also has a connotation of being insincere and exaggerated. Avoid rhetorical excess and theatrics; such tactics reduce your credibility.[11]

Reason over rhetoric means that counsel should:[12]

- support facts with evidence;

- support the law with authority;

- support conclusions with facts and law; and

- support the justice of your cause with policy and logic.

Be subtly rhetorical. Use the power of simplicity. Use the power of language. An effective turn of phrase or choice of words can be very persuasive. Justice Binnie provides this story:[13]

> He recalled once having tried to convince a judge that a concrete shelf in a swimming pool was a hazard. But when defence counsel focused on it as a "safety ledge" designed to prevent children falling into the deep end, pretty soon, everyone was calling this thing the "safety ledge" and it wasn't the "killer concrete" that [the client] had broken his neck on.

---

[11] Linda Rothstein, "Advocacy at the crossroads" (Winter 2010) 29 Advocates' J No. 3, 11-15 at para.38.

[12] For a further discussion on reason over rhetoric see Linda Rothstein's article on advocacy *ibid.* at para. 37.

[13] Justice Binnie as reported by Brad Daisley, "Focus the key to winning cases, Binnie tells seminar," The Lawyers Weekly, Vol. 20, No. 12, July 21, 2000.

Justice Binnie's story underscores the power of language. Think about the words you use. Words can create powerful images. Language is a weapon – use it – but with moderation.

## 2.3   A Submission is Not a Speech

This third principle complements the first two points. Consider the context in which you are making your submission. You are speaking to an audience of one. Do not preach to that one person. Talk to the judge. Engage in a conversation, which is what one person does when talking with another. Therefore, your tone and tenor should be conversational. Better still: try to involve the judge in reasoning through the case with you. The two examples below illustrate the difference between making a speech and engaging the judge.

| *A Speech* | *A Talk* |
|---|---|
| Your Honour, throughout the history of the English Criminal Law there is a golden thread, and that is that the prosecution must prove its case beyond a reasonable doubt. Lord Sankey said this over almost 70 years ago in the case of *Woolmington v. D.P.P.*[14] and it has stood the test of time and is still good law. In the case before you the Crown has failed to prove its case on identification. . . | Your Honour, the key issue in this case is identification and it is important to review the Crown's evidence on identification to see whether they have proven identification beyond a reasonable doubt. Keep in mind, Your Honour, there is no eye-witness to the actual break and enter. The Crown relies on circumstantial evidence, which they say links Mr. Smith to the break and enter. When we look at those links. . . |

## 2.4   Practice

Preparation begins with practice. An effective oral presentation takes enormous work. The presentation needs to be carefully honed in terms of what is said and how it is said. Often one is deceived by watching "natural" speakers, who can communicate so effortlessly. There is nothing "natural" about such presentations. The speakers have worked hard to be natural. Do not be afraid to rehearse your submissions and do not apologize for so doing. That is precisely what you should do. Take the time to practice. In the hurly-

---

[14] *Woolmington v. D.P.P.*, [1935] A.C. 462.

burly of the criminal courts, this might mean no more than taking five minutes to slip into an interview room to collect your thoughts and outline an argument. Become comfortable with the words you use and work on how to use them. Your voice is a potent weapon. Think about emphasis, pace and the power of silence after making a point.

One thing that you can work on and eliminate is distractions. Certain mannerisms or habits of speech can be very distracting. True, you need to be yourself, but not at the expense of distracting your listener. There are many irritants:

- Pointing of the finger or pen;

- Clicking or fidgeting with your pen;

- Chewing gum;

- The gunslinger, hands-in-pockets confrontation posture;

- Walking around the court.

I suggest that you videotape a submission. What you see can be excruciating. The videotape is cruel but honest. You will soon see certain bad habits. Some counsel like to start every question with "and" or "okay." Others, to fill in the silence, have an "ers" or "ums" habit. All these things can be fixed and removed once you are aware of them.

Sir Winston Churchill, perhaps the greatest orator of the 20th century, laboured long and hard over his speeches. Interestingly, he had a slight speech impediment in that he had a lisp, making it difficult for him to pronounce words beginning and ending in "s." He worked on and overcame this impediment. When one looks at his speeches, the phrasing in them, the pace and the power of language, is beautiful. A wonderful example is his famous "We Shall Fight on the Beaches" speech. The time was June of 1940. France was falling to the Nazis and the British Army had just been rescued from Dunkirk. Churchill spoke to Parliament and this is how he ended his speech – enjoy his use of language:[15]

> We shall go on to the end, we shall fight in France, we shall fight on the seas and oceans, we shall fight with growing confidence and growing strength in the air, we shall defend our Island, whatever the cost may be, we shall fight

---

[15] For a collection of Winston Churchill speeches, see The Churchill Centre at *http://www.winstonchurchill.org*

on the beaches, we shall fight on the landing grounds, we shall fight in the fields and in the streets, we shall fight in the hills; we shall never surrender, and even if, which I do not for a moment believe, this Island or a large part of it were subjugated and starving, then our Empire beyond the seas, armed and guarded by the British Fleet, would carry on the struggle, until, in God's good time, the New World, with all its power and might, steps forth to the rescue and the liberation of the old.

## 2.5    Talk – Do Not Read

The least effective speakers are the readers. No matter the value of their content, it will be lost in the delivery. This is the most common mistake committed by new counsel. They are nervous and, as a result, they retreat into their notes. The notes, which should be a reference point, just an aid, become an unnecessary crutch. The nervous speaker seeks the safety of the notes and so the reading begins. Reading, no matter how good a reader you are, is not effective. Eye contact engages and involves the listener. In order to relate to the listener, you need to look at the person. Look at them and talk to them.

The problem lies in what you bring with you to the podium. If you bring a full verbatim script, invariably you will get caught and start reading. I recommend you adopt point form heading notes. The headings remind you of your structure. You glance down, see the heading and then naturally tell the judge, in your own words, what it is you want to say under that heading. This is "point and shoot" delivery. You look down, see the point, look back up and deliver. Some speakers use no notes. Few of us can. If you can, without your delivery looking memorized or contrived, great. Do not, however, feel that the use of notes is a sign of weakness — it is a sign of preparation and organization.

## 2.6    Be Strong but Reasonable

As an advocate you are advancing a position. You must have conviction in order to give your argument conviction. Consider the following exchange between a judge and counsel:

**Judge**: Are you saying that your client was not drunk?

**Counsel:** It is our position that the evidence adduced at trial is not sufficient to support a finding that the plaintiff was intoxicated.

This answer is weak. It is prefaced by counsel saying, "It is our position." Moreover, it is too long-winded. A stronger, sharper answer is called for.

"That is exactly what we are saying" or "That is correct" or "Yes." Do not be afraid to answer simply and directly. Counsel are often too timid. You are familiar with your case and if your case postulates that your client was not drunk, tell the judge that. It is both refreshing and compelling to give a straight, simple answer to a question.

Know in advance the strengths and weaknesses of your position. In this way, you will know what you can and cannot concede. The "stand at all costs," "fight to the death" approach rarely works. You need to know when to fight and when to retreat. At one hearing, where the accused appealed a conviction for criminal negligence causing death, I observed defence counsel steadfastly refuse to concede that her client was in any way negligent in causing the death. The court pursued the point. "Are you saying that your client was not negligent at all?" Counsel refused to budge. One judge persisted. "Not negligent even in a civil sense?" Counsel remained firm. The judges shrugged their shoulders and shook their heads. The admission of civil negligence was not fatal to her case and, given the facts, was really beyond dispute. Criminal negligence refers to negligence of a different kind and degree from civil negligence; it requires a measure of "moral turpitude" to make negligent conduct criminal. Counsel's stubborn stand cost her a large measure of credibility with the court. She was being unreasonable.

## 2.7    Make it Simple

There is power in simplicity. A strong message is clear and simple. Good advocates focus on what really matters. They cut through complexity, discarding inconsequential information and zeroing in on the important facts. They are able to tell the judge what the case is about.

Professor Irving Younger, in his essay "In Praise of Simplicity," put it very well:[16]

> Ladies and gentlemen, I am here to speak up for simplicity. I lament the law's lack of it. I condemn the perversion that turns it into a sin. I preach the faith that simplicity is good in itself.

Good communicators are able to take complex situations and put them into simple terms. For example, in *R. v. Duarte*, the police had set up an informer in an apartment and audio-visual equipment was installed to record any conversations. Alan Gold, in challenging the admissibility of the re-corded conversations, argued that it is one thing for a young man to talk

---

[16]    Irving Younger, "In Praise of Simplicity" (1984), N.Z. L.J. 277.

about his sexual conquest the night before, which is a risk his partner always has to face, however, it is quite another thing for the young man to have recorded the session and shown all! Gold captured, in this simple way, the heightened violation of privacy. He also captured the ear of the Supreme Court of Canada. Justice La Forest wrote in *Duarte*:[17]

> In other words, the law recognizes that we inherently have to bear the risk of the "tattle-tale" but draws the line at concluding that we must also bear, as the price of choosing to speak to another human being, the risk of having a permanent electronic recording made of our words.

Simplicity includes not only what is said — the message — but how it is said. There is freshness and strength in using simple language. Unfortunately, lawyers often fall into the trap of "sounding like lawyers." All professions have their jargon. Avoid it. Keep this principle in mind: the more you sound like a lawyer the less effective you are.

## 2.8    Only Strong, Short Quotes

A submission should be in your own words. Do not look for someone else to speak for you. In other words, do not "over-quote." Some counsel are so insecure and afraid to tell the judge any law that they constantly refer to cases and rely on quotes to make their point for them. The result is that their talk gets bogged down in the material. What you need is the confidence to tell or summarize the law for the judge and, if asked, to be ready with case authority. But there is no need to lead with the case authority; keep it in your back pocket. Consider the examples below.

---

[17] *R. v. Duarte* (1990), 53 C.C.C. 3d 1 (S.C.C.).

| Letting the Cases Speak for You | Speaking for Yourself |
|---|---|
| Your Honour, in *Hunter v. Southam*, the Supreme Court of Canada held, and Your Honour, I am quoting from the bottom of page 114 [*pause as judge finds the reference*] Justice Dickson (as he then was) wrote, "The State's interest in detecting and preventing crime begins to prevail over the individual's interest in being left alone at the point where credibly-based probability replaces suspicion." That is our point. The police officer only had a suspicion . . . | Your Honour, a police officer's suspicion is not good enough to justify a search. The officer must have reasonable grounds for the search. In this case. . . |

If you cannot say it any better then, by all means, use a quote, provided that the quote is short and strong. In oral presentations, the simple truth is that long quotes are not remembered. Therefore, apply a three-line rule: if the quote is more than three lines, do not use it. The one-line quote is best of all.

## 2.9  Be Organized

Any submission needs structure and the judge needs to know how the submission is structured. Provide a roadmap of your argument for the judge. If there are three issues that you want to address, then say so and list them. Headings and signposts are good. A "heading" is just that, a "heading," and does not go into too much detail. Keep your headings short so that the judge can easily write them down. Let the judge know when you are moving from one issue to another. This is a perfect time for the judge to ask questions. I also suggest that for each issue you prepare a self-contained argument that has its own introduction, body and conclusion. The reason for this is that the judge may interject and say, "I do not need to hear you on that point, but I am interested in the third issue." With a self-contained argument you can move on, instead of saying, "But my submissions on point two directly apply to what I have to say on the third point."

## 2.10  Cut to the Chase

Brevity is appreciated by all. Mr. Justice Estey is credited with providing this simple advice on presenting oral argument:

*Be brief. Be clear. Be gone.*

Identify the key issue and get to it. People retain the most at the start and at the conclusion of any talk. Therefore, starting strong and getting to the point is very important. Arguments in the Supreme Court of the United States provide an excellent example. Counsel appearing before that Court have strict time constraints, usually a half hour. The standard opening is to say, "May it please the Court: What is at issue in this case is . . ." Should counsel not identify the key issue or issues early on, it is not long before the justices intervene. This indeed is the problem. If counsel do not show that they have command over the issues in the case and do not provide a clear order for their argument, then judges will likely intervene and counsel will lose control over their argument.

## 2.11   Be Heard

You will be nervous before your submission — the adrenalin will be pumping. As a result you might tend to speak too quickly. Slow your speech down. Let your message sink in. Also make certain that your message is heard. Speak distinctly and in a "courtroom voice" that is strong and projects.

Certain people naturally speak fast; they have a machine gun delivery. If that is you, then you must control it. Develop a "burst and pause" cadence. Speak and then pause to allow the listener to digest your burst of words. New counsel fear silence. Don't. A pause is refreshing for the listener. It allows the listener to rest or think. It also creates emphasis. Follow the pen is sage advice and if the judge is writing points down pause to allow the judge to do so.

Your voice is also a tool of persuasion. Use it. Linger over or stress certain words through the tone of your voice.

## 2.12   Start Strong: Finish Strong

Education researchers have observed that people retain the most at the start and at the conclusion of any talk. The start of any presentation is important. First impressions are important. Getting off to a good start breathes confidence into the presenter. The beginning of the submission is when you have a most attentive listener. You need to maximize this moment. A tried and true way to start is to begin by telling the listener your focus, your key point and what your talk will be about.

Similarly you need a strong ending. Not a summary — an ending. Bookend your submission. Reiterate your opening. Reiterate what the case is all about. An ending is not a summary; it is the time to close your book, look the judge in the eye and tell the judge why your case should prevail. Always have an ending. The ending should be short, crisp and strong.

## 3.   USING TECHNOLOGY

We are a visual society. Yet, the court tradition is an oral one. There is value in combining and complementing oral presentations with visual aids. Technology allows us to create and project graphic imagery as never before. Diagrams and flowcharts can be created with ease; digital documents and photographs can be enlarged and zoomed-in for effect. Use technology to make your presentations more engaging.

The technology need not be complicated. For example, a court document camera (ELMO) that projects the documents onto a screen, if available, is a wonderful way to focus on key documents and allows you to circle and highlight on the document itself. It also allows you to determine what documents you show and when. In other words, there is no set presentation or order of documents.

However, be wary. Technology is not to be used to replace your submission and it ought not to become the focal point of your submission. Visual aids are indeed intended to be "aids" in presenting.

### 3.1   Technology Basics

Whatever technology you use, outlined below are certain basics to follow:

1.   Become comfortable with the technology. You need to know how to work the technology or have someone with you who can.

2.   Make sure the technology can be used in the courtroom. Does the courtroom have a projector? Is your computer compatible with the projector?

3.   Test it. Do not trust a technician's assurances that it will work.

4.   Give notice to opposing counsel that you will be using certain visual aids. Notice diffuses objections; whereas surprise invites objections.

5.   Provide copies for opposing counsel and for the judge.

6.  Have a back-up. Technology is wonderful when it works, but is a disaster when it doesn't.

## 3.2   PowerPoint Presentations

As an educator I am very familiar with PowerPoint in the classroom and have used it extensively. It is a wonderful tool that unfortunately is much abused. Like so many, I over-used it. Now I use it far more selectively and to better effect.

PowerPoint is intended to present a visual. It is not intended to provide text. Yet most users of PowerPoint fill their slides with text and, worse still, they then proceed to read from the slides. A PowerPoint is intended to make a "point"; it is not intended to provide the viewer with a complete set of notes.

What about PowerPoint in the courtroom? Certainly PowerPoint is increasingly being used in jury trials. For example, experts use PowerPoint to assist them in explaining their science to the jury and PowerPoint can be used in closing arguments. Keep in mind that jurors do not interrupt and ask counsel questions, but judges sitting alone do. For that reason I do not think that PowerPoint is well-suited to judge alone trials in terms of providing a base template for a closing argument. Where it may have a place is in ordering and displaying certain visuals such as diagrams, flowcharts, and photographs.

Whatever the future uses of PowerPoint, outlined below are suggested rules from my experience as a PowerPoint user and misuser:

*   Cut the text. Focus on visuals.

*   One point per slide.

*   Apply the rule of 12: no more than 12 slides for any presentation. This means that your slides are indeed brief points and not notes. It also means that you can easily print the 12 slides on one page (six slides per side) as a handout.

*   Use a visually clear font such as Arial at a size no less than 24. Have a simple yet professional design. Do not use "bells and whistles." No zooming in or fading out. No sound effects. No moving text.

*   Respect colour contrast. What you see on the computer screen may not display well when projected. Avoid gaudy colour combinations. A dark

blue background works well with white lettering. Dark lettering works well on a light background.

- Be consistent. Do not change font, slide design or colours.

- If you want people to be attentive, know how to mute the visuals or fade to black so that the audience focuses on you. Do not run the PowerPoint presentation while you are talking.

- Know how to move forward, backward and to specific slides.

- Practise presenting the PowerPoint and test your presentation in the room, with the equipment you will be using.

- Remember the PowerPoint presentation should complement your presentation, not replace it.

- Always have a back-up should the technology fail.

# 6

# A TRIAL BOOK

- **Preparing a Trial Book**

---

The best preparation is of no value if it gets lost at trial. You must be in a position to use your preparation at the required moment and this necessitates organization. Your trial material is organized into a trial book or trial brief, which contains all you need to conduct the trial. In fact, the test of a good trial book is whether a lawyer, who is unfamiliar with the case, could take the matter to trial using the trial book alone.

There is no mystery to a trial book. It simply organizes your material for ready access. The material is placed in 8-1/2 x 11 three-ring binders. I do not recommend that you cram everything into one gigantic, cumbersome and unwieldy binder. A number of binders, depending on the complexity of the case, is suggested. Label the binders, or use different colours of binders. The key is to be able to find what you need when you need it.

Some lawyers use a divider method where separate file folders are used to organize the material. The divider method is better suited to cases with a large amount of material. Whereas the three-ring binder holds all in place, the drawback with using dividers is that your material is loose within each folder and loose material can easily get misplaced. While it may be irritating to open and close the binder continually, James McElhaney, in his book, *Trial Notebook*, observed that to some lawyers the "snap of the binder eventually produces a fearful anticipation on the part of the opponent as surely as Pavlov's bell made his dogs expect that dinner would be served."[1] So it should, if you are well prepared.

---

[1] J. McElhaney, *Trial Notebook*, American Bar Association (1981), p. 21.

Another option is an electronic trial book. There are commercially produced programs on creating an e-trial book.[2] Interestingly, one of the most important words of caution (should you try the electronic mode), is to have back-up such as a three-ring binder and hardcopies.[3] One difficulty in using your laptop is speed. Usually it is much quicker, especially in examining a witness, to used tabbed documents rather than downloading documents from your laptop. Test it. Find out what works best for you.

What goes into a trial notebook? There is no one formula.[4] You may well develop your own organization. The most important thing is that the material is organized for you and that you can find what you need when you need it. The outline below is my own organization of a trial notebook.

## 1.   PREPARING A TRIAL BOOK

### 1.1   Title Page

| | |
|---|---|
| Style of Cause: | Smith v. Jones |
| Cause of Action: | Assault & Battery |
| Date of Incident: | 11th March 2015 |
| Client Address & Phone: | |
| Opposing Counsel: | |

In a criminal case, the charge is specified and broken down into its respective elements. As the trial progresses, the required elements can be checked off.

While normally you would expect to find a table of contents and index following the title page, this is not always possible. It is difficult to number the pages in your trial book successfully because new documents and new information keep interjecting and indexing is redundant in that all of the

---

[2] See eg. Bruce Olson, "The trial lawyers's electronic notebook", which uses Microsoft office OneNote, found at http://office.microsoft.com/en-ca/onenote-help/the-trial-lawyer-s-electronic-notebook-HA010385354.aspx .

[3] See *The Trial Notebook* ebook, which is a free ebook downloaded from http://www.theattorneycasefile.com/ .

[4] For various descriptions of trial books: see McElhaney, *ibid.*, at pp. 20-26; T. Mauet, D. Casswell and G. Macdonald, *Fundamentals of Trial Techniques*, 2nd Can. ed. (1995), pp. 343-349.

material should be clearly *tabbed*. Divider tabs separate the major topics and secondary tabs refer to individual witnesses or matters which are organized in some sequence, be it alphabetical, order of appearance, or chronological. An index may be desirable for specific headings, for example, an index for documents or for exhibits.

## 1.2    Fact Summary

A summary of the facts helps to refresh your memory or to familiarize new counsel with the case. The summary should refer to relevant documents and witness testimony. Its purpose is to provide a short overview of the case. An excellent adjunct is to prepare a calendar of events, which will help you to put the evidence in context.[5]

## 1.3    Legal Memorandum

You know the facts. You also must know the law. Include any memoranda prepared on the law or points of evidence. The legal memorandum should outline your theory of the case as well as assessing your opponent's case. Include copies of any relevant statute law relied upon.

## 1.4    Court Documents

Place in chronological order all court documentation: statement of claim, statement of defence, motions, orders. Matters of process, procedure and notice arise and you will need to be able to respond by referring to the applicable pleading, motion or order.

## 1.5    Trial Chart

Like the evidence chart, which was described in Chapter 1, the purpose of the trial chart is to organize the law, exhibits and witnesses. It is a checklist to ensure that you are in a position to prove all the necessary elements required under the law. The trial chart is made up of three columns (see the chart on the following page):

---

[5] R. Manes and V. Edwards, *Manes Organized Advocacy*, 2nd ed. (1988), at p. 13-2.

| Elements of Law | Witness | Exhibit |
|---|---|---|
| Negligence: | | |
| (a) Faulty brakes | Mechanic — Smyth Passenger — Morris — testify defendant said brakes failed | Car repair estimates |
| (b) Excessive speed | Police officer — Gyles | Accident Report — skid mark measurements |
| | Witness — Stokes — estimated speed 80 km/h | Diagram of accident scene |

### 1.6   Trial Plan

Once you are aware of what you must prove and what evidence you must call, next you must consider the order of presentation. The trial plan lists the order of witnesses. It is wise to include their addresses, home and work telephone numbers in order to contact them on short notice if need be. Briefly outline their evidence in a few points. Also consider your opponent's case and whom you anticipate he will call and in what order. One suggestion is to include an estimate of time, which will give your client an idea of the length of trial.[6] This is also helpful in arranging court time.

### 1.7   Documents

Include copies of all relevant documents. Chronological order is recommended, and if there are a large number, an index should be prepared and placed at the start of this section. I would not file documents intended to be introduced as exhibits in this section. Rather, documents going in as exhibits should be kept in a separate binder or folder. The reason for this is twofold: convenience and order. When it comes time to introduce the exhibit through a witness, if your exhibits are filed in the same binder as your outline of the witness examination, then you must jump from the examination section of the binder to the document section and too often you can

---

[6] J.C. Bouck, "Planning and Presenting a Civil Case" (1976), 34 Advocate 275, at p. 276.

lose your place. It is preferable to leave the trial binder open at the examination section and turn to your exhibit binder.

Further, by keeping your own set of ordered documents, you will always have ready access to a document when needed. In contrast, if you keep the exhibits in your document section, you may displace some of the documents in the rush of introducing the exhibit.

Fortunately, the practice today is for most documents to go into trial by consent. An exhibit book is prepared and filed with the court.

No matter how documents or other types of real evidence are introduced into evidence at trial, it is necessary for counsel to keep a record of the exhibit number. In your document section, if an index is prepared, the exhibit number can be marked alongside the respective document. But a separate exhibit list should be kept by counsel in a convenient place, for example, on a page attached to the front cover of the trial book, or taped to the counsel table. It is important that you know where the exhibit list is and need not fumble for an exhibit number only to be told the number by the judge, who obviously is better organized than you.

One last matter, include extra copies of the exhibit. One will be filed as an exhibit, probably the original. One should be available for the judge to follow as you use the exhibit in court. And one should be kept for you. Keep in mind a further back-up copy is in your document section. Do not fear the duplication. The most important thing is that you are prepared to use the material at trial, and if this requires copies filed under different headings, do it.

## 1.8    The Opening

You have prepared your opening in advance. It is there either in point form or in full. The danger in having your opening written out in full is that at the start of trial you are nervous and will seek the safety of reading your opening. DO NOT READ YOUR OPENING STATEMENT. What is critical is that you have prepared the opening in advance and are in a position to make a favourable first impression on the judge.

## 1.9    Witness Statements

For each witness you have a separate background sheet, with name, address, telephone number, employment, a separate outline of evidence and a separate list of exhibits to be tendered through the witness. Any statement from the witness is included and prepared as an exhibit if need be. Key points are highlighted in your work copy. Never put a marked or highlighted copy before a witness. Use clean copies only.

Your direct examination is organized by way of a narrative that you will elicit from the witness, or point form pieces of testimony, or a complete list of questions and answers. New lawyers will be tempted to adopt the latter approach, but beware, because "scripted" testimony, if not well done, looks "scripted" and loses its naturalness and, with that, its credibility. A common practice is to use only one side of a page for the direct examination outline, thus leaving the other side for the answers you receive. Answers to be used in argument can then be easily written in. Another option is simply to leave spaces between questions to allow you to write the response.

## 1.10    Opposing Witnesses

Include any background that you know. Include any statements of the witness and prepare the statements as exhibits. If you anticipate the opposing party will testify, include the examination for discovery, if short. If the examination for discovery is too long to include, then prepare a summary, with an index, of important parts of the party's testimony. Exact statements, where important, should be included. You are now in a position to impeach the witness as to prior inconsistent statements should the opportunity arise.

As with the direct examination, you outline the areas on which you intend to cross-examine. The half-page method, once again, is recommended for recording witness answers.

## 1.11    In a Civil Case: Portions of Examination for Discovery to be Read In

You have already gone through the examination for discovery of the opposite party and have marked questions and answers that you will read in. Now make a list of those questions and answers and page numbers. Follow this list when reading in.

## 1.12    Evidentiary Issues

Critical areas of evidence can be anticipated and prepared for. In this section of the trial book your evidentiary briefs are filed (three copies: one each for you, your opponent and the judge). Relevant cases are included or your verbal argument on the specific evidence issue. One suggestion for new lawyers is to make a list of common evidentiary objections and post that in a prominent place on the counsel table. The list will help to jog your evidentiary memory at trial when you think something is not quite right with the testimony, questioning or evidence, but you cannot readily put your finger on the problem.

## 1.13    Closing Argument

Some lawyers recommend that you do not start preparing your closing address until the trial is well underway. After all, they admonish, the evidence will never come out as planned.[7] I disagree. I believe that there is wisdom in knowing where you are going, or your hoped for goals, before you begin the trial. In fact, there is much to be said for starting your trial preparation with the closing and working backward. By so doing, your goals are clearly established and you can better tailor your trial evidence and tactics to the achievement of those goals. I recognize the danger, however, that you may become too wedded to your argument and be unwilling to adjust that argument to accord with the actual evidence. What you must do is always remember that your argument is based on *the evidence adduced at trial* and not on the evidence that you *assume* will be presented. But the danger of "inflexibility" must be weighed against the formidable challenge of creating a closing during the course of a trial. Counsel, especially new counsel, have enough on their minds without the added burden of drafting a closing. Therefore, to my mind, it is far better to have a "draft" closing ready for final editing at trial.

## 1.14    List of Authorities

It is helpful for the judge to be provided with key cases you relied upon in argument. The cases, if more than one or two, should be tabbed and put in a binder or bound and a copy prepared for your opponent. Such a practice culminates your preparation for trial.

On the eve of trial, go through the trial using your trial book. Do you have everything? Do you know where everything is? If you do, then you are ready for trial.

---

[7] Manes, *supra*, note 5, at p. 13-5.

# 7

# THE RUNNING
# OF A CIVIL TRIAL

- **The Order of a Civil Trial**

Regulation of a civil trial is governed by the rules of the Court and by common law.[1] In Ontario and Manitoba, Rule 52.07 mandates the order of evidence and the order of addresses by counsel on opening and closing. Generally, a civil trial proceeds as follows:

## 1.   THE ORDER OF A CIVIL TRIAL

**1. Preliminary Matters**

(a)  Appearances
(b)  Amendments to the Statement of Claim
(c)  Amendments to the Statement of Defence
(d)  Opening Statements
(e)  Tendering of Exhibits
(f)  Order for Exclusion of Witnesses

**2. Plaintiff's Case**

(a)  Direct Examination of a Witness
(b)  Cross-examination of a Witness
(c)  Re-examination of a Witness

---

[1]  Throughout this chapter I will refer to the Ontario Rules of Civil Procedure and the Manitoba Queen's Bench Rules, which are similar, keeping in mind that the rules of court in other provinces do vary. See, for example, the British Columbia *Supreme Court Civil Rules*, BC Reg 168/2009, Rule 12-5(72).

> (d) Judge's Questions of a Witness
> (e) Reading in from Defendant's Examination for Discovery
>
> **3.   A Motion for Non-Suit**
>
> **4.   Defendant's Case**
> (a) Defendant's Opening
> (b) Defendant Adduces Evidence
> (c) Reading in from Plaintiff's Examination for Discovery
>
> **5.   Rebuttal Evidence by the Plaintiff**
>
> **6.   Closing Arguments by Plaintiff and Defendant**

## 1.1   Preliminary Matters

### (a)   The Appearances

The presiding judge enters the court and the clerk calls the court to order. Everyone stands. The judge bows to counsel and takes his seat. Counsel sit down. The judge then needs a few moments to settle in, arrange his papers, pleadings, trial book and writing materials. *You wait.* Finally the judge, when ready to proceed, will look to plaintiff's counsel, which is your cue to begin, or the judge will formally ask for "the appearances." Plaintiff counsel then stands and says:

> My Lord (Lady), my name is Holmes (surname only). H-O-L-M-E-S, initial O. My colleague's name is Darrell. D-A-R-R-E-L-L, initial C. We appear for the plaintiff(s) and are ready to proceed.

Defendant's counsel immediately follows with a similar introduction.

### (b)   Any Amendments to the Statement of Claim

If there are amendments to the statement of claim, counsel for the plaintiff(s) says:

> My Lord, I have one or two amendments to make to the statement of claim. My friends have notice of this application. The first amendment relates to paragraph 4 in which I would like the phrase "or should reasonably have been expected to know" inserted immediately after the phrase "the defendant knew" in the second line of the paragraph. The second amendment involves the

addition of a new paragraph in the pleading which I have numbered 6(a). I have prepared the proposed amendment in written form and would tender it to Your Lordship at this time. (*Copy of paper containing paragraph 6(a) should be handed to clerk.*) In effect, this amendment raises an allegation of estoppel as against the corporate defendant.

### (c)   Any Amendments to the Statement of Defence

Defendant's counsel follows a similar procedure regarding any proposed amendment to the statement of defence (see item b). In the event that the plaintiff does not move for an amendment of the statement of claim but the defendant wishes to introduce an amendment to his pleading, immediately after the identification of counsel, the defendant's counsel says:

> My Lord, before my friend proceeds with the presentation of the plaintiff's case, the defendant(s) has (have) an application to amend the statement of defence. Notice of the application has been given to my friends. The amendment relates to paragraph . . .

### (d)   The Opening Statements

At this point in the trial, after the appearances and after any amendments, the plaintiff *and the defendant* may make an opening address (R. 52.07).[2] Another option is to open *after* the agreed upon exhibits are tendered or to tender the exhibits as part of your opening. The advantage of opening after the exhibits are tendered is that your opening will be presented closer to the actual calling of your evidence and you also have a number of documents already before the court that you can refer to in your opening statement. The opening is a brief statement outlining the parties, the cause of action, the facts, the issues and witnesses to be called. It is an opportunity to introduce and inform the judge of your case. Opening statements will be dealt with in detail in Chapter 9.

### (e)   Tendering of Exhibits

Usually the parties have agreed upon a number of exhibits that go in at this time "by consent." Plaintiff's counsel introduces the exhibits immediately before or after the opening or as a part of the opening. The latter approach can be a very effective way of moulding critical documents or

---

[2] Please note that under the British Columbia Court Rules, defendant counsel can only open after the close of the plaintiff's case. See *Supreme Court Civil Rules, supra* note 1 at Rule 12-5(72).

diagrams into the "story" of the case. Each exhibit would be duly marked and numbered pursuant to the rules of the Court.

(i) *Statement of Admitted Facts* — Often tendered as a "by consent" document is a "Statement of Admitted Facts," the format of which is outlined on p. 118. The statement of admitted facts is an agreement between the parties as to certain facts not in dispute and is designed to facilitate the trial by saving the parties expense and court time caused by the calling of needless witnesses. The statement of admitted facts should not, however, be used to pre-empt the testimony of witnesses important to your case whose testimony concerns facts at issue. The evidence of a witness is far more vivid for the judge than the simple reading of the statement of admitted facts.

Let us consider an automobile accident case. You would not want to call the local meteorologist to testify that on the day of the accident the temperature was 15°C and the sky was clear. Surely those facts could be agreed upon. The situation would be different if the temperature were in dispute. Say the temperature at the time of the accident was 1°C and that the accident occurred in a low-lying area where the temperature may have been colder causing freezing or frost on the road. In this case, you would not agree to the 1°C temperature as a fact. On the contrary, it may well be important for you to call a meteorologist to give testimony as to the recorded temperature and the possibility of colder variation at the accident site.

Another illustration comes from the *Waite v. Stewart* problem in Chapter 2. There is no question that Stewart kicked Waite in the head. The plaintiff, however, must still prove causation. The defendant admits causation, which is obvious. So, too, counsel should be able to agree as to the physical scene of the fight: the size of the parking lot, lighting available, location of the cars. A diagram, if it would assist the court, is agreed to and prepared. Agreement should also be reached as to the extent of the plaintiff's injuries. The fact that the plaintiff suffered a broken jaw is not seriously in dispute. Once the plaintiff, through the pre-trial discovery process, verifies the injury, is there any reason for the defendant to contest this fact? There is not. In fact, it is in the interests of the defendant to admit this fact in order to minimize testimony on the injury, which would only emphasize the plaintiff's pain and suffering.

To illustrate the wisdom of admitting that which you cannot dispute, note the case of *Harper v. Bolton*, which involved a personal injury claim.[3]

---

[3] *Harper v. Bolton*, 124 S.E. 2d 54 (So. C.S.C., 1962).

The plaintiff had lost an eye in the automobile accident. Defendant's counsel should have admitted this fact because at trial the following occurred during the direct examination of the doctor who treated the plaintiff:

**Q.** Incidentally, do you happen to have the eye?
**A.** Yes, I do.

**Q.** Will you let me have it, please?
(*Witness hands small vial containing human eye to Mr. Dallis.*)

**Q.** That is the eye that you removed from Theresa Harper?
**A.** From Theresa Harper, yes.

**Mr. Dallis:** We would like to offer this in evidence, if the Court pleases.

At this point defendant's counsel objected; however, it was pointed out that the defendant had denied the extent of the injuries and demanded strict proof thereof. The judge then pressed defendant's counsel for an unqualified admission that the plaintiff had lost her eye:

**The Court:**  Do you admit in open court that the eye was removed?

**Mr. Nelson:**  From what the doctor has said, *I don't think there can be any doubt about it.*

**The Court:**  No, sir, I asked you if you admit that.

**Mr. Nelson:**  If the doctor testified to that, I do admit it.

**The Court:**  We will receive the eye in evidence.

Surely, the loss of the eye was beyond question and the refusal by counsel to admit that fact cost him credibility with the court and now the eye was there to stare at the jury throughout the trial. Not surprisingly, a verdict was returned for the plaintiff.[4]

It is to the benefit of both counsel to conduct the trial crisply and judges will be most appreciative of counsel who by prior agreement narrow the facts and law in dispute. But always be "cautiously agreeable." Scrutinize with care any admission that you are prepared to make and check the admission with your client. Caution is dictated because, as with any formal

---

[4] A new trial was ordered on appeal based in part on the error in allowing the eye to be placed in evidence before the jury.

admission, it is binding and will not be easily withdrawn should you be mistaken.

The formality in tendering the statement of admitted facts is as follows:

My Lord, agreement has been reached between counsel on certain facts and I would like to tender into evidence a statement of admitted facts.

*(Give to the clerk — a number will be assigned to the exhibit.)*

*(Paraphrase the facts.)* My Lord, the agreed facts include . . . *(Go through the numbered list of agreed facts.)*

Where counsel are not prepared to agree to certain facts and you are of the view that they are doing so unreasonably, R. 51 provides for a formal request to admit facts or documents. Under the rule, failure to admit the requested facts or documents may impact on costs.

---

## THE QUEEN'S BENCH

### WINNIPEG CENTRE

BETWEEN:

### SIMON FISHER,

Plaintiff

and

### MORSE CATCHER,

Defendant.

## STATEMENT OF ADMITTED FACTS

The parties to this action are prepared to admit the following facts at the trial of this action:

1.

2.

3.

Dated at Winnipeg, Manitoba, this _____ day of _____ .

_____ Solicitor for the Plaintiff

_____ Solicitor for the Defendant

*(ii) Statement of Agreed Damages* — In many personal injury actions, only one of the two principal issues, either quantum of damages or liability, goes to trial. Agreement as to damages narrows the case down to the single issue of liability.

By way of example, return to *Waite v. Stewart*. In that case there are four distinct liability and quantum issues:

- liability for the kick;

- quantum of general damages for the broken jaw;

- proof that the injury caused the plaintiff's loss of employment; and,

- quantum of employment income and career opportunity loss.

Each of these issues is quite distinct. Agreement on quantum for the actual injury, treatment and period of recovery is certainly likely. Loss of employment and career opportunity are more difficult to quantify, but if agreement could be reached as to the quantum of this loss it would save the calling of considerable evidence on that issue. The trial could then be focused on the liability and proof.

Even if counsel are not prepared to agree to all damages, at least the special damages should be agreed upon prior to trial. The agreement on damages is called a "Statement of Agreed Damages" and a sample is provided on p. 120. Defence counsel sign the statement, which clearly leaves liability in issue, and defendant's counsel may reiterate this point when the agreement is tendered:

> My Lord, if I may, with respect to the statement of agreed damages the defendant is *only* agreeing to the amount of the special damages listed. *Liability* and *general damages* remain in issue.

The formality in tendering the statement of agreed damages is as follows:

> My Lady, agreement has also been reached regarding the amount only of certain damages . . . *(usually refer to headings in statement of claim)* and the amount agreed is . . .

THE QUEEN'S BENCH

WINNIPEG CENTRE

BETWEEN:

SIMON FISHER,

Plaintiff

and

MORSE CATCHER,

Defendant.

STATEMENT OF AGREED DAMAGES

The Defendant, without admitting any liability for the same, is prepared to admit the following special damages:

1.

2.

3.

Dated this _____ day of _____ , in the City of Winnipeg, Manitoba.

_____
Solicitors for the Plaintiff

_____
Solicitors for the Defendant

*(iii) Other Exhibits* — Sketches of the accident scene, documents, photographs and other pieces of physical evidence where there is consent are introduced into evidence by plaintiff's counsel at the start of trial. The formality remains the same:

> My Lord, the next evidence I would like to tender is a sketch of the accident scene (to scale or not to scale), which is also agreed upon by my friend.

As each exhibit is tendered to the clerk, the exhibit will be assigned a number and that exhibit, whenever used during the trial, should be referred to by its exhibit number. Counsel, therefore, need to keep a list of the exhibits and their numbers.

Where there are a number of documents, they should be put into an indexed document book, generally prepared by counsel for the plaintiff. If these documents are agreed upon to be entered by consent, then this book can be tendered as one exhibit. The individual documents are referred to as Exhibits 1-k, 1-f, 1-m . . . 1-z. This saves having to go through the tedious and time-consuming ritual of tendering each document separately.

*(iv) By Operation of Law* — Certain documents do not need the consent of the opposite party to be introduced into evidence. Medical reports are admissible pursuant to the respective provincial Evidence Acts.[5] Plaintiff counsel says:

> My Lady, next I would like to tender pursuant to s. 50 of the Manitoba Evidence Act a medical report prepared by Dr. _____ , a copy of the report has been duly given to my friend.

### (f)  Order for Exclusion

In virtually all trials, an order for exclusion of witnesses is made, which is provided for in R. 52.06. The purpose of exclusion is twofold: First, to prevent witnesses from shaping their testimony to what they have heard from other witnesses. Second, it is a means of exposing fabrication by witnesses giving evidence for the same side. Contradictions in testimony where there should be consistency speak to collusion.[6]

The parties to the action are not excluded. However, counsel can move by way of R. 52.06(2) to have the party give evidence *before* his witnesses. Take the situation where a party to an action intends to call his wife to confirm his version of events. The husband can sit in the courtroom and hear his wife's evidence and tailor his testimony accordingly. To preclude this from happening, opposing counsel can move under R. 52.06(2) for the husband to testify first and, most importantly, in the absence of the wife.

Counsel may also request that a particular witness be allowed to watch the proceedings. For example, a psychiatrist expert may wish to be fully

---

[5]  *Manitoba Evidence Act*, R.S.M. 1987, c. E150 (also C.C.S.M. c. E150), s. 50, and the Ontario *Evidence Act*, R.S.O. 1990, c. E.23, s. 52.

[6]  See Wigmore, *Evidence* (Chadbourn rev. 1976), paras. 1837-1842.

informed of the surrounding facts in order to give expert testimony on the state of mind of the defendant at the time of the incident. Once excluded from the courtroom, the witnesses are not to consult with one another about their testimony nor with anyone else about prior testimony given in court. An exception is made for counsel who, as officers of the court, may contact witnesses during the trial, but are honour-bound not to divulge what has transpired in court.[7]

## 1.2    The Plaintiff's Case

### (a)    *Direct Examination of a Witness*

With the preliminary matters complete, plaintiff's counsel calls his first witness:

> I call as my first witness, the plaintiff, Robert John Doe.

The witness is sworn to give evidence under oath or by way of affirmation. The oath and affirmation are as follows:[8]

> **Oath**:  I swear that the evidence to be given by me shall be the truth, the whole truth and nothing but the truth. So help me God.

> **Affirmation**:  I solemnly affirm that the evidence to be given by me shall be the truth, the whole truth and nothing but the truth.

You should check with your witnesses prior to trial as to how they wish to be sworn.

Your direct examination then begins. At the conclusion you say:

> I have no further questions, My Lady.

### (b)    *Cross-examination of a Witness*

Defendant's counsel is afforded the opportunity to cross-examine the witness. The cross concludes in the same way as the direct.

---

[7]  See *R. v. O'Callaghan* (1982), 25 C.R. (3d) 68 at 75 (Ont. H.C.).

[8]  See *Manitoba Evidence Act, supra*, note 5, ss. 15 [re-en. 1987-88, c. 44, s. 9(1)] and 16, Ontario *Evidence Act, supra*, note 5, ss. 16 and 17, and *Canada Evidence Act*, R.S.C. 1985, c. C-5, s. 14.

### (c)   Re-examination of a Witness

Plaintiff counsel may then re-examine the witness. Do so sparingly. Re-examination is not intended for plaintiff's counsel to conduct the direct examination anew. It is intended to address new matters raised in cross-examination. It is not to be used as a device to split your direct examination. You are expected to conduct a thorough direct examination in the first place. Effective re-examination, however, can be most useful. It affords you the last word with the witness and can be used to clarify contradictions raised in the cross-examination and in this way rehabilitate a discredited witness. If you do re-examine, keep it brief:

> My Lady, I have one or two questions I would like to put to the witness in re-examination.

If you have no re-examination, simply say:

> I have no re-examination, My Lady.

### (d)   Judge's Questions of a Witness

Before the witness is allowed to step down from the stand the judge may have some questions to put to the witness. Witnesses should be told as a part of their preparation to wait in the witness box until excused by the judge. If the judge has asked some questions, he will give counsel an opportunity to ask any questions arising from his questions. If there are none, the witness is excused.

This procedure repeats itself for each witness called by the plaintiff.

### (e)   Reading In of Excerpts from Examination for Discovery

After you have called all of your witnesses you may decide to read *into evidence* portions of the examination for discovery of the *defendant*. At this time you would "file" the examination for discovery of the defendant. "File" is the correct term under the rules (Manitoba R. 34.17, Ontario R. 34.18). To "file" the examination simply means that the examination is made available for the judge. The examination is not an exhibit. The examination is filed for possible reference by the judge, who will read only the portions referred to at trial, either through cross-examination or read in by counsel.

The rules of court make this abundantly clear:

Manitoba R. 34.17(3) [Ontario equivalent R. 34.18(4)]: The transcript of an examination in an action shall not be given to or read by the trial judge until a party refers to it at the trial, and the trial judge may read only those portions referred to by a party.

Only the portions of the examinations referred to become evidence. Plaintiff counsel tenders the examination for discovery of the *defendant*:

My Lord, I would now file the examination for discovery of the defendant pursuant to the rules of the court.

Anything you read in from the examination testimony of the defendant becomes part of your case. Rule 31.11 governs: [Outlined below is the Manitoba Rule, the Ontario Rule is worded slightly differently.]

31.11 (1) At the trial of an action, a party may read into evidence as part of the party's own case against an adverse party any part of the evidence given on the examination for discovery of,

(*a*) the adverse party; or
(*b*) a person examined for discovery on behalf of, or in addition to, the adverse party, unless the trial judge orders otherwise,

if the evidence is otherwise admissible, whether the party or person has already given evidence or not.

**Qualifying Answers**

31.11(3) Where only part of the evidence given on an examination for discovery is read into or used in evidence, at the request of an adverse party the trial judge may direct the introduction of any other part of the evidence that qualifies or explains the part first introduced.

Reading in causes some confusion in the minds of new lawyers, who think that if you are counsel for the plaintiff, you read in from the plaintiff's examination for discovery. *Wrong!* If you were to read in from your party's examination that would be self-serving evidence. By comparison, the prior testimony of the defendant, or adverse party, is an admission made by the party that can be introduced into evidence. Look at the examinations for discovery as property. Plaintiff's counsel owns the examination for discovery of the defendant and defendant's counsel owns the examination for discovery of the plaintiff. And you cannot use the other's property to read in!

Prior to trial, you review the examination transcript in detail. Questions and answers that advance your case are identified for reading in. *Beware!*

You may be bound by any inconsistent evidence read in, and you must exercise great care in your selection. If a response is ambiguous and can be interpreted against you, then do not read it in.[9]

Remember, you cannot read in from the examination for discovery unless the transcript is first filed. The procedure for reading in is as follows:

My Lord, at this point I would like to read in certain questions and answers from the defendant Jones' examination for discovery, filed with the court, as part of the plaintiff's case.

I read in all of page 1, the caption, style of cause, and appearances. (*This identifies the examination for discovery as being applicable to the action now on trial.*)

On page 12, I read in questions and answers numbered 6 to 10 inclusive. (*Counsel then reads in those questions and answers verbatim.*)

**Q.6** What is your position with International Company?

**A.** I am the president of the company.

(*At the conclusion of reading in you read in the examiner's certificate, which verifies the accuracy of the examination transcript.*) I also read in the examiner's certificate on page 32.

Always read the complete question and answer into the record. Under R. 31.11(3) opposing counsel can request that other portions of the discovery be read in to complete or explain the portion counsel proposes to read in. You should anticipate these requests and be prepared to respond. If the request for additional reading in is accepted, then you can elect to *withdraw* your proposed question and the unwanted additional evidence.

At the end of your evidence you say:

M'Lord, that concludes the case for the plaintiff.

### 1.3   A Motion for Non-suit

A motion for non-suit (to dismiss the action) may be made at the conclusion of the plaintiff's case by the defendant.[10] The defendant must

---

[9] For a classic example of this mistake, see *Silverman Jewellers (1974) Ltd. v. Traders Gen. Ins. Co.* (1977), 3 C.P.C. 129 (Man. Q.B.).

[10] See *McKenzie v. Bergin*, [1937] O.W.N. 200 (C.A.), where the Ontario Court of Appeal ruled that the trial judge "should not, of his own motion, undertake to non-suit."

satisfy the trial judge that, given the evidence, no jury, acting judicially, could find in favour of the plaintiff. Should the defect be one of inadvertence, a discretion rests with the trial judge to remedy the defect under R. 52.10:

### Failure to Prove a Fact or Document

52.10 Where, through accident, mistake or other cause, a party fails to prove some fact or document material to the party's case,

(*a*) the judge may proceed with the trial subject to proof of the fact or document afterwards at such time and on such terms as the judge directs; or

(*b*) where the case is being tried by a jury, the judge may direct the jury to find a verdict as if the fact or document had been proved, and the verdict shall take effect on proof of the fact or document afterwards as directed, and, if it is not so proved, judgment shall be granted to the opposite party, unless the judge directs otherwise.

The law with respect to a motion for non-suit is not uniform across Canada. The key question is whether the defendant is obliged to elect whether or not to call evidence before any motion is heard. The Ontario practice is that the motion for non-suit should not be entertained until the defendant makes such an election. "If the defendant elects to call evidence, the judge reserves on the motion until the end of the case. If the defendant elects to call no evidence . . . then the judge rules on the motion immediately after it has been made."[11] Justice Laskin is of the view that at least in Ontario bringing a non-suit motion is of little practical value:[12]

A non-suit motion adds to the time and expense of a trial. And because of the election requirement, it has little practical value. Perhaps a defendant bringing the motion sees a tactical advantage in being able to argue first. To succeed on the motion, however, the defendant must show that the plaintiff has put forward no case to answer, in most lawsuits an onerous task. Why not simply take on the less onerous task of showing that the plaintiff's claim should fail?

In other jurisdictions, putting the defendant to an election is not necessarily mandated; it depends upon the type of non-suit motion. A distinction is made between a motion of *No Evidence* and a motion of *Insufficient Evidence*.

In a motion of no evidence, the defendant alleges that the plaintiff has failed to present any evidence on a necessary element of the action and,

---

[11] See *FL Receivables Trust 2002-A (Administrator of) v. Cobrand Foods Ltd.*, 2007 ONCA 425 (Ont. C.A.) at para. 13.

[12] *Ibid.* at para. 14.

therefore, the plaintiff's action fails in law. The Manitoba Court of Appeal in *Lou Petit Trucking v. Petit* accepted the following statement of the law:[13]

> If the case is one where some essential ingredient may be lacking, the judge may entertain a motion for dismissal at the end of the plaintiff's case without requiring the defendant to close his case if his motion does not succeed. The judge, at that point, is being asked to decide, as a matter of law, not of fact, whether, even if all the evidence of the plaintiff is accepted, any case has been made out.

A motion of insufficient evidence, however, is different. Here the issue concerns the sufficiency in fact of the evidence presented by the plaintiff. The defendant challenges the facts as being insufficient and before such a challenge is entertained the defendant should be put to his or her election as to whether to call evidence.

The rules of court in British Columbia are helpful because they clearly differentiate between these two motions. The applicable Rules of the British Columbia Supreme Court provide as follows:[14]

### No evidence application

12-5(4) At the close of the plaintiff's case, the defendant may apply to have the action dismissed on the ground that there is no evidence to support the plaintiff's case.

### Defendant need not elect whether to call evidence

12-5(5) A defendant is entitled to make an application under subrule (4) without being called upon to elect whether or not to call evidence.

### Insufficient evidence application

12-5(6) At the close of the plaintiff's case, the defendant may apply to have the action dismissed on the ground that the evidence is insufficient to make out the plaintiff's case.

### Defendant must elect not to call evidence

12-5(7) Unless the court orders otherwise, an application under subrule (6) may be made only after the defendant has elected not to call evidence.

---

[13] *Lou Petit Trucking Ltd. v. Petit* (1990), 64 Man. R. (2d) 139 at 144 (C.A.), citing Hamilton J. in *Jehle v. Petaski*, [1977] 1 W.W.R. 438 (Man. Q.B.).
[14] *Supreme Court Civil Rules, supra* at note 1.

At times, the distinction between a no evidence motion and a motion of insufficient evidence will not be clear. If in doubt, the Manitoba Court of Appeal holds the view that the defendant should be put to his election.[15]

## 1.4    Defendant's Case

### (a)    Defendant's Opening

Under R. 52.07 the defendant may make an opening at the start of his case provided he has not already done so immediately following the plaintiff's opening. This is a question of strategy and will be considered further in Chapter 9.

### (b)    Defendant Adduces Evidence

The procedure for the calling and examination of witnesses, as outlined for the plaintiff's case, is repeated for the defendant.

### (c)    Defendant Reads In from the Examination for Discovery of the Plaintiff

At one time it was suggested that a defendant was precluded from reading in from the plaintiff's examination for discovery if the plaintiff gave evidence.[16] The view was that the witness must be faced with the statements while testifying and thereby given an opportunity to explain. This position was premised on the "rule" from *Browne v. Dunn*, which mandates that where counsel intends to impeach a witness by presenting contradictory evidence, the evidence should be put to the witness.[17]

A distinction needs to be made between reading in for the purpose of using "admissions" against a party and reading in for the purpose of "impeachment." Rule 31.11(2) regulates use of the examination for discovery for impeachment and requires, as with any previous inconsistent statement, that the witness be confronted with the inconsistency.[18] Rule 31.11(1) is concerned with admissions and it should be noted that in this new rule the reading in from the discovery applies even when the party adverse has

---

[15] *Lou Petit Trucking Ltd. v. Petit, supra,* note 13, at p. 144. See also *Laufer v. Bucklaschuk,* [2000] 2 W.W.R. 462 (Man. C.A.).

[16] See W.B. Williston and R.J. Rolls, *The Law of Civil Procedure* (1970), Vol. 2, at pp. 884-886.

[17] *Browne v. Dunn* (1893), 6 R. 67 (H.L.).

[18] The procedure for examination on prior inconsistent statements is outlined in ss. 20 and 21 of the Manitoba and Ontario *Evidence Acts, supra,* note 5.

"given evidence." Mr. Justice Holland of the Ontario High Court faced this issue directly in *Int. Corona Resources Ltd. v. Lac Minerals Ltd.* when, at the close of the defendant's case, counsel for the defendant sought to read in "lengthy extracts" from the examinations for discovery of plaintiff witnesses.[19] Mr. Justice Holland allowed the reading in, with these observations:[20]

> The new Rule is a departure from the prior practice and clearly permits evidence to be read in even though the party or person has given evidence . . .
>
> By reason of the provisions of the Evidence Act . . . it appears that counsel for Lac can only read in those parts of the examination for discovery . . . which are admissions and those parts that go to credibility so long as the provisions of the Evidence Act were complied with when the witness was in the box in connection with such parts.

The authority, therefore, to read in from the plaintiff's examination for discovery, even if the plaintiff has testified, is recognized, but Mr. Justice Holland also recognized the potential for abuse and advised counsel:

> *It is to be hoped that counsel for Lac will refrain from reading in paragraphs from the examinations for discovery that have been fully dealt with in examination-in-chief and cross-examination because to do so would be unnecessary and repetitive.* [Emphasis added.]

In most instances, reading in from the plaintiff's examination will be "unnecessary and repetitive" and therefore should only rarely be done.

When confronted with a damaging admission read in by the defendant, plaintiff's counsel always has the option of recalling the plaintiff in rebuttal to explain the admission.[21]

## 1.5    Rebuttal Evidence

Plaintiff counsel has a right to call evidence in reply to evidence presented by the defendant (see R. 52.07). Rebuttal evidence should not be used to "sandbag" or split your case. You are expected to give a complete presentation of your case in the first instance and the pleadings and discovery make you aware of the evidence that you need to adduce to meet the

---

[19] *Int. Corona Resources Ltd. v. Lac Minerals Ltd.* (1986), 8 C.P.C. (2d) 39 (Ont. H.C.).

[20] *Ibid.*, at pp. 41-42.

[21] *Stout v. Carter* (1965), 54 D.L.R. (2d) 384 (B.C. S.C.).

defendant's case. Accordingly, you will not be allowed to introduce evidence that you should have adduced as part of your original evidence. Proper reply evidence, therefore, should be restricted to clear instances of new issues raised by the defendant or unrefuted contradictions arising from the defendant's case. The defendant, in turn, has a right of *surrebuttal* to address *new* issues raised by the rebuttal evidence.

### 1.6    Closing Arguments by Plaintiff and Defendant

At the close of evidence, the judge hears argument from the parties. The order of presentation in trials before a judge alone has the plaintiff addressing the court first, followed by the defendant, with the plaintiff accorded an opportunity to reply.

The case is then left with the trial judge for judgment. A decision may be made quickly through an oral judgment; the judge may make certain orders, with written reasons to follow; or, as in most cases, the judge's decision is reserved.[22]

The trial is over.

---

[22] The British Columbia Rules of Court provide for a right of reply and a response to the reply. See *Supreme Court Civil Rules*, *supra* note 1 at Rule 12-5(72), which reads:(c) at the close of all of the evidence, the party who began may address the jury or the court, and the opposite party may then address the jury or the court and the party who began may then reply and the court may allow the opposite party to be heard in response to a point raised in the reply.

# 8

# THE RUNNING
# OF A CRIMINAL TRIAL

- **Fundamental Principles of a Criminal Trial**

- **The Order of a Criminal Trial**

A criminal trial is a fascinating amalgam of law, procedure and evidence. It is both a complex and dynamic process, where experience is a distinct advantage. Experienced counsel know the court, the judge and what to expect as the trial unfolds. In other words, they know the game and the rules of the game. To offset this advantage and avoid being taken advantage of, new counsel need to become familiar with the running of a criminal trial. This chapter outlines a criminal judge alone trial, starting with key principles, and then walks through the various stages of the trial.

## 1. THE FUNDAMENTAL PRINCIPLES OF A CRIMINAL TRIAL

I suggest that there are four fundamental tenets of a criminal trial.

*First*, a criminal trial is accusatorial.

*Second*, our trial system is adversarial.

*Third*, a criminal trial is a search for truth.

*Fourth*, justice demands that the accused receive a fair trial.

These principles mould and direct a criminal trial.

## 1.1    A Criminal Trial is Accusatorial

"He who asserts must prove." This maxim guides a criminal prosecution. The Crown alleges that the accused has committed a crime and the Crown bears the burden of proving that allegation beyond a reasonable doubt. The presumption of innocence as found in section 11(d) of the *Charter* enshrines this principle.[1] Section 11(d) is violated whenever an accused may be convicted while a reasonable doubt exists. Reverse onus provisions, which place the onus on the accused to prove a defence or negate an element of an offence, violate the *Charter*. For example, s. 16(3) of the *Criminal Code* places the burden of proof on an accused to prove mental disorder on a balance of probabilities. Similarly, an accused raising automatism must establish that defence on a balance of probabilities.[2] Although the reverse onus provisions in both of these examples violate the *Charter* both are saved under section 1, as being reasonable limits in a free and democratic society.

The threshold "beyond a reasonable doubt" is high and the Crown faces a formidable task in building a case to prove each element of a crime to such a degree. The fundamental reality is that accused persons who are "likely guilty" or "probably guilty" go free. That is our system and it reflects our revulsion in wrongfully convicting an innocent person.

We are all very familiar with the phrase "beyond a reasonable doubt." At one time, it was thought best not to try to explain, define or embellish the phrase. That is no longer the case. The Supreme Court of Canada in *R. v. Lifchus* mandates further explanation be given to juries.[3] The Supreme Court provided a model jury charge. The principles contained in the charge are as follows:

- A reasonable doubt is not an imaginary or frivolous doubt;

- It is not based upon sympathy or prejudice;

- It is based on reason and common sense derived from the evidence or lack of evidence;

- Even if you believe the accused is probably guilty or likely guilty, that is not sufficient;

[1]  See *R. v. Oakes* (1986), 24 C.C.C. (3d) 321 (S.C.C.).
[2]  See *R. v. Stone* (1999), 134 C.C.C. (3d) 353 (S.C.C.).
[3]  *R. v. Lifchus* (1997), 118 C.C.C. (3d) 1 (S.C.C.).

- It is virtually impossible to prove anything to an absolute certainty and the Crown is not required to do so;

- In other words, in order to convict, what is required is something less than absolute certainty and something more than probable guilt.[4]

A special instruction applies in all trials where the accused testifies. This is especially important in "he said/she said" cases. In such trials it is not a simple matter of whom you believe. You may have no doubt that the accused is lying or mistaken, but still be left in doubt about whether the complainant is telling the truth. For example, in a sexual assault case, the accused testifies that the complainant freely consented to the sexual activity. Because of contradictions and evasions in his testimony, you do not believe him. However, when the complainant testified, she too was not entirely convincing. She admitted to drinking heavily and there was fuzziness in her recollection of events. Even if you do not believe the accused, has the complainant convinced you beyond a reasonable doubt of the crime? In such situations, trial judges sitting alone, like jurors, must comply with the following "W.D. instruction:"[5]

1) First, if you believe the evidence of the accused, obviously you must acquit.

2) Second, if you do not believe the testimony of the accused but you are left in reasonable doubt by it, you must acquit.

3) Third, even if you are not left in doubt by the evidence of the accused, you must ask yourself whether, on the basis of the evidence which you do accept, you are convinced beyond a reasonable doubt by that evidence of the guilt of the accused.

## 1.2 The Trial is Adversarial

Our trial system is premised on the belief that the truth will best come out when the respective interested parties present, test and challenge evidence before an impartial judge, who then decides the case. In the adversarial system, counsel raise the issues, provide the applicable law, highlight weaknesses in their opponent's case and enforce the rules of the trial. Judges are

---

[4] This last elaboration comes from *R. v. Starr* (2000), 147 C.C.C. (3d) 449 at para. 242 (S.C.C.).

[5] *R. v. W.(D.)* (1991), 63 C.C.C. (3d) 397 (S.C.C.).

reluctant to interfere in counsel's case. To be sure, judges will intervene to ensure a fair trial, but in terms of the evidence presented and witnesses called, those matters rest largely with the counsel involved.

The adversarial system works well when equally competent counsel conduct the trial. It works less well when an unrepresented litigant is involved. In this situation, the trial judge is expected to assist the unrepresented party in properly conducting the trial.[6] Yet, what judges find even more difficult are the "under-represented litigants." In these situations a person has counsel, albeit sub-par, and the trial judge is loath to interfere precisely because the accused is represented. The message then is clear — our adversarial system requires competent counsel, familiar with the trial process, prepared on the facts, knowledgeable on the law and informed as to the rules of the trial.

### 1.3    A Criminal Trial is a Search for Truth

"The ultimate aim of any trial, criminal or civil, must be to seek and to ascertain the truth."[7] Both sides present evidence designed to reconstruct past events. Perfect reconstruction is not possible; we simply cannot replay the past and must do the best we can with the evidence available.

The rules of evidence and of trial practice facilitate the finding of the truth. Failure to appreciate this fact leads to misapplication of the rules, injustice and, ultimately, loss of truth. So it is that our rules of evidence are currently being reformed in order to better pursue truth. The trend in the law of evidence in Canada, in fact, is to eschew fixed rules in favour of a more flexible approach precisely in order to do justice in individual cases. The best example is the Supreme Court's decision in *R. v. Khan*, where the Court created the new principled basis for the admitting of hearsay evidence.[8]

### 1.4    An Accused is Entitled to a Fair Trial

As a principle of fundamental justice, an accused has the right to a fair trial. A "fair trial" need not be a "perfect" one, or the most advantageous trial possible from the accused's perspective. What constitutes a fair trial takes into account not only the perspective of the accused, but the practical

---

[6] See *R. v. McGibbon* (1988), 45 C.C.C. (3d) 334 (Ont. C.A.) and *R. v. Phillips* (2003), 172 C.C.C. (3d) 285 (Alta. C.A.); affirmed [2003] S.C.J. No. 56.

[7] *R. v. Nikolovski* (1996), 111 C.C.C. (3d) 403 at para. 13 per Cory. J. (S.C.C.).

[8] *R. v. Khan* (1990), 59 C.C.C. (3d) 92 (S.C.C.).

limits of the system of justice and the lawful interests of others involved in the process. What the law demands is not perfect justice, but fundamentally fair justice. At the same time, occasional injustice cannot be accepted as the price of efficiency.[9]

Implicit in this principle of "fairness" is that the state will treat the accused fairly. Abusive and unfair tactics by the state will not be condoned – even if it means the exclusion of highly probative evidence. We see this intertwined with the exclusion of evidence under s. 24(2) of the *Charter*, where evidence obtained in a manner that infringes the *Charter* and its admission could bring the administration of justice into disrepute.[10] For example, a confession may be excluded simply because the accused was not read his full section 10(b) *Charter* rights. Notwithstanding the fact that the statement was given voluntarily and is reliable, the state is obliged to fairly inform the accused of his right to counsel and failure to do so is unacceptable.

We accept then that the state may be precluded from introducing otherwise relevant evidence against an accused. Such is the price to ensure that the state acts within the law and treats its citizenry fairly. On the other hand, it would be wrong to deny an accused the right to present relevant evidence going to innocence. An accused has the fundamental right to make full answer and defence. Professor David Paciocco put forth this proposition: "While the law can justifiably sacrifice truth about guilt in the interests of other pursuits, it can never justifiably sacrifice the truth about innocence."[11]

Therefore, the law of evidence is not symmetrical. Limitations are placed upon the introduction of Crown evidence, which do not apply to the defence. For example:

- The Crown is prohibited from introducing bad character evidence of the accused, unless it falls within the similar fact exception. Yet, there is no general prohibition on the accused presenting bad character of a Crown witness.

---

[9] This paragraph paraphrases McLachlin C.J. in *R. v. Find* (2001), 154 C.C.C. (3d) 97 at para. 28 (S.C.C.).

[10] See Chapter 15.

[11] D. Paciocco, "Truth and Proof": The Basics of the Law of Evidence in a 'Guilt-Based' System" (2001) Can. Crim. Law Rev. 71 at 78.

- Full disclosure of the Crown's case to the defence is demanded. Yet, the defence has no reciprocal duty to disclose its case.[12]

- A judge has a judicial discretion to exclude relevant and material evidence offered by the Crown where its probative value is outweighed by its "prejudice." Yet, defence evidence should only be excluded solely where the risks of prejudice *substantially* outweigh its probative value.[13]

- Rules of exclusion should be relaxed where necessary to allow the defence to introduce relevant evidence going to innocence.[14]

The fundamental principle is that it would be wrong to prevent an accused from introducing otherwise relevant evidence that goes to innocence.[15] The key is relevant evidence; an accused has no right to introduce irrelevant evidence.

## 2.   THE ORDER OF A CRIMINAL TRIAL

Counsel will look in vain for a comprehensive statute that outlines the order of a criminal trial. Rather, you must piece together, as best you can, a number of disjointed sections in the *Criminal Code* that pertain to trials.[16] Generally speaking, a criminal trial proceeds as follows:

---

[12] *R. v. Stinchcombe* (1991), 68 C.C.C. (3d) 1 (S.C.C.).

[13] *R. v. Shearing* (2002), 165 C.C.C. (3d) 225 at para. 107-109 (S.C.C.).

[14] *R. v. Brown* (2002), 162 C.C.C. (3d) 257 at para. 117 (S.C.C.).

[15] See *R. v. Brown, ibid.*, where it was recognized that in appropriate cases solicitor-client privilege would have to give way to the accused's ability to make full answer and defence.

[16] See s. 557 "Taking of Evidence" (Trial without a jury) and s. 646 "Taking Evidence" (Procedure in jury trials). Both these sections refer to the procedure found in Part XVIII, which pertains to preliminary inquiries. Under Part XVIII, s. 537 deals with the powers of a justice in conducting a preliminary inquiry and s. 540 concerns the taking of evidence at the preliminary. Other sections that pertain to the trial process include s. 645 (Trial adjournments and pre-trial motions); s. 650 requires that an accused be present in court during the course of his or her trial unless removed by the court or permitted to be absent; s. 651 outlines the order of addresses.

## The Order of a Criminal Trial

1. **Appearances by counsel**

2. **Any preliminary matters [amendments to indictment or information; any pre-trial motions; order for exclusion of witnesses]**

3. **Opening statement by the Crown**

4. **Admissions by the defence**

5. **Crown calls evidence:**
   i)   witness takes stand
   ii)  direct examination of witness
   iii) cross-examination of witness by defence
   iv)  re-examination of witness [*if necessary*]
   v)   judge may question witness
   vi)  next witness called

6. **Crown closes case**

7. **Defence may make motion of no evidence to stop the trial**

8. **Defence opens case with opening statement**

9. **Defence calls evidence [*as above*]**

10. **Defence closes case**

11. **Crown may seek to call further evidence**

12. **Closing submissions by counsel:**
    i)  Defence makes submissions first if the defence called evidence
    ii) Crown makes submissions first if the defence has not called evidence

13. **Judge reserves decision or gives decision orally from the bench**

14. **If found guilty, the court may immediately turn to sentence and, after hearing submissions from counsel sentence the accused, or the judge may adjourn the matter to allow counsel to prepare for a sentence hearing.**

## 2.1    Appearances by Counsel

At the start of a trial counsel introduce themselves. The presiding judge enters the court and the clerk calls the court to order. Everyone stands. The judge usually bows to counsel and takes his seat. Everyone sits down. The judge then needs a few moments to settle in, arrange his papers, trial book and writing materials. Counsel wait. Finally the judge, when ready to proceed, will look to counsel, which is the cue to begin, or the judge will ask for "appearances." Counsel stand and say something like:

---

**Crown**: "Your Honour, Joan Smith, appearing for the Crown."

**Defence**: "Your Honour, my name is Grant Mitchell, I act for Mr. Jackson, who is present, and I am prepared to proceed."

*or*

"For the monitor, my name is . . . . ."

"For the record, my name is . . . . ."

---

If acting as defence counsel, indicate to the judge that your client is present. Remember, your "client" has a name and is not "the accused."

### (a)    Where Should the Client Sit?

It is important for defence counsel to personalize their clients. That is also one reason to have the client either seated at the counsel table or nearby. Many courtrooms, particularly older jury courtrooms, have a "prisoner's dock," which often is the loneliest, coldest, and most uncomfortable seat in the court.[17] A trial judge has discretion to permit the accused to sit at the counsel table rather than in the dock. The discretion should be exercised in a manner that balances the interests of a fair trial and courtroom security.[18]

For those clients who are out of custody it should be accepted practice for them to sit with their counsel. Obviously, those accused who are detained pending trial pose greater concern. Some constitute a security risk; some do not. Absent security concerns, the accused should be allowed to sit with

---

[17] See Lynal Doerksen, "Out of the Dock and Into the Bar: An Examination of the History and Use of the Prisoner's Dock" (1990), 32 C.L.Q. 478.

[18] *R. v. Lalande* (1999), 138 C.C.C. (3d) 441 (Ont. C.A.) at para. 19.

counsel. Such a practice should not be regarded as exceptional, although I appreciate that there is a line of authority to the contrary.[19] As a matter of course, the chief investigating police officer in serious crime cases often sits with Crown counsel or within close proximity. Surely an accused should have the same opportunity. This has nothing to do with some sort of stigma attached to the prisoner's dock; it has everything to do with trial fairness and the perception of trial fairness. By having the accused seated at the counsel table they are given direct and immediate access to their counsel to consult, assist and question.

Even more importantly, it intimately involves the accused in the entire trial process. Commissioner Kaufman in the *Morin Inquiry* recommended that: "Absent the existence of a proven security risk, persons charged with a criminal offence should be entitled, at their option, to be seated with their counsel, rather than in the prisoner's dock."[20] This recommendation makes sense.[21] Of course, another option is to do away with the prisoner's dock entirely, which evidently is the case in Nova Scotia. Edward Greenspan had this to say: "I think the prisoner's boxes in this country ought to be destroyed. I do not know how anyone sits in that box looking innocent."[22]

## 2.2   Preliminary Matters

Prior to the start of the trial proper, the court may deal with a wide variety of pre-trial motions. The above motion to allow the accused to be seated at the counsel table is but one example. Even in judge alone trials, it is becoming increasingly commonplace to hold pre-trial evidentiary hearings. For example, in a drug case, the key issue is the admissibility of the drugs seized. If the drugs are excluded, the Crown has no case and deciding

---

[19] Courts in Ontario are divided. For a summary of the law and differing emphasis see: *R. v. Davis*, 2011 ONSC 5567 (Ont. S.C.J.) and *R. v. C. (G.)*, 2013 ONSC 2904 (Ont. S.C.J.).

[20] The Honorable Fred Kaufman, *Report of the Kaufman Commission on Proceedings Involving Guy Paul Morin* (1998), recommendation 83.

[21] In Ontario it appears that the Ministry of the Attorney General has adopted the policy with respect to accused persons who are not in custody and who present no security concerns, that while the ultimate decision rests with the presiding judge, the Crown should normally consent to the accused person being permitted to sit at the counsel table should he or she request to do so. See *R. v. Lalande* (1999), 138 C.C.C. (3d) 441 at para. 19 (Ont. C.A.).

[22] Edward Greenspan, "Making Sure the Accused Does Not Become "The Star Witness" for the Prosecution," Ontario Criminal Lawyers' Association Papers at para. 33 (an address to the Criminal Lawyers' Association, Toronto, Ontario November 21-22, 1997.)

this point decides the trial.[23] Amendments to the indictment or information to rectify minor defects that do not mislead or prejudice the accused are commonly made at this time.[24]

## (a)   Exclusion of Witnesses

An order for the exclusion of witnesses is normally made prior to the taking of evidence, and should be done prior to the Crown making any opening submissions. Such an order is provided for in s. 537(1)(h) where it appears "that the ends of justice will be best served by so doing." In the vast majority of cases, the ends of justice are best served by excluding witnesses, especially where credibility is at issue. The purpose of the exclusion is to prevent the shaping of witness testimony. A common sense reality is that witnesses may be influenced by what they hear from other witnesses. The order is usually granted as a matter of formality, which is the way it should be. In one case, a provincial court judge presiding over a preliminary inquiry refused to grant a requested and non-contested order for exclusion of witnesses. The judge took the view that there was a presumption that witnesses would come to court with the intention of telling the truth to the best of their recollection. Counsel seeking the order, therefore, needed to show why this "presumption" should be overruled. Counsel made a number of arguments, including the simple question, "Why not?" Indeed, why not exclude the witnesses? The judge was found to have erred.[25] The Court of Appeal ruled that, generally speaking, if counsel request the exclusion it ought to be granted and any exceptions will be few and far between.

In *R. v. M. (A.)*, the trial judge allowed the mother of the child complainant in a sexual assault case to remain in the courtroom.[26] The mother subsequently testified. On appeal it was found that the trial judge should have excluded the mother. The trial judge allowed the mother to remain solely on the complainant's request. There was no evidence to show that the child was unable to testify without her mother being present. Moreover, the mother could have testified first. The Appeal Court also noted that the mother's testimony was in fact conditioned by her daughter's evidence.

The practice and law with respect to the exclusion of witnesses is as follows:[27]

---

[23] *Charter* motions will be discussed in more detail in Chapter 15. Pre-trial motions are provided for in s. 645(5) of the *Criminal Code*.

[24] See s. 601 of the *Criminal Code*.

[25] *R. v. Collette* (1983), 6 C.C.C. (3d) 300; affirmed 7 C.C.C. (3d) 574n (Ont. C.A.).

[26] *R. v. M. (A.)* (1993), 26 C.R. (4th) 379 (Que. C.A.).

[27] *Dobberthien v. The Queen* (1974), 18 C.C.C. (2d) 449 at 454-455 (S.C.C.).

1) The trial Judge may order any witness, other than the accused, excluded from the courtroom. Such a direction will ordinarily apply to all witnesses whose names are listed on the indictment, to any other persons who may be called by the prosecution, and to witnesses who may be called by the accused.

2) Unless otherwise directed by the Judge, such a witness must remain outside the courtroom until all of the evidence, including that given in rebuttal is completed.

3) If a witness nevertheless remains in Court:

   a)   he is not necessarily disqualified, although, in certain circumstances, the trial Judge may exclude his evidence;

   b)   the weight, if any, to be given to his evidence is for the jury, or for the Judge, if there is no jury, to decide.

Note that should a witness disobey the exclusion order, this does not mean that the witness's evidence is to be excluded, but is a factor that goes to weight.

The accused is not excluded. Counsel may also request that other witnesses be allowed to remain in the court. Crown counsel may wish to have the chief investigating officer remain throughout the trial. Certain expert witnesses may remain in order to better present their evidence. For example, a psychiatrist may wish to be fully informed of the surrounding facts in order to give expert evidence on the state of mind of the accused at the time of the incident.

Once excluded from the court, the witnesses are admonished not to talk with one another about their testimony, nor with anyone else about prior testimony given in court. Should witnesses breach this order, once again, this goes to weight and does not prevent them from testifying.[28]

The non-communication order does not apply to counsel. In *R. v. O'Callaghan*, the trial judge banned *all* communication with the excluded witnesses.[29] Defence counsel sought to be exempt from the ban; the judge refused. Such an order went too far. Counsel, as officers of the court, may

---

[28]  See *R. v. Power* (1989), 88 N.S.R. (2d) 178 (C.A.).
[29]  *R. v. O'Callaghan* (1982), 25 C.R. (3d) 68 (Ont. H.C.).

contact witnesses during the trial, but are honour bound not to divulge what has transpired in court.

## 2.3    Opening Statement by the Crown

The Crown does not have a statutory right to make an opening address, but through custom and tradition it has a right to do so.[30] The purpose of an opening is to outline the case for the trial judge. It informs the judge of anticipated legal issues and of the evidence to be called. Unfortunately, Crown counsel often do not make any opening in judge alone trials. As will be discussed later, this is a mistake, and Crown counsel should make an opening in every trial.

In civil trials, a defendant may make an opening either immediately after the plaintiff's opening, or after the plaintiff's case and prior to the presentation of the defendant's case. Section 651(2) of the *Criminal Code* gives the accused the right to make an opening. Traditionally, a defence opening is made after the Crown closes its case and the defence decides to present evidence. However, there is discretion in the trial judge to permit counsel for the accused to open immediately after the Crown, but this discretion should be exercised only in special or unusual circumstances.[31] Special circumstances include:[32]

- The trial is expected to be lengthy with complex factual issues;

- It would be helpful to hear the position of the defence prior to hearing any evidence;

- In a retrial, where there is relative certainty about what the witnesses will say;

- There is competing and significant expert evidence;

- Credibility of the Crown witness(es) is central to the case and the opening would help to focus this issue.

---

[30] See *R. v. Vitale* (1987), 40 C.C.C. (3d) 267 (Ont. D.C.); *R. v. Campbell*, 2002 CarswellOnt 3528, [2002] O.J. No. 4042 (S.C.); and *R. v. D. (A.)* (2003), 180 C.C.C. (3d) 319 (Ont. S.C.J.).

[31] *R. v. Dalzell, ibid.,* at para. 16. See also *R. v. Rojas*, 2003 CarswellBC 1715, [2003] B.C.J. No. 1632 (S.C.), where the Court questions the jurisdiction to allow a defence opening at the start of a trial.

[32] Taken from *R. v. Dalzell, supra* note 31, at para. 19 and *R. v. Campbell, supra,* note 30, at para. 6.

There are problems with the defence making an opening at the start of a trial. First, trials are unpredictable. The defence can anticipate what the Crown can prove, but cannot be sure.

Second, such an opening may allude to what the defence hopes to achieve in cross-examination of the Crown witnesses. Uncertainties abound and the risk is high that defence counsel may well fall short; a fact the Crown is at liberty to comment on in closing.

Third, openings are intended to outline the evidence called by the defence but, in a criminal trial, the defence may not call any evidence.

Fourth, openings are not intended to be argument. It is a difficult for defence counsel to present an opening at the start of a trial without crossing the line into argument.

In at least one case the judge allowed the defence to open only upon undertaking to call evidence.[33] But most courts do not consider such an undertaking necessary.[34] Nor should it be — an accused should not be called upon to indicate whether or not he is going to call evidence until after the Crown has presented a case to meet. Should the defence make an opening at the start of the trial, then the defence will not be permitted a second opening should it elect to call evidence at the conclusion of the Crown's case. Moreover, even if defence witnesses are not called, the defence may be called upon to close first.[35]

## 2.4    Admissions by the Defence

Under s. 655 of the *Criminal Code* an accused may admit facts in indictable cases for the purpose of dispensing with proof of them. Under common law, counsel may do the same for summary conviction offences.[36] An accused does not have an unqualified right to make admissions; the Crown must be willing to accept the admissions made. For this reason, the document prepared is often called "Agreed Statement of Facts," signed by counsel for the Crown and defence.

The purpose of s. 655 is to facilitate the trial. One advantage for defence counsel in agreeing to certain admissions is that it does help to focus the trial and can be used by the defence to make a *de facto* opening statement.

---

[33] See *R. v. Edwards* (1986), 2 W.C.B. (2d) 200 (Ont. H.C.).
[34] See *R. v. Sood*, 1997 CarswellOnt 40, [1997] O.J. No. 5385 (Gen. Div.).
[35] See the undertakings in *R. v. Campbell, supra,* note 30 at para. 13.
[36] See *Castellani v. The Queen,* [1970] 4 C.C.C. 287 (S.C.C.).

For example, the defence may accept that on a certain date the accused imported a controlled drug into the country. Identity is accepted. The quantity and type of drug is accepted. The importation is accepted. The only issue is duress and the trial is now focussed on that issue.[37]

Much trial time can be saved through wise and expedient concessions. Certainly prior to any trial, Crown and defence counsel should talk and explore ways to streamline the trial. Where it is obvious that certain documents are admissible, little is to be gained by calling witnesses to authenticate the obvious. For example, photographs of the scene may be admitted by consent – without the need to call the police photographer. Or, the Crown may have served notice seeking to admit certain documents as business records under s. 30 of the *Canada Evidence Act*. If the defence accepts these documents as authentic, then there may be little need to call the keeper of the records.

### 2.5    Crown Calls Evidence

With the preliminaries complete, the Crown calls evidence. Wide discretion is accorded to the Crown in presenting its case. There is no obligation on the Crown to call all witnesses "essential to the narrative." In fact, there is no duty on the Crown to call the complainant or victim.[38] There is, in our law, no right for the accused to face his accuser. In most instances, the Crown prosecutor will call the complainant or victim, not because she has to, but because their evidence is essential to establish the case. Should the prosecutor decide not to call a particular witness, this gap may weaken the Crown's case, but that is for the prosecutor to consider. Decisions on how to present the case against an accused must be left to the Crown's discretion absent evidence that this discretion is being abused. No requirement that the Crown call witnesses with material evidence and simply make them available for cross-examination should be imposed, nor should a trial judge ever order the Crown to produce a witness.[39]

Should the Crown refuse to call a witness it is always open to the defence to call the witness. The defence may be reluctant to do so, especially if the witness is not co-operative. Moreover, should the defence call the witness, then the defence will have to make closing argument first and lose the opportunity to have the last word.[40] In this situation, an option is for the trial judge to call the witness. A trial judge in a criminal case has a limited

---

[37]  See *R. v. Ruzic* (2001), 153 C.C.C. (3d) 1 (S.C.C.).
[38]  The leading case is *R. v. Cook* (1997), 114 C.C.C. (3d) 481 (S.C.C.).
[39]  *R. v. Cook, ibid.*, at para. 56.
[40]  See section 2.11.

discretion to call witnesses without the consent of the parties. This step may be taken if, in the opinion of the trial judge, it is necessary for the discovery of truth or in the interests of justice. The discretion should only be exercised rarely and then with extreme care, so as not to interfere with the adversarial nature of the trial procedure or prejudice the accused.[41]

A witness's testimony is to be taken under oath.[42] This means that witnesses are to give evidence under oath or by way of affirmation. The oath and affirmation are as follows:[43]

---

**Oath:** I swear that the evidence to be given by me shall be the truth, the whole truth and nothing but the truth. So help me God.

**Affirmation:** I solemnly affirm that the evidence to be given by me shall be the truth, the whole truth and nothing but the truth.

---

You should check with your witnesses prior to trial as to how they wish to give their evidence. For example, an oath need not be taken by swearing on the Bible.[44] Where there is a question as to the capacity of a person to testify, then counsel will need to consider and apply s. 16 of the *Canada Evidence Act*. Children under 14 years of age do not take an oath or make a solemn affirmation; rather they give evidence after promising to tell the truth.[45]

### (a)    Direct Examination by Crown Counsel

Counsel begin by announcing to the court the witness called:

"Your Honour, I call as my first witness, Robert John Doe."

The direct examination then begins. Counsel who call a witness are bound by certain rules of trial practice. Counsel is not to lead the witness improperly in giving evidence; nor, as a starting point, is counsel to attack the credibility of the witness. The examination ends with counsel saying something like:

---

[41] See *R. v. Finta* (1994), 88 C.C.C. (3d) 417 at 528-533. For application of this discretion, see *Re Giroux and The Queen* (2002), 166 C.C.C. (3d) 427 (Alta. Q.B.).

[42] See ss. 540(1)(a), 646 and 802(3) of the *Criminal Code*.

[43] See ss. 13 and 14 of the *Canada Evidence Act*.

[44] See *R. v. Kalevar* (1991), 4 C.R. (4th) 114 (Ont. Gen. Div.)

[45] See section 16.1 of the *Canada Evidence Act*.

"Thank you, Mr. Doe. I have no further questions at this time, Your Honour."

Do not use the television gambit, "Your witness."

### (b)    Cross-Examination by Defence Counsel

An accused has the right, protected by ss. 7 and 11(d) of the *Charter*, to cross-examine Crown witnesses.[46] This right was affirmed in *R. v. Lyttle*, where Justices Major and Fish commenced their joint judgment with the following statement of principle:[47]

> Cross-examination may often be futile and sometimes prove fatal, but it remains nonetheless a faithful friend in the pursuit of justice and an indispensable ally in the search for truth. At times, there will be no other way to expose falsehood, to rectify error, to correct distortion or to elicit vital information that would otherwise remain forever concealed.

> That is why the right of an accused to cross-examine witnesses for the prosecution — without significant and unwarranted constraint — is an essential component of the right to make full answer and defence.

The practice in Canada is to follow the "English Rule," which allows the cross-examiner to inquire into any relevant matter, as compared to the "American Rule," where cross-examination is limited to subjects or topics that were covered in direct examination and to matters relating to the witness's credibility. It follows then that the American objection "Beyond the scope of the direct" is not known in our law.

### (c)    Re-examination by Crown Counsel

At the conclusion of the cross-examination, Crown counsel may re-examine the witness. Re-examination is not intended to be a continuation or reiteration of the direct examination. Counsel are expected to put their case in on direct. Re-examination is intended to address new matters raised in cross-examination, or with matters raised in cross-examination that require explanation.[48] One common use of re-examination is to counter the suggestion of recent fabrication. In this situation, the Crown may raise the fact that the witness made a prior consistent statement, which ordinarily would be barred in direct examination.

---

[46] Please note that pursuant to s. 486.3 of the *Criminal Code* an unrepresented accused may not personally cross-examine certain witnesses.

[47] *R. v. Lyttle* (2004), 180 C.C.C. (3d) 476 at para. 1-2 (S.C.C.).

[48] *R. v. Evans* (1993), 82 C.C.C. (3d) 338 at 349 (S.C.C.).

Re-examination is not the time for counsel who called the witness to raise new matters or expand in more detail upon areas that should have been dealt with fully on direct. The judge may, however, in his discretion grant leave to introduce new matters in re-examination and the opposite party may then cross-examine on the new facts.[49]

### (d)    Judge's Questions of a Witness

The general rule is that a judge may ask a witness questions of clarification and amplification, but should not intervene in the questioning of a witness to such an extent as to give the impression of taking on the role of counsel.[50] Justice Lamer (as he then was) put it in these terms:[51]

> First of all, it is clear that judges are no longer required to be as passive as they once were; to be what I call sphinx judges. We now not only accept that a judge may intervene in the adversarial debate, but also believe that it is sometimes essential for him to do so for justice in fact to be done. Thus a judge may and sometimes must ask witnesses questions, interrupt them in their testimony and if necessary call them to order.

The most appropriate time for the trial judge to ask questions is after counsel have questioned the witness. Therefore, anticipate that before the witness is allowed to step down from the stand the judge may have some questions for the witness. Witnesses should be told as part of their preparation to wait in the witness box until excused by the judge. If the judge asks questions of the witness, counsel will be given an opportunity to ask further questions arising from the judge's questions.

### 2.6    Crown Closes Its Case

The Crown cannot split its case. An accused has a constitutional right to know the case to be met before answering the Crown's case.[52] The fundamental principle is that the Crown must produce in its own case all the clearly relevant evidence it has. The Crown cannot hold back part of its case, allow the defence to call evidence, and then buttress its case by introducing further evidence in reply. The rule prevents the accused being taken by surprise. The rule also provides a safeguard against the importance of a piece of evidence, by reason of its late introduction, being unduly

---

[49] *R. v. Moore* (1984), 15 C.C.C. (3d) 541 at 568 (Ont. C.A.).

[50] See *James v. Canada,* 2000 CarswellNat 3057, [2000] F.C.J. No. 2135 at para. 52 (C.A.).

[51] *R. v. Brouillard* (1985), 17 C.C.C. (3d) 193 at para. 17 (S.C.C.).

[52] See: *R. v. Latimer* (2001), 150 C.C.C. (3d) 129 at para. 47 (S.C.C.).

emphasized or magnified in relation to the other evidence.[53] As we shall see, the Crown is allowed to call evidence in reply, but the courts carefully scrutinize the introduction of reply evidence.

## 2.7    A Defence Motion of "No Evidence"

At the close of the Crown's case the defence may make a motion of "no evidence." In a jury trial, the same motion is called a motion for a directed verdict of acquittal. Should the defence motion succeed, the trial stops and the accused is acquitted. When a motion of no evidence is made, the accused is entitled to have the motion ruled upon prior to being put to his election whether to call evidence or not.[54]

The phrase "no evidence" is somewhat of a misnomer. As Chief Justice McLachlin observed, the distinction between "no evidence" and "some evidence" is nonsensical. Rather, the question always to be asked is "whether there is sufficient evidence to permit a properly instructed jury to reasonably convict."[55] On a motion of no evidence, the judge is to assume that the evidence adduced by the Crown is true. The judge is not to assess the credibility of witnesses. If a witness testifies that she saw the accused commit the crime then that is direct evidence of the crime and is to be accepted – notwithstanding frailties in the evidence of the witness. If there is direct evidence on each element of the crime alleged, the motion is denied and the trial proceeds. If there is an absence of evidence on any element, then the motion will be granted and the case against the accused dismissed. In cases based on circumstantial evidence, the trial judge must engage in a limited evaluation or weighing of the inferences sought to be advanced by the evidence. If the evidence is rationally capable of supporting the infer-ences the Crown seeks to be made, then it is for the jury to say whether or not those inferences should actually be drawn and the case proceeds.[56]

In judge alone trials, new counsel often get confused between a motion of no evidence and argument at the end of the day that the Crown has not proven its case beyond a reasonable doubt. It can happen that the arguments immediately follow one another, but they are separate and distinct. Defence counsel at the close of the Crown's case makes a motion of no evidence arguing that the Crown has presented "no evidence" on a required element of the crime. The trial judge denies the motion, deciding that there is "some evidence" upon which a properly instructed jury could reasonably convict.

[53] *R. v. Biddle* (1995), 96 C.C.C. (3d) 321 at para. 14 (S.C.C.)
[54] *R. v. Boissonneault* (1986), 29 C.C.C. (3d) 345 (Ont. C.A.).
[55] *R. v. Charemski* (1998), 123 C.C.C. (3d) 225 at para. 21 (S.C.C.).
[56] See *R. v. Charemski, ibid.*, at para. 33.

Defence elects to call no evidence. The trial proceeds immediately to final submissions. The argument now is that, although there may be some evidence to support conviction, there actually is insufficient evidence to find the accused guilty beyond a reasonable doubt. The trial judge is now free to assess the credibility of the Crown witnesses and factor in the frailties of their evidence.

## 2.8    Defence Opens Its Case

The making of an opening statement is provided for in s. 651(2) of the *Criminal Code*. Unfortunately, in judge alone trials, defence counsel all too often make no opening statement. They should. They are missing an opportunity to inform the judge of their case. More will be said on defence opening statements in Chapter 9.

## 2.9    Defence Calls Evidence

The procedure for the calling and examination of witnesses, as outlined for the prosecution, is repeated for the defence with counsel, of course, reversing roles. In terms of the order of witnesses, there is no rule that the accused must be called first. The British position is that the accused should be called first. The obvious concern is that the accused, having sat through and listened to the other defence witnesses, will be able to mould his testimony accordingly. However, the British position is not the law in Canada. The Canadian position is well stated by Justice Branca in *R. v. Smuk*:[57]

> The accused, or counsel for the accused, is totally and completely free to decide whether or not the accused will or will not testify and if he does in what order or sequence he will be called to testify either before or after the witnesses who are called to testify for and on his behalf. The Court cannot under any circumstances insist that an accused should testify first no more than the Court can order the accused to testify. It is to be remembered that until the accused is found guilty at the conclusion of the trial by the jury there is a presumption in our law that he is innocent and when he testifies presumably he testifies as a witness of truth and his evidence like that of any other witness must be carefully weighed and considered after the evidence has been given in Court. His evidence cannot be prejudged and no advantage or disadvantage is to be attributed to his evidence *in advance* because he testifies after defence witnesses have testified for and on his behalf. . .[Emphasis added.]

---

[57] *R. v. Smuk* (1971), 3 C.C.C. (2d) 457 at 462 (B.C.C.A.). See also *R. v. Angelantoni* (1975), 28 C.C.C. (2d) 179 (Ont. C.A.).

Edward Greenspan, in writing on defence trial strategy, took the position that there is good reason for calling the accused towards the close of the defence case and that he would rarely call his client first.[58] However, a downside in not calling the accused first, especially where credibility is critical, is that it may reduce the weight of the accused's evidence. It is a factor a trial judge may take into account; it is open to the trial judge to conclude that the accused's evidence has been deliberately tailored to conform to the evidence of other defence witnesses.[59] A further reality is the practice of the court. Judges may be used to seeing the accused called first, which is the norm in Manitoba. Counsel who deviate from this "custom" must be prepared to answer to the judge, who in judge alone trials, ultimately assesses the credibility of all witnesses.

## 2.10    Crown Seeks to Call Further Evidence

After the defence closes its case, the Crown may seek to call further evidence in "reply" or to "reopen" its case. "Reply" or "rebuttal" evidence needs to be distinguished from the Crown "reopening" its case. Applications to adduce rebuttal evidence and to reopen the case are "close cousins," but not "identical twins."[60]

"Reply" or "rebuttal" evidence by the prosecution is restricted to evidence to meet new facts introduced by the defence. It is based upon the adversarial system and fairness. The Crown is allowed to reply to evidence raised in the defence case, otherwise a distorted or unfair picture will be left to the trier of fact. It is permitted "to insure that at the end of the day each party will have had an equal opportunity to hear and respond to the full submissions of the other."[61] The Crown may be allowed to call evidence in rebuttal after completion of the defence case, where:

1)    the defence has raised some new matter or defence which the Crown has had no opportunity to deal with; and,

2)    the Crown could not reasonably have anticipated.

But rebuttal will not be permitted regarding matters that merely confirm or reinforce earlier evidence adduced in the Crown's case, which could have

---

[58] E. Greenspan, "The Preparation of the Trial Brief and the Planning of Trial Strategy and Tactics (Criminal)", in *Advocacy*, a symposium presented by the Canadian Bar Association – Ontario in Collaboration with the Law Society of Upper Canada (1982), 35 at 41-42.

[59] See *R. v. Gagnon*, [1999] B.C.J. No. 1158 (Prov. Ct.).

[60] *R. v. G. (S.G.)* (1997), 116 C.C.C. (3d) 193 at para. 39 (S.C.C.).

[61] *R. v. Aalders* (1993), 82 C.C.C. (3d) at 229 (S.C.C.).

been brought before the defence was made.[62] The allowing of reply evidence is a matter within the discretion of the trial judge and the Crown should seek leave to call the evidence.

Often the Crown will seek to present reply evidence to contradict statements made by the accused. When this occurs, the collateral fact rule is triggered. The Crown will not be allowed to call evidence on collateral matters.[63] The accused's answer is final. Where the matter concerns an issue essential for the determination of the case, then the Crown may be allowed to call evidence in rebuttal. Justice Cory in *R. v. Aalders* explained:[64]

> It is true that the Crown cannot split its case to obtain an unfair advantage. Nor should the Crown be able to put in evidence in reply on a purely collateral issue. However, it is fit and proper that reply evidence be called which relates to an integral and essential issue of the case. In such circumstances, it would be wrong to deprive the trier of fact of important evidence relating to an essential element of the case. The course of a trial, particularly a criminal trial, must be based upon rules of fairness so as to ensure the protection of the individual accused. However, the rules should not go so far as to deprive the trier of fact of important evidence, that can be helpful in resolving an essential element of the case.

When the Crown applies to "reopen" its case, it deviates from the adversarial process. The evidence that the Crown now seeks to introduce is relevant and, in a perfect world, should have been introduced as part of the Crown's case. Traditionally, the Crown was only allowed to reopen its case if the evidence arose *ex improviso* — in other words, if "some matter arose which no human ingenuity could have foreseen." That is no longer the law. The focus has shifted. Now the "paramount" question to be resolved upon an application to reopen the Crown's case is whether the accused will be prejudiced in his or her defence.[65] Emphasis is on the protection of the accused's interests. The fact that the Crown is not at fault in failing to discover evidence will often be irrelevant to the presence or absence of prejudice to the accused.

The bottom line is that a trial judge has a very narrow discretion to allow the Crown to "reopen" its case. It should only be permitted in those very exceptional cases where the absence of prejudice to the accused is manifestly obvious. Two examples were given by Justice Cory in *R. v. G.*

---

[62] *R. v. Brown* (1999), 137 C.C.C. (3d) 400 at para. 12 (Ont. C.A.).

[63] The collateral fact rule is discussed in more detail in Chapter 14.

[64] *R. v. Aalders, supra,* note 61 at 230.

[65] See *R. v. G. (S.G.), supra,* note 60 at para. 29-45.

*(S.G.)*.[66] The first example shows how the conduct of the defence directly or indirectly contributes to the Crown's failure to lead the particular evidence before the close of its case. In this instance it does not lie in the mouth of the accused to claim prejudice where the failure of the Crown to adduce the particular evidence arises from the actions of the defence. The second example shows how the Crown makes an omission or mistake on a noncontroversial issue that is purely formal or technical, and has nothing to do with the substance of the case.

## 2.11    Closing Submissions

Under s. 651(3) of the *Criminal Code*, where the defence does not present evidence, defence counsel is entitled to address the court last. Where the defence presents evidence, the prosecution is entitled to address the court last. This section was challenged under the *Charter*. It was argued that s. 651(3) violated the accused's right to make full answer and defence in that the defence could not adequately respond to the Crown's case in its entirety. Inherent in the challenge is the belief, which is not universally accepted, that there is power in having the last word and being able to respond to the Crown's argument. The Supreme Court of Canada, in a marginally thin 5:4 decision, upheld the section.[67] Even the majority, however, conceded that it might be preferable to modify the current order of addresses. Most common law jurisdictions allow the accused to address the court last or adhere to a three-step order: prosecution (first) – defence (second) – prosecution (reply). The majority did note that a trial judge has an inherent power to allow the defence to reply in clear cases where the Crown's closing has been unfair.[68] The order of addresses in jury trials is more critical than in judge alone trials. I think that it is fair to say that often judges will allow counsel to make brief replies in order to fully understand the case presented on its facts and in law. Such flexibility is to be encouraged as it allows both sides full opportunity to respond to all arguments presented.

After both sides have presented argument, the case is left with the trial judge for decision. The judge may render a decision on the spot, or reserve.

## 2.12    Moving to Sentence

Should the trial judge find the accused guilty, the next phase in the criminal process is sentencing. In relatively minor cases, counsel should

---

[66] *Ibid.*
[67] *R. v. Rose* (1998), 129 C.C.C. (3d) 449 (S.C.C.).
[68] *Ibid.*, at para. 136.

anticipate that a sentencing will take place immediately following the guilty verdict and prepare accordingly. Counsel will be given an opportunity to make submissions on sentencing and, if need be, file evidence or call witnesses. A sentence hearing is more informal and relaxed than a trial proper. For example, the rules of evidence are relaxed and much evidence is admitted simply through the submissions of counsel. In certain cases, counsel may wish an adjournment to prepare properly for sentencing. Courts are reluctant to grant lengthy adjournments. Section 720 of the *Criminal Code* states that a court "shall" sentence an offender "as soon as practicable" after a finding of guilt.

# 9

# OPENING ADDRESSES

- **The Content of an Opening Address**

- **The Plaintiff's Opening**

- **The Defendant's Opening**

- **A Criminal Case: Crown Opening**

- **A Criminal Case: Defence Opening**

The importance of the opening address in jury trials is stressed repeatedly in writings on trial advocacy.[1] We are told that first impressions count and we must strike while the jury is fresh and attentive.

Ought not the above comments also apply for a trial before judge alone? Is not a judge also influenced by first impressions? Is not a judge also most fresh and most attentive at the start of a trial? Yet the opening address in non-jury trials all too often is ignored.

For example, in Manitoba, where I am most familiar, it will be very rare for the Crown to make an opening of any kind in the Provincial Courts. Counsel seem to assume that there is no need. The judge knows the procedure, so just get on with calling evidence. Such is not good practice. Opening addresses are made in jury trials, administrative hearings, and should definitely be made in judge alone trials. John Sopinka stated, "No case should commence without an opening statement of some kind."[2] He is correct. There is value in setting the scene for the judge. Even in the most straight-

---

[1] See, *e.g.*, Thomas Mauet, *Fundamentals of Trial Techniques* 2nd Can. ed. (1995), p. 23.

[2] J. Sopinka, *The Trial of an Action* (1981), p. 58.

forward of cases, there is room for counsel to stand and inform the court that it is indeed straightforward.

# 1.   THE CONTENT OF AN OPENING ADDRESS

The purpose of an opening is to put the legal and factual issues in a context for the judge, and, I might add, also for opposing counsel. Essentially you articulate your theory of the case and provide a roadmap. There is no established format for an opening. Much will depend upon the case, the court and the judge. Certain judges are impatient at the start of the trial and want to proceed to the evidence, others are not. A Superior Court trial is also far different from a trial in the Provincial Court. In Provincial Court it is safe to say that an opening should be short and to the point.

It is helpful to look at the opening address from the judge's perspective. Ask yourself, "If you were the judge what would you like to know at the start of the trial? What would help you to understand the case and the evidence?"

## 1.1   Things to Avoid

### (a)   Overstatement

It is important to recognize that the opening is not the time to try and "sell" your case. The harder you try to sell your case in the opening, the less effective you are and the more improper is the opening. Therefore, cut the rhetoric. An impassioned plea packaged in rhetorical eloquence will not impress a judge. Persuade through clarity. Strive to assist and inform the judge about your case and in so doing your case will sell itself.

Moderation in claims and in tone is essential. First, judges are not keen at the start of a trial to hear a rousing speech. Second, opposing counsel will seize upon any overstatement. Therefore, it is far better to understate than overstate. In other words, it is better to exceed expectations than fail to meet those expectations.

### (b)   Too Much Detail

Do not try to do too much in the opening. You will only alienate the judge, who wants to hear from the witnesses and not from you. In the case of *C.N.R. Co. v. di Domenicantonio*, plaintiff counsel took two and one-half days in opening, although stripped of interruptions, it was only eight pure hours of opening! On appeal one justice was not amused and could "see no justification for an eight-hour opening address in any trial."[3]

The opening is not the time to present your evidence. It is a blueprint or map of your case where you introduce your story and cast of witnesses. It is a time to highlight and direct the judge to particular points, but is not the time to pre-empt your witnesses by giving their evidence for them.

At the end of your opening, the judge should know who you are calling as witnesses, when you are calling them and, in general terms, why you are calling them. The judge, therefore, has your trial agenda and knows what to expect and what to look for as the evidence unfolds. Present an outline of your case — not a treatise.

### (c)   Argument

The opening is not the place for argument. Argument is saved for the closing. Your purpose in the opening is to set the case for the judge. Issues can be raised and identified for consideration by the judge, but this is not the time to argue those issues.[4]

Nor is it appropriate to anticipate defences. Your primary goal in the opening is to outline your case. For example, as Crown you may not know what the defence is. Defence counsel may simply be relying on the fact that you cannot prove your case. Unless a defence is clearly raised and before the court, Crown counsel should avoid any reference to what the defence may or may not be.

## 2.   THE PLAINTIFF'S OPENING

The following is a general guide for a plaintiff's opening in a civil case:

- Provide a broad context.

- Introduce the parties.

- State the cause of action.

- State the facts — highlight your witnesses and evidence.

---

[3] *C.N.R. Co. v. di Doenicantonio* (1988), 49 D.L.R. (4th) 342 at 365 (N.B.C.A.).

[4] A good summary on the law with respect to jury opening is found in *Brophy v. Hutchinson*, 2003 BCCA 21 (B.C. C.A.).

- Assist the court with the legal issues.

- Address any defences.

- Outline the relief sought.

### 2.1   Provide a Broad Context

A judge will be most attentive in the first few minutes of your presentation. Capture that moment. In a few words or sentences, what is the trial about? What is your theory of the case? Cut through the legalisms and tell the court why your client is in court. Generally I recommend a broad brush approach. In other words, concentrate on giving the trial judge a factual and legal context in which to consider the evidence.

### 2.2   Introduce the Parties

How do the parties fit into the picture? In particular, you want to *personalize* your client. You want to explain why your client comes before the court.

### 2.3   State the Cause of Action

The cause of action lies at the heart of any case. It provides the basis for liability and provides the framework around which facts and law will be built. Therefore, I suggest that you state the cause of action early.

### 2.4   State the Facts — Highlight Your Witnesses and Evidence

The opening address is not the time to present your evidence! Should you go too far, expect the impatient judge to say, "Counsel, I would prefer to hear the evidence from your witnesses and not from you." The opening is a time merely to introduce your story and your cast of witnesses. Use the opening to highlight and direct the judge to particular points. Do not pre-empt your witnesses by giving their evidence for them.

Look as well for points that give credence to a witness's testimony:

- She was *the only person not drinking at the party*;

- He was the *first* person to arrive at the scene;

- Dr. Smith was the plaintiff's family physician for *20 years*;

- Professor Wigmore has written a *leading text* on the subject.

I strongly encourage you to use exhibits in your opening. If you have a prepared sketch of the scene, and there is no objection to its admissibility, then use the sketch to describe the scene to the judge. The judge will then be in a far better position to understand the evidence that follows.

Similarly, there is room to use other documents in your opening. If you are relying upon a clause in a contract, then show the judge the clause. The judge can see and read the clause; it is there in concrete terms. If the case spans a period of time, providing the judge with a chronology would be helpful.

At the end of your opening, the judge should know who you are calling as witnesses, when you are calling them and, in general terms, why you are calling them. The judge, therefore, has your trial agenda and knows what to expect and what to look for as your evidence is presented.

You are to be fair in your review of the facts. Opposing counsel can object, and ought to do so, if you misstate the facts. Do not give counsel that opportunity. Moreover, if you do misstate the facts, you lose credibility with the court.

Nor should you refer to evidence that may be inadmissible. If there is a question as to the admissibility of evidence, leave that evidence out of your opening. Stay with the evidence that you can prove and that is admissible.

## 2.5   Assist the Court with the Legal Issues

I have used the phrase "assist the court." In the opening, you outline the legal issues to the judge. You do not argue those legal issues. Argument is saved for the closing. Your purpose in the opening is to set the case for the judge. You are not there to argue the law at this time. Let the evidence speak for itself. In other words, save the closing argument for your closing argument. The opening is the place to identify the legal issues for the judge and, if invited by the judge, to explain the law. Once again, it is not the place to argue the law. One way to assist the judge in understanding the legal issues is for you to have prepared a legal brief on the law or an outline of the legal issues with copies of the leading cases. This material can be given to the judge at the opening for review of the law during the recess or over the midday break, or, as is increasingly the case, is provided as part of the pre-trial material.

The law, the facts and the evidence are all intertwined. There is no one way of organizing these three critical strands. You may find it best to deal with each in turn. However, I recommend you try whenever possible to interrelate a legal issue with the facts and the evidence. The legal issue provides your heading and the facts and evidence explain how you will prove that issue.

## 2.6    Address Any Defences

The primary goal in your opening is to present *your* theory of the case. You are under no obligation to present the other side's case in *your* opening address. Plaintiff's counsel, as part of their duty to raise the legal issues, need to refer to defences raised by the defendant, but that is all. You need not go into the evidence that supports the defendant's position. Let defendant's counsel present their own opening:[5]

> It has been suggested that when dealing with matters that are in dispute it is necessary to refer to the evidence of your opponent. It is submitted that there is no obligation to outline the defendant's evidence . . . On the other hand, in defining an issue, counsel will often state what his opponent's position is in order to explain the issue.

Nor should you anticipate who the defendant will be calling and how you, through cross-examination, will elicit favourable evidence for your case. The opening is confined to your evidence. You do not comment on the defendant's anticipated evidence.

Although it is not necessary for you to raise evidence unfavourable to your case in the opening, tactically it is wise to confront and defuse key weaknesses in your case upon which the defendant will rely. Otherwise the judge will think that you presented a one-sided portrait of the facts and you lose credibility. It also will pre-empt defendant's counsel from rising and saying:

> The plaintiff, in opening, never mentioned one key fact . . .

## 2.7    Outline the Relief Sought

Lastly, tell the court briefly what the relief issues are and, if quantum of damages is at issue, tie the quantum issue to the facts and evidence that you will adduce at trial.

---

[5] John Sopinka, *The Trial of an Action* (1981), p. 60.

You will note that I have excluded a conclusion. I do so because, in opening before a judge alone, I think that the standard jury conclusion is redundant. Before a jury, counsel conclude their opening by saying something like:

> At the end of all the evidence in this case, I will be asking you to return a verdict in favour of the plaintiff and against the defendant.

The judge knows that this is why you have brought the action. By the end of your opening, the judge should also know your cause of action, witnesses to be called, legal issues and relief sought. It is time to get on with the trial. Simply end your opening by advising the judge that you are prepared to move on:

> Your Honour, that concludes my opening address, and with the leave of the court I am now ready to call the first witness for the plaintiff.

## 2.8   A Sample Plaintiff's Opening

---

**Sample Opening**

Consider the case of *Waite v. Stewart*: See Chapter 2.

***Plaintiff Opening in Waite v. Stewart***
***(Assume Manitoba where "My Lord" is used)***

My Lord, may it please the court I would like to make a brief opening statement. The plaintiff, Richard Waite, brings this action in assault and battery against the defendant. The assault and battery involved a fight. But this case is not about a fight — it is about excessive force. For the evidence will show that there really was not much of a fight. Only two blows were struck. Both by the defendant. Both kicks. The first kick struck Mr. Waite in his stomach. Mr. Waite bent over. He will testify that he was winded and was holding his stomach. The defendant then kicked Mr. Waite a second time — this time in the face. This second kick to the head broke Mr. Waite's jaw. It is this second kick that gives rise to our claim of excessive force.

*[Your theory of the case and cause of action is put to the judge right at the start.]*

*(cont'd)*

---

Mr. Waite, who is a television broadcaster, and the defendant played on opposing teams in a recreational hockey game that was played at the Highlander Sports Complex here in Winnipeg in the evening of March 13, 2015. The fight occurred in the parking lot of the sports complex after the two had left the game.

*[Note the personalizing of the plaintiff. The plaintiff is referred to by name. The defendant is not.]*

To assist your Lordship we have prepared a diagram of the parking lot area where the fight occurred. I tender this diagram by consent and ask that it be marked as an exhibit *[Marked as an exhibit]*. The diagram shows the East side of the sports complex. It is to scale with the lighting marked. The fight occurred in the parking lot roadway to the North of the line of cars parked on the North East side of the building.

*[The scene is set for the judge by using the diagram. See page 247.]*

We will be calling two witnesses: Mr. Waite and Mr. Edward Gore. Mr. Waite will testify that he was cut above the eye by the defendant in the hockey game. As a result of the injury Mr. Waite left the game. As he was leaving the sports complex to go to work he noticed the defendant and Mr. Waite decided to talk to him. Mr. Waite will then describe the events leading up to the two kicks and the breaking of his jaw.

*[The description of Mr. Waite's evidence is cursory. I do not want to pre-empt Mr. Waite's actual testimony.]*

My Lord, we will also be calling Mr. Edward Gore, who was with Mr. Waite at the hockey game. Mr. Gore was an eyewitness to the fight and I ask your Lordship to pay particular attention to what Mr. Gore has to say about the two kicks administered by the defendant to Mr. Waite.

*[Focus is maintained on the two kicks. I am not giving Mr. Gore's evidence, but the judge is certainly on notice as to the critical area of Mr. Gore's evidence.]*

*(cont'd)*

Mr. Waite and Mr. Gore are the only witnesses that we will call. My learned friend and I have come to an agreement with respect to damages and no witnesses need be called on that issue. I tender now the agreement as to the quantum of damages, which is the sum of $40,000, and I ask that it be marked as an exhibit [*Marked as an exhibit*]. As the agreement shows the defendant is agreeing only to the quantum of damages, liability remains at issue. My Lord, the plaintiff also abandons any claim for punitive damages.

*[This illustrates how the opening helps to narrow the issues for the judge to consider.]*

Although the case only concerns liability, there are a number of legal issues to consider. First, as has been mentioned, there is the issue of excessive force. A second issue is that of informed consent. The defendant was trained in karate and used that training in kicking Mr. Waite. May it please the court I would like to tender by consent a copy of the defendant's karate record provided by the Western Canada Karate Association. [*Exhibit marked*]. Your Lordship will note that the defendant began his training in 2012 and by the time of the fight with Mr. Waite the defendant had a brown belt level 1 in karate. Mr. Waite had no knowledge of the defendant's karate training. The question is raised as to whether Mr. Waite's lack of knowledge as to the defendant's karate training vitiates any consent he may have given to fight.

*[Numbers are used to list the issues, making it easy for the judge to follow. Watch the judge and go slowly to enable the judge to write the issues down. The karate record is incorporated into the opening to highlight the defendant's karate record.]*

The defendant also raises two defences: self-defence and provocation. With respect to the issue of provocation there is a real question as to whether or not provocation can go to reduce compensatory damages, and those are the only damages now being sought.

*[The defences are mentioned without further comment. There is no need for the plaintiff to elaborate upon issues raised by the defendant. The judge is on notice as to the issues and that is all that is required.]*

*(cont'd)*

> My Lord, to assist with the legal issues I have prepared a book of authorities, my learned friend has already received a copy. [*Handed to the clerk — not marked as an exhibit*]. The book includes the leading cases on each of the issues. The authorities are arranged according to issue, which are listed in the table of contents and arranged using different colour tabs. At the start of each of the issues there is a short summary on the applicable law.
>
> [*Providing the book of authorities at the start of the trial gives the judge an early opportunity to review the law.*]
>
> My Lord, that concludes my opening address, and with the leave of the court I am now ready to call the first witness for the plaintiff.

## 3.   THE DEFENDANT'S OPENING

Defendants should always make an opening. Why vacate the floor to the plaintiff? You obviously have a case to present or else there would be no need for the trial. Tell the judge your side of the dispute. This is most important if you have an affirmative defence to raise. Therefore, in a civil case (at least in Manitoba and Ontario)[6] the primary question for defendant's counsel with respect to an opening statement is not whether to make an opening, but when. You have the option of immediately following the plaintiff's opening, which may be wise when presenting an affirmative defence, or you may wait until you present your case. By waiting you gain the advantage of hearing the plaintiff's case to which you can respond specifically in your opening.

The fact that you are presenting after the plaintiff's opening or case must be taken into account. As a general rule, the defendant's opening should be short and to the point. There is no need for you, as defendant's counsel, to review the cause of action, the facts of the case or the law. Presumably these areas were all covered in the plaintiff's opening and *DO NOT NEED REPEATING!* This is even more so should the defendant's opening be done at the close of the plaintiff's case. Remember the trial is now half over, and by this time the judge has a pretty good idea of what the

---

[6] As mentioned in Chapter 7, under Court Rule 52.07 in Manitoba and Ontario, the defendant may either open immediately after the plaintiff's opening or after the plaintiff's case is closed and prior to the defendant presenting evidence. In British Columbia, the defendant may only open after the close of the plaintiff's case. See Supreme Court Civil Rules, B.C. Reg. 168/2009, Rule 12-5 (72).

trial is all about — you are, in other words, not dealing with a blank slate. What I suggest that you do is concentrate on directing the judge's attention to a few key points — either factual or legal issues — and clarify the defendant's position on those issues. Then highlight and outline the witnesses that you will be calling.

There is a temptation to open your case by attacking the plaintiff's case. Do not do this. Keep in mind that the purpose of the opening is to inform the judge about your case — an outline of the who, what and when of your case. It is not the time to argue the case. Save your attacks for the closing.

## 3.1   A Sample Defendant's Opening

---

### *Defendant Opening in Waite v. Stewart*

### *(Assume Ontario where "Your Honour" is used.)*

*[Done at the end of the plaintiff's case.]*

Your Honour, this case is about provocation, consent and self-defence. We will be calling two witnesses: Mr. Stewart and Mrs. Gloria Rice. And to be blunt, Mr. Stewart's recollection of the events surrounding the fight with the plaintiff differs markedly from what Your Honour has heard in the plaintiff's case. There is then an issue as to credibility to be resolved on certain very important facts. Fortunately, we are not left simply with the word of one party against the other.

The second and final witness that we will call is Mrs. Gloria Rice, who witnessed the fight and who, is the only *independent observer* as to what transpired. As Your Honour listens to Mrs. Rice's evidence, I invite Your Honour to compare it to what the plaintiff has said transpired and to Mr. Stewart's description of events.

I am now prepared to call Mr. Stewart as our first witness.

*[The defendant's openiing is brief, strong and has focus. Note that the judge was invited to compare Mrs. Rice's evidence to the evidence of the parties. The judge was not told that Mrs. Rice's evidence was*

*(cont'd)*

---

> *consistent with that of Mr. Stewart and therefore his version of events is the more credible. Let the judge come to that conclusion. Your task in the opening is to direct the judge's attention. The time for suggesting conclusions is in the closing:*
>
> > *"In my opening address I invited Your Honour to compare the evidence of Mrs. Rice — the only independent witness to the events — to the evidence of the respective parties. I submit that her evidence is completely consistent with what Mr. Stewart says occurred."]*

## 4.   A CRIMINAL CASE: CROWN OPENING

Opening statements are most often reserved for jury trials; rarely do you hear an opening statement made by either the Crown or defence in a criminal trial before judge alone. Perhaps it is the time constraints. Many Crown attorneys put in one or two trials in a given day and they just do not have time to prepare an opening statement — no matter how brief. The practice then is that opening statements are not given. Practices can change.

The elements of a good opening statement in a criminal case are the same as in civil trials. Crown counsel must, however, be very careful in the giving of an opening. The case *R. v. Griffin* provides a good example.[7] Here, the trial judge ordered a mistrial following upon the wrongs committed by the Crown counsel in her opening statement. Although this case involved a jury, the principles to be followed by Crown counsel are the same for a non-jury trial. The fundamental principle being that Crown counsel must be impartial and should exclude any notion of winning or losing. "The Crown should take the position of advocate for no particular person but rather should conceive his or her duty to assist the court."[8] The following specific wrongs were cited:

---

[7] *R. v. Griffin*, [1993] O.J. 2573 (Ont. Gen. Div.) per Marshall J., October 19, 1993.
[8] *Ibid.*, at para. 27.

- The use of inflammatory and vindictive language is improper.

- The Crown should not impart his or her personal opinion as to the guilt or innocence of the accused.

- The impression should not be given that an investigation by the state has established guilt.

- Crown counsel should not appear nor regard themselves as one struggling for a conviction.

- Crown counsel should not attempt to argue the case or argue the case by the use of rhetorical questions.

- Crown counsel should only refer to admissible evidence.

To this list we can add these further "wrongs:"[9]

- It is wrong to use language to infer that the character of the accused is in question.

- It is wrong to use language suggesting strongly that the accused has a case to answer, i.e., "explain or else."

From the foregoing you might think that Crown counsel must be so circumspect that any opening given must necessarily be ineffective. Not so. There is power in a clear and simple statement of one's case. Outlined below is an opening statement given by the Crown in a double murder case in Winnipeg. See how the Crown counsel put his case to the jury:[10]

> My Lord, members of the jury, this trial concerns a scheme of murder for profit, and the victims were the accused's sister and his wife. The two acts of murder are separated in the indictment into the two counts you heard read and in time by about three and a half years. Nevertheless, say the prosecution, they form a single scheme, a part of a scheme.

---

[9]  *R. v. Hamilton* (1991), 10 C.R. (4th) 385 (Ont. Gen. Div.).
[10]  Crown Counsel's opening statement in *R. v. Khan* (1996), 108 C.C.C. (3d) 108 (Man. C.A.).

The charges made against the accused are two in number, as I've said, and are both murder in the first degree. Murder in the first degree, you will learn from My Lord in due course, can be committed in several ways. The prosecution say in this case that the deaths are murder in the first degree because they are planned and deliberate; planned in the ordinary sense of that word, that there was a scheme or a plan, and deliberate in the sense that the plan was considered, the consequences were considered and the risks were considered.

The plan was a simple one; to insure the victim for a sum of money, well in excess of what was required, and then, shortly afterwards, to put her to death . . .

The Crown's theory of the case is clearly outlined for the jury. Counsel is letting the facts speak to the jury without unnecessary rhetoric.

What is advocated in this chapter is that Crown counsel should – as a bare minimum – do a "quick opener." Even in the simplest of cases there is room for an opening. Consider this most routine of cases – a shoplift. The accused is charged with theft of a bottle of perfume valued at $57.50. The Crown's only witness is a security guard, who worked at the department store, saw the theft and arrested the accused. The police were called and the accused made no statement to the attending officers. What can you say to the judge by way of an opening? Consider the example below.

---

### Sample Opening Address in a Shoplift Case

Your Honour, to assist you. This case is a shoplift. It occurred at the Eaton Department Store on Main Street. We will be calling only one witness, Laura Nystrum. Ms Nystrum works as a security guard for Eaton's. She observed the defendant take a box of perfume out of a display cabinet and put it into a bag she was carrying. Before leaving the store, the defendant was then seen to reach into her bag and take the box that contained the perfume out and leave it on a shelf. The defendant was stopped when she left the store and the unboxed bottle of perfume was found in her bag. So, Your Honour, this is a one-witness case and I am now ready to call Ms Nystrum.

---

The example above would take no more than one minute. The judge would now have a good understanding of the Crown case and, knowing that it rests on the evidence of one witness, take particular interest and care in assessing Ms Nystrum's testimony. The attraction of the above opening is that it is simple and direct. Unnecessary clutter is avoided. This is not a legal case. Emphasis is on a factual context. Detail and explanation is left out. You do not need to tell the judge everything. Provide an outline and let the judge fill in the blanks as the evidence unfolds. For example, there is no need to explain to the judge the import of removing the perfume bottle from the box. The judge already knows the security barcode is on the box and not on the bottle. That will come out in evidence.

## 4.1   There is Wider Scope in Opening Before a Judge Alone

In opening before juries there are certain rules.[11] One fundamental rule is that Crown counsel is not to refer to any evidence where admissibility is likely to be contested. A non-jury trial is different. The trial judge is both trier of fact and arbiter of the law. This means that issues concerning the admissibility of evidence can be raised with the trial judge in the opening. In fact, raising these issues and explaining how the Crown proposes to deal with the evidence is most appropriate. Consider the example below.

---

### *Sample Opening Raising Admissibility Issues*

Your Honour, if it please the court, I would like to make a brief opening. The charge before Your Honour is one of break and enter of a dwelling-house. On July 15 of last year Mrs. Mable Stewart, who is 78 years of age, heard a knock at her door. It was at approximately 11:00 pm. She went to the door and with the chain latch still fixed opened the door a crack. At that moment, a man rammed the door and burst into her home. He had a knife and told her to sit down. He demanded money. She pointed to her purse. He then cut the phone line. Told her to stay put and searched through the house. He took a DVD, some jewellery and a silver cutlery set. He then left after telling her not to say anything or leave the house because he had friends watching. Now Mrs. Stewart is feisty and she carried a mobile phone on her person. After her attacker was out the door, she phoned the police.

*(cont'd)*

---

[11]   See Justice Dan Ferguson, "The Law Relating to Jury Addresses" 16 Advocates' So. J., No. 2, 19-23 (July, 1997).

> Officers Jurgens and Martin were on patrol in the area and received a dispatch to attend to Mrs. Stewart's home and to be on the lookout for a male, dark complexion, carrying a bag. Half a block away from Mrs. Stewart's home, the officers saw the defendant walking down the street. He was carrying a bag. The officers stopped and Officer Jurgens got out of the patrol car to talk to the defendant. Officer Jurgens recognized the defendant. Officer Jurgens asked the defendant if he would open his bag. The defendant refused. The officers then searched the defendant's bag and found Mrs. Stewart's possessions.
>
> Your Honour, My Friend has advised me that the defence contests the admissibility of the items seized. What I propose is to call Mrs. Stewart first and as part of her evidence have her identify the items found in the bag carried by the defendant. At that time, the items can be marked for identification only. Then I will call Officers Jurgens and Martin and we can enter into a *voir dire* into the admissibility of the seized items. At this stage, I only anticipate calling these three witnesses as part of the Crown's case.

### 4.2    Telling A Story

Both of the examples presented in this section on Crown openings cut through the legal mumbo jumbo to tell a story. Storytelling, in a courtroom sense, is a powerful tool. As listeners, we are used to hearing stories from which we paint mental pictures. Both examples, therefore, use a narrative format. Counsel, as narrator, tells the story of what Ms Nystrum saw that day at Eaton's or what happened to Mrs. Stewart when her home was broken into. This is an approach that is interesting, because stories are inherently interesting. A story then, simply told, lies at the heart of a "quick opener."

There is no set format for an opening, as there are countless stories to tell. Much will depend upon the case, the court and the judge. The key is to be succinct and helpful. Even the most harried of Crowns can do a "quick opener" and even the most impatient of judges can hardly complain about a well-crafted, short, crisp opening.

## 5.    A CRIMINAL CASE: DEFENCE OPENING

In a non-jury criminal trial, it is rare indeed for the defence to make an opening statement. This tradition deserves re-thinking. There is value in simply telling the judge that the defence intends to call such-and-such witnesses. In other words, it is useful to tell the judge how you are going to run your defence. There is value in informing the judge of the defence or defences upon which you will rely. The opening should not be long. There is no need to set the trial scene; we are halfway through the trial. There may, however, be a need to set the scene from the defendant's perspective. The point is that you have an opportunity to assist the court in understanding and following your evidence and most defence counsel are not taking advantage of that opportunity.

In presenting the opening, the principles that apply to Crown openings apply as well to the defence. A tone of quiet understatement is recommended. The opening should be a short, crisp outline of your defence evidence. Who are you calling as witnesses? What is the import of your defence? A word of caution. No doubt you will be tempted to respond to the Crown's evidence – to argue in reply. This is not the time. Save argument for closing.

In Chapter 1 we discussed the case of *R. v. Vandergraaf*, in which the accused was charged with assault with weapon involving a jar of peanut butter.[12] A spectator at a National Hockey League game was injured by a flying jar of peanut butter. It was a judge alone trial. Mr. Vandergraaf was convicted at trial, but the conviction was overturned on appeal. Let us return to the trial and look at a sample defence opening.

---

### *Sample Defence Opening*

Your Honour, we will be calling evidence. I will be calling Mr. Vandergraaf as our only witness. Mr. Vandergraaf will tell you that he did throw a jar of peanut butter following the hockey game. He actually did not see where it landed, however, most importantly he will tell you that when he threw the jar he fully intended to see it splatter on the ice. He never intended for it to strike or hurt anyone. Your Honour, I now call Mr. Vandergraaf to the stand.

---

[12] *R. v. Vandergraaf* (1994), 93 C.C.C. (3d) 286 (Man. C.A.).

**Problems**

1. Prepare an opening statement for the plaintiff in *Mary White v. Wilber John*. Refer to the problem at the end of Chapter 2.

2. Prepare an opening statement for the defendant in *Mary White v. Wilber John*. Refer to the problem at the end of Chapter 2.

3. Select a well known case from tort or criminal law. Look to the facts, evidence and witnesses in that case. Prepare an abbreviated opening statement either for the plaintiff (Crown) or defendant (defence).

# 10

# CLOSING ARGUMENT

- **Things to Avoid in Closing**

- **The Structure of a Closing**

- **Arguing the Facts**

- **Arguing the Law**

- **Arguing Policy**

- **Arguing Second**

- **A Right of Reply**

- **Ending your Argument**

---

The closing is the culmination of the trial. All that has gone on before in the trial should be directed towards how it will be used in closing. For this reason, in preparation for the trial, it makes sense to work backwards from the closing. After you have garnered your facts and law, outline your closing. This will then provide a blueprint for the trial proper. In direct examination, you will know which facts you need from each witness to make your argument in closing. In preparing for cross-examination, your closing will tell you what you want to say about the credibility and validity of your opponent's evidence; it will identify your targets in cross-examination. Finally, you cannot make an opening without knowing your closing. The two go hand in glove. In sum, the closing encapsulates your trial plan.

It follows that the closing must be prepared, at least in outline form, prior to the start of the trial. I totally reject the view that the closing is left to the end, to develop as the trial unfolds. There is a saying, attributed to

Yogi Berra, "If you don't know where you are going, when you get there you are sure to be lost." Such is the fate of a trial without direction. The outline is there and you fill it in as the trial proceeds. In a way, it provides a helpful checklist as you progress through the case. Fully 80 to 90 per cent of the closing argument should be completed *before* the trial starts. You have decided on the organization of your argument. You have decided on the case authorities upon which you rely. You know, for the most part, the evidence in support of your argument. The last 10 to 20 per cent of your closing is the actual evidence adduced at trial, which can never be fully anticipated. If you have prepared adequately, there will be few surprises.

Along with the preparation of your argument, there is the preparation of argument aids. In many instances, the pre-trial memoranda are forwarded by consent of counsel to the trial judge and become the trial briefs. Or a separate trial brief, outlining the issues and your position on them, is prepared and made available to the judge at the start of the trial. A book of case authorities is prepared, properly bound and tabbed, and the portions relied upon are highlighted. I suggest that you use a line in the margin to identify certain passages. In this way, each copy will already be marked and will spare you having to go through and colour highlight the specific passages in each copy. For lengthy cases where you are only going to refer to a few pages, there is no need to photocopy the entire case. Copy the headnote and the relevant pages. Books are prepared for both the judge and opposing counsel.

A closing before a trial with judge alone is not the same as a jury address. Beware. Most texts on trial advocacy deal with closing arguments before juries. You have a different audience. In closing before a jury, you concentrate on the facts. In closing before a judge alone, you review the law and the facts. Do not make the mistake of assuming that the judge only wants to hear law. Far too often counsel dump law on the judge and do not adequately address the facts of the case. These lawyers have too much common law and not enough common sense.[1] Few cases are won on the law alone. The law is there to *apply* to the facts of the case.

It is important also to take advantage of your audience. In arguing before a judge alone you have the advantage of being able to "scout" the judge. Some judges are fact-based. Some judges are law-based. Some judges have written the authoritative text on the area that you are now arguing. Some judges have no background in the applicable area of law. Ask col-

---

[1] J. Arnup, "Advocacy"(1979), 13 Law Soc. U.C. Gaz. 27 at p. 39, quoting a comment by O.C. Mazengarb.

leagues, ask the court reporters and ask the clerks about the judge. In this way, you may better be able to tailor your final argument to fit the character of the presiding judge.

The order of address in a non-jury trial also is different from a jury trial. Generally the plaintiff argues first, irrespective of whether the defendant has called evidence, and a right of reply is accorded to the plaintiff.[2] In a criminal trial the order of argument before a judge alone is different: counsel for the prosecution is entitled to argue last unless the defence calls no witnesses.[3]

Having said that you prepare the closing in advance, it is also true that you cannot be too wedded to it. I have seen too many students who, in preparing for their trials, write out verbatim their closing and read it at the end. The prepared script inevitably does not reflect the evidence that actually was adduced at trial. The result is that counsel argues on the basis of "anticipated" evidence and the question most asked by the trial judge is, "Where is that in the evidence, counsel?" The closing cannot be prepared in totality; it is a framework that needs to be filled out by the evidence.

There is always need for flexibility. In fact, at times, the trial plan may have to be jettisoned completely. I'll share with you an experience I had as an articling student. I represented an enterprising 13-year-old charged with theft of bathtubs. I called the case "The Bathtub Caper." My client saw some bathtubs lying in the back lane by the garage of a residence. He got the help of an adult who had a truck to pick up the tubs and transport them to a local scrapyard. The proceeds from the sale were then split between the two. I prepared the case, none too confidently, on the basis that my client thought these tubs were left in the back lane as abandoned garbage. Of course, he made no inquiries to check. I was an expert on "abandonment" and "colour of right." A new defence soon arose at trial – identification. The Crown called the adult driver to testify as to what he knew about the tubs and who engaged him to transport them. Fortunately for my client, the adult had a poor memory and could only recall that "a kid" took him to the tubs and helped him. To the adult, all "kids" looked alike and he was unable

---

[2] The Manitoba Queen's Bench Rules specifically provide for this order and right of rebuttal, R. 52.07. In Ontario, the Rules of Civil Procedure address only the order for a jury trial, R. 52.07, where the defendant argues last only if no evidence is presented by the defendant. The practice for non-jury trials is different and the plaintiff generally argues first. See J. Sopinka, *The Trial of an Action* (1981), at p. 112. In British Columbia, under the rules, there is a right of reply and sur-reply, see *Supreme Court Civil Rules*, B.C. Reg. 168/2009, Rule 12-5 (72).

[3] See *Criminal Code*, R.S.C. 1985, c. C-46, s. 651.

to identify my client. Out went the "abandonment" defence and in came identification. The plan to call my client was put on hold. All my research on abandonment was for naught, but my client was acquitted. My experience is not unique. The courtroom is an unpredictable place and counsel need to adapt to the evidence.

# 1.  THINGS TO AVOID IN CLOSING

In addressing juries there are certain egregious errors that will either result in a mistrial or act as successful grounds of appeal. In judge alone trials, these same errors are not as "fatal," nevertheless they constitute things to avoid as a matter of poor tactics and advocacy.[4]

## 1.1   Misstating the Evidence

Besides being ethically irresponsible, it is tactically unwise to mislead the court in any manner. First, opposing counsel will probably pounce on your misstatement. Second, you lose credibility with the judge. Integrity is the most important attribute that you bring to an argument. Should you lose that, then the credibility of your entire argument is brought into question.

## 1.2   Not Informing the Court of Binding Authority

Counsel have an obligation to assist the court with the law. The *Code of Professional Conduct* specifically mandates that a lawyer must not "deliberately refrain from informing the tribunal of any binding authority that the lawyer considers to be directly on point and that has not been mentioned by an opponent."[5]

## 1.3   Referring to Facts Not in Evidence

You cannot introduce facts not in evidence. The one exception is for facts accepted by way of judicial notice. Judicial notice dispenses with the need to prove facts that are clearly uncontroversial or beyond reasonable dispute. However, inferences to be made from the facts are certainly within the realm of argument.

---

[4] See Mr. Justice Dan Ferguson, "The law relating to jury addresses" (Juy 1997) 16 Advocates' Soc. J. No.2, 19.
[5] The Law Society of Upper Canada, *Rules of Professional Conduct* (2014), section 5.1-2(i). Comparable provisions are found within the governing rules of the respective law societies.

## 1.4    Using Impassioned Rhetoric

One definition of argument is "reasoning." Reason with the judge. Impassioned pleas are rarely effective and often annoying. Persuasion is found in the eloquence of a simple argument, presented well, which outlines the applicable law and is supported on the facts.

## 1.5    Stating Your Personal Beliefs

Let the facts and the law speak for themselves. Your personal opinion is of no moment. Avoid using "I believe" or "I think." It may seem a cruel comment, but courts are not generally interested in what "you think" or what "your opinion" is of the law. You may value your opinion, but the court does not. Alan Dershowitz, the well-known Harvard Law School professor and equally well-known media commentator, forgot this point. He acted for former heavyweight boxing champion Mike Tyson on appeal of his rape conviction. In Dershowitz's submission before the appeal court seeking bail for his client, he said, "I will resign from this case if he breaks his bail. We will drop our appeal. That's how strongly I feel." To which the prosecutor replied, "So what?"

## 1.6    Making Personal Attacks

It is appropriate to attack the legal position of opposing counsel; it is entirely inappropriate to attack opposing counsel personally. Such attacks will brand you as arrogant.

## 1.7    Not Answering Questions from the Bench

Do not be afraid of questions from the judge. Fear silence instead. You have no idea what the silent judge is thinking; you have no idea whether the judge is with you, against you, or what, if anything, is troubling the judge. A silent court leaves counsel in limbo and you will only find out how well or poorly your submissions fared when judgment is rendered. Therefore, do not fear questions.

Anticipate that you will be asked questions and, above all, answer them when asked. The matter is of concern to the judge and the judge expects an answer. If you will be dealing with the question later, advise the judge of that but, at the same time, give a short answer to the question with an assurance that you will be providing a more detailed response later on in your argument.

## 2.   THE STRUCTURE OF A CLOSING

A good argument in closing meshes the facts, law and policy. There is no one standard formula. Each case is different. Certainly most cases are fact-driven. Other cases are law-driven and, in rare cases, you have an opportunity to make law. You need to be flexible enough to fit the argument to the case, but regardless of the argument, a structure there must be.

A recommended structure is as follows:[6]

1.   An opening

2.   A statement of the points in issue

3.   Issue 1
        Review of applicable evidence
        Review of law related to the evidence
        Conclusion

4.   Issue 2

5.   Issue 3

6.   End to your closing

Whatever your argument you need to show the judge your structure; you need a roadmap. A sound and simple way to start your argument is by telling the judge how you have structured it. This will allow you to maintain control over the argument, in that the judge is confident that you know where you are going. Number your issues and provide a heading for each. Consider the example on the following page.

---

[6] See as well, John Sopinka, "Appellate Advocacy," 11 Advocates' Soc. J., No. 1, 16-20 (March 1992).

## Opening Your Closing Argument

Your Honour, this case falls to be decided on three issues:

1) Was the defendant driving? [*Wait for the judge to write the heading down.*]
2) If the defendant was driving, was he intoxicated? [*Wait.*]

Finally, if Your Honour finds on these first two points, the Crown must still prove, and this is the third issue:

3) Did the defendant's impairment cause the accident and death of Mr. Williams? [*Wait.*]

The Crown must prove all of these elements. Your Honour, I will now turn to the first issue. Was the defendant driving?

In a "one issue" case, counsel should directly deal with the issue. For example, in a shoplift case where the defendant denies intending to steal the item, Crown counsel might well begin by saying:

Your Honour, there is only one issue in this case. Did the accused intend to steal the DVD disc? She says she merely forgot pay for it. The facts say differently. . ...

Where you have more than one argument, the general rule is start with your strongest point. Show the judge that you know the strength of your own case. By starting with weaker points, you lose the judge's patience and your own credibility with her. Now, it is not always possible to start every argument with your strongest point – logic may dictate otherwise. Consider the opening sample, above, where three issues were identified. Your strongest point actually is causation. The Crown may have real difficulty in proving that the defendant's impairment was a contributing cause to the accident. However, to start with this point almost seems to concede points 1) he was driving and 2) he was impaired. There is a logical sequence: 1) Was he driving? 2) If so, was he impaired? and 3) If so, did the impairment cause the accident?

I suggest that for each issue you prepare a stand-alone argument that has its own introduction, body and conclusion. In this way, you can easily move from one argument to another. Should your argument be an interrelated mass it is more difficult for you to abandon your predetermined course and you are left struggling when the judge interjects by saying, "I really don't need to hear from you on the second point, but what concerns me is point three. Please address that point."

At the conclusion of each issue, advise the judge that you intend to move on to the next issue:

> Your Honour, subject to any questions that you might have, that concludes my submissions on the issue of intoxication. I will now turn to the next issue, which is . . .

As a rule of thumb, present your argument before attacking the other side's position. To use a military analogy: "Secure your beachhead before advancing inland." To do otherwise gives too much credence to the opposing viewpoint. After all, you were so concerned about it that you addressed it right from the start. Moreover, you are being negative. You are criticizing before being constructive. Better to start positively. Start by showing the judge why your position is correct. It will then be easier to convince the judge that your opponent is wrong.

An argument is not a story, where you keep the judge in suspense until the ending. At the start of your argument, state your position. This is called "point first" argument.[7] It helps to frame your argument and gives it strength and focus. Reasoning follows to support your position.

## 3.   ARGUING THE FACTS

The presiding judge has sat through the entire trial. She has taken extensive notes. She is familiar with the evidence. There is no need for you to relive the entire trial. A chronological or witness-by-witness review of the evidence is unnecessary. On the other hand, do not assume that the judge has seen all that you have seen or views the evidence in the same way you do. It is equally inappropriate to say, "I do not propose to review the evidence because Your Ladyship has just heard it."[8] Take a simple example. Recall how often you come out of a theatre only to find that your interpretation of the play is completely at odds with that of a friend who sat right next to you and who saw the same play. People see and interpret things

---

[7]   See The Honourable John Laskin, "Forget the Windup and Make the Pitch: Some Suggestions for Writing More Persuasive Factums," 18 Advocates' Soc. J. No. 2 at 3-12 (1999).

[8]   Sopinka, *supra*, note 2, at p. 113.

differently. Your function as counsel in closing argument is to convince the judge that your interpretation of the facts is the more compelling.

Your first task in arguing the facts is to highlight particular pieces of the evidence. Not all evidence is of equal value. Identify the pivotal points and draw those to the judge's attention. Underline their importance and in this way these facts may take on a new significance for the judge. Emphasize points. If you rely on a document, refer the judge to the document and read the salient points from it. This is visual and aural reinforcement. Should you be at a trial where a running transcript of the testimony is prepared, refer to the transcript of the witness's testimony. Read from that transcript. Have the judge see and hear what the witness said. Should you not have a running transcript, this is where your note-taking comes to the fore, in that you have recorded certain verbatim statements that you now "quote" to the judge.

Your second task is to assist the court in resolving disputes presented by the evidence. Many trials are won or lost on credibility. It is your responsibility to convince the judge that your witnesses are more credible than those witnesses called by your learned friend. Support your witnesses by the evidence. Cite corroboration. Cite consistency. Cite impartiality. Correspondingly, challenge the opposing side's evidence. Raise inconsistency. Raise bias. Raise contradictions. These were your very objectives when you examined the witnesses and are now to be expressly used in closing.

Your third task is to tie the pieces of evidence together to create a crisp, complete and convincing case. Each piece of evidence viewed in isolation means little. Closing is the time to mould all the pieces of evidence into your theory of the case. Outlined below are some suggested techniques.

## 3.1   Be Specific

There is power in specific detail. For example, it is one thing to say that the accused kicked the victim on the ground "repeatedly." It is quite another to say that an eyewitness saw the accused kick the victim "eight" times, "three" kicks which were to his head, as he was lying on the ground.

Use the evidence. Use of direct quotes and of exhibits can be very effective.

---

### *Using Evidence in Closing*

**Use the Witness's Evidence**

Your Honour will recall that Mrs. Morgan, who was seated at the next table when the fight broke out, testified that she saw the accused swing at Mr. Innocent with, in her words, a "strong" right hand fist that struck Mr. Innocent on the left side of his face. She then said that Mr. Innocent "collapsed" to the floor and that it was, once again in her words, "obvious to all that Mr. Innocent was unconscious." Once Mr. Innocent was on the floor, the accused commenced to kick him. . ..

**Use the Exhibits**

Your Honour, if I can refer you to the photographs of Mr. Innocent taken at the hospital. These are exhibit 2. [*Wait until the judge has them*] You will see the extent of his injuries. You will see the injuries to both sides of Mr. Innocent's face. These injuries are consistent with Mr. Innocent being kicked in the face. . .

---

## 3.2    Build on Undisputed Facts

In many cases, there is much evidence that is not in dispute. A useful technique can be to list the undisputed evidence in support of your position. A solid foundation of "objective," undisputed evidence gives credence to your argument.

## 3.3    Use the Other Side's Evidence

It is expected that your witnesses will give favourable evidence. It is not expected that the opposing side's witnesses will assist your cause. Look for confirmation of your case through the opposing witnesses. It is also especially powerful to point out that this was the witness' evidence given in direct examination.

## 3.4    Concentrate on Credibility

You need to win the credibility issues at trial. Courts of Appeal are very reluctant to overturn findings of credibility. Therefore, a high priority in many cases is to show that your witnesses are the more credible. In support of your witnesses, cite corroboration, consistency and impartiality.

In challenging the other side's evidence, raise inconsistency, bias and contradictions.

### 3.5   Use Visual Aids Where Appropriate

Visual aids may assist. Where the trial is complex, or the money trail is convoluted, or the cast of characters is confusing, a flowchart and chronologies are helpful. Even a listing of points on a white board, although primitive, may be effective. Where appropriate, look to such visual aids.

Whatever medium you use, it is fundamental that you are comfortable with it. For example, should you decide to use digital images of exhibits, make sure that your computer is compatible with the courtroom projector system (assuming the courtroom has such a system). Test it. Make sure it works and you know how to make it work. Technology is wonderful – when it works.

A second reality about using technology is to give opposing counsel notice. Usually it is not a problem, but as a matter of courtesy opposing counsel should not be surprised and giving notice diffuses most objections.

## 4.   ARGUING THE LAW

Depending on the legal issue, you may well be the expert on the law and the judge will need your assistance. For example, in the "Bathtub Caper Case," referred to earlier, I would imagine that I knew more about "abandonment" than the trial judge, who may well have been hearing this defence for the first time. In this situation, your task is to explain the law. On "run-of-the-mill" legal issues, the judges are for the most part very familiar and need little assistance. No detailed explanation on the law is required. Incidentally, most cases fall into this latter category.

Arguing the law is not a legal memorandum verbalized. Nor is it a review of the law. This is a common mistake made by new counsel who feel obligated to canvass the law beginning with the *Magna Carta*. There is no need. You can assume that the judge is familiar with general principles of law. What you must do is to *apply the law to the facts*. This demands that you focus your legal argument upon the case at hand.

Show discrimination by being selective in the cases you use. Citing case upon case is ineffective. Imagine being forced to watch a bricklayer at work. Day after day, brick after brick, you watch. That would be tedious in the extreme. What you are interested in seeing is the final product — the building. It is the same with the law. What is the principle that underlies the cases you have researched? What propositions of law does the line of authorities expound? This is what you tell the judge. Zero in on the few *foundation cases* and address those. Other supporting authorities may be included in your trial brief, but should only be referred to in passing in your argument:

> My Lord, that proposition of law is accepted not only by the Court of Appeal in this province, but also by the Courts of Appeal in Saskatchewan, Alberta, British Columbia and New Brunswick. (*If asked for those authorities you are prepared to provide them.*) Or . . . And a list of those authorities is provided at paragraph 10 of our trial brief on page 3.

In discussing the foundation cases, provide a context. If the facts are on point, say so. If not, say so. The context of the case is most important if you are going to distinguish the case on the facts or challenge it on the law.

Another useful case to provide to the court is the *summary case*. This is a decision that summarizes the applicable law. You cite it not as a precedent necessarily, but as a source to assist the judge to familiarize himself with the pertinent law:

> My Lord, the law on this issue was thoroughly canvassed by Mr. Justice Berger in *Holt v. Verbruggen*, which is a 1981 decision of the British Columbia Supreme Court and is found at 20 Canadian Cases on the Law of Torts at page 29 (*or . . . is found at tab 4 of our book of authorities*). I note as well that there is an excellent annotation to this decision by Professor Osborne.

When you quote from a case keep it short. A long quote will only detract from your oral presentation. This is oral argument, not a reading session. Strive for a sharp, short quote that captures in vivid fashion what you want to say. Keep in mind that the words of Lord Denning or of Chief Justice Dickson carry far more weight than your own. Whenever you do quote, introduce the quotation with a correct citation:

> My Lord, I quote from the case of *Murphy v. Culhane*, a 1976 decision of the English Court of Appeal. That case is cited at 1976, 3 All England Reports at page 533 (*or . . . is provided at tab 2 of our book of authorities*). I refer Your Lordship to page 535 of that decision, where Lord Denning, Master of the Rolls, in writing for the entire court, stated . . . (*If the case is provided . . . I refer to the highlighted portion of the case at the bottom of page 535. I quote . . .*)

Do not leave the quote hanging. Integrate the quoted proposition of law with the facts of your case and show how the quote has direct application to your case. Otherwise the quote has little meaning.

A common mistake for new counsel is to rely on the cases to make their argument for them. An effective oral argument is you talking and not having the cases talk for you. John Sopinka put it this way:[9]

> Unless there is a binding authority on all fours in your favour, do not lead with the cases. Lead with the logic of your argument, which will be supported by the cases: show the court that what you are saying makes sense.

Constantly citing and quoting from authorities breaks up your argument. Just tell the judge the law and keep your supporting authorities in your "back pocket." The difference in approaches is illustrated below.

| *Cases Talking* | *You Talking* |
|---|---|
| Your Honour, we rely on the common law defence of necessity, which was found in the decision of *R. v. Morgentaler* (1976), 20 C.C.C. (2d) 449 (S.C.C.) to be preserved under section 8(3) of the Criminal Code. I did not include the *Morgentaler* case, however, section 8(3) is found at page 3 of my book of authorities. There are three elements to the defence of necessity. I refer you to the decision of *R. v. Latimer* (2001), 150 C.C.C. (3d) 129 (S.C.C.) where the Supreme Court of Canada accepted the following elements. Your Honour at page 147. . .1) imminent peril or danger; 2) the absence of a reasonable legal alternative; and 3) proportionality between the harm inflicted and the harm avoided. | Your Honour, we rely on the defence of necessity. There are three elements to the defence: 1) imminent peril or danger; 2) the absence of a reasonable legal alternative; and 3) proportionality between the harm inflicted and the harm avoided. [*Should the judge ask for authority, counsel has it in her "back pocket."*] |

---

[9] John Sopinka, *Appellate Advocacy, supra*, note 6.

Telling the judge the law makes for a clean, crisp and concise argument. You will then only rely on cases when they are truly necessary. Obviously, should the judge query your statement of law or appear doubtful in any way, then you will cite and provide appropriate authority. Make no mistake, you have the authority, but you are not necessarily leading with it in your argument.

## 5.  ARGUING POLICY

Policy addresses the wisdom of the law. The question for counsel to answer and mould into their argument is, "Why is the law the way it is?" Policy questions are concerned with issues beyond the result of the particular case at hand. In fact, policy argument can be used to defuse the apparent justice of ruling in one party's favour. The response is, "Yes it may work hardship for the particular party, but the sanctity of the rule must be upheld because . . ." Conversely, policy can be the most persuasive means of over-turning legal precedent that is against you. Question the rationale of the law. Is the rationale of the law still relevant? Can the policy concerns be addressed in alternative ways? Does the law fly in the face of practical realities? If your answer to any of these questions is "yes," then you have a basis on which to challenge the law. Policy concerns especially come to the fore where legal precedent ends. Here policy can provide the rationale for extending the law. Issues of policy have taken on increased importance in the era of the *Canadian Charter of Rights and Freedoms*. Application and analysis of the *Charter* is based on a "purposive approach."[10] Policy arguments are ideal vehicles for examples or hypotheticals. The Supreme Court of Canada's decision in *R. v. Smith* is a classic in this regard.[11] The accused was charged and convicted of importing a narcotic having a "street value" of between $126,000 and $168,000.[12] He was sentenced to eight years imprisonment. A challenge was brought against the *minimum* seven-year sentence for importing a narcotic. The Supreme Court of Canada found that the minimum sentence violated s. 12 of the *Charter* (protection against cruel and unusual treatment or punishment). The court was not concerned with Mr. Smith. The judges were concerned with the hypothetical, "young person who, while driving back into Canada from a winter break in the United States, is caught with only one, indeed, let us postulate, his or her first 'joint of grass'."[13] This hypothetical highlighted the injustice of the seven-year minimum sentence under law.

---

[10] *Dir. of Investigation & Research, Combines Investigation Branch v. Southam Inc.* (1984), 41 C.R. (3d) 97 (S.C.C.).

[11] *R. v. Smith* (1987), 58 C.R. (3d) 193 (S.C.C.).

[12] *Ibid.*, at p. 201.

[13] *Ibid.*, at p. 220, per Lamer J.

Occasionally cases take us beyond the limits of precedent and policy may well be our only guide. For example, in *R. v. Salituro*, the Supreme Court of Canada ruled that spousal incompetency did not apply where, although there was a valid marriage in law, the spouses were irreconcilably separated.[14] As the Court noted, where spouses are irreconcilably separated, there is no marital harmony to preserve and the rationale for preserving spousal incompetency ceased to apply. Policy dictated the result.

*R. v. Jobidon* provides a good example of where policy helped to resolve competing lines of authority.[15] Jobidon was charged with manslaughter. He had killed a man in a "fair fistfight" outside of a bar. The appeal courts throughout the land split as to whether or not such fights were consensual and, therefore, did not constitute an illegal assault. A majority in the Supreme Court accepted the policy argument; it was difficult to see any redeeming policy reason to sanction bar brawls.

*Smith, Salituro* and *Jobidon* were cases that ended up in the Supreme Court of Canada. Most cases do not. Therefore, although policy is important to understand, it may not be overtly argued that often. Most cases fall to be determined on the facts. I will put it this way. Policy makes for good discussion in the classroom, but may not be so applicable in the courtroom.

## 6.   ARGUING SECOND

In arguing second, the important point is that the argument responds to what has gone on before. You have the advantage of hearing the other side's argument and of observing the judge's reaction. Use this advantage. In your argument, respond to the concerns raised by the trial judge. Seize upon these concerns. For example:

> As Your Honour noted, the Crown's case really rests on the testimony of Mr. Wells and there are some serious questions about his evidence . . .

There will be times when you need to respond directly to an argument raised. For example:

> My learned friend relied on the case of *R. v. Smith* in support of his position. However, the court in that case was careful not to deal with the point now before us. I refer Your Honour to page 17 of the case, paragraph 25, where Justice Commons said. . .

---

[14]   *R. v. Salituro* (1991), 68 C.C.C. (3d) 289 (S.C.C.).
[15]   *R. v. Jobidon* (1991), 66 C.C.C. (3d) 454 (S.C.C.).

However, I caution against starting your argument by addressing points raised in the argument just completed. Going into the trial you had prepared a structured, logical argument. To go off on a "tangent" in response to a comment made by your opposing counsel can lead you into peril. As often as not, you are so eager to respond that you abandon your game plan. The start of your argument is perhaps the most important moment, yet you are starting by addressing a point raised by your opponent. Resist the urge to immediately respond. Start with your position, your argument, and respond to the points raised as they fit within your argument.

## 7.    A RIGHT OF REPLY

The right of reply is not to be abused. Just as with re-examination, the purpose of reply is to respond to new areas raised by the defendant in argument. It is not an opportunity for you to repeat all of your arguments. The last word is important. Take advantage of your right of reply. Prepare for it. You know your theme, your theory of the case. Capture that theme in a short, strong statement. Then wait for the defendant to give you an opening to respond, as will invariably happen. Respond to the matter and weave in your prepared comment:

> My Lord, I have one matter to address in reply. My learned friend has relied upon the case of *X v. Y*, but that case was decided before *M v. N* and never addressed the policy issue underlying the law. The policy of just compensation for damages caused was not even raised. That is why the case of *X v. Y* should not be followed and that is why in this case (prepared line) *the plaintiff is entitled to just compensation for injuries caused by the defendant.*

Do not trivialize the reply. Do not respond to a whole list of minor errors or disagreements. The reply should be succinct and strong.

The value in having the right of reply is that it essentially removes the need for you to interrupt and object during the defendant's closing. Objections during closing argument should be rare. You object only when opposing counsel makes *grievous* misstatements of the law or facts. Otherwise save your response for reply.

## 8.    ENDING YOUR ARGUMENT

Your closing must have an ending. This is the time to close your book, put the notes away, look the judge in the eye and give a short, succinct statement of your position. Try to capture in a few sentences your position and the reason why the court should rule in your favour.

Conclude by saying: "Your Honour, subject to any questions that you may have, that concludes my submission."

---

**Problem**

Consider the case of *Waite v. Stewart*. Refer to Chapter 2, the direct examination of Richard Waite contained in chapter 11, and the problem at the end of Chapter 12. You are now in closing argument. One issue is that of *provocation* and whether provocation can go to reduce *general* damages as well as *punitive* damages. Refer to the following legal authorities:

> *Murphy v. Culhane*, [1976] 3 All E.R. 533 (C.A.)

> *Holt v. Verbruggen* (1981), 20 C.C.L.T. 29 (B.C. S.C.)

> *Landry v. Patterson* (1978), 93 D.L.R. (3d) 345 (Ont. C.A.)

> *Coote v. Antonenko* (1986), 46 Sask. R. 161 (Q.B.)

> *Check v. Andrews Hotel Co.* (1974), 56 D.L.R. (3d) 364 (Man. C.A.)

> *Lane v. Holloway*, [1967] 3 All E.R. 129 (C.A.)

> *Shaw v. Gorter* (1977), 2 C.C.L.T. 111 (Ont. C.A.)

Argue as plaintiff's counsel.

Argue as defendant's counsel.

Maximum time limit for argument is 15 minutes.

---

# 11

# PUTTING IN YOUR CASE: DIRECT EXAMINATION

- **Witness Preparation**

- **Leading Questions**

- **Principles of Direct Examination**

- **Re-examination**

- **A Sample Direct Examination**

"Putting in your case" means presenting to the judge your theory of the case. In so doing, two considerations prevail, legal requirements and persuasive requirements. First, your case must adduce all of the essential elements necessary to support the cause of action and relief sought. Get the facts in. Your trial brief lists the legal requirements and your evidence. You will win few cases, however, if your primary objective is simply to avoid a non-suit. More is required. Persuasion is essential. You strive to convince the judge that your theory of the case and the evidence introduced in support of it is more believable, more credible, more *just* than that of your opponent.

To my mind, a persuasive case is presented efficiently. The case has focus. The evidence is honed. Ask yourself this basic question, "What is the case all about?" The answer tells you what is important and what is not important. You then concentrate on what really matters. Unfortunately, when you look at many trials, you find a deluge of superfluous detail. What has happened is that the counsel involved have not culled the evidence. In preparing for any trial you may well accumulate a large amount of information. You are not obliged to use it all. Look to what the judge needs to know and then select the evidence that best conveys this information. Unnecessary detail clutters up your case, obscures the critical points you want to make and wastes court time.

Your case ultimately rests upon your witnesses. Evidence is presented through witness testimony and this chapter is about how to conduct efficient and effective direct examinations. First, it discusses witness preparation. Generally speaking, the better the witness is prepared, the better is the testimony. Second, you want to present a "clean" examination, which is not open to objection. In order to do this, you need to know what you can and cannot do in direct examination. Therefore, you need to understand the law on leading questions. Third, certain suggested approaches and techniques will be offered on how to conduct more effective direct examinations.

## 1.   WITNESS PREPARATION

Witness preparation involves helping witnesses *present* their evidence better. The focus is on *how* the witnesses give their evidence and not on *what* that evidence is. Counsel's task is to help witnesses tell their story — the true story. To have witnesses *change* their testimony crosses the line from proper preparation to unethical fabrication.

In terms of what amounts to proper preparation of witnesses, it is worthwhile to examine the two extremes, the English practice and the American practice. In England, the barrister only interviews the client and expert witnesses. Other witnesses are interviewed by the instructing solicitor. One argument commonly put forth to justify this practice is that there is concern that the barrister, through inadvertence or by design, could suggest to witnesses what their evidence ought to be in order to win the case.[1] Is this then to say that the instructing solicitor is less able or less prone inadvertently or unscrupulously to taint the witness's evidence? I think not.

The English practice is unduly restrictive. In many cases there are witnesses, other than the client, who are key to the success of the case. These witnesses need to be properly prepared for giving their evidence and, in most instances, that task can only be done by the person who is going to conduct the examination of the witness.[2]

---

[1] Sir Malcolm Hilbery, *Duty and Art in Advocacy* (1946), p. 11.

[2] See the comments of Sir David Napley, *The Technique of Persuasion*, 4th ed. (1991), pp. 46-47, who is of the view that the English practice is "outmoded and should be abolished." The Attorney General in the United Kingdom is now moving to allow Crown prosecutors to interview key witnesses. A consultation paper was prepared for the Crown Prosecution Service in 2003 on "Pre-trial Witness Interviews by Prosecutors." Refer to the Crown Prosecution Service website at *www.cps.gov.uk*

The American approach represents the other extreme. One need only refer to the countless books written on leading American trials to see how the witnesses are "rehearsed" in the giving of their testimony.[3] Witnesses are run through mock direct and cross-examinations, sometimes before mock juries, over and over again until the "script" is right. The trick, it seems, is to be scripted without appearing to be so. In my view, the American approach is prone to excess and is too liable to abuse. As with so many things, a middle course is the right course.

When does proper preparation become improper perjury? The line is difficult to draw at times, but what is important is that counsel respect that line. Consider this example. You are interviewing a critical eyewitness. The witness is having difficulty recalling certain key pieces of evidence. What do you do? Showing the witness a copy of an earlier statement he himself or she herself made in order to refresh the memory is proper. However, to refresh the witness's memory through statements made by other persons taints the witness's evidence. In this situation you are giving the witness a memory aid that invites the witness to recall what others have said occurred, and in testifying a real question is raised as to whether this is truly the witness's own evidence.

An example of witness tainting is found in the case of *R. v. Buric*.[4] The police were investigating a murder in a "cold case" going back some ten years. They arrested P and charged him with first degree murder. P made a deal with the Crown and pled guilty to the lesser offence of conspiracy to commit murder and received a sentence of nine years. In exchange, he became the key Crown witness. Needless to say, P was a streetwise, unsavory criminal. In order to induce him to turn on others involved, the police showed P statements from other witnesses. Only after seeing these statements and reading about what they had to say, did P give a statement to the police and the deal was made for him to testify. Unfortunately, the police did not keep accurate records of their dealings with P. The trial judge found that in these circumstances the tainting made P's evidence manifestly unreliable, had affected trial fairness, and refused to allow P to testify. On appeal it was found that the trial judge had erred in preventing P from testifying. According to the majority, the tainting issue was one of weight, for the jury, and not admissibility. Nevertheless, *Buric* stands as an egregious example of what not to do in preparing a witness.

---

[3] An example of the American approach to preparing a witness can be found in James McElhaney, *Trial Notebook*, 2nd ed. (1987), pp. 31-42.

[4] *R. v. Buric* (1996), 106 C.C.C. (3d) 97 (Ont. C.A.); affirmed 114 C.C.C. (3d) 95 (S.C.C.).

The same problem arises when there are numerous witnesses to an event and there are disagreements or inconsistencies with their evidence. How are inconsistencies among the witnesses to be handled? One American author suggested a "group" approach, whereby all the witnesses would be brought together to see and hear each other's evidence. According to the writer, the advantage of the group approach was that it made for "a united front, a dovetailing of testimony, and a uniformity of narration."[5] The so-called "advantage" of using the group approach is really its major disadvantage. The group approach invites group evidence. There is too much danger that witnesses when interviewed together will adapt their evidence to what they have seen or heard others say. The witnesses should be interviewed separately. One exception is for experts who may need to hear what other experts have to say — the same is not true for the lay witness.

The need for care in preparing witnesses should not deter counsel from ensuring that their witnesses are properly prepared to testify. Witness preparation is essential. You will accomplish little if you are thoroughly prepared but your witnesses are not. They give the evidence, not you. Proper witness preparation involves four areas:

1)   preparation of the testimony,

2)   preparation of the presentation,

3)   preparation for the court, and

4)   preparation for the cross-examination.

## 1.1   Preparation of the Testimony

Your goal is to prepare the witnesses so that they are completely at ease with what they must say, without being "scripted."

1)   Have the witnesses review their prior statements or testimony given. They must know to what they have already attested.

2)   Provide an overview of the case so that the witnesses know where they fit into the case and how their testimony is relevant.

3)   Highlight the key parts of their testimony.

---

[5]   E. Low, *How to Prepare and Try a Negligence Case* (1957), pp. 70-74, as quoted in Gary Bellow and Bea Moulton, *The Lawyering Process* (1978), p. 683.

4)  Go through the direct examination with the witnesses so that they are familiar with you, your questions and your organization.

5)  Go over rules of evidence, which may confuse the witness:

    • You cannot *lead*. Explain what a leading question is and that the witness may have to "help" where it is difficult to ask a question in a non-leading way.

    • Go over *opinion* and *conclusion* evidence. Emphasize to the witness that the court wants factual evidence from the witness and not opinion.

    • Explain *hearsay*. Nothing can throw a witness off more than to be told that "You cannot tell us what Mr. Morris said."

6)  Help witnesses tell what they really mean. Some witnesses appear inconclusive when they are not. They may have a habit of saying, "I suppose" or "I guess," when what they really mean is, "I know it was him."

### 1.2    Preparation of the Presentation

Besides what the witness will say, you must also be concerned with how it is said. A truthful witness can come across as a "damned liar" to the trial judge. In particular, when a trial presents conflicting testimony, credibility is critical and you must do all you can to help your witness tell the truth so as to be believed.

1)  Witnesses should speak up and keep their heads up. Look at the questioner when answering the question.

2)  They must keep their composure. Be relaxed, but not flippant. Be polite.

3)  Witnesses must know which exhibits are being introduced through them. Go through the foundation requirements for the introduction of the exhibit. If a diagram is used, the witness must become familiar with that diagram and its use.

4)  Go over what the witnesses should wear. The court process deserves respect. Without going into detail, perhaps the best advice to give to your witnesses in terms of what to wear is to say, "Dress as though you were going for a job interview."

### 1.3    Preparation for the Court

Counsel are nervous. Witnesses often are even more nervous. The unknown breeds fear and most witnesses have never testified in court before. You have an obligation to make them comfortable.

1) Go over the trial process with your witnesses. Go through the direct, cross- and re-examination steps with them. Let them know at what point during the trial you anticipate calling them. Assist them with parking or transportation to the court.

2) Describe the court and the various players in the trial. Use a diagram, video or, for a particularly nervous witness, go to the actual courtroom. If need be, have the witness watch part of a trial.

3) Go over some of the small details that can throw a witness. Will the witness swear or affirm? Does the witness stand or sit? Where will the witness have to wait before being called?

### 1.4    Preparation for the Cross-examination

What witnesses fear most is the cross-examination. You must prepare them as best you can for questioning by the opposing counsel. Most importantly, go over inconsistencies in the witness's evidence or between that witness and others. See if the inconsistencies can be explained. Sometimes the witness simply was mistaken earlier and will have to say so. In these circumstances, it is better to admit error rather than have the witness painted as evasive or untrustworthy. Finally, conduct a mock cross-examination or have a colleague do so. Experience under fire is the best teacher. The following are suggested rules for witnesses to abide by on cross:

1) Listen to the questions.

2) Do not lose your temper.

3) Do not become argumentative. Often a witness will come off the stand proud of how, "That lawyer was sure put in his place." I doubt it. Most likely the witness simply came across as an obnoxious, difficult witness whose testimony will be given little weight.

4) When asked a question:

   • If you do not know the answer, say so.

- If you do not understand the question, say so, and it will be repeated.

- If you do not remember, say so.

- If you know the answer, say so.

5) Do not volunteer information. Answer only the question asked.

6) Do not be forced into answering yes or no. If you cannot answer yes or no, say so. You are entitled to explain.

7) If an objection is made, you are to stop talking. Your counsel does not want you to answer that question. Wait for the ruling from the judge.

The last piece of advice you give to a witness is — tell the truth.

## 2.   LEADING QUESTIONS

A direct examination is not a narrative or soliloquy. You do not simply call the witness and ask "What happened?" and then sit down. The witness's evidence is brought out through your questions, which guide, direct and highlight the witness's testimony. The witness tells a story through your questions. The format of a direct examination then is question and answer.

In terms of questioning your witness, it is trite law that the party who calls a witness is generally not permitted to ask the witness leading questions. The rule is: Do not lead your witness. The principle behind the rule is that in direct examination you are presenting witnesses favourable to your case, who are sympathetic towards your client and who are susceptible to your suggestions. Therefore, suggestions on your part are not permitted. "A leading question then is one that suggests to the witness the answer desired by the examiner."[6] There are two types of leading questions, a question that suggests the answer and a question that assumes a fact in dispute.

**Suggestive of an answer**

The "suggestive" question may be blatant or subtle.

***Blatant:***   "You saw a man over six feet tall and weighing over 200 lbs., didn't you?" The suggested answer is clear.

---

[6] *McCormick on Evidence*, E. Cleary (ed.), 3rd. ed. (1984), at p. 11.

***Subtle:***    "Did you or did you not see a man over six feet tall and weighing over 200 lbs.?" This question gives the witness the option, yes or no. Does it really? Are you not really expecting a "yes" answer? Why? Because by giving certain characteristics you are expecting the witness to agree with your description.

One test for a leading question is "whether an ordinary man would get the impression that the questioner desired one answer rather than another."[7] You must avoid being too *specific* in your questions because the specific question begs for a specific answer. Let us carry our question to the specific extreme:

> Did you or did you not see a man over six feet tall, weighing 200 lbs., with red hair, horn-rimmed glasses and a mole on his left cheek?

You obviously expect a "yes" answer. The proper question can be simply phrased:

> Please describe the man you saw.

## Assumption of a fact

> How fast was the man running when he left the bank?

The question is not objectionable if the witness had already testified as to observing a man running from the bank. The question is objectionable if there is no evidence before the court that the man was *running*. Counsel has assumed that fact.

It is important to recognize that the answers to leading questions are not inadmissible in evidence. They simply have little weight.[8] The reason is apparent: the testimony has been directed through counsel and is tainted. A good illustration is *R. v. Williams*.[9] In this case the accused was charged with possession of stolen goods. The case against the accused turned on the identification of the accused by a pawn dealer, who was sold the stolen goods.

> **Q.** Did you purchase them?
> **A.** I did, yes.

---

[7] *Ibid.*

[8] See E. Ratushny, "Basic Problems In Examination And Cross-Examination" (1974), 52 Can. Bar Rev. 209 at p. 212.

[9] *R. v. Williams* (1982), 66 C.C.C. (2d) 234 (Ont. C.A.).

**Q.** On what date, sir?
**A.** I believe it was on the 20th of August.

**Q.** How much did you purchase them for?
**A.** 45 dollars.

**Q.** All three?
**A.** Yes.

**Q.** From whom did you purchase them?
**A.** That boy there. Well, he was one of the boys, one of the group of boys that came in.

**Q.** I see and you gave whom the 45 dollars?
**A.** I gave it to one of those boys there.

**Q.** Which boy?
**A.** Well the boy in the background, he was there also.

**Q.** *But the accused, do you know who the accused is?*
**A.** That boy there, sitting down.

**Q.** *Right, he was one of them?*
**A.** Yes and a few more other boys.

**Q.** *I see and you gave him 45 dollars.*
**A.** That's right. [emphasis added]

The direction by counsel is apparent. Mr. Justice Martin, writing for the court, allowed the appeal after determining that the identification was valueless "having regard to the way in which the answers identifying the appellant were elicited from the identifying witness."[10]

A very helpful case on leading questions is *R. v. Rose*.[11] It is quite apparent that the Crown counsel prosecuting the case did not understand what a leading question was. For example, he asked his witness the following question:[12]

> **Q.** Now, my information is that the police had set surveillance on yourself and on the 19th of August you got into a motor vehicle with Mr. Rose. The 21st of August you got into a motor vehicle with Mr. Rose.

---

[10] *Ibid.*, at p. 236.
[11] *R. v. Rose* (2001), 153 C.C.C. (3d) 225 (Ont. C.A.).
[12] *Ibid.* at 231.

Defence counsel objected – leading. To wit, the Crown counsel replied:

> Well, this is information I have and I'm asking this witness to either confirm
> or deny it. If he confirms it, it will become a fact. If he denies it, it won't
> become a fact. I don't think it's leading at all. It's information I have and I'm
> asking him to confirm it or deny it. It's not suggesting the answer.

The question is leading. It is suggestive of the answer. The fact that the
Crown is telling the witness that his information is such and such suggests
that it is true and the witness ought to accept it. Moreover, counsel is putting
facts to the witness, rather than having the witness provide the facts. This
is leading.

Later on in the case, Crown counsel improperly led another witness
by referring to a prior statement that she had given to the police. Crown
counsel presented the witness with the written statement that she had given
to the police. He then referred to what she had said in the statement in
framing his questions to her. In essence, the statement acted as a script. Here
are some excerpts:[13]

Q. And you told Constable Mills that you had another motor vehicle . . .

Q. And you told Constable Mills that, you stated Evon helped to buy the car,
it was just in my name, is that . . .

Q. And Constable Mills asked you, who drives it and who owns it now as far
as you're concerned and you stated, "He drives it and I signed it over to
him, so as far as I know, Evon said he's going to sell it."

This is a common mistake made by new counsel, who think that they can
use the witness's own statement in the direct examination of that witness.
No. This is improper. Not only is this leading the witness, but it violates
two other rules of evidence. First, it is hearsay. The witness is testifying as
to an out-of-court statement she gave, which is being introduced for its truth.
Second, if it is going in to show consistency with her in-court testimony,
then it is inadmissible self-serving evidence. Statements are not to be used
in such a fashion. You use the statement in planning your direct examination
and your hope is that the witness will give evidence consistent with her
statement. But you do not mention the statement. The statement is not used
to frame your questions. You simply ask the witness for the information:

Do you own a car?

---

[13] *Ibid.* at 235.

Who owns the car?

Who drives the car?

In our example, Crown counsel could only use the statement in two circumstances:

1) If the witness has a failure of memory then the statement may be used to refresh the witness's memory, and

2) If the witness says something inconsistent with her statement and the Crown moves to cross-examine her under s. 9(2) of the *Canada Evidence Act* (see Chapter 16.) The statement, however, cannot be used to guide the examination.

## 2.1 Avoiding Leading Questions

Here is a rule of thumb to assist new counsel in avoiding leading questions. Begin a question with: *who, what, where, when, why* and *how*. Do not begin a question with: *did* or *were*.[14] The problem with starting a question with "did" or "were" is that invariably you are converting a statement into a question. See the examples below.

---

### *Examples of Leading and Non-Leading Questions*

**No:** Did you see Mr. Waite outside the sports complex?
**Yes:** Who did you see outside the sports complex?

**No:** Did you see Mr. Waite hit the defendant back?
**Yes:** What did Mr. Waite do after being hit?

**No:** Did you take Mr. Waite to the hospital?
**Yes:** Where did you take Mr. Waite?

**No:** Did the fight take place before 8:00 pm?
**Yes:** When did the fight occur?

**No:** Were you going to play hockey at the sports complex?
**Yes:** Why were you at the sports complex?

**No:** Was Mr. Waite winded by the kick to the stomach?
**Yes:** How did Mr. Waite appear when he was kicked in the stomach?

---

[14] John Olah, *The Art and Science of Advocacy* (1991), pp. 9-17.

## 2.2    Re-Formulating the Rule on Leading

It is incorrect to say that counsel cannot lead in direct examination. As we have seen, answers to leading questions are not inadmissible, but may be given less weight. Obviously, if you lead on critical areas then you actually are reducing the value of the answers you receive – as occurred in *R. v. Williams, supra.* At times I have observed student counsel lead their witnesses from start to finish. When asked why they did so, they often reply that opposing counsel did not object. What they fail to realize is that through their questioning they have weakened their evidence. The judge wants to hear from the witness and not from counsel.

It follows that if you do not care about the weight to be given to certain answers, then, by all means, lead. It is permitted to lead on introductory matters. "Do you reside at 209 Elm Street?" Such questions are allowed in order to save time.

It is permitted to lead on undisputed matters. For example, the date and location of an accident is really not at issue. What is at issue is the manner of driving. In a criminal prosecution, Crown counsel will cut right to the chase with an eyewitness to the accident:

Q. I understand that you are a second year law student at the university, is that correct?

Q. On September 29th, 2015, in the morning, you were driving to the university, is that correct?

Q. As you got to the corner of University Crescent and Markham Drive did you observe a car pedestrian accident?

*At this point, you stop leading. It is time for the witness to give evidence.*

Therefore, good direct examiners certainly do ask leading questions. In fact, if you are fortunate enough to watch a trial conducted by senior counsel, you might well be surprised by the number of leading questions asked without objection. The reason is simple — counsel are leading on unimportant matters and this moves the trial along. The trick is to know when to lead and when not to lead. Here is the re-formulated rule:

> **Lead When It Doesn't Matter.**
>
> **Don't Lead When It Does Matter.**

## 2.3   Directional Leading

It is permitted to direct a witness to a specific subject area that the lawyer wishes to examine on. Such direction is good, if not essential. For example, in a murder case, the Crown calls the next door neighbour to identify the accused's car parked in front of the victim's home the day the victim disappeared. The scene is set. The witness testifies that he was at home that day doing yard work. Crown counsel then asks:

**Q.** Did you see a car parked in front of the victim's house?

This is a directional question and is proper. The witness's mind is turned to the topic, without any further specifics. How else would counsel get the information? The question "What did you see?" could lead anywhere. What is objectionable is if counsel goes on to give specifics:

**Q.** Did you see a pink, BMW convertible in front of the victim's home?

To summarize, "general" direction on a topic is proper; "specific" direction on a topic is improper.

Robert Keeton gives another excellent example. In an automobile accident case, the driver of the truck involved made an admission following the collision. Counsel want to direct the witness to the statement:[15]

> . . . and surely it is leading in an absolute sense to ask, "Did the truck driver say anything?" It is leading in the sense that it suggests to the witness that the lawyer wants testimony as to the truck driver's comments rather than testimony just then as to something else that happened immediately after they collided. But questions that merely direct attention to the subject matter about which the lawyer wants the witness to testify are not regarded as "leading" in law; if such questions were not permitted, it would be almost impossible to conduct an examination on any basis other than simply asking the witness to tell what he knows about the lawsuit.

---

[15] R. Keeton, *Trial Tactics and Methods*, 2nd ed. (1973), at p. 50.

It is also permitted to direct a witness to a specific statement if it is intended to *contradict* the testimony of a prior witness:[16]

> **Q.** Mr. Blank, you were present when an exchange of words took place between Mr. Smith and Mr. Jones in Mr. Smith's office?
> **A.** Yes.
>
> **Q.** Will you tell us what was said on that occasion?
> **A.** Well, Mr. Smith called Mr. Jones a thief and Mr. Jones said, "Well you can't prove it."
>
> **Q.** Mr. Brown has testified that when Mr. Smith called Mr. Jones a thief, Mr. Jones said, "You are a liar." Is that correct?
> **A.** No, Mr. Jones didn't say you are a liar, he said, "You can't prove it."

## 2.4    Leading When the Witness is Having Difficulty

It is permitted to lead a witness who is unable to answer a question without leading. Witnesses do forget or the questions may be of such a complicated nature that leading is necessary. The Rules of Court in civil cases provide for leading in such circumstances. For example, in Manitoba Rule 53.01(2) applies:[17]

> 53.01 (2) Where a witness appears unwilling or unable to give responsive answers, the trial judge may permit the party calling the witness to examine the witness by means of leading questions.

In criminal cases, counsel may lead where it is necessary to do so in the interests of justice.[18] This power should not be used lightly because the response to your leading question, although admissible, may be given little evidentiary weight by the presiding judge.

## 2.5    Refreshing the Witness's Memory

Trials occur months, if not years, after the incident that gives rise to the litigation. A witness's memory is fragile and the law recognizes that witnesses will need to refresh their memories. It is impossible to control how witnesses refresh their memories prior to testifying. Any manner of means may be used. As mentioned earlier in this chapter, it is good practice

---

[16] A. Martin, "The Examination of Witnesses," in Examination of Witnesses II, Continuing Legal Education Seminar, p. 3.01, at p. 3.03 (Vancouver, 1986).

[17] See also: Ontario, Rules of Civil Procedure, r. 53.01(4); British Columbia, Rules of Court, r. 40(21).

[18] *Reference re R. v. Coffin* (1956), 114 C.C.C. 1 at 22 (S.C.C.).

to show witnesses their prior statements or transcripts of their testimony so that they can recall what they said. Abuse may occur, as happened in *R. v. Buric, supra.* It is open to the cross-examiner to explore what means were used by the witness to refresh memory and expose any impropriety.

Once in court, the judge regulates the refreshing process. Witnesses are nervous, especially the uninitiated, and they will forget. The law enables counsel to attempt to refresh the memory of a witness. Wigmore identified two types of refreshing memory: 1) "Present Recollection Revived" and 2) "Past Recollection Recorded."[19] In the former, the memory of the witness is revived. The refreshing instrument has rekindled the witness's recollection and the witness now can testify by way of "present" memory. With "past recollection recorded" the memory of the witness is not revived. The memory is dead. The witness can only testify as to what is recorded in the document. The document is in substance the evidence and courts should be careful to ensure that the record is accurate and reliable. The distinction that Wigmore makes generally goes unnoticed in Canadian courts, however, it is a valid distinction in principle that deserves consideration.

### (a)    Present Recollection Revived

The traditional approach to reviving a witness's present memory was outlined by the Ontario Court of Appeal in *R. v. Gwozdowski,* where the following principles were taken from *Phipson on Evidence*:[20]

> A witness may refresh his memory by reference to any writing made or verified by himself concerning, and contemporaneously with, the facts to which he testifies; but such documents are no evidence *per se* of the matters contained
> . . .

> The writing may have been made either by the witness himself, or by others, providing in the latter case that it was read by him when the facts were fresh in his memory, and he knew the statement to be correct . . .

> The document must have been written either at the time of the transaction or so shortly afterwards that the facts were fresh in his memory. A delay of a fortnight may not be fatal; but an interval of several weeks, or six months, has been held to exclude.

The American position on "present recollection revived" suggests broader latitude for the type of "reviving" material: "Any writing or thing

---

[19] Wigmore, *Evidence* (Chadbourn rev. 1970), para. 758.
[20] *R. v. Gwozdowski* (1973), 10 C.C.C. (2d) 434 at 437 (Ont. C.A.).

may be used to stimulate and revive a recollection."[21] Wigmore accepted this comment on the law:[22]

> Common experience, the work of Proust and other keenly observant literary men, and recondite psychological research, all teach us that memory of things long past can be accurately restored in all sorts of ways. The creaking of a hinge, the whistling of a tune, the smell of seaweed, the sight of an old photograph, the taste of nutmeg, the touch of a piece of canvas, may bring vividly to the foreground [of] consciousness the recollection of events that happened years ago and which would otherwise have been forgotten. If a recollection thus reawakened be then set down on paper, why should not that paper properly serve in the courtroom, as it does in everyday life, to prod the memory at still a later date?

According to Wigmore, the fact that the "revival material" was not written by the witness or not made contemporaneously with the observation is no fault. To date, Canadian courts have been wary of accepting Wigmore's liberal interpretation for refreshing of memory.[23] Times may be changing. The Wigmore approach certainly was approved of by Justice Binnie in *R. v. Fliss*.[24]

*Fliss* is an interesting case. The accused was charged with murder. The police conducted an undercover operation, whereby Fliss was invited to join a criminal organization. During the course of the operation, Fliss disclosed to the undercover officers that the police did not like him because they thought he had committed a murder. This was the undercover officer's opening. He suggested to Fliss that through his underworld contacts he could find someone suffering a terminal illness to make a false confession and get Fliss off the hook. All that Fliss had to do was provide sufficient detail to make the confession believable. Fliss took the bait. He took the undercover officer to where the killing occurred and described the killing in detail. The officer was "wired" and the conversation with Fliss was recorded. At trial, the judge found that the police had insufficient grounds to get the authorization to record the conversations and the recording and transcript were ruled inadmissible. The police officer was, however, allowed to testify as to his recollection of what Fliss had told him and use the inadmissible transcript to refresh his memory.

---

[21] 3 Wigmore, *Evidence*, Chadbourn rev. (1970), para. 758, p. 125.
[22] *Ibid.*, at p. 128, taken from Frank J. in *Fanelli v. U.S. Gypsum Co.*, 141 F.2d 216, 217 (2nd Circ., 1944).
[23] See *R. v. Dimmer* (1983), 37 C.R. (3d) 227 (Alta. Q.B.).
[24] *R. v. Fliss* (2002), 161 C.C.C. (3d) 225 (S.C.C.).

Justice Binnie made the following observation, which closely reflects Wigmore's view:[25]

> There is also no doubt that the officer was entitled to refresh his memory by any means that would rekindle his recollection, whether or not the stimulus itself constituted admissible evidence. This is because it is his recollection, not the stimulus, that becomes evidence. The stimulus may be hearsay, it may itself be largely inaccurate, it may be nothing more than the sight of someone who had been present or hearing some music that had played in the background. If the recollection here had been stimulated by hearing a tape of his conversation with the accused, even if the tape was made without valid authorization, the officer's recollection – not the tape – would be admissible.

Therefore, it was acceptable for the officer to refresh his memory of what was said by reading the inadmissible transcript of the conversation. Of importance, the transcript is not made an exhibit. The refreshing document does not become evidence; it only assists the witness in giving his testimony, which is the evidence. What was unacceptable in *Fliss* was for the officer to read verbatim from the transcript. The result was to allow the prosecution to put into evidence indirectly what the exclusion order forbade it from doing directly.

The steps involved in refreshing the memory for a witness are outlined in the table following:

---

### *Refreshing Memory*

1) **Witness has forgotten evidence.**

2) **"Cue" the witness that there is more evidence:**

**"Do you recall anything else?"**

3) **Provide a foundation for the refreshing document:**

**— Made or authenticated by the witness**

*(cont'd)*

---

[25] *Ibid.*, at para. 45.

---

— **Made near the time the events recorded**

— **No changes to the document**

— **Document would assist memory**

4) **Ask permission for the witness to review the document.**

   **[*Opposing counsel may object*]**

5) **Witness reads document [*silently to self*] to refresh memory.**

6) **Ask again about the forgotten evidence.**

7) **Witness gives "refreshed" evidence.**

---

*Note*: 1) the refreshing document does not become evidence,

2) the witness does not read from the document,

3) the witness gives evidence from his or her present memory,

4) the trial judge rules as to whether or not the witness will be allowed to refresh memory, and,

5) opposing counsel is given an opportunity to challenge the refreshing.

Once a document is used to refresh a witness's memory, opposing counsel has a right to inspect the document. This will mean that if a privileged document is used to refresh the witness's memory, the privilege will be lost. Opposing counsel may then cross-examine the witness using the document. Depending upon the scope of the cross-examination on the document, the trial judge has a discretion to make the document an exhibit if necessary for the trier of fact to understand or fully appreciate the cross-examination.

The most common use of notes is by police officers. An illustration is provided below:

**Q.** Officer O'Brian, what time did you arrive at the bank?

**A.** I'm really not sure, at about 10:00 p.m. I guess.

**Q.** Would anything help you remember?
**A.** Yes.

**Q.** And what is that?
**A.** I took notes.

**Q.** When were those notes taken?
**A.** At the end of my shift later that night.

**Q.** And were these notes made by you?
**A.** Yes.

**Q.** My Lord, may the witness refer to his notes?

**Court:** Yes.

**Q.** Officer O'Brian, have the notes refreshed your memory?
**A.** Yes — I arrived at the bank at 10:05 p.m.

### (b)   Past Recollection Recorded

Past recollection recorded applies when the witness has no present memory and must rely upon the record. This is what happened in *Fliss* when the police officer started to read verbatim from the transcript of the conversation. Certainly the officer had a present recollection of the "gist" of what Fliss had told him. As the officer pointed out, it is not every day that a person sits down and tells you how they killed someone. But the officer testified at a level of detail that suggested "encyclopedic recall." Justice Binnie gave this example:[26]

> I said, "Do you want me to explain to you exactly how this is going to work or not?" And there was a pause, and he said, "Yeah, I do." I said, "Huh?" And he said, "Yeah."

The officer could not possibly remember this detail. He was reading from the transcript.

The Court then turned to consider "past recollection recorded." To rely on past recollection recorded, Justice Binnie approved of four criteria put forth by Wigmore:[27]

---

[26] *R. v. Fliss, supra*, at para. 54.
[27] *Ibid.* at para. 63.

1) The past recollection must have been recorded in some reliable way.

2) At the time, it must have been sufficiently fresh and vivid to be probably accurate.

3) The witness must be able now to assert that the record accurately represented his knowledge and recollection at the time. The usual phrase requires the witness to affirm that he "knew it to be true at the time."

4) The original record itself must be used, if it is procurable.

On the facts, the third criteria was not met. The undercover officer read the transcript the day after the recording. Presumably he had at that time a good recollection of it, but he never swore to it. He never expressly acknowledged the accuracy of the transcript. Moreover, he could not vouch for the entire transcript – yet the trial judge allowed him to read in portions, which he could neither recall nor verify as accurate. Justice Binnie refused to treat this as simply a matter of form over substance. This sends a clear message to the courts that if you are going to allow such a record to be read into evidence, the dictates of the above criteria must be strictly met. Once these criteria are met, the record is the evidence and it ought to be introduced as an exhibit.[28]

### (c)    Using Court Transcripts to Refresh Memory

A court may allow witnesses to refresh their memories by looking at court transcripts of their past testimony perhaps from a preliminary inquiry, prior trial or examination for discovery.[29] The "contemporaneity" requirement is not enforced. Nor is there need for the witness to verify that the transcript is accurate. The steps for refreshing as outlined in section 2.5(a) are followed.

### 2.6    Leading When the Witness is Adverse

It is permitted to lead a witness who is declared adverse or hostile. Unlike in direct examination, leading questions are permitted in cross-examination and, in essence, once a witness is found to be adverse or hostile

---

[28]  There are differing views as to whether the record should be made an exhibit. For a more detailed discussion on past recollection recorded see D. Paciocco and Lee Stuesser, *The Law of Evidence*, 7th ed., (2015) at pp. 459-463.

[29]  See *Reference re R. v. Coffin* (1956), 114 C.C.C. 1 (S.C.C.).

counsel calling the witness may cross-examine the witness. Note that the concerns regarding bias and susceptibility of the witness to suggestion vanish when the witness turns adverse or hostile. Dealing with adverse witnesses is explained in more detail in Chapter 16.

## 3.  PRINCIPLES OF DIRECT EXAMINATION

This part outlines basic principles of direct examination. It does not thoroughly cover the topic and the new lawyer is advised to consult some of the more comprehensive books or articles on direct examinations, of which there are many. Nor does this part concern itself with special types of direct examination, such as the hostile witness (see Chapter 16). I will assume that your witness is co-operative, as are most of the witnesses you call. With the "regular" witness in mind, there are certain *basic rules* for counsel to follow in direct examination.

---

### *Basic Rules for Direct Examination*

1) **The witness testifies — not counsel.**

2) **Counsel orders the testimony.**

3) **Be natural**

4) **Ask simple questions using simple language.**

5) **One question at a time.**

6) **Personalize the witness.**

7) **Volunteer weaknesses.**

8) **Get the facts — not just opinion**

9) **Make sure the judge gets it.**

10) **Be brief.**

---

**Rule 1:    The Witness Testifies — Not Counsel**

Thomas Mauet put it very well. "After all, a witness will be believed and remembered, because of the manner and context of his testimony, not because the questions asked were so brilliant."[30] Counsel should be in the background and attention should be focused on the witness. Therefore, counsel should not seize the spotlight through their own actions or words. For example, if you start pacing while your witness is testifying, you will distract everyone from concentrating on what the witness is saying. As counsel, you do dominate any trial and you must repress this dominance in favour of your witnesses. On direct let your witness tell the story, let the witness talk and you, like everyone else in the courtroom, listen to what is said. Be passive. In contrast, on cross-examination you are expected to dominate.

## Rule 2:    Counsel Orders the Testimony

Do not be mistaken as to the meaning of rule 1. An unbridled witness is disaster. You rein in the witness. You choreograph the testimony. You first need your script of the examination. This can take a variety of forms. A point form outline of areas that you want covered and their order is one option. Other lawyers rely on a narrative of the witness's testimony and simply frame the questions from the narrative. New lawyers may feel more secure with a complete set of questions and answers. This approach provides security, but creates the danger that your questions and the witness's responses look "scripted" and spontaneity is lost. Another suggestion is the "paragraph method" where you prepare the testimony by groups of questions, each on a common topic, and each with an introductory topic sentence intended to steer the witness on to the next area.[31] Whatever your choice, your job is to keep the testimony moving in a logical, understandable manner, with emphasis on the points that you want emphasized. To this extent you keep the witness under control.

---

[30]  T. Mauet, D. Casswell, G. MacDonald, *Fundamentals of Trial Techniques*, 2nd Can. ed. (1995), at p. 58.

[31]  J. McElhaney, "The Paragraph Method" (April 1989), 75 A.B.A.J. 96-97.

| Paragraph Method | |
| --- | --- |
| *Questions:* | *Answers:* |
| Topic: Background<br>• Age:<br>• Married?<br>• Children?<br>• Work?<br>• How long?<br>• Do before?<br>• Ever in trouble before? | |

You direct the witness to the topics you want covered. Your questions act as guideposts. Do not be afraid of telling both the witness and the court where you are going. For example:

> **Q.** Mr. Waite, you have told us about having your jaw broken. Let's turn to that injury and get a little more detail. . . .

Headings are good in written work, so too in a direct examination.

## Rule 3:    Be Natural

The testimony should unfold as though the witness were telling a story. It is natural. The testimony is to appear natural and spontaneous even though you have prepared to the hilt.

Now we do not expect you to weep when your client weeps, but empathy with your witness is to be expected. Pay attention, and appear to be interested in what your witness has to say because, if you are not interested, do not expect anyone else in the courtroom to be either! One sure "give away" that your answers are scripted is to take the script with you from the podium to question the witness. Or, if you are using a question and answer format, checking off as the answers are given. All spontaneity is lost. Disguise your preparation better than this. Appear to be natural.

## Rule 4:    Ask Simple Questions Using Simple Language

Questions asked should be brief and in plain English. Just because you are a lawyer does not mean that you have to sound like one. Avoid legal jargon, it impresses no one. Questions simply put and readily understood are the most impressive. Below are some examples of "lawyer talk" versus "plain talk."

| Lawyer talk | Plain talk |
|---|---|
| What, if anything, happened next? | What happened next? |
| Would you indicate, please, at what distance the plaintiff's motor vehicle was from yours when you first observed it? | How far away was the other car when you first saw it?[32] |
| What did you then do with respect to the operation and control of your motor vehicle? | How did you drive your car?[33] |

## Rule 5:   One Question at a Time

A corollary to asking a simple question is to ask only *one* question at a time. More than one question at a time only confuses. Consider the following:

> **Q.** Did you notice anything unusual or was it too dark to see?
> **A.** Yes.

"Yes" to what — that the witness noticed something unusual or "Yes" it was too dark to see?

## Rule 6:   Personalize the Witness

In order to make the witness's testimony trustworthy, you must show that the witness is a person to be trusted. Background information on the parties to the action is crucial. For corporate parties, it is essential that you personalize the company representatives and thereby give the company a human face.

---

[32] Taken from J. McElhaney, *Trial Notebook* (1981), at p. 99. Professor McElhaney provides an interesting list of lawyerisms.
[33] Taken from I. Younger, "The Art of Cross-Examination," A.B.A. Litigation Monograph Series (1976), at p. 22.

Edward Greenspan speaks of a need to cultivate a favourable "atmosphere" in the courtroom towards your client:[34]

> Affect the atmosphere to the benefit of your client by every legitimate means. For example, convey at every turn, that you personally believe in your client's innocence. You don't say it outright, but you must imply it throughout the trial.

> Take the time to go over to the prisoner's dock and talk to your client to give the impression he is not a pariah . . . At lunchtime, walk with your client down the corridor so the jury will see that you treat him as a human being. Have some family members there to humanize your client. These are important trial tactics.

Keep in mind, that for some witnesses, no or very little personalization is warranted. For example, it is a waste of court time to delve into the background of an eyewitness, who is simply there to tell what she saw.

## Rule 7:    Volunteer Weaknesses

By admitting certain weaknesses in your evidence, you enhance your credibility with the court. In so doing, you are saying that you have nothing to hide and nothing to fear in the case at trial. You also defuse the potential damage from exposure in cross-examination. Now, if the subject is raised again in cross, the witness can reply:

Yes, I have already admitted that.

In direct examination you also decide on when to raise the weakness and can "bury it" in the middle of the examination.

Think carefully, however, before you reveal any such evidence. There is no reason to drag your client through the mud if your opponent has no idea about the dirt. The first question, then, is does your opponent know? Second, is there any real reason to raise the issue? The weakness may be a trivial one and there is little to be gained by throwing stones at your own witness. Third, can you block the evidence through a timely objection? If so, you do not want to raise the matter as a part of your direct. Wait for the

---

[34] *Supra*, note 10, at p. 39. E. Greenspan, "The Preparation of the Trial Brief and the Planning of Trial Strategy and Tactics (Criminal)," in Advocacy, a symposium presented by the Canadian Bar Association — Ontario in collaboration with the Law Society of Upper Canada (1982), at p. 39.

matter to be raised on cross-examination and then object. If overruled, you can then answer the matter in re-examination.

One troubling issue that often arises in criminal cases is that the Crown is forced to call witnesses who have in fact given a number of statements inconsistent with what they now say in court. This was precisely the case in *R. v. Pinkus*.[35] The accused was charged with murder. The Crown called the former girlfriend of the accused. She would testify that the accused admitted to shooting the victim. Yet, for two years, she had told the police that the accused had nothing to do with the shooting. The Crown wanted to raise her inconsistent statements and have her clarify why she changed her story. The trial judge refused to allow the Crown to do so and termed it akin to "oath-helping." With respect, it is difficult to see how this practice amounts to oath-helping or bolstering the credibility of your witness. Rather, as the Crown stated, he simply wanted to show the jury his witness "warts and all." Diffusing matters that can make fodder in cross-examination is a common and accepted court practice. For example, counsel often lead with the prior criminal records of their clients or witnesses to blunt the impact of the cross-examination. This does not forestall the cross-examiner from going over the same ground. The trial judge took the position that the trier of fact is "assisted to a greater degree when the initial questions are asked by the cross-examiner rather than the examiner."[36] Ironically, this leaves it open for the Crown now to re-examine the girlfriend on why she changed her mind and to have the last word.[37]

### Rule 8:    Get the Facts — Not Just Opinion

The witness is there to testify as to facts observed, except for the expert, the witness's opinion is of little value. For example, in *Waite v. Stewart*, an eyewitness may be of the opinion that Stewart did not need to kick Waite the second time, but that opinion is of no importance. Counsel need to obtain from the witness the facts which led to that opinion. The witness may be of the opinion that Waite "wanted to fight." That is an opinion. Get the facts — what did Waite do to suggest that he wanted to fight?

Another common situation occurs when a witness is called in an impaired driving case to testify as the accused's intoxication. The statement, "the driver was impaired" is an opinion. Get the facts:

---

[35] *R. v. Pinkus* (1999), 140 C.C.C. (3d) 309 (Ont. S.C.).
[36] *Ibid.*, at 316.
[37] See *R. v. Sammy*, [2002] O.J. No. 5486 (C.J.), where the judge followed *Pinkus* and ruled that because the Crown could not raise the prior inconsistent statement as part of its case in direct, then so doing in re-examination was proper.

**Q.** Why do you say he was impaired?

**A.** He reeked of alcohol. He could hardly speak and when he did speak he slurred his words and made no sense. His eyes were all bloodshot. He could not stand and fell down twice before just sitting on the ground. He also threw up all over himself.

The facts make your case.

## Rule 9:    Make Sure the Judge Gets It

Do not rush through the testimony. In fact, you will have to concentrate on controlling the speed of the testimony. The judge attempts to record as much of the evidence as possible. All will be for naught if the trial judge cannot keep up with the testimony. Remember this is the first time that the judge has ever heard the witness's story. You know it well. The witness knows it well. The judge does not. Therefore, allow the judge time to digest what is being said and to write it down. Heed the observation of Richard Harris K.C.:[38]

> There is nothing more common with beginners than going *too fast*. They are frequently told by the judge that they forget that he has to take down the answers; and the importance of your evidence looking well on the judge's notes cannot be exaggerated . . . When the evidence is coming well, there is no doubt a great temptation to let it run too fast, but you must take care it does its proper work, otherwise it will be like a rush of water which shoots over the mill-wheel instead of turning it.

Although Harris' observation was made over 60 years ago, it is still true. The most common fault that I see with student counsel is that they go through the evidence too quickly and fail to get out the necessary facts. Examinations that should take 15-20 minutes are done in five. Here are certain techniques to assist you in slowing down and getting the necessary detail:

* Pause after the answer. Work on what might be called the "direct examiner's three-step:" question, answer, pause / question, answer, pause.

* Do not be afraid of silence. New counsel are terrified of "dead air." Don't be. Do not be afraid to take your time to formulate your question or let an answer really sink in.

---

[38]  Richard Harris K.C., *Hints on Advocacy*, 17th ed. (1937), p. 39.

- Slow your witness down. It is perfectly permissible to interrupt your own witness. If the witness is talking too fast or giving too much information all at once, stop the witness and remind him that the judge has to take note of his evidence.

- Use a "loop-back" approach. Should a witness give a gush of information, loop-back and ask more specific questions that arise from the witness's narrative. For example, a witness has described a fight that she witnessed in a gush of testimony. Go back: "Now you mentioned you saw the accused throw a beer bottle. Where did he throw it? Where was he looking when he threw it? What did he say when he threw it?"

- Make certain that the witness speaks up. Tell the witness to speak up. Try not to examine the witness from too close a proximity; this will only invite a muted conversation between the two of you. If necessary, move yourself and the podium away from the witness. Remember as well that witnesses will respond to your tone and voice and, if you are speaking too softly, they will respond in turn.

As you are examining the witness, keep a watchful eye on the judge. Is the judge listening intently? Did the judge write down that last statement? Take your time. Make certain that the evidence is heard.

**Rule 10:    Be Brief**

Brevity is always appreciated by the judge. You know where you are going with your witness. Get on with it! Home in on the key points. Too much time is wasted because witnesses testify for too long on areas not pertinent to the case. Be concise. Be precise. Be brief.

## 4.   RE-EXAMINATION

Counsel are expected to put their case in on direct. Re-examination is not designed for counsel to present the second half of their evidence. Its purpose is to clarify matters raised in cross-examination to ensure that the witness's evidence is fairly and completely received. The witness is afforded an opportunity to explain an answer given in cross-examination — where an explanation is needed. For example, in cross-examination, a witness is questioned about giving a prior inconsistent statement to the police. In re-examination, counsel may ask the witness why he made the prior inconsistent statement or the circumstances surrounding the taking of the statement.

Re-examination is not the time for counsel who called the witness to raise new matters or expand in more detail upon areas that should have been dealt with fully on direct. However, the trial judge does have the discretion to allow the counsel calling the witness to examine upon new areas. Leave to do so must be sought and, if granted, opposing counsel will be given an opportunity to cross-examine the witness on the new areas raised.

The Ontario Court of Appeal in *R. v. Candir* summarized the law on re-examination as follows:[39]

> It is fundamental that the permissible scope of re-examination is linked to its purpose and the subject-matter on which the witness has been cross-examined. The purpose of re-examination is largely rehabilitative and explanatory. The witness is afforded the opportunity, under questioning by the examiner who called the witness in the first place, to explain, clarify or qualify answers given in cross-examination that are considered damaging to the examiner's case. The examiner has no right to introduce new subjects in re-examination, topics that should have been covered, if at all, in examination in-chief of the witness. A trial judge has a discretion, however, to grant leave to the party calling a witness to introduce new subjects in re-examination, but must afford the opposing party the right of further cross-examination on the new facts: *R. v. Moore* (1984), 15 C.C.C. (3d) 541 (Ont. C.A.), at p. 568.

In many cases, it may be wiser not to re-examine. If you have been hurt in cross-examination, re-examination may only serve to highlight the injury. Or some counsel, through a sense of misguided importance, use the re-examination to correct trivial inconsistencies. Don't. The effective re-examination is *short* and *strong*.

In re-examining a witness, you are not allowed to lead. The witness is *yours* and the rules against putting suggestions to *your* witness remain. You are permitted, however, to lead the witness to the topic of re-examination, to focus the testimony. Use a directional question to direct the witness to the topic. Once there, stop directing, and ask the open-ended question. Consider this short, but most effective, re-examination:[40]

> [*The expert witness was cross-examined about various economic surveys that forecast lower inflation rates than suggested by the expert. One of these surveys was the P & M report.*]

> **Q.** Now, apparently one of the favourite studies of my friend . . . is the [P & M] report. Do I understand from your answers to his questions that that is an annual report that comes out each year?

---

[39] *R. v. Candir*, 2009 ONCA 915 (Ont. C.A.) at para. 148.
[40] The Seventh Annual Advocacy Symposium presented by the Canadian Bar Association — Ontario and the Law Society of Upper Canada, 6th and 7th May 1988, Toronto, at p. 47.

**A.** It is.

[*The witness is directed to the topic.*]

**Q.** And has it, each year, attempted to predict the long-term inflation rate?
**A.** It has.

**Q.** And what has its track record been?
**A.** Not too hot.

**Q.** Thank you very much.

The re-examination can also be anticipated and prepared for. Consider the case where you are defending a corporate defendant being sued for injuries to a youngster, who trespassed onto the company property. Following the accident, the company hired a person to be on the premises 24 hours a day. Your position is that this remedial action by the corporation is inadmissible going to the issue of negligence in the boy's case. In some jurisdictions in Canada, remedial evidence is not allowed, in others it is admissible. You have no intention of raising the matter in direct. After all, your view is that it is inadmissible evidence. In cross-examination of the corporate president, opposing counsel raises the remedial action. You object. Your objection is overruled. In re-examination you reply:

> **Q.** Mr. Jones, in cross-examination you testified that after the accident your company hired a security person to be on the premises 24 hours of the day. Is that correct?
> **A.** Yes.
>
> **Q.** Why did you decide to hire the security person?
> **A.** Well, we were as shocked as anyone about the boy's injuries. We never dreamed that anyone would climb over an eight-foot high fence, with barbed wire at the top and with signs posted about the danger. We wanted to make absolutely certain that this could never happen again. So out of an abundance of caution I ordered the security person hired.
>
> **Q.** I have no further questions in re-examination.

You had the last word and you used it effectively.

## 5. A SAMPLE DIRECT EXAMINATION

Consider the direct examination of Richard Waite (Chapter 2). Waite is the plaintiff in this assault action. In preparing your direct, you want to emphasize that Waite was the victim of *excessive* force. You want to create a "sympathetic" atmosphere towards Waite by showing that although he agreed to a fight, he certainly did not *deserve* or expect to be beaten as he was. The actions of the defendant are to be highlighted for their *brutality*, which will support your claim for punitive damages. We will assume that no agreement has been reached on damages. The portion of the direct examination that follows takes us from introductory background through to the incident and to the injury sustained by Waite:

---

**Richard Waite, Sworn:**

**Q.** Mr. Waite, you are the plaintiff in this action?
**A.** Yes.

**Q.** The action is in battery. Who committed the battery?
**A.** The defendant, James Stewart.

**Q.** What happened?
**A.** He kicked me in the face and broke my jaw in two places.

[*Note*: *The first question was not: "Your name is Richard Waite and you reside at . . . " There is no need to confirm the witness's name, which is recorded on being sworn. Nor is there a need for any kind of gratuitous greeting such as, "Good morning, Mr. Waite." Save such greetings for outside the courtroom. Also, this opening is designed to cut to the heart of the case.*]

**Q.** Before we turn to that, Mr. Waite, I'd like you to tell us a little about yourself. Where do you live?

[*Note:* *The open ended question "Tell us about yourself" was quickly focused. Otherwise the witness may start rambling about his life. In the early stages of the testimony, it is better for counsel to help the witness by asking simple specific questions.*]

**A.** At 392 Morningside Drive in Winnipeg.

**Q.** Are you married?
**A.** Yes.

**Q.** Any children?
**A.** Yes, a three-year-old daughter.

*(cont'd)*

---

**Q.** And what do you do for a living?
**A.** I'm a television broadcaster with CKZ-TV.

**Q.** Please tell the court what you do as a broadcaster.
**A.** I have two prime responsibilities. First, I have a regular television assignment and read the news at 10:30 p.m. each weekday evening. Second, during the day much time is spent reporting and preparing news stories for release on any of our television newscasts.

**Q.** How long have you been a broadcaster?
**A.** I've been involved in the broadcast industry for almost seven years.

**Q.** What did you do before becoming a broadcaster?
**A.** I worked as a public relations officer with the Department of Tourism for the province of Manitoba for five years.

**Q.** Mr. Waite, as a broadcaster, have you always been with CKZ-TV?
**A.** No. I started with CKBI-TV in January of last year, but was laid off in June and then I started work with CKZ-TV in July.

[*The above background serves the purpose of putting the witness at ease. It also establishes that Waite is a responsible, working, family man, which is certainly not the portrait of a "street fighter." The background on employment would be returned to later when employment loss was considered in detail.* **Note:** *In a criminal prosecution much of this background would be omitted.*]

**Q.** Now, Mr. Waite, let us turn to the night of 13th March of last year, did you have to work?
**A.** Yes, I was scheduled to do the 10:30 news.

**Q.** Did you do the news that night?
**A.** No — earlier in the evening I had my jaw broken.

**Q.** Let's turn to how that happened. I understand you were playing hockey at the Highlander Sports complex on Ellice Avenue in Winnipeg?
**A.** Yes.

*(cont'd)*

[*Direction and transition question. The question is leading, but all matters referred to are not in dispute.*]

**Q.** Was this an organized or unorganized hockey game?
**A.** It was a league game. Part of a recreation league called "Old Timer Fun Hockey." The league has eight teams made up of players over 21 years of age, who are looking for a little exercise.

**Q.** How long have you played in the league?
**A.** I've played in the league for three years.

**Q.** Describe the game that night.
**A.** Well, that game was unusually rough. The league has a non-contact rule.

**Q.** What do you mean by a "non-contact rule?"
**A.** No body checks are allowed and, if you fight, then you are automatically suspended for three games. For a second fight you are kicked out of the league.

**Q.** Please go on.
**A.** The game was pretty rough. There were a lot of penalties. Slashing, high-sticking, that sort of thing. In the third period, with about ten minutes left in the game, I was hit with a stick above my right eye that caused a cut.

**Q.** How did that happen?
**A.** I was in front of the opposing team's net when their defenceman, Stewart — [*points*]

**Counsel**: Indicating the defendant James Stewart.
**A.** Yes. He was pushing me from out in front of the net and was using his stick and he caught me with the stick above the right eye.

**Q.** What happened after you were hit?
**A.** I went down. The cut was bleeding pretty good. Somebody gave me a towel and I held it to my head. Stewart was given a penalty and since it drew blood he was kicked out of the game. There was only ten minutes left and I decided to get cleaned up. I had to work that night.

*(cont'd)*

**Q.** What did you do next?
**A.** I went to the dressing room and got cleaned up.

**Q.** How badly cut were you?
**A.** Not that bad, no stitches were required. I just put a bandage on the cut.

*[This portion of the examination provides the context for the fight to follow. It also shows that the defendant was the aggressor on the ice.]*

**Q.** After you got cleaned up, what did you do?
**A.** I put my gear together and was ready to head to work. As I was loading my car, I saw Stewart heading for his car. So I decided to go and talk to him.

**Q.** What were you going to talk about?
**A.** Well, he was young and I had not seen him play in the league before. I just wanted to let him know that he was playing too aggressive a hockey for us. The league was fun and he was playing too tough.

**Q.** What happened next?
**A.** He was loading his gear into his trunk and I called out to him that I'd like to talk to him.

**Q.** Do you remember what you said?
**A.** Yes, I said, I'd like to talk to him about the game.

**Q.** Go on.
**A.** He just ignored me. So I called out the same thing. He closed his trunk and was heading to his car door. By this time I was right behind him and I pulled at his sleeve. It was his right arm and I pulled at him to turn around and face me.

**Q.** Did he turn and face you?
**A.** Yes.

**Q.** Then what happened?
**A.** I said again, I'd like to talk to him about the game. And he said, "Shove off, I've got nothing to talk to you about." And he pushed me.

*(cont'd)*

**Q.** Describe the push.
**A.** He used both hands and pushed me in the chest.

**Q.** How much force was used?
**A.** A considerable amount. The push caused me to step back.

**Q.** What happened next?
**A.** I shoved him back and that is when he slipped and fell. As he was getting up, he said, "If you want a fight — you've got it."

**Q.** Mr. Waite, you said that he slipped and fell. What caused his fall?
**A.** He just slipped in trying to move away from me. The parking lot was pretty slippery.

**Q.** What did you do after he told you he wanted to fight?
**A.** I had already turned away because I could see that he didn't want to listen to reason. When I got into the lane of the parking lot I turned to see him following me. He said, "Come on big guy." And he had his fists up like a fighter. I put my hands up as well to protect myself.

**Q.** At this time, after he said, "Come on big guy," what was going through your mind?
**A.** I thought that I had no choice. This guy was coming at me and I had to defend myself.

**Q.** What happened next?
**A.** Well, he was coming at me so I took a swing at him, to stop him. I missed. Then he kicked me in the stomach and knocked the wind right out of me.

**Q.** Describe how you felt at this time?
**A.** I couldn't breathe. I was doubled over holding my stomach. Then he kicked me again, this time in the face.

**Q.** My Lady, may the witness leave the witness box? I would like to have him show his position after the first kick.

**Her Ladyship:** Any objection, counsel? [*to defendant's counsel*]

*(cont'd)*

**Defendant Counsel:** M'Lady, the witness is perfectly able to describe his position. I see no need for these theatrics.

**Plaintiff Counsel:** M'Lady, this is not theatrics. Rather, it is important for Your Ladyship to see Mr. Waite's exact position at this time. The demonstration will, in fact, be clearer for the court than a verbal description and should assist the court in understanding what occurred.

**Her Ladyship:** I agree. I think that it will assist me. I will allow the demonstration.

[*Plaintiff counsel, through the demonstration, slows the trial down to emphasize the plaintiff's helplessness after the first kick. Note, as well, how the examination rapidly went through the plaintiff's own provocative behaviour in confronting the defendant in the parking lot. Let the defendant emphasize this in cross-examination.*]

**Q.** Mr. Waite, please show the court how you were positioned after the first kick.

**Counsel:** Mr. Waite is in a doubled over position. He is kneeling, holding his stomach with both hands. M'Lady, I believe that that is an accurate description of the plaintiff's position for the record.

**Her Ladyship:** I agree.

**Q.** Mr. Waite, how far was your head from the ground at this time?
**A.** I was bent right over, my head would only have been a couple of feet from the ground.

**Q.** Before you return to the witness box, where was the defendant at this time?
**A.** He was right in front of me.

**Q.** Thank you, Mr. Waite, you may return to the witness box. Mr. Waite, you told the court that you were kicked a second time in the face. Where exactly?
**A.** He kicked me in the lower right jaw. His foot was coming up and hit me in the jaw.

*(cont'd)*

**Q.** At this time, what were you doing?
**A.** Nothing. I couldn't do anything. I was simply holding my stomach.

**Q.** Were you moving in any direction?
**A.** No.

**Q.** As you were bent over, holding yourself, did you say anything?
**A.** No. I couldn't speak.

**Q.** Did you make any sounds at this time?
**A.** Yes, I was gasping for my breath, deep gasps.

**Q.** How much time passed between the first and second kick?
**A.** There was a pause, a good couple seconds.

**Q.** What happened to you after you were kicked in the face?
**A.** I fell to the ground. The pain was awful. I was just lying there in a pool of blood.

**Q.** Describe how it felt to be kicked in the face.
**A.** The pain was terrible. It was like my face had exploded. I heard the crack of bone and knew that my jaw was broken. Blood was pouring out of my mouth. Fortunately, people came to help me.

**Q.** Who were these people?
**A.** A friend of mine, Edward Gore, and a woman bystander.

**Q.** What did Mr. Stewart do?
**A.** He did absolutely nothing. He didn't try to help me at all. He simply left.

**Q.** So you are on the ground and the defendant has left. What happened next?
**A.** My friend, Edward Gore, helped me. He wrapped my jaw in a towel and took me to the Health Science Centre.

**Q.** How long did it take you to get to the hospital?
**A.** About 10 to 15 minutes.

**Q.** How were you feeling at this time?
**A.** I was in a great deal of pain. The pain was shooting up my jaw. I couldn't talk and I was swallowing blood.

*(cont'd)*

**Q.** What happened when you got to the hospital?

**A.** Edward took me to the emergency ward. There I had to wait for almost an hour before being taken in for x-rays. I just sat in the emergency holding my jaw. A nurse gave me a new towel.

**Q.** Were you given anything for the pain?

**A.** No. They couldn't in case I had to have surgery. The pain was unbearable.

**Q.** So you are in the waiting room, then what happened?

**A.** The x-ray was taken and a doctor told me that the jaw was broken in two places. He asked my permission to operate and set the jaw. I nodded my agreement. And I was operated on within another hour. I was put under and the next thing I remember is seeing my wife in the recovery room.

**Q.** How long were you in the hospital?

**A.** They released me at noon the next day.

**Q.** That would be on March 14th?

**A.** Yes.

**Q.** What was done to set your jaw?

**A.** My jaw was immobilized by wires.

**Q.** Mr. Waite, you say that your jaw was wired. I show you a photograph, tab E, M'Lady. Do you recognize this photograph?

*[Note: Counsel does not ask for permission to approach the witness. Counsel simply approaches.]*

**A.** Yes. It is a photograph of me.

**Q.** When was it taken?

**A.** It was taken by my wife on March 14th, when I was brought home from the hospital.

**Q.** Is it an accurate and fair representation of how you looked at that time?

**A.** Yes it is.

*(cont'd)*

**Counsel:** M'Lady, I ask that this photograph be entered as an exhibit.

**Her Ladyship:** Exhibit 7.

**Q.** The photograph shows that your face was swollen. Is that accurate?
**A.** Yes. At times I could hardly see because of the swelling.

**Q.** How long did this swelling last?
**A.** It lasted for a full week.

**Q.** Mr. Waite, the photograph also shows a wire in the corner of your mouth. What is that?
**A.** That is how the jaw was wired.

**Q.** And how was the wire attached to your jaw?
**A.** Pins were drilled into the jaw bone and the wires were fastened to the pins.

**Q.** How long was your jaw wired like this?
**A.** For two months.

**Q.** And how were the wires removed?
**A.** I had to have a second operation two months later to remove the pin supports and this was done on May 15th.

**Q.** How long were you kept in hospital at this time?
**A.** I spent a half day at hospital.

**Q.** During these two months were you on any medication?
**A.** Yes. I was given a pain prescription for the first week and after that I regularly took over the counter pain killers. I also had to take penicillin when I developed an infection in my gums.

**Q.** Mr. Waite, describe what it was like for you for these two months.
**A.** It was terrible. I had to eat everything with a straw. I lost 10 kilos. I had a great deal of pain. My jaw constantly throbbed. I couldn't talk really. I couldn't participate in my normal sports.

*(cont'd)*

*[Note the use of the photograph to highlight the injury to Mr. Waite. Questions were also asked using the photograph in order to keep it before the court for a period of time. The remainder of the direct examination is omitted. Areas yet to be covered include the effect of the injury on his life for the two months, residual effects, effect on employment and loss of career opportunities. Let us turn to the conclusion of the examination.]*

**Q.** Mr. Waite, I just want to return to the fight for a moment. Have you been involved in fights before?

**A.** No. The last time I had a fight was in elementary school.

**Q.** Why did you fight the defendant?

**A.** I don't know. It's not my nature. I guess I wasn't thinking. It was the heat of the moment.

**Q.** Were you aware that the defendant had martial arts training?

**A.** No.

**Q.** Did the defendant ever say anything about this before or during the altercation?

**A.** No.

**Q.** Would you have fought the defendant had you known about the martial arts training?

**A.** No. I am no fighter.

**Q.** Mr. Waite, have you taken any fight training of any kind?

**A.** No, I'm no fighter. The results of this fight show that.

**Q.** That concludes my direct examination, M'Lady.

*[At the **start** of the plaintiff's case counsel read in from the defendant's examination for discovery extracts where the defendant admitted to extensive martial arts training. The purpose of doing this at the **start** of the trial was to impress upon the judge the defendant's skill in fighting, with devastating consequences to the plaintiff.]*

# 12

# USING EXHIBITS

- **Introduction of Exhibits**

- **Marking an Exhibit "For Identification"**

- **Use of the Exhibits at Trial**

- **Introducing Photographs**

- **Using Diagrams**

An exhibit, if properly used, is a powerful adjunct to the spoken testimony heard at trial. Simply put, we are better watchers than listeners and visual aids help us to perceive and retain information.[1]

An exhibit is also permanent, whereas a statement has a fleeting lifespan. An exhibit can be probed and examined by the trier of fact long after a witness has finished testifying. Counsel need to cater to this reality. Photographs, "a day in the life" video, diagrams, overhead projections, demonstrations, models and summaries can say things better and in far shorter time than the drone of testimony. In this sense advocacy is like good teaching, the lawyer involves the judge in the case much like a teacher involves students in learning. Here is an example from a master of the courtroom, Melvin Belli, who, in describing one of his early cases, learned a valuable lesson about "real" evidence:[2]

---

[1] See S. Mader, "Communicating Complex Medical Issues: A Visual Approach" Paper presented at the Trial Lawyers Association of British Columbia, *Persuasion and the Complex Case - Strategies to Simplify Challenging Medical/Legal Cases,* 07 December 2012, at p. 5.
[2] M. Belli, *My Life on Trial* (1976) at pp. 105-107.

Ernie Smith was a black, a convict at San Quentin who had kicked another convict in the head in the prison yard and killed him. He looked like a killer to me . . .

Smith told me he'd been in a fight with a con named Artie. "I knocked him down", Smith said, "but then he had a knife and was going to throw it at me. So I stomped him."

"Whoa", I said. "What?"

"I stomped him."

"No, not that. You said he had a knife?"

"Yeah. Every con in here carries a knife."

" 'Every con in here carries a knife?' That's crap, and you know it. Now we better find something sensible to hang a murder rap on or, brother, we've had it." . . .

I wanted to talk to the captain of the guard, Ralph New.

"Ralph", I asked, "was it possible for Arthur Ruis to have had a knife out there in the yard?"

"Possible?" he said. "Here are some of the weapons we've found." And with that, he opened a great, big, deep drawer, full of the most evil collection of weapons I'd ever seen . . .

I put New on the stand and got him to tell me about the knives. Then I went over to the counsel table and picked up the entire drawer and started back toward New, asking the judge's permission to introduce the drawer's contents into evidence.

To this day, I don't remember if I made my next move deliberately or whether it was an accident, but I really did stumble. I spilled the knives right there on the floor in front of the jury. I looked up at the judge, and he had a little smile on his face. He was shaking his head. I couldn't have found a better way of bringing home a point to the jury. So I made the most of it. I took my time picking up the knives, one by one, and as I would grab one, I would look at it and shake my head and put it back in the drawer . . .

I had learned a valuable lesson, one taught by Captain Kidd at Boalt, but only half realized: that jurors learn through *all* their senses, and if you can tell them and show them, too, let them see and feel and even taste or smell the evidence, then you will reach the jury.

Exhibits are a powerful communication device for judges as well. However, any exhibit must be introduced and used properly in court. If used improperly, exhibits can detract from the trial and cause confusion. Problems with exhibits are mostly the fault of counsel, who are not familiar with how to introduce or use the exhibit as evidence. Outlined below are general principles on how to avoid such confusion.

## 1.  INTRODUCTION OF EXHIBITS

Prior to trial you need to plan how your exhibits will be introduced into evidence. There are three ways: through operation of law, through agreement and through a witness. In the first two cases the exhibits are introduced at the start of the trial, as outlined in Chapters 7 and 8. Parties are urged to consent to the introduction of documents. Little is gained by counsel who persist in demanding needless witnesses be called to verify undisputed materials, except wasted time and the ire of the presiding judge. At one trial in which I assisted, opposing counsel would not consent to our introduction of a large, and I must say beautiful, diagram of the accident site. We were forced to call the draftsman who prepared the diagram. This was at the start of the trial. The judge was not pleased for, in his words, "The diagram looked very nice and would be very helpful." The diagram was admitted and opposing counsel came off as a most disagreeable sort, which is not a good way to begin a trial.[3]

The tendering of an exhibit that is not going in by consent involves five distinct steps:

---

### *Tendering Exhibits*

**1) Introduce It**

**2) Show It**

**3) Prove It [Provide a Foundation]**

**4) Mark It**

**5) Use It**

---

[3] For a case dealing with the admissibility of demonstrative aids see *Reis v. Doman*, 2004 CarswellOnt 5503 (Ont. S.C.J.).

First, *introduce the exhibit* to the judge, opposing counsel and the witness: Mr. Witness I am going to show you a letter dated . . .

Provide enough information so that all concerned are aware of what it is that you intend to tender as an exhibit. Second, either *show the exhibit* that you intend to introduce to opposing counsel in open court or make it clear that opposing counsel has already inspected or has a copy of the exhibit. Opposing counsel is now on notice and in a position to object to the admissibility of the particular exhibit. Third, *lay a proper foundation* for its admissibility. A proper foundation rests on three points:

1. The exhibit is *relevant*: the exhibit is of some probative value in proving a fact at issue. In base terms, the exhibit must have "something to do with the case."[4] Or, if the exhibit is being introduced purely as an aid in the giving of testimony, it must be established that it will, in fact, assist the witnesses.

2. The exhibit is *authentic*: the exhibit is what it purports to be. In the case of "real" evidence related to the case, it must be shown that the evidence has not been tampered with. In the case of "demonstrative aids," it must be shown that the exhibit does not unfairly distort the scene or evidence in any way.

3. The witness is qualified: the witness can verify the authenticity of the exhibit.

The fourth step is to *mark the exhibit*. When a proper foundation has been laid for an exhibit then it can be tendered into evidence and marked as an exhibit. Usually a number is attached. It is best to question the witness about the exhibit only after it is tendered and marked. Do not forget to tender the evidence as an exhibit!

The fifth step is to *use the exhibit*. For the exhibit to have impact, for it to be remembered, it needs to be used in court.

Let us take, for example, the introduction of photographs. You intend to introduce through an eyewitness a series of photographs of an accident scene taken eight months after the accident. In most instances, the calling

---

[4] J. McElhaney, *Trial Notebook* (1981), at p. 46.

of the photographer is not necessary. After all, the eyewitness, if familiar with the scene, can attest to the accuracy and fairness of a photograph as it pertains to the time of the accident.

---

[*The accident involved an injury to a small boy who fell off a set of climbing bars on to a concrete pad.*]

**Q.**     Mr. Smith, you testified earlier that you were with your children at the playground. How often did you visit the St. Michael playground?

**A.**     We regularly went there. Two or three times per week and we've been doing that for the past three to four years and still do.

[**Note:** *You have picked a strong witness who really knows the playground.*]

**Q.**     I'm going to show you a photograph. My Lady, tab K in the document book, my learned friend has been provided with a copy of this photograph. Do you recognize the photograph?

**A.**     Yes ... it's a picture of St. Michael playground taken from the west.

**Q.**     Mr. Smith, is this a fair and accurate photograph of the playground as it appeared on 13th October 2014?

**A.**     Yes it is. Nothing has changed.

**Counsel:**   My Lady, I tender the photograph as an exhibit.

**or:**    My Lady, I ask that the photograph be marked as an exhibit.

**Judge:**   Any objections? [*None*] Marked as Exhibit 17.

**Exhibit 17:** Photograph of St. Michael playground taken from the west.

## 2.   MARKING AN EXHIBIT "FOR IDENTIFICATION"

It is not always possible to authenticate an exhibit fully through one witness, and a series of witnesses is required. If this is the case, the exhibit is marked first "for identification" and on "final authentication" is marked as an exhibit in the cause. The purpose of marking for identification is simply to keep track of the exhibit. If the exhibit marked for identification is never tendered into evidence then it does not become evidence in the cause. Exhibits "for identification" are usually labelled by letter and once they are introduced into evidence they are given a number.

For certain exhibits there is need to show a chain of custody from retrieval of the exhibit to the courtroom. This is called "continuity." For example, during the course of a search of the accused's home, a computer disk is found. The disk contains child pornography and the Crown relies on the disk to prove that the accused possessed child pornography. The chain of custody proceeds from the police officer who initially seized the disk, who then gave it to the officer in charge of the investigation, who in turn gave it to a technician to view and record the disk's contents, then returned it to the officer in charge, who placed it in his secure evidence locker pending trial. In most cases continuity is not an issue and defence counsel will concede such. If continuity is at issue, then the Crown would need to prove that the disk as played in court was the disk originally seized from the accused's home and that it had not been tampered with. All those who took control of the disk would need to be called. The disk would be marked for identification until its continuity was established and only then would it be introduced as evidence.

---

*[A draftsman prepares a diagram of St. Michael playground. The draftsman is not able to testify that the diagram is an accurate portrayal of the playground on the date of the accident.]*

**Q.** Mr. Johns, are you familiar with St. Michael playground on 9th Street in the city?
**A.** Yes, I am.

**Q.** How is that?
**A.** You asked me to go there and measure and diagram the playground.

**Q.** When did you go to the playground?
**A.** On 15th May 2015.

*(cont'd)*

**Q.** Mr. Johns, I show you a diagram. Do you recognize it?

**A.** Yes. That is the diagram that I prepared for you of St. Michael playground. My initials and the date 15th May 2015 are in the lower right hand corner.

**Q.** Is the diagram an accurate depiction of the playground on that date?

**A.** Yes.

**Q.** Is the diagram to scale?

**A.** No.

**Q.** Why didn't you make the diagram to scale?

**A.** Drawing to scale is extremely time-consuming and costly. And for the purposes of showing the relative location of the play equipment, benches and trees it really is not necessary. All the major items were measured and placed in position as accurately as possible.

**Counsel:** My Lady, I ask that the diagram be marked as Exhibit A for identification.

**Judge:** Exhibit A for identification.

*[Later in Mr. Smith's testimony. See above.]*

**Q.** Mr. Smith, I'm showing you a diagram marked as Exhibit A for identification. Do you recognize it?

**A.** Yes, it is a diagram of St. Michael playground.

**Q.** Is the diagram a reasonable and accurate depiction of the playground as it was on 13th October 2014?

**A.** Yes it is.

**Q.** Would the diagram help you explain your testimony?

**A.** It sure would.

**Counsel:** My Lady, I tender Exhibit A for identification as the next exhibit.

**Judge:** Any objections. *[None]* Marked as Exhibit 22.

## 3.   USE OF THE EXHIBITS AT TRIAL

As mentioned earlier, where many documents are involved, you are encouraged to co-ordinate the introduction of these materials into evidence with opposing counsel. Most should go in by consent. A brief of documents is prepared for the judge and all counsel. Should all the documents contained in the brief be agreed upon, then have the brief marked as an exhibit, with the individual tabbed documents becoming Exhibits 1-A, 1-B, 1-C and so forth.

If there are only a few exhibits, then Crown counsel or plaintiff counsel at the start of the trial can introduce them "by consent" one at a time and have them marked individually as exhibits. Provide copies of the exhibits to the trial judge so that he or she can follow along as the actual exhibits are used in the trial.

---

**Counsel**:

Your Honour, there is agreement as to certain exhibits and I tender the following exhibits by consent. First, there is the Certificate of Analysis of Blood Alcohol dated May 23, 2015 . . . .

---

With exhibits already admitted by consent, the process is streamlined and there is no need to authenticate, prove or mark the exhibit. Simply call for the exhibit and put it before the witness. Getting the documents before the court in the above fashion is one thing, but counsel next must consider how best to bring particular documents to the judge's attention. Little will be gained if a key document is lost among the many documents introduced. Highlight the document. Weave the document into your examination. Consider the illustration below:

---

[*In a contract case, mistake of fact is alleged by the plaintiff. The defendant is being examined in chief and he has just testified that he met with the plaintiff to sign a contract.*]

Q. Mr. Smythe, I'm showing you Exhibit 6 [*pause, check to see if the judge has located the document.*] Do you recognize this document?
A. Yes.

*(cont'd)*

> **Q.** And what is it?
> **A.** It is the contract that Burt Jackson and I agreed to on 12th July 2015.
>
> **Q.** On page 2 of the contract at the bottom there are two signatures. Do you recognize these signatures?
> **A.** Yes, one is my signature and the other is Burt Jackson's.
>
> **Q.** Were you present when Mr. Jackson signed the contract?
> **A.** Yes, I was.
>
> **Q.** Did it appear that Mr. Jackson read the contract before signing?
> **A.** Yes, he took a few minutes to go through it and then signed it. I did the same.

The judge has now been directed to the contract and the fact that the plaintiff read and then signed the contract has been highlighted. It is not recommended that you then go on and have the witness summarize or interpret the document. Such is open to objection: the witness is being asked for a conclusion, or the document "speaks for itself."[5]

## 4.   INTRODUCING PHOTOGRAPHS

Photographs should be essential exhibits in many trials. In personal injury cases, a photograph literally is worth a thousand words in describing the plaintiff's injuries and in vividly placing those injuries before the court.

The admissibility of photographs or videotapes depends upon

1)   their accuracy in truly representing the facts;

2)   their fairness and absence of any intention to mislead; and,

3)   their verification on oath by a person capable of doing so.

The person verifying the photograph does not need to be the person who took the photograph. For example, I can be shown a picture of my house taken by someone else and I can verify that it is an accurate photograph of my house. The steps involved in tendering a photograph are as follows:

---

[5]   R. Keeton, *Trial Tactics and Methods*, 2nd ed. (1973), at p. 68.

---

### *Tendering Photographs*

1) Show the witness the photograph;

2) Ask if the witness recognizes the photograph.

3) How does the witness recognize the photograph?

4) Is the photograph a fair and accurate depiction of what is shown on such and such a date?

5) Ask for the photograph to be marked as an exhibit.

6) Use the photograph to ask the witness further questions.

[*Remember: the process is streamlined if the photograph is already an exhibit by consent and all of the above steps are not necessary.*]

---

## 5.   USING DIAGRAMS

Unlike a contract or other document that forms part of the "real" evidence in a case, other exhibits are used primarily for illustrative purposes.[6] Proper use of such materials must be planned and prepared for. The witness must be shown the exhibit prior to trial and become familiar with it. The procedure involved in introducing and marking the exhibit should be fully explained to the witness.

Before any witness will be allowed to use a diagram it must be established that the witness is familiar with the scene, that the diagram is a fair representation of the scene and that it would assist the witness in giving his or her testimony to refer to the diagram. The steps are outlined below:

---

[6] The status of "illustrative evidence" is not clear. Some courts view the diagrams as fully admissible into evidence. Other courts do not admit such material into evidence, but treat the devices as "illustrative only."

---

## Using Diagrams

1) Establish that the witness is familiar with the scene.

2) Show the witness the diagram. Ask the witness if he or she recognizes it?

3) Is it a fair representation of the scene as it was on such and such a date?

4) Would it assist you in giving your testimony to refer to the diagram?

5) Use the diagram.

---

Of importance, counsel directs and puts on the record how the diagram is to be marked. An example is provided below:

---

[*Recall that Mr. Smith has already authenticated the diagram of St. Michael playground which was introduced into evidence. Counsel is now going to have Mr. Smith go back over his earlier testimony to impress upon the court the position where he actually was seated and from where he observed the accident.*]

**Q.** My Lady, may the witness approach the diagram?

**Judge:** Yes.

**Q.** Mr. Smith, you indicated in your testimony that you were seated on a bench. Would you use this black felt pen to mark an "X" on the bench where you were seated? [*Witness marks*]

**Q.** Mr. Smith, you also said that you saw the plaintiff's mother seated on a bench. Would you mark with an "O" the bench where she was seated? [*Witness marks*]

---

You must also plan how to use any illustrative devices to best effect. One way is to have witnesses go through their testimony in general fashion and then take them back to the diagram to reinforce their testimony. In other cases, the early use of a diagram is essential to explain a complicated scene or fact situation. Whatever you do, strive for a logical flow in the testimony and remember that the use of a diagram interrupts that flow. Avoid having the witness engage in courtroom gymnastics as he or she bounces back and forth from the diagram to the witness box.

Above all, remember the judge is your audience. Far too often counsel and the witness will engage in their own private and intimate conversation while huddled around the diagram. The witness is intent upon showing counsel what he or she means and that is wrong. The task of counsel is to focus the witness on showing the judge.[7]

You must also give consideration to how the witness will mark the diagram. Far too often at the close of trial a diagram looks like a muddled battlefield plan. "Xs and Os", crosses and arrows, zigzag chaotically across the paper. Different colour markers, one for each witness, may help but in many cases the net result is simply multi-coloured chaos. Where more than one witness is to mark a diagram and where consistency in marking is important, consider two options. Clear overlays can be used, a fresh transparent overlay for each witness. In argument, the overlays can be transposed and thereby compared. Or separate clean diagrams can be used for each witness. In both instances, the individual overlay or clean diagram would be marked as a separate exhibit: 1-A, 1-B, 1-C, 1-D. Remember, just as with the testimony of a witness, you want the visual evidence of your witness to be as clear and understandable as possible for the judge.

A key point with using any illustrative aid, whether it be a diagram, chart or model, is that the trial judge must see it. Having the witness mark a letter-sized diagram placed in front of the witness is quite ineffectual in that it always needs to be passed to the judge to see. Think about how you can have the witness use the diagram and at the same time have the judge follow along. BIG is the operative word. Diagrams need to be big. This can be done in a variety of ways:

1) through an actual enlargement of the diagram,

2) through a computer document projector, which may be available in the courtroom, or

3) through a simple overhead projector and clear transparency.

---

[7] For a humorous anecdote, see Mr. Justice Robert Reid's article, "Some Surprising Things Judges Learn About Evidence" (1986), 5 Adv. Soc. J. 31 at p. 36.

A second key point is that a record must be kept for the Court of Appeal of any use made of the diagram by the witnesses. A transcript, as below, is of no value:

**Witness:**    I saw the accused go in this door.

**Question:**    Where were you when you saw him go through the door?

**Witness:**    I was right about here.

*(You must ensure that the Court of Appeal knows which "door" and where "here" is.)*

**Counsel:**    For the record the witness has indicated the northernmost door on the Main Street side of the store.

**Counsel:**    For the record the witness pointed to the west side of Main Street directly opposite the northernmost door of the store. *(Then ask the witness how far she was away from the accused at this time.)*

If the witness has actually marked a diagram, following your clear directions, and the marked diagram is going to be tendered as an exhibit then there is little point to put the marking on the record. In the example given earlier, where Mr. Smith marked the St. Michael playground, there was no repetition "for the record" of his markings.

# 6.    PROBLEM — DIRECT EXAMINATION

**1.    You are to prepare and conduct a direct examination of JAMES STEWART.**

*Refer to:*

Chapter 2, section 6 — Sample Pleadings for the issues before the court.

The DIRECT EXAMINATION OF RICHARD WAITE (Chapter 11, section 5).

POLICE STATEMENT.

KARATE RECORD (*Note:* At the examination for discovery James Stewart admitted its accuracy. The document is tendered by consent as EXHIBIT 4.)

BACKGROUND:

*Age:* 22     *Height:* 5' 10"     *Weight:* 165 lbs.

*Student:* Third year engineering

*Address:* 389 Beaverton Street (Lives at home with parents). Stewart started playing in the recreation hockey league in January. The injury to Waite in the game was purely accidental.

RE INCIDENT: After the game Stewart wanted nothing to do with Waite, who was being abusive (see police statement). In Stewart's view, Waite was "spoiling for a fight." Stewart defended himself. The kicks were designed to immobilize Waite quickly.

RE KARATE: Stewart views karate as a defensive sport. He has never been advised that he must warn anyone about his karate training; on the contrary, he has been told not to tell people because that can encourage attackers to test the so-called "karate expert."

## POLICE STATEMENT OF JAMES STEWART

Last night I played at the Highlander in a recreational hockey league. In the course of the game I accidentally hit a guy with my stick just above the right eye. After the game, I'm loading my gear into my car and the guy who I'd cut in the game approaches me. He says, "You got no stick now, big boy. Let's see how brave you are now." I told him that I didn't want any trouble. His reply was, "You got it." Then he says something like how would you like to get hit in the face with a stick. He then flicked his hand in my face, brushing his gloves across my face a couple times. And then he pushed me against the car. I tried to ignore him and get into my car but he blocked my way. He then pushed me a couple more times and finally I fell into a snow bank by the car. As he was pushing me he said, "Let's see how tough you are." With the last push I blew my stack and I said something like, "Let's go to it." He then turned and walked into the parking lot lane and I followed. We circled for a moment or two. He threw a punch at my head. I then gave him a defensive body blow to the abdomen. That winded him. I finished him off with a light chop to the side of his head. He fell to the ground and a friend took care of him. I left.

**Q.** Mr. Stewart, are you trained in karate?

**A.** Yes I am. I've taken karate for three years and I have my brown belt.

*Signed:* James Stewart          Date: 14th March 2015

*Witness:* Sgt. E. Meese

---

Western Canada Karate Association
3535 Portage Avenue
Winnipeg, Manitoba
R3M 0P2

October, 2015

> RE: JAMES STEWART
> 389 BEAVERTON STREET
> WINNIPEG, MANITOBA

Outlined below is the Associations record for Mr. JAMES STEWART:

| | |
|---|---|
| Sept. 15, 2012 | Register Karate Association |
| Oct. 30, 2012 | White Belt Awarded |
| Jan. 27, 2013 | Yellow Belt Awarded |
| Mar. 15, 2013 | Participant Mid-West Karate Tournament |
| May 17, 2013 | Orange Belt Awarded |
| Oct. 13, 2013 | Green Belt Awarded |
| Nov. 20, 2013 | Participant Manitoba Karate Tournament (3rd place Green Belt) |
| Feb. 22, 2014 | Participant Mid-West Karate Tournament (2nd place Green Belt) |
| May 14, 2014 | Purple Belt Awarded |
| Dec. 10, 2014 | Brown Belt (Level 1) Awarded |
| Feb. 24, 2015 | Participant Mid-West Karate Tournament |
| May 6, 2015 | Brown Belt (Level 2) Awarded |
| Sept. 17, 2015 | Brown Belt (Level 3) Awarded |

I certify that the record is accurate and complete as of October 2, 2015.

Yours Sincerely,

K.C. Chop
Secretary
Western Canada Karate Association

**2.  Prepare and conduct a direct examination of G. Rice.**

Rice is called as a witness for the Defendant in *Waite v. Stewart*. Refer to:

The Police Statement (provided).
The Diagram (provided).

The diagram has been consented to by counsel and is Exhibit 1. The markings that you have are taken from the interview you had with the witness prior to trial. You are to assume that the diagram, Exhibit 1, is blank.

Background:

*Age:* 32
*Address:* 82 Smythe Road        Winnipeg
*Occupation:* Salesperson        Safe Shopping Canada
              (four years at present position).
*Married:* One child (six years old)

Rice does not know either the plaintiff or the defendant. Rice is a regular curler at the Highlander and knows the building well.

Statement of G. Rice

At around 8:45 on 13th March I was at the Highlander Sports Complex for curling. I was removing my curling gear from the trunk of my car when I saw two men in argument. I was across the parking lot from them some 70 to 80 feet away. One of the men was really baiting the other. He was saying to the other man things like, "You've got nobody or no stick to protect you now." He then pushed the man and slapped the man across the face a couple times and then pushed the man into a snow bank. The other man got up and the two went into a lane to fight. The one man who was doing all the baiting swung at the other. He missed. The other man then kicked the man in the stomach. The man doubled up. It looked like he had the wind knocked out of him. Then the other man kicked the man again, this time in the face. The man fell to the ground. Another man ran up to help him and so did I. The man who kicked him, turned, got into his car and left.

*Signed:*      G. Rice                              *Date:* 14th March 2015
*Witness:*     Sgt. E. Meese

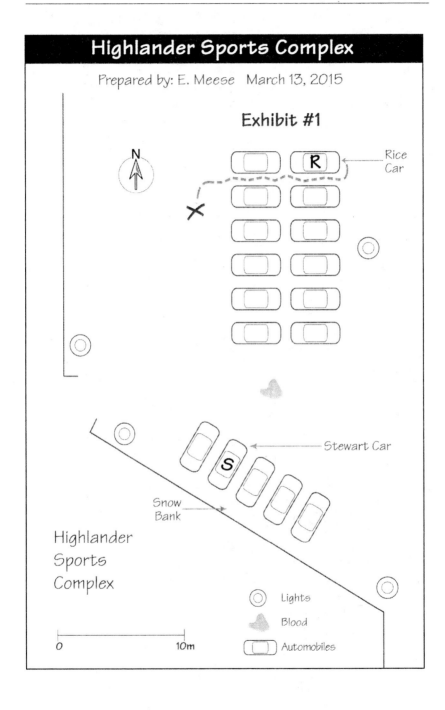

**Highlander Sports Complex**

Prepared by: E. Meese   March 13, 2015

Exhibit #1

N

Rice
Car

R

X

Stewart Car

S

Snow
Bank

Highlander
Sports
Complex

Lights

Blood

Automobiles

0                    10m

# 13

# PRINCIPLES OF CROSS-EXAMINATION

- **The Purpose of Cross-examination**

- **Preparation for Cross-examination**

- **The Decision to Cross-examine**

- **Principles of Cross-examination**

- **Sample Cross-examination**

Cross-examination is a terrifying challenge for new counsel. Anxiety is created because it is in cross-examination that counsel are most vulnerable. We all know that the cross-examination is a highlight of a trial. Counsel move to centre stage and are expected to perform. This is the "unscripted" portion of the trial where counsel and the witness match wits and we expect the lawyer to win. This is the true fear of cross-examination, the fear of *personal* failure by counsel or the fear of *embarrassment*, as Irving Younger puts it:[1]

> Most trial lawyers have vivid recollections of their first cross-examinations, regardless of how long ago they have taken place. Probably, you wanted the ground to open beneath you so that you could sink in, have the ground close up around you, and never be heard from again. If it was a criminal case, your client would go to jail for a long, long time because of your cross-examination.

---

[1] Younger, "The Art of Cross-Examination," Proceedings of a speech at the American Bar Association's Annual Meeting in Montreal, Canada, 12th August 1975, American Bar Association (1976), at p. 16.

If it was a civil case, your client would pay out a lot of money because of your cross-examination. More importantly, you had exposed yourself to public scorn. You had embarrassed yourself.

Cross-examination is difficult and there will be failures. You are new counsel and you will make mistakes and disasters will befall you. Take solace. The importance of cross-examination to your case is overrated. This is not to say that I disagree with Wigmore, who in his treatise on evidence stated that cross-examination "is beyond any doubt the greatest legal engine ever invented for the discovery of truth."[2] Certainly the opportunity to cross-examine an opposing witness is fundamental to our system of trial, but in reality few witnesses are utterly devastated by cross-examination. Most cases are won in your direct and the cross-examination acts only to confirm the evidence presented in direct. Exceptions are criminal defence lawyers, who, because in many cases they call no evidence, must rely upon putting their case to the judge through the cross-examination of the Crown's witnesses. I will make suggestions for new counsel on how to avoid disasters. My purpose is to provide you with seed principles on cross-examination to be nurtured in your practice.

There is much that counsel must do on their own to hone their cross-examination skills. Read. Look to books on cross-examination. Refer to books by or about masters of the courtroom. Observe. Should you have the luxury of time, go to court and watch *any* lawyers, not just "senior" lawyers, at work. You will learn by watching the techniques of others, both good and bad. Finally, you need experience. You learn best by doing and the painful mistakes you make will be etched on your memory, never to be repeated. It is suggested that the minimal experience necessary for one to be a good cross-examiner is 25 jury trials.[3]

Let us begin by asking what is it about cross-examination that makes it difficult and terrifying for counsel? I suggest that it is fear of the unknown and there are two "unknowns." First, counsel do not know the witnesses whom they are cross-examining. Second, counsel do not know what those witnesses will say. What counsel must do is minimize these "unknowns." You do so through proper preparation and planning, which are the essential principles that support a good cross-examination.

Preparation aims at gathering information about the opposing witnesses and their evidence. In a civil case, this is achieved through the discovery process. In a criminal case, defence counsel will rely upon the

---

[2] 5 Wigmore, *Evidence*, Chadbourn rev. (1974), para. 1367, p. 32.
[3] Younger, *supra*, note 1, at p. 17.

preliminary inquiry and disclosure by the Crown. The more you know about the witnesses and their evidence, the less you have to fear in cross-examination.

Planning aims at structuring the cross-examination so as to elicit information from the witnesses that you want raised and to avoid giving the witnesses the opportunity to testify on matters that you do not want raised. Plan to *control* the witnesses and their evidence. You determine the agenda and you ask the questions. Proper planning, therefore, is concerned with deciding what questions to ask and how to ask them. Without such a plan you lose control over the witness and you enter the dangerous domain of "unknown" testimony.

## 1.   THE PURPOSE OF CROSS-EXAMINATION

Robert Keeton classified the goals of cross-examination into four groups:[4]

1.   discrediting the testimony of the witness being examined,

2.   using the testimony of this witness to discredit the unfavourable testimony of other witnesses,

3.   using the testimony of this witness to corroborate the favourable testimony of other witnesses, and

4.   using the testimony of this witness to contribute independently to the favourable development of your own case.

Other commentators simplify the goals of cross-examination into:[5]

1.   eliciting favourable testimony from the witness, and

2.   discrediting the testimony of the witness.

Of importance is that cross-examination is not necessarily aimed at destroying the witness.

Unfortunately, perhaps because of watching too much television, or perhaps because of a misguided sense of their own importance, many new

[4] R. Keeton, *Trial Tactics and Methods*, 2nd ed. (1973), at p. 94.
[5] R. Salhany, *Cross-examination: The Art of the Advocate* (1988), at p. 7.

counsel assume that cross-examination means "attack." They are tenacious, ferocious bull dogs, frothing at the mouth, straining at the leash, ready to pounce on the witness at the command, "That concludes the direct examination." Upon hearing those words, the lawyer is unleashed with the client in the background yelling, "Go get 'im, Fido!"

Very few witnesses deserve that kind of treatment. Such a cross-examination for most witnesses is tactically misplaced, questionably effective and totally unprofessional. Our professional code of conduct admonishes counsel not to "needlessly abuse, hector or harass a witness."[6] You, as cross-examiner, wield an enormous amount of power over a witness; you ask the questions and the witness must answer them. What you ask and how you ask it can be very humiliating and intimidating for the witness. Do not abuse your power.

Cross-examination need not be and only rarely should be "cross." Coax favourable testimony out of the witness. Even if your objective is to discredit the witness, little will be gained by a blatant, frontal attack on the witness. This is what the witness expects, once again a product of too much television, and it is difficult to bludgeon a witness into submission. Be subtle. Go gently. Remember Aesop's fable of "The Wind and the Sun:"[7]

> The Wind and the Sun were disputing which was the stronger. Suddenly they saw a traveller coming down the road, and the Sun said: "I see a way to decide our dispute. Whichever of us can cause that traveller to take off his cloak shall be regarded as the stronger. You begin." So the Sun retired behind a cloud, and the Wind began to blow as hard as it could upon the traveller. But the harder he blew the more closely did the traveller wrap his cloak round him, till at last the Wind had to give up in despair. Then the Sun came out and shone in all his glory upon the traveller, who soon found it too hot to walk with his cloak on. *Kindness effects more than severity.*

Let the witnesses expose themselves by being cross or angry. In contrast, you are the epitome of politeness, sincerity and integrity.

Remember, also, that most witnesses are truthful and are trying to help the tribunal resolve the issues before it. Use the witness's willingness to help. The "help me out" approach is non-confrontational and is most effective at eliciting favourable testimony for your case.

---

[6] See e.g., The Law Society of Upper Canada, Rules of Professional Conduct, Rule 5.1-2(m); Law Society of Manitoba, Code of Professional Conduct, Rule 5.1-2(m).

[7] J. Jacobs, *The Fables of Aesop*, N.Y. (1966), at pp. 142-143.

By way of example, assume that the Crown has called an eyewitness to a fatal stabbing. The witness's evidence is that the stabbing was done deliberately and not in self-defence, but the witness could not identify the attacker. You know that the Crown will be calling two other witnesses, who were as far away from the affray as this witness, but who will identify your client. You want to establish the difficulties in seeing accurately at the time. This is a perfect witness to help you do so because she has already testified that she could not see who the attacker was:

Q. Ms Smith, there are just a few matters I'd like you to help me with. You were directly across the street from where the stabbing occurred, is that correct?
A. Yes I was.

Q. That would be about 25 metres away?
A. It would.

Q. You mentioned there were a number of young men involved. How many would you say?
A. There were at least 12 to 15.

Q. So there could have been more?
A. Yes.

Q. Many of them wore the same type jackets, didn't they?
A. Yes they did.

Q. And they were all pretty close to the same ages, teenagers, would that be right?
A. Yes they were.

You are gathering ammunition to challenge the subsequent testimony of the other eyewitnesses.

## 2.    PREPARATION FOR CROSS-EXAMINATION

### 2.1    Knowing Your Goals

Deciding what questions to ask of a witness flows from your theory of the case and from your appreciation of the opponent's theory of the case. Before trial you ask yourself: Why is that witness being called? How will that witness help their case? How will the witness hurt your case? From these questions you go on to consider: How can the witness help your case? And, how can you discredit the witness's expected testimony?

Through this process you select areas for cross-examination. These are your targets. List them. Then structure your cross-examination around them. The fewer targets the better. The simple fact is that a judge, like any person, can only retain so much information and, by being selective, you direct the judge to the few damaging areas you want highlighted. Such focus can be most effective.

Imagine the following moot problem that involved a negligence action against an anaesthetist brought by a patient alleging injury caused by the improper administration of an anaesthetic during an operation. The anaesthetist, during the course of the plaintiff's operation, was also supervising a second operation in a separate operating room. While the anaesthetist was away, a nurse monitored the anaesthetic. The nurse is called by the defendant to give evidence that she was an experienced operating room nurse and had monitored the anaesthetic for the defendant in many other operations. What is it you want to focus on? I suggest that you want to emphasize that a nurse and not a doctor was left in charge of the anaesthetic:

**Q.** Nurse Jones, you're not a doctor are you?
**A.** No.

**Q.** You've never gone to medical school?
**A.** No.

**Q.** Nurse Jones, so you cannot be a specialist in anaesthesia?
**A.** I'm not.

**Q.** And as a nurse you're not allowed to administer an anaesthetic, are you?
**A.** No.

**Q.** Only a doctor is allowed to administer an anaesthetic, isn't that correct?
**A.** Yes.

The one fact that is implanted in the mind of the judge is that Nurse Jones is not a doctor and, no matter how competent or experienced she may be, she could never have the necessary skill or qualifications to replace the doctor, who should have been present.

A real example is taken from the murder case of *R. v. Deacon*, where the eminent Harry Walsh, Q.C., was one of the counsel for the accused.[8] Much of the evidence against the accused was circumstantial, including

---

[8] Taken from the transcript of the case heard before a judge and jury 28th October to 2nd November 1946.

casts of footprints taken from the scene. Harry Walsh, in his cross-examinations of the Crown witnesses, invariably asked, "What size of boots were you wearing?" He also obtained concessions that a number of the officers had milled around the scene prior to the taking of the footprint casts. The net result was that by the conclusion of the Crown's case the jury had an image of thousands of feet stomping about the crime scene, which was precisely what was desired by the defence in order to minimize the impact of the footprint evidence linking the accused to the murder scene. Unfortunately for Deacon it was not enough, and he was found guilty of the murder.[9]

Harry Walsh, when he repeatedly asked the Crown witnesses, "What size of boots were you wearing?" had a purpose, and you too must have a purpose for every question you ask.[10] The ultimate purpose is to elicit evidence for use in closing argument. If a question has no purpose — don't ask it! If you do, trouble will surely follow:[11]

> I have always gone on the principle "Leave well alone." A friend of mine, a brilliant counsel (now unfortunately deceased) named W.B. Campbell, was defending a man at the Old Bailey for murder of a barmaid. Not a single word was said by any witness called by the Crown of any previous threat by the prisoner, but Campbell, confident of getting a favourable answer, put to the licensee of the house the following question: "Did you ever hear the prisoner threaten the deceased woman before the date of the alleged murder?" and the publican replied: "*Yes, many times*, although I never thought the threat serious." The prisoner was convicted and afterwards executed. Poor Campbell came up to see me in a dreadful state of dejection, saying he wished he had never come to the Bar, and it took me a long time to console him.

## 2.2 Knowing the Evidence

In preparing for cross-examination, it is fundamental that you thoroughly familiarize yourself with the evidence. You have the means. In a civil case, through the discovery process, you have the transcripts from the examinations for discovery and you have the relevant documents. In most instances, you have witness statements as well. If you do not have a statement from an anticipated opposing witness, you should endeavour to get one. There is no property in witnesses and there is nothing to stop you from speaking to the witness, although there is no corresponding obligation on the witness to speak to you. If the witness is critical or has critical documents

---

[9] *R. v. Deacon* (1947), 3 C.R. 265 (S.C.C.).
[10] K. Evans, *Advocacy at the Bar* (1983), at p. 138.
[11] Taken from Wigmore, *supra*, note 2, at para. 1368, p. 47.

but proves uncooperative, you have certain legal remedies. Under R. 31.10, with the court's leave, you may examine for discovery the witness. Under R. 30.10 the court may order the production of any relevant document in the possession of a non-party.

In a criminal case you have the preliminary inquiry transcript and have the right to broad disclosure from the Crown. The Supreme Court of Canada, in *R. v. Stinchcombe*, has established the principle that the Crown is under a general duty to disclose all information within its control unless it is clearly irrelevant or privileged.[12] This information, however, is only made available upon request.

Interviewing Crown witnesses is also available to the defence. However, caution is recommended in that these witnesses may misconstrue your questions as undue "pressure." I suggest that if you do intend to talk with any Crown witness then make certain that someone from your office is present both to take any statement, because you do not want to be placed in the position of calling yourself to give testimony about the taking of the statement should the witness contradict and deny the statement, and to refute any allegation of impropriety.

Knowing the evidence is the prerequisite for planning the cross-examination. It will dictate the areas to be covered in cross and it will dictate how you approach the witness. By knowing the witness's prior statements in minute detail, you are also in a position effectively to impeach and control the witness. I would go so far as to say that you are to know and be able to recall the prior statements made by the witness better than the witness can. If you do, you have an enormous advantage over the witness. If you do not, then you will be taken advantage of by the witness. If the cross-examiner is not prepared, witnesses get away with misstatements, inaccuracies and contradictions. That same witness, when confronted by prepared counsel, will be caught time and time again. Documents, in particular, provide a firm and irrefutable base from which to contradict or to commit a witness.[13]

Ironically, for new counsel, your first trials are likely to be ones where you will have the least amount of information. You will win your litigation "spurs" in the provincial courts handling criminal and highway traffic matters. There is no preliminary inquiry and the thoroughness of the police investigation and witness statements is minimal at best. In these cases you

---

[12] *R. v. Stinchcombe* (1991), 68 C.C.C. (3d) 1 (S.C.C.). For a more detailed discussion on *Stinchcombe*, see Chapter 4.

[13] D. Napley, *The Technique of Persuasion*, 3rd ed. (1983), at p. 132.

face a large number of "unknowns." Still, the more "unknowns" you alleviate, the better prepared you will be.

To be effective, the out-of-court preparation must be combined with in-court preparation. You must listen carefully to what the witness says in direct. It is not necessary that you write everything down; you know what is important and what is not. But a few choice verbatim statements used by you in cross-examination or in your closing are the mark of a good advocate. Far too often, new counsel do not listen to the direct. They are busy "rehearsing" for their cross, and when their time comes they dive into their prepared cross-examination oblivious to what the witness has just said. The direct testimony of the witness helps to mould the cross-examination. Certain issues, where you anticipate contradiction, may be conceded by the witness and there is no need for you to cross on those issues. On the other hand, new avenues may reveal themselves and you must be flexible enough to address them.

Besides listening to the witness, watch the witness. Size the witness up, and consider how you can take advantage of any perceived character weaknesses. The impression you allow the witness to leave with the court can be as important as that witness's testimony.

A beautiful illustration was given by Gilbert Gray, Q.C., at the Seventh Annual Advocacy Symposium. Mr. Gray was called upon to cross-examine the designer of a car that had a fold down rear seat providing access to the trunk. A child climbed into the trunk from the rear seat, locked himself in the trunk and suffered a severe brain injury from suffocation. Before starting his cross-examination, Gilbert Gray, Q.C., in typical understated English fashion, told the audience that he had not the "foggiest notion" as to how to approach the witness because he had not "wood shedded" the witness in any way. He had only observed him in direct examination, but what he perceived was an assertive and self-confident witness. Watch how this characteristic is used to advantage:[14]

Q. And you are a man of firm opinions and strong view, are you not?
A. I would say so.

Q. Sometimes outspoken?
A. Yes.

---

[14] "The Seventh Annual Advocacy Symposium" presented by the Canadian Bar Association — Ontario and the Law Society of Upper Canada (6th and 7th May 1988, Toronto), p. 81 at pp. 83-84.

**Q.** You say what you mean, and you mean what you say.
**A.** I try to.

**Q.** And you weigh your words carefully, especially if you are dealing with proceedings, judicial proceedings?
**A.** Yes.

**Q.** Would you just, please, look out at the jury and say whether you weighed these words carefully. "Parents who leave children alone in a car should be shot."
**A.** Yes. I've weighed that very carefully. That is my opinion . . .

**Q.** And then, when you say "leave a child in a car alone," you mean even for the fleeting second or for a period of time?
**A.** I would say even for a fleeting second. That is, I can envisage, of course, dropping a letter off in a mail box, something of that nature, and you leave the car to put it in, but at that time you can still see the car and you see that nothing has happened. But, if you leave a child unattended and you cannot see them within the vehicle, I think indeed you're asking for great trouble.

**Q.** Asking for great trouble?
**A.** Yes.

**Q.** If the car is on the level, with the brake on, ignition key out, windows just, say, ajar, safety strap fastened around the child, would you still shoot the parents? Look at the Toronto jury, please.
**A.** If they left a child unattended, maybe cat-o-nine tails if not shooting.

**Q.** And why would you shoot the parents?
**A.** Because a motor vehicle is a couple of tons of danger, and you have to · respect that . . .

**Q.** . . . Well, now the reason why you think it may be dangerous is that children tend to be mischievous is that right?
**A.** Yes, and inquisitive.

**Q.** And they lack foresight. Boys will be boys.
**A.** Yes.

**Q.** And wherever there is an allurement, for example an interesting hiding hole. Children like hiding, don't they?
**A.** Yes, very much.

**Q.** Then you don't need an engineer or a jury to tell you that such is an enticement for a child?
**A.** It is an enticement.

**Q.** And, when you open one of the seats forward, there is an obvious enticement and allurement?
**A.** Yes.

**Q.** And you knew it?
**A.** Yes.

Gilbert Gray, Q.C., caught the witness making an exaggerated statement
and he perceived that the witness would stubbornly cling to his absurd
position before admitting his mistake. Even if the witness did admit his
mistake, that too is a victory for the cross-examiner. Mr. Gray let the witness
wallow in his overstatement for the jury to digest fully and any juror who
was a parent would be thinking, "What utter nonsense." The witness is
discredited.

Part of your trial preparation includes a visit to the scene, which can
only improve your understanding of the evidence and place you in a better
position to cross-examine witnesses. If you are not familiar with the scene,
witnesses can take advantage of your ignorance. In contrast, it is an intimidating prospect for a witness to be confronted by an examiner who has
"been there" and knows the scene as well as, if not better, than the witness.

**2.3    Knowing Yourself**

The focus in cross-examination, unlike the direct, is on the cross-
examiner. You are fully exposed for judicial scrutiny and it is important
that you do not appear bogus. Be true to yourself. Be comfortable with
yourself and know your strengths, weaknesses and limitations. Don't try to
be someone you aren't. If you're not folksy, don't try to be. If you're not
flamboyant, don't try to be. If you're not aggressive, don't try to be.

Having said this, there also must be flexibility within yourself to adapt
to the variety of witnesses you will confront. Experienced police officers
are assertive on the stand and can make the inexperienced counsel cower.
You cannot allow this to happen. In response, you must be stronger. In
contrast, the tough examiner must tone down aggressive questioning when
examining a child witness or sympathetic witness. No judge likes to see
counsel attack a "nice" witness and such a tactic merely engenders sympathy
for the witness and brings discredit upon you. You are your client's "rep-
resentative" and it is fundamental that you foster a favourable impression.
Your "style" must be appropriate to the case and to the witness; this you
consider before you cross-examine the witness.

## 3.   THE DECISION TO CROSS-EXAMINE

You do not have to cross-examine a witness. In fact, the wisest course of action with many witnesses is to say, "I have no questions, M'Lady." Before cross-examining a witness, therefore, you must pause and ask yourself, "What can I achieve in cross-examining this witness?" If the witness has not hurt your case, do not cross-examine. Why cross-examine if the witness has actually provided you with favourable testimony; leave well enough alone. If you do not know "why" you are cross-examining the witness, then you should not be doing it.

Pause. Ask for a moment to review your notes. You will be granted that indulgence by the court. The message — think before you cross.

Now it is also true that in certain instances the law requires that you cross-examine witnesses. This is the case whenever you are going to challenge the credibility of a witness through contradictory evidence. For example, in *Penney v. Manitoba Public Insurance*, the plaintiff brought an action for disability benefits.[15] The insurance company denied benefits, claiming that he was faking his disability. The plaintiff took the stand and testified that he was disabled. His medical expert testified that he was disabled. The insurer then, as part of its case, introduced a videotape showing the plaintiff doing what he claimed he could not do. The Court of Appeal was not amused. If you are going to contradict a witness, fairness demands that the contradictory evidence be put to the witness in cross-examination. This is the rule in *Browne v. Dunn* and will be discussed further in Chapter 14 on impeachment.

## 4.   PRINCIPLES OF CROSS-EXAMINATION

I use the term "principles" of cross-examination. Other writers refer to the "rules" of cross-examination and Irving Younger used a certain allegoric licence in dispensing his "Ten Commandments" of cross-examination.[16] A "rule" or "commandment" has too strong a connotation, whereas a "principle" is sufficiently general to accommodate the needed flexibility and exceptions that go to make a good cross-examination. One cannot be too categorical or too absolute in talking about cross-examination and say you must *always* do this or you must *never* do that. Flexibility and a quick mind are two essential attributes that enable the cross-examiner to seize the unexpected opportunities when presented. Having made this proviso, the prin-

---

[15] *Penney v. Manitoba Public Insurance Corp.* (1992), 81 Man. R. (2d) 145 (C.A.).
[16] Younger, *supra*, note 1.

ciples listed and explained below constitute good advice and are to be ignored or deviated from by new counsel at their peril.

---

### *Principles of Cross-Examination*

1) **Be Brief**

2) **Simple Questions Simply Asked**

3) **Use Leading Questions**

4) **Know When to Stop**

5) **Do Not Allow the Witness to Repeat the Direct**

6) **Do Not Quarrel with the Witness**

7) **Plan Your Questions**

8) **Listen Carefully to the Witness's Answer**

9) **Start Safe and Finish Strong**

10) **Seize the Moment**

---

Behind the principles there is a common theme and that is *control*. The principles in one way or another suggest various means of controlling the witness and, thereby, the information that comes out in cross-examination.

Gilbert Gray, Q.C., remarked that the English approach to cross-examination is not so much to control the witness:[17]

> Control him! How different it is in England where we say, "Give him his head," "Let him have enough rope so that he'll hang himself" . . . And it is astonishing to me that you don't get an impression of gross unfairness when people are being cut short — indeed gagged.

Do not misinterpret Mr. Gray's comment, "Give him his head," because the English barrister, like any good cross-examiner, points the witness in desired

---

[17] Advocacy Symposium, *supra*, note 14, at p. 98.

examination directions. The barrister controls the direction the "head" is moving. But I agree with the admonition not to cut off the witness. It is rude and Gilbert Gray, Q.C., went on to observe:[18]

> In England, the commonest judicial phrase you would have heard in the symposium so far would be, "Let the witness answer. Stop interrupting." "Mr. Gray, what are you trying to keep out?" "Let the witness have his head. You can ask him questions about it."

A Canadian judge would respond in a similar fashion. You have asked the question and you should not prevent the witness from giving an answer to your question. Your control comes from the questions you ask and not from muzzling the witness.

## 4.1    Principle 1: Be Brief

"Be brief" ranks first in importance, yet it is the principle most often breached by counsel. Irving Younger suggests one reason to be brief: "Chances are, you are screwing up. The shorter the time you spend on your feet, the less you will screw up."[19] A second reason he gives is that of retention. A judge, like a juror, can only absorb so much information.

Your cross-examination has focus. You know your targets. These points you want to highlight. If you belabour an area or cross-examine on too many peripheral points, all impact will be lost.

You know where you want to go and what you want to achieve in cross-examination. Ask your questions aimed at those goals — then stop.

## 4.2    Principle 2: Simple Questions Simply Asked

The surest way for you to lose focus in your cross-examination is by asking long questions. No one, including the judge and the witness, knows what you have asked. Keep your questions short. As a guide, use one line per question.

One form of long question is "the summary question." The cross-examiner thinks that by repeating what seems to be inconsistent testimony, he is highlighting to the court the lack of credibility to be given to that testimony.

---

[18] *Ibid.*
[19] Younger, *supra*, note 1, at p. 21.

Let us use the case of *Waite v. Stewart* (Chapter 2) and the cross-examination of the plaintiff, who was kicked in the face by the defendant:

**Q.** Now Mr. Waite, you say that Mr. Stewart deliberately kicked you in the face?

**A.** Yes.

**Q.** But you were doubled over, head down, holding your stomach, and in pain — so you weren't looking at the defendant at this time, were you?

**A.** No I wasn't. I was in too much pain.

The repetition of the earlier evidence serves no purpose. In fact, through the repetition, you are reinforcing the fact that the plaintiff was helpless when kicked by your client the second time. Keep it simple and focused on what you want:

**Q.** Mr. Waite, after you were kicked the first time, you weren't looking at the defendant, were you?

**A.** No.

A second type of long question is "the complex question." Unfortunately, often as not the complex question is phrased in complex language. The net result is an incomprehensible question:

**Q.** You were proceeding in a westerly direction in the south median lane on Willow Street, which is an east-west artery in the city, when as you were approaching the intersection of 7th Avenue, at about 4:50 p.m., you saw the incident that brings you before this court, and the sun would be in your eyes at this point. Isn't that correct?

What exactly is the question? The cross-examiner may say that, "I was asking about the sun being in the witness's eyes." But that is not the simple question. The question contains a number of statements that, standing on their own, could be "the question." In cross-examination ask one question at a time. If you do not, the ambiguity allows witnesses to waffle and evade and you lose control. For example, in the above question the witness may reply:

**A.** I don't understand your question. [*A legitimate response*] *or*

**A.** I don't think I was in the south median lane. [*Evasion, you were focusing on the sun*] *or*

**A.** It wasn't 4:50; it was 4:45. [*Further evasion*]

Break the question down into simple parts and focus on what you want to achieve:

> **Q.** Mr. Smith, you were driving west on Willow Street, isn't that correct? [*Whether the witness was in the median lane or not has no relevance to the "sun" issue, nor is there need for the added complexity of east-west artery.*]
> **A.** Yes.
>
> **Q.** And that was about 4:50 p.m., wasn't it?
> **A.** I'd say closer to 4:45.
>
> **Q.** Okay, and it was clear that day?
> **A.** Yes.
>
> **Q.** Now at that time of year (*looking at note*) the sun sets at 5:07 p.m. Would you agree with that?
> **A.** That sounds about right. I don't know exactly.
>
> **Q.** So you must have been driving right into the sun, isn't that right?
> **A.** Yes, that's right.

Simple questions also allow you better control of the witness. It is difficult for a witness to evade a direct question simply put. If the witness does evade the question, ask the simple question again. If the witness still refuses to answer, ask that same simple question again. By this time the judge is well aware that the witness is being evasive and you are in a position to clamp down on the difficult witness. Keith Evans provides this example:[20]

> I watched a co-defending barrister some time ago conduct his entire case with sweetness and light, turning away almost all of the evidence with smiles and admissions. He stripped the prosecution case down to its bare essentials and showed, by so doing, that it was mostly composed of conjecture and inference. Just one witness stood out. A detective sergeant said that the defendant had admitted all, not in writing, just in a cell interview. None of the suspect's rights had been given to him, no solicitor's visit, no telephone call. The barrister began as gently as he had with all the other witnesses. But the detective sergeant didn't like the "short question, short answer" method. He began making speeches. Suddenly the advocate was quite different. Half-way through the second answer he broke in, "Officer!"
>
> **A.** Sir?
>
> **Q.** Been in the police force long?

---

[20] Evans, *supra*, note 10, at p. 136.

**A.** Fifteen years.

**Q.** Given evidence before?
**A.** Many times.

**Q.** Capable of understanding a simple question are you?
**A.** Yes.

**Q.** I'll repeat my last question.

## 4.3    Principle 3: Use Leading Questions

In cross-examination the witness is in many instances hostile or at least unsympathetic towards your side. Therefore you should suggest answers to the witness and you should lead. To put it another way, you tell the witness what to say. Now this is not always possible nor is it always desirable. At times an open-ended question will have to be asked in order for you to find out needed information, or at times an open-ended question can be asked for effect. But before you ask an open-ended question, assess the risks. This is especially critical when you are asking an open-ended information question. Before asking such a question, consider the importance of the information to your case and how damaging an unfavourable answer could be to your case.

For example, in a burglary identification case the owner of the house returned to find two men running out the back door. She has identified your client by name. Your client has told you that he never knew the owner at all, although they lived in the same neighbourhood. You have already established in cross-examination that the owner's opportunity to see the burglars lasted for a fleeting moment when they had their backs to her. She says your client turned to look back and that is when she recognized him.

**Q.** Mrs. Smith, you identified Mr. Jones by name earlier?
**A.** Yes.

**Q.** But you never knew him at all before this did you?
**A.** No.

**Q.** How did you know Mr. Jones' name?
**A.** Well, when I described the man to the police officer he said, "Sounds like Jones," and when we reviewed the photographs I recognized Jones.

**Q.** So you got the name from the police officer?
**A.** Yes.

What you have shown is that the identification is further tainted by the police officer's suggestion and you have uncovered a further fruitful avenue for cross-examination. In asking, "How did you know Mr. Jones' name?" there was little downside risk because the witness must have obtained that information from some secondhand source, either the police or another person, which would go to taint the identification. Even if the witness had said that she knew Jones by name, the argument challenging her identification on the grounds of opportunity to perceive had in no way been compromised.

The concern with an open-ended question is that it allows the witness to explain, and that is precisely what you do not want a witness to do on cross-examination. You are asking for trouble when you ask:

- What do you mean?

- Explain that?

- Why do you say that?

- How could you have seen that?

- What happened?

You are simply allowing the witness to repeat answers from direct examination and you have lost control over the witness. After all, how can you stop the witness from giving a damaging narrative when you have asked, "What do you mean?" and the witness is answering *your* question? You got exactly what you deserved.

Having said that, as a general principle, you ask leading questions, there is nothing more agonizing than listening to counsel try to turn *every* statement into a leading question. The questioning becomes stilted:

**Q.** You say that you left the dance at 12:30, isn't that right?
**A.** Yes.

**Q.** And you were drinking during the dance, isn't that right?
**A.** Yes.

**Q.** As I recall in your direct testimony you said that you had four or five beer, is that correct?
**A.** Yes.

**Q.** And you chose not to drive, isn't that right?
**A.** Yes.

**Q.** In fact you turned the keys of your car over to Winston White, isn't that right?
**A.** Yes.

**Q.** And the reason you did that was because you had too much to drink, isn't that right?
**A.** Yes.

I do not deny that the cross-examiner in the above example is making the point, but I suggest that the questioning could be rephrased for better effect. Try for more variety in your questioning. Try for more naturalness. One way is through the use of your voice. Inflection in your voice turns a statement into a question without the need for "Isn't that right?" Consider the following simple line of questioning:

| The Question Approach | The Statement Approach |
|---|---|
| You got up at 7:00, isn't that correct? | You got up at 7:00? |
| You then had a shower, correct? | You showered? |
| After that you had breakfast, didn't you? | You had breakfast? |
| You then got dressed, isn't that right? | You got dressed? |
| You walked to the train station, right? | You walked to the train station? |
| Didn't you then catch the 8:15 train into the city? | You caught the 8:15 train into the city? |

Return to the earlier cross-examination. The cross-examiner obviously knows the answer to certain of the above questions and so there are opportunities to use open-ended questions to effect. Let us try the cross-examination again:

**Q.** Now you left the dance at around 12:30, right?
**A.** Yes.

**Q.** And you'd been drinking at the dance?

**A.** Yes.

**Q.** In fact, you testified that you had four or five beer?
**A.** Yes.

**Q.** And when you left the dance you headed to your car?
**A.** Yes.

**Q.** And I take it that you drove your car? [*You know that this is not the case.*]
**A.** No.

**Q.** No. So who drove your car? [*You also know the answer to this question.*]
**A.** Winston White.

**Q.** And the reason Winston drove was because you had too much to drink, isn't that right?
**A.** Yes.

## 4.4    Principle 4: Know When to Stop

Illustrations of the "one question too many" are legion. My personal favourite comes from Irving Younger:[21]

The case is a criminal prosecution for atrocious assault or assault in the first degree. The theory of the prosecution is that the defendant and the victim got into a fight. In the course of the fight, the defendant got his teeth around the victim's nose and bit it off. Horrible, but it is possible. The teeth are very sharp, the jaws are the strongest voluntary muscle in the body and the nose is only cartilage. One can bite it off.

The prosecution rests upon the testimony of an eyewitness who testifies that it happened just that way. The defense lawyer cross-examines:

Question:  "Where were the defendant and the victim when the fight broke out?"
Answer:    "In the middle of a field."

Question:  "Where were you?"
Answer:    "On the edge of a field."

Question:  "What were you doing?"
Answer:    "Bird watching."

Question:  "Where were the birds?"

---

[21] Younger, *supra*, note 1, at p. 30.

Answer:    "In the trees."

Question:    "Where were the trees?"
Answer:    "On the edge of the field."

Question:    "Were you looking at the birds?"
Answer:    "Yes."

Question:    "So your back was to the people fighting?"
Answer:    "Yes."

Now what do you do? You stop and sit down. And what will you argue in summation? He could not have seen it. His back was to them. You have challenged the perception. Instead, you ask the one question too many:

Question:    "Well, if your back was to them, how can you say that the defendant bit off the victim's nose?"
Answer:    "Well, I saw him spit it out."

That is the kind of answer you will get every time you ask the one question too many.

Do not ask for an explanation where none is needed. Once you have obtained the admissions you require to make your argument — stop. The only explanation to be given is your explanation in closing. There is no need to allow the witnesses to explain their testimony. In particular, this is a cardinal rule when questioning occurrence witnesses, as was the case in the Younger example. Once their perception is discredited — stop.

## 4.5    Principle 5: Do Not Allow the Witness to Repeat the Direct

The hallmark of poorly prepared counsel executing poorly planned cross-examinations is that the counsel invites the witnesses to repeat their direct examination. I cringe when I hear counsel begin their cross-examination with:

**Q.** Mrs. Witness, where did you say you lived?
**A.** 654 Willow Street.

**Q.** How long have you lived there?
**A.** For some 16 years.

**Q.** Turning to the day of the accident, why were you going into the city?
**A.** As I've already said, I had to buy a birthday present for my daughter.

And so the cross-examination proceeds.

Counsel reviews the witness's background and the events leading up to the particular incident with little or no purpose or direction. The only result that flows from such a cross-examination is that the judge has now heard the witness's evidence for a second time and is not likely to forget it.

## 4.6    Principle 6: Do Not Quarrel with the Witness

Quarrelling with a witness is of the counsel's own making. In certain instances a deliberately provocative question is put to the witness in the full recognition that the witness will disagree:

> **Q.** Mr. Defendant, I put it to you that you were drunk when you got into your car to drive home that evening?

Your point here is not to get the admission, but to highlight your position, which is that the defendant was drunk that evening.

Most quarrels, however, are the result of ambiguous questions put by counsel. Given the ambiguity, the witness has room to manoeuvre and to challenge the question. Take the questioning in principle 3 on the alcohol consumed and suppose the following question was asked:

> **Q.** You were drinking heavily at the dance, weren't you?
> **A.** I wouldn't say heavily. I had my usual. I am not a heavy drinker.

The quibbling has begun. Why? Because you asked a vague question calling for the witness's agreement with your definition of "heavy" and the witness was not going to co-operate. There was no need for this quarrel. Whether the witness termed his drinking "heavy," "light" or "moderate" was of no import. The key fact was that the witness had consumed "four or five beer" and that is all you needed and that is what you should have asked. In your closing argument you can attach your own adjective to describe the drinking without fear of rebuke from the witness.

Quarrelling with the witness often arises when counsel want the witness to make their argument for them. For example, in a criminal prosecution for assault with weapon, the accused calls a friend who witnessed the altercation. Note the cross-examination below:

> **Q.** In direct you testified that the accused had a beer bottle in his hand, isn't that correct?
> **A.** Yes.

**Q**. In fact he had that bottle in his right hand, didn't he?
**A**. Yes.

**Q**. And he was holding the neck of the bottle, wasn't he?
**A**. Yes.

**Q**. And there is no mistake about this is there, he then hit Mr. Smith over the head with the bottle?
**A**. Yes.

**Q**. Mr. Smith had nothing in hands that you saw?
**A**. No.

**Q**. And it was the accused who walked towards Mr. Smith, isn't that right?
**A**. Yes.

**Q**. Mr. Smith never advanced towards the accused?
**A**. No, but he did turn to face him.

**Q**. Well, I put it to you that it was the accused who was the aggressor.

---

*[**NO**. This is going to invite an argument with the witness. You do not need the witness to make your argument for you. In closing you will say that based on the facts the accused was the aggressor. If you ask this type of question, don't look for the witness to make your argument.]*

---

**A**. No, you can't just look at the moment before the attack. Smith had pushed and threatened a number of us throughout the evening. He also had a pool cue leaning on the table beside him. At any moment I thought he was going to pick up that pool cue and swing it.

## 4.7    Principle 7: Plan Your Questions

The craft of cross-examination is to frame the questioning in such a way that the wary witness provides favourable testimony without truly appreciating that fact until it is too late to retract. This requires a careful cross-examination strategy. The frontal attack on a witness will be easily diverted. You must be subtle. You must be indirect. You must be ingenious. Remember, you argue by way of inference and all that you want from the witness is the necessary foundation of facts to support the inference that you will advance in final argument. You need not get the witness to confirm the inference — only the foundation of facts.

In an estate action, the closest surviving relatives of the testator contest the will of "Old Uncle Tom," who happened to give the bulk of his estate to an environmental group. The will is contested primarily on the ground of lack of testamentary capacity. The will was made by the testator in holograph form on 26th December 2014. A direct question, asked as such, will only result in a direct denial:

> **Q.** Uncle Tom appeared to know what he was doing when you last saw him on 25th December, isn't that right?
> **A.** No, I wouldn't say that. Uncle Tom was a very sick man at this time. His mind wasn't right.

Let us be subtle:

> **Q.** Mr. Nephew, Uncle Tom lived out on Concession Road 25, isn't that right?
> **A.** Yes.

> **Q.** And you tried to talk him into moving into town, didn't you?
> **A.** I sure did.

> **Q.** In fact you've been trying to get him to move for years?
> **A.** Yes.

> **Q.** But he wouldn't listen to you I take it?
> **A.** You're right.

> **Q.** He loved it out in the country, didn't he?
> **A.** Yes, he did.

---

[*Stop. You have your concession. He loved the country and wanted to preserve the countryside through support for the environmental group. His bequest to that group made perfect sense.*] . . .

---

> **Q.** Now I understand that on Christmas Day in 2014 you had a family gathering at your home, is that right?
> **A.** Yes.

> **Q.** And in the afternoon you and other family members played chess?
> **A.** Yes.

> **Q.** Do you play a great deal of chess, Mr. Nephew?
> **A.** Yes I do.

> **Q.** Would you agree with me that it is a game of considerable skill?

**A.** Yes I would.

**Q.** Who did you play with that afternoon?
**A.** Cousin Frank and Uncle Tom.

> [*Stop. You have achieved your limited purpose of showing that the day before writing the will Uncle Tom had the ability of mind to play chess, the inference being that Uncle Tom had the necessary capacity of mind to write a will the very next day.*]

Sequencing of questioning is an important art in cross-examination. A safe way is to sequence to a conclusion. You list facts through your questioning that lead to a conclusion. If your facts are compelling, the conclusion in some respects is really of no moment; you do not care whether the witness agrees with you or not. A riskier approach is to put the conclusion to the witness in order to invite a review of the contrary facts. This approach is riskier because the witness is in "disagreement mode" and may well be reluctant to admit any of the facts you summarize. The table below outlines the two approaches.

A police officer is on the stand in a theft case. Intoxication is a defence to theft. The officer in his report and testimony states that "the accused had been drinking, but was not intoxicated." Defence counsel challenge this position and suggest that their client was very intoxicated.

| Sequencing to a Conclusion | Sequencing from a Conclusion |
| --- | --- |
| Q. Officer, when you arrested Mr. Smith you smelled alcohol on his breath?<br>A. Yes. | Q. Officer, when you arrested Mr. Smith he was drunk, wasn't he?<br>A. No – he had been drinking, but I would not say he was drunk. |
| Q. As I understand it, he also slumped down leaning against your patrol car?<br>A. Yes, he rested against the car. | Q. So your position is he was not drunk?<br>A. Yes.<br>Q. Well, let's review the facts. You smelled alcohol on his breath?<br>A. Yes. |

*(cont'd)*

Q. And when he spoke to you he slurred some of his words?
A. Yes.

Q. When you drove him to the police station, he threw up in your car – didn't he?
A. Yes.

Q. When you got to the police station the first thing you did, according to your report, was to get him a cup of coffee?
A. Yes – he wanted a cup of coffee.

Q. Yes, and when you came back with the coffee he was asleep in the witness room, wasn't he?
A. He'd dozed off.

Q. Officer, Mr. Smith was sleeping it off, wasn't he?
A. I don't know why he fell asleep.

Q. Officer, he fell asleep because he was drunk, isn't that he case?
A. That is not my opinion.

Q. He slumped down, leaning against your patrol car?
A. Yes, he rested against the car.

Q. His speech was slurred?
A. At times, but not always.

Q. He threw up in your patrol car?
A. Yes, but that has happened before with people seated in the back seat.

Q. The first thing you did when you got to the police station was to get him a cup of coffee?
A. Yes – he wanted a cup of coffee.

Q. And when you returned to the witness room with the coffee he was asleep?
A. Yes – it was early in the morning and he'd dozed off.

Q. Officer, smell of alcohol, unsteady on one's feet, slurred speech, throwing up, need for coffee, need for sleep, are all indicia of intoxication, aren't they?
A. In some cases, yes.
Q. Well, officer I am going to put it to you again, Mr. Smith was drunk, wasn't he?
A. No, he was not.

## 4.8    Principle 8: Listen Carefully to the Witness

Do not rush your cross-examination. Listen to and digest the answers given by the witness. Has the witness really answered your question? If not, ask it again. Has the witness raised a new avenue for cross-examination? If so, pursue that line of inquiry. Do not, in other words, become preoccupied with worry about your next question. Listen to the answer before asking your next question. The basic principle is that you will learn far more by listening than by talking.

It is fundamentally important that you listen and ensure that the witness has actually answered your question. If your question is clear, and the witness should know the answer, then you should expect an answer and not allow the witness to evade.

> **Q.** You were pouring drinks for your guests?
> **A.** Yes I did pour some drinks.

> **Q.** You poured drinks for Mr. Jones, right?
> **A.** I poured drinks for a number of people.

*ASK THE QUESTION AGAIN.*

> **Q.** You poured drinks for Mr. Jones, right?
> **A.** There were a lot of people at the party.

*ASK THE QUESTION AGAIN. There is nothing wrong with the question. Do not re-phrase the question.*

> **Q.** Sir, I am going to ask the question again. You poured drinks for Mr. Jones, right?
> **A.** Yes I did.

*Another good retort when a witness is being evasive and gives a non-responsive answer is to say:*

> **Counsel:** I didn't ask you that. [*or*] I didn't ask you how many people were at the party.

*Then ask your question again:*

> **Q.** You poured drinks for Mr. Jones, right?

Do not fear silence in the courtroom. There is no requirement that your questions be rapid fire. In fact, your questions should be deliberately paced to allow the judge to fully digest their import. Listen and think before you ask your next question. Take your time.

### 4.9    Principle 9: Start Safe and Finish Strong

This principle recognizes the primacy of retention. We recall more at the start and at the end of an event, therefore it is important to start favourably and to end positively. By this I do not suggest that you immediately go after the witness. On the contrary, in cross-examination you strive for admissions first and impeachment can wait because, if you put the witness on the defensive from the start, gaining subsequent admissions will be all the more difficult. There are, of course, exceptions and in certain instances you may wish to establish control early. An excellent example of this was shown by John Sopinka, Q.C. (as he then was) in a demonstration at the Seventh Annual Advocacy Symposium. He was cross-examining an expert witness and his stated goal was:[22]

> I just want to get across to the jury that this expert has made some mistakes; that he has made some assumptions that aren't valid; and that they have reason to look with skepticism on his evidence. Then I call my own evidence to deal with the matter.

He began his cross-examination as follows:

> **Q.** You have made certain assumptions in your report, and you have been given certain background information on which to base those assumptions. Is that correct?
> **A.** Yes.
>
> **Q.** And you would agree that, to the extent that the information or the assumptions are wrong, your report is, to that extent, wrong?
> **A.** A change in the assumptions would change the figures in the report.
>
> **Q.** Do you have a quarrel with the word "wrong?" If your assumptions are wrong to that extent, your report is wrong. Is that correct?
> **A.** Yes.
>
> **Q.** Thank you. Now let's examine some of the assumptions . . .

The establishing of control is important with certain witnesses. In the above, it was important for John Sopinka to show that he was not going to permit any distracting quibbling. A simple question was asked and a simple answer was expected. Police officers, similarly, often need to be brought under rein. I observed a student do the following in a moot trial:

> **Q.** Mr. Police Officer, you rely on your notes. Is that correct?
> **A.** Yes I do.
>
> **Q.** Without your notes it would be difficult for you to recall the events surrounding a given incident. Is that not the case?

---

[22] Advocacy Symposium, *supra*, note 14, at pp. 33-34.

**A.** Yes.

**Q.** So, officer, you are concerned about keeping accurate notes?
**A.** That is correct.

**Q.** And it is important for you to accurately record the names and addresses of witnesses. Is that correct?
**A.** Yes.

**Q.** Officer, will you look at the top of page 2 of your notes. Officer would you tell the court how you spelled "Freda?"
**A.** I spelled it, F-R-I-E-D-A.

**Q.** That is wrong, isn't it officer?
**A.** Yes, it's wrong.

**Q.** And what address do you have down for Freda?
**A.** 2110 6th Street.

**Q.** What if I told you that the address for Freda is 2118 6th Street, your address for Freda would also be wrong, wouldn't it officer?
**A.** Yes.

The police officer's credibility was slightly marred, but, more importantly, the officer was shown that any inconsistency or inaccuracy would be pounced on by the counsel. The message: this was not a counsel to fool with.

Think about starting your cross-examination on a safe area, one where you know what the answers should be and can successfully exert control if necessary. The reason for choosing a safe beginning is that it helps to establish a tone of control on your part. By comparison, should you select a difficult area and struggle, witness confidence grows and they will be more difficult to control.

In ending the cross-examination, what you must avoid is the negative last impression. Give thought to a few final questions that will end the cross-examination on a positive note. Take this wonderful example from the suit, referred to before, that was brought against the defendant car manufacturer for the defective rear seat access to the trunk. In earlier evidence it was brought out that a safety device that could have prevented the accident could have been put in place for the cost of about $65. In the cross-examination of an executive with the defendant car manufacturer, plaintiff counsel concluded with the following:[23]

---

[23] *Ibid.*, at p. 80.

**Q.** Okay. Thank you. Now, by the way, do you have any children? I think you said you have two children.
**A.** Yes, I do.

**Q.** And I take it that you would be willing to spend $60 more for a car to make absolutely sure that those children were safe from any harm. Isn't that correct, sir? Is that a correct statement?
**A.** No, it is not.

**Q.** I have no further questions. Thank you.

The witness was in a no win situation. To reply "Yes" would mean that the company should have put the device in the car and passed the cost on to the consumer. Yet, to say "No" shows a cold, uncaring person, who places money over the safety of children. Regardless of the answer, a powerful ending is guaranteed.

## 4.10   Principle 10: Seize the Moment

The true art of cross-examination is not simply the asking of the right questions; the questions must also be asked in the right way. You want to impress upon the mind of the judge the few points that are the focus of your cross-examination, otherwise a damaging thrust can be wasted. You must seize the moment and by that I mean capture the attention of the presiding judge. One medium for doing so is through demonstrative evidence. Documents can be used in a similar fashion. In the case of *Waite v. Stewart* (Chapter 2), the defendant was very proficient at karate and you have the record of his extensive karate training (see the problem on direct examination) — use it:

**Q.** Mr. Stewart, you have some karate training. Is that correct?
**A.** Yes.

**Q.** And before March of 2015 you had been taking karate training for how long? [*An open-ended question deliberately asked to lure the witness into giving an incorrect answer.*]
**A.** Just two years.

**Q.** And you were pretty good at karate, weren't you? [*Also deliberately ambiguous to entice the witness to quibble.*]
**A.** I enjoyed the sport, but I don't know how good I was at it.

**Q.** Well, Mr. Stewart, let's look at your karate record. Could I have Exhibit 3 please. M'Lady I am referring to tab "F" in the document binder. Mr.

Stewart, take a look at this document, which was provided by the Karate Association. Is it an accurate record of your karate history?

**A.** Yes it is.

**Q.** So you started karate in September of 2012, some 2-$\frac{1}{2}$ years prior to March of 2015?

**A.** Yes.

**Q.** And in March of 2015 you had your Brown Belt Level 1?

**A.** Yes.

**Q.** And the only belt level higher than a brown belt is a black belt. Is that correct?

**A.** Yes.

**Q.** And on 24th February 2015 the record shows that you had participated in a karate tournament. Is that correct?

**A.** Yes.

**Q.** The record also shows that you placed third in a karate tournament in 2013 and second in a karate tournament in 2014. Is that not correct?

**A.** Yes.

What you have done is to keep the judge focused on the document, which highlights the defendant's extensive karate training.

The same effect is achieved through thoughtful questioning of a witness. Rather than going for the witness's jugular vein on a vulnerable point, why not extricate the damaging testimony in a slow and excruciating fashion so that the point lingers before the judge? Professor James Jeans poses the case of a 20-year-old defendant who is the driver of an automobile involved in a personal injury accident suit.[24] He has been driving for four years and has never had a licence. Now you could immediately confront the witness with this fact, but Professor Jeans suggests a more subtle approach:

**Q.** Mr. Jones, of course, at the time of the accident you did have a licence. Did you not?

**A.** No.

[*Pause*]

**Q.** Well, you have been driving for four years. Have you sir?

---

[24] J. Jeans, "Jeans on Trial Advocacy: Cross Examination," a videotape produced by the National Institute for Trial Advocacy (1980).

**A.** Yes.

**Q.** Did your licence expire?
**A.** No.

**Q.** Did you ever have a licence?
**A.** No. I never had a licence.

Your incredulity in hearing that a person has been driving for four years without a driver's licence would be shared by the judge.

"Lingering effect" is one approach, but the reverse is also equally effective. A devastating single question may be all that is required and will certainly be remembered by the judge. For example, in a criminal prosecution the accused raises an alibi. The Crown has presented three eyewitnesses and there is some circumstantial evidence linking the accused to the crime. The accused calls his mother to support his alibi. In cross-examination the prosecutor asks:

**Q.** The accused, seated there, is your son, isn't he?
**A.** Yes.

Nothing else needs to be said.

### 4.11    Putting It All Together

Keeping the principles of cross-examination in mind, you are now in a position to start drafting your cross-examination. Begin by listing your targets — what you hope to achieve from the witness. These targets provide your headings. Under each heading you then list the facts which go to "hit the target." These are the facts you anticipate eliciting from the witness. The facts are gleaned from the witness's statements. Carefully review these statements as they help to frame your cross-examination. The facts provide your questions. You tell the witness the facts you want. Cross reference the facts to the witness's statements. In this way, should the witness deny a fact, you are in a position to contradict or impeach the witness. Outlined below is a sample draft cross-examination.

## 5.    SAMPLE CROSS-EXAMINATION

The case is a simple shop-lifting, theft charge, which would be dealt with in Provincial Court. The item stolen is a one litre bottle of eye solution worth $30.00. You represent the accused, who has entered a plea of not guilty. You are to plan the cross-examination of the Crown's key, and probably only witness, the security officer.

## 5.1    Defence Case

The accused is a university student. He was looking for a particular brand of eye solution, which he thought was supposed to be on sale at the particular pharmacy. He went to the pharmacy's eye care area, which is quite large, and looked for the brand on sale. He must have placed the bottle in his open book bag, which held a number of his university texts, whilst he was looking. He went to the store cashier and asked about the brand. The cashier knew nothing about it. She checked the store flyer and did not find the brand on sale. He then left the store. Next he was confronted by the security officer. The officer asked him if he would come back into the store office. The accused accompanied the officer, having no idea what was wrong. In the office he was asked to empty out his bag and it was only at this time that he saw the bottle. He recalls saying, "I forgot all about that, I must have put the bottle in my bag as I was looking for my eye solution." The officer then told the accused that the police would be called. He continued to protest his innocence. The officer did not listen to the accused. The officer just said that it was "Store policy to see that all shoplifters were charged." The police were called.

## 5.2    Prosecution Case

The security guard provided the following report: the officer observed the accused in the store. Accused spent a number of minutes by the eye care area. The officer was suspicious because the accused was carrying an open bag. He was seen to put a bottle into the bag. The bottle was one litre of "Allergen Eye Solution" valued at $30.00. He remained in the eye care area for a few more minutes, went to the front cashier and then left the store without paying for the bottle of eye care solution. Once outside the store he was stopped and asked to return to the store office. The accused co-operated. The bag was emptied on to a table and the bottle was retrieved. The accused denied knowledge. The police were called.

## 5.3    Target

There is a tendency to immediately think of attacking the security officer. Yet, the security officer is simply doing his job. Rather than attacking him, consider how his evidence can help your case. Your theory is that the taking of the bottle was an innocent oversight. With this officer then the target is:

*To elicit evidence consistent with innocent taking.*

## 5.4    The Facts to Frame Your Questions

Your client's version of events is consistent with what the officer says happened. What you want to do is to re-interpret the events by putting forth your theory of the case. Consider the facts that are consistent with innocent taking:

*Facts consistent with client looking for something:*

The eye care area is large.

There are lots of different eye care products.

Your client was at that area for a long time.

Client looked at a number of different items.

*Facts inconsistent with intent to steal:*

He went to the cashier rather than directly leaving the store.

Item put in the bag was large, rather than a small item easy to hide.

Bag was left open.

Client was co-operative upon arrest.

*Client's theory of the case:*

What he told the officer, protesting his innocence.

Store policy to prosecute everyone.

## 5.5    Drafting Your Questions

The facts provide you with your questions. The questions may then be put in point form or written out in more detail.

| Point Form | Scripted |
|---|---|
| Been to store<br>Large eye care area | I have been to your store and it has quite a large eye care area doesn't it? |
| Half an aisle | In fact, there is half an aisle simply devoted to eye care products isn't there? |
| Lots of products | And in that half aisle there are lots of different eye care products? |

---

*Information is power. Telling the witness that you have been to the store puts the witness on notice that you are prepared.*

---

| | |
|---|---|
| Client spent time there | Sir, isn't it the case that Mr. Andrews spent virtually all his time at the eye care area? |
| Actual time — number of minutes | You testified that he stood there for four to five minutes? |
| Items off shelves | In that time he took a number of items off the shelves, didn't he? |
| Look at them | Yes, and he would look at them? |
| Put back | Then put them back? |
| At times items both hands | At times he might have one item in one hand and one in the other? |
| Obvious, looking for something | Sir, it is obvious he was looking for something? |

*The last question calls for an opinion from the witness. But note the sequencing of the questions. The earlier factual questions point to this conclusion. This conclusion is also your theory of the case, which you are putting to the judge. Keep in mind, however, that this question or opinion is not necessary. You have the facts to put this conclusion to the judge in closing argument.*

| | |
|---|---|
| Bottle in bag | It was during this time that you saw Mr. Andrews put the bottle in his bag, correct? |
| Remained in area | It is also correct that after putting bottle in bag, Mr. Andrews remained in the eye care area for a time? |
| Continued to look | During that time he continued to look at various items? |
| Not directly leave store | Now after leaving the eye care area he did not directly leave the store, did he? |
| Went to cashier | He went to the cashier? |
| No purchases | And as far as you know he never purchased any items? |
| No need for him to go to cashier | Then there was actually no need for him to go to the cashier? |
| Spoke with | In fact he spoke with the cashier for a time? |
| Never spoke with cashier | You never spoke with the cashier about what he talked to her about? |
| After speaking left | After speaking with the cashier Mr. Andrews then left the store? |
| Bottle large | Now the bottle of eye solution found in his bag is large, isn't it? |

*(cont'd)*

| | |
|---|---|
| In bag open | And when Mr. Andrews emptied his bag in the office, the bag was open at that time? |
| Never closed | So after Mr. Andrews put the bottle in his bag, he never closed it? |
| Other items | There were also other items in the bag? |
| Books | Specifically there were a number of books, weren't there? |
| Stopped co-operative | When you stopped him outside the store he was co-operative? |
| Never ran | He never tried to run away, did he? |
| Never baulked | In fact, he never baulked at all about going with you to the store office? |
| "I forgot all about that bottle..." | Once the bag was emptied, Sir, did he not say, "I forgot all about that bottle in my bag as I was looking for my eye solution." |
| Protested innocence | In fact, whilst in the office he continued to protest his innocence, didn't he? |
| Nothing you could do | But there was nothing you could do, right? |
| Store policy | Your store policy is simply if a person leaves the store without paying for an item the police are called, right? |
| Prosecute all | Prosecute all shoplifters? |
| Why here today | And that, Sir, is why we are here today? |

*Note that all of the above questions were leading. The security officer was told what to say. What he was told to say came from his statement and what your client told you. The approach is non-confrontational, but you have highlighted the evidence that is consistent with innocent taking.*

## 6.   PROBLEM

1.   Prepare and conduct a cross-examination of **Richard Waite**. Refer to:

**Chapter 2** for a summary of the issues.

**Waite's Direct Examination** contained at the end of Chapter 11.

**Stewart's Evidence** found in Problem 1 (Chapter 12).

# 14

# IMPEACHMENT

Wigmore, in his treatise on evidence, likened impeachment to explanation:[1]

> In short, the whole process of impeachment or discrediting of a witness, as known to practitioners, is nothing but *the general logical process of explanation*. So, too, the process of corroboration or support of a witness is the logical process of closing up the possible avenues of explanation, and thus making the proposed inference more and more necessary and unavoidable.

The witness has made an assertion and in cross-examination you seek to adduce evidence that will assist you to *explain away* that assertion.

---

[1] 3A Wigmore, *Evidence*, Chadbourn rev. (1970), para. 874, at pp. 636-637.

You explain away the evidence of a witness either by attacking the *integrity of the witness* or by attacking the *integrity of the testimony* or both. These are distinct targets. An attack upon the integrity of a witness is a personal attack. You put into issue the character of the witness in that you are challenging the witness's veracity or impartiality. You adduce evidence of bias, interest, corruption, prejudice, prior convictions, prior bad acts (if admissible) and reputation as to veracity. At the end of the day, you argue that *the witness* is not credible.

In contrast, an attack on the integrity of the testimony is more impersonal. You challenge the capacity of the witness to observe, recall or communicate accurately. You allege not that the witness is a liar or biased but that the witness is mistaken.

Wigmore's substitution of "explanation" for "impeachment" is useful because what you are seeking to do in your cross-examination is to obtain evidence to support your explanation in closing. Far too often counsel put the explanation to the witness, for the witness's response:

> **Q.** Officer Smith, you left so many things out of your report, how is it possible to trust the accuracy of your recollection?

> *or*

> **Q.** You have a real interest in seeing the defendant win this case, perhaps enough of an interest to twist the facts in the defendant's favour?

Do not expect the witnesses to agree with your explanation. They will resist:

> **A.** Unimportant matters I left out. But I recorded the important facts. The most important fact being that your client told me that he killed that girl!

> *or*

> **A.** If the defendant wins this case, my company may make more money. But that has nothing to do with what I've said today. You wanted the truth and you got it. I don't "twist" facts for anyone — including you.

Putting your explanation to the witness is not necessary. You have obtained the needed evidence to support your inference and there is little to be gained, other than an argument, by putting your explanation to the witness. Save your explanation for the judge:

> My Lord, I would submit that the evidence brings into question the credibility of Mr. Smith . . .

## 1.   THE RULE IN *BROWNE v. DUNN*

However, having said this, if you intend to contradict the testimony of
a witness, you must give the witness an opportunity in cross-examination
to explain the contradiction. You must confront the witness with your
contradictory evidence. This rule was laid down by the House of Lords in
*Browne v. Dunn*, where Lord Herschell stated:[2]

> Now, my Lords, I cannot help saying that it seems to me to be absolutely
> essential to the proper conduct of a cause, where it is intended to suggest that
> a witness is not speaking the truth on a particular point, to direct his attention
> to the fact by some questions put in cross-examination showing that that
> imputation is intended to be made, and not to take his evidence and pass it by
> as a matter altogether unchallenged, and then, when it is impossible for him
> to explain, as perhaps he might have been able to do if such questions had
> been put to him, the circumstances which it is suggested indicate that the story
> he tells ought not to be believed, to argue that he is a witness unworthy of
> credit. My Lords, I have always understood that if you intend to impeach a
> witness you are bound, whilst he is in the box, to give him an opportunity of
> making any explanation which is open to him; and, as it seems to me, that is
> not only a rule of professional practice in the conduct of a case, but is essential
> to fair play and fair dealing with witnesses.

The case of *R. v. K. (O.G.)* provides a good example of the rule at
work.[3] The accused was charged with two counts of sexual assault. The
accused said the complainant consented to the sexual acts. The complainant
said "no consent." In cross-examination of the complainant, defence counsel
never put the accused's version of events to her. The trial judge found this
to be most unfair. Southin J.A. agreed and succinctly stated the law as
follows:

> It is not fair to a witness to adduce evidence which casts doubt upon his
> veracity when he has not been given an opportunity to deal with that evidence.[4]

What flows from this unfairness? In *Browne v. Dunn*, the Court ruled
that the plaintiff, having failed to cross-examine the witnesses on a critical
area, was barred from urging the jury to disbelieve their evidence and that
the jury was now obliged to accept their testimony. This is not to say that
in every case where there is a failure to confront, counsel is precluded from
challenging the testimony, or that the unimpeached witness's evidence is

---

[2] *Browne v. Dunn* (1893), 6 R. 67 at 70-71 (H.L.).
[3] *R. v. K. (O.G.)* (1994), 28 C.R. (4th) 129 (B.C. C.A.).
[4] *Ibid.*, at p. 135.

to be accepted. This may occur, but the rule is not so absolute.[5] There is no prescribed consequence as a matter of law. Certainly the trial judge may weigh the failure to cross-examine against the cross-examining party, but is not obliged to do so.[6] The effect of the failure depends on the circumstances of each case. In certain instances, the failure may be remedied by recalling the witness and having the contradiction put to her. Justice Moldaver in *R. v. McNeill* suggests that recalling of the witness is the first option to explore.[7] Furthermore, the rule does not go so far as to preclude the calling of contrary evidence. But keep in mind that, under sections 10 and 11 of the *Canada Evidence Act* and the provincial equivalents, before being allowed to contradict a witness by introducing prior inconsistent statements, counsel must lay a proper foundation, which includes confronting the witness in cross-examination with the making of the inconsistent statements.

You may confront the witness directly:

**Q.** I put to you . . .

**Q.** I suggest . . .

You do not expect the witness to agree with your "suggestions," but that is not the purpose of the questions. You are confronting the witness with your contrary position and at the same time you are highlighting your case for the judge. Or, you may confront the witness indirectly:

**Q.** Earlier you said that you saw Mr. Williams strike the deceased over the head with *what appeared* to be a baseball bat?
**A.** Yes.

**Q.** You weren't certain it was a baseball bat?
**A.** No.

**Q.** It could have been a piece of lumber?
**A.** Yes.

**Q.** It could have been a metal bar?
**A.** I guess so.

**Q.** The fight between the deceased and the other man occurred on the north side of the parking lot — right?
**A.** Yes.

---

[5] *Penney v. Manitoba Public Insurance Corp.* (1992), 81 Man. R. (2d) 145 (C.A.).
[6] See *R. v. K. (O.G.)*, *supra*, note 3.
[7] *R. v. McNeill* (2000), 144 C.C.C. (3d) 551 (Ont. C.A.). This case provides an excellent review of the law on the rule.

**Q.** And you were standing near the south end of the parking lot?
**A.** Yes.

**Q.** According to the diagram, which is to scale, that would put you some 50 metres away from the fight. Are my calculations correct?
**A.** Yes.

**Q.** There are trees that fringe the north side of the parking lot, are there not?
**A.** Yes.

**Q.** And there are no lights in the parking lot?
**A.** There are no lights.

**Q.** The fight occurred at approximately 1:00 a.m. in the morning?
**A.** Yes.

**Q.** So it was dark?
**A.** Yes.

**Q.** Yet, you say that you saw Mr. William's face from where you were?
**A.** Yes.

**Q.** Now two other people were standing with you, Susan Brown and Tom White?
**A.** Yes.

**Q.** They were right beside you?
**A.** Yes.

[*You will be calling Susan Brown and Tom White, who both were unable to make out the face of the attacker from where they were standing.*]

Do not overwork the rule. It is not necessary for you to go over every single detail to be contradicted. The rule is intended to deal with unfairness arising from failure to cross-examine on important issues.[8]

## 2.   THE COLLATERAL FACT RULE

Wide leeway is given to the *questioning* in cross-examination. Counsel are allowed to explore matters directly related to the issues before the court, primary relevancy, and to probe areas affecting the credibility of witnesses, secondary relevancy. However, in general, when a cross-examiner asks a question purely going to credibility the witness's *answer* is *final*. This is the

---

[8]   *R. v. Johnson*, 2010 ONCA 646 (Ont. C.A.) at para. 79.

collateral fact rule — *you will not be permitted to contradict a witness on a collateral matter.* The reasons behind the rule are based on policy:[9]

> (1) There is a reason of unfair surprise; one might contrive and charge upon the witness an error of any kind, time, or place, and it would obviously be unfair to expect him to be prepared to refute it, except so far as it bears directly upon the matter in litigation . . . (2) There is a reason of confusion of issues; for the necessity of investigating each error alleged would add to the trial so much consumption of time and confusion of issues as to be intolerable.

Let us take the example of an eyewitness to a motor vehicle accident. She was standing on the corner waiting to cross when the accident occurred. She has testified that she had just left a bank and was walking to her car. You have evidence that she had just left a department store:

> **Q.** You're certain that you had just left the bank?
> **A.** Yes.

Now, the fact that she was mistaken about the bank may imply that she does not remember well what occurred that day; there is some probative value to the inconsistency. But consider the court time. You would have to call the department store salesperson, but to what purpose? Is the inconsistency that important? No. However, what if you have evidence that the witness had just left a local tavern and you have witnesses who will testify that she was drinking all day?

> **Q.** You weren't at Charlie's Bar?
> **A.** No.
>
> **Q.** You weren't drinking there that afternoon?
> **A.** No.

Should you be left with those denials? No. Intoxication goes directly to the witness's testimonial powers and directly to the issue of what really occurred. This evidence should be considered by the judge.

The difficulty with the collateral fact rule is in application and in deciding what is or is not a collateral fact. The leading case is *A.G. v. Hitchcock*, where Pollock C.B. outlined the following test:[10]

> [I]f the answer of a witness is a matter which you would be allowed on your part to prove in evidence — if it has such a connection with the issue, that you

---

[9]  Wigmore, *supra*, note 1, at para. 1002, pp. 960-961.
[10]  *A.G. v. Hitchcock* (1947), 154 ER 38 at 42 (Ex Ch).

would be allowed to give it in evidence — then it is a matter on which you may contradict him.

*Hitchcock* has spawned two different approaches to collateral facts. Wigmore rephrased the test from Hitchcock as follows: "Could the fact, as to which error is predicated, have been shown in evidence for any purpose independently of the contradiction?"[11] In other words, if the only basis for presenting the evidence is that it contradicts the opponent's witness, it is inadmissible, but if it assists the trier of fact in some other way, it is admissible. This assistance includes facts relevant to a material issue and facts that go to discredit a witness's credibility. If we return to our example of the eyewitness to the accident, the evidence of drinking goes to impeach the witness's ability to have perceived the incident accurately. Under this test, the evidence has "independent" relevance beyond proving that the witness lied or was mistaken about his drinking.

The second approach, illustrated in Phipson's text on evidence, is more restrictive.[12] It prohibits proof of contradiction going to credibility. Proof may only be given on matters relevant directly to the substantive issues in the case. Under the Phipson approach, evidence about the credibility of a witness is collateral, and a party cannot call evidence to contradict a witness on a collateral matter unless it fits within one of several stated exceptions. These include proof of (1) bias, interest, or corruption; (2) previous convictions; (3) evidence of reputation for untruthfulness; or (4) expert evidence on problems that could affect the reliability of the witness's evidence.

The difficulty with the Phipson approach is that it invites the "pigeon-holing" of evidence and, if rigidly applied, excludes valuable evidence going to credibility.

In deciding on what collateral test to apply, I suggest we turn to first principles. The collateral facts rule is not based on lack of relevancy or probative value, otherwise the questions asked would not be allowed. Allowing proof on collateral matters is excluded because it may confuse the trier of fact by engaging distracting side issues, take up too much valuable court time, or unfairly surprise a witness, who is not prepared to answer questions on "collateral" matters. Where the evidence sought to be admitted has sufficient value, or the competing concerns are absent, the evidence is not collateral. The generally recognized "exceptions" illustrate the point. Bias, interest, and corruption all go directly to the witness's credibility and are important in assessing the witness's evidence. Physical or mental defects

---

[11] Wigmore, *Evidence in Trials at Common Law*, Vol. 3A, para. 1003.
[12] *Phipson on Evidence*, 15th ed. (London, 2000) at para. 12-33.

that go to the witness's reliability are important. The witness's reputation for truthfulness goes to the heart of the witness's evidence. The exception for prior convictions may have less relevance, but there is ease of proof; all that a party need do is file the certificate of conviction.

Categorizing is not the correct approach. Instead of looking at the "type" of relevancy of the offered evidence, we need to look at the value of the evidence. The key question ought to be: Is the evidence offered of sufficient value and of sufficient importance to the issues before the court that we ought to hear it having regard to the necessary court time required, potential confusion of issues, and any unfairness and prejudice to the witness?[13]

Wigmore made this exact point many years ago:[14]

> In general, the exclusionary rule is too strictly enforced. "Everything," said Lord Denman, "is material that affects the credit of the witness." The discretion of the trial court should be left to control. It is a mistake to lay down any fixed rule which will prevent him from permitting such testimony as may expose a false witness. History has shown, and every day's trials illustrate, that not infrequently it is in minor details alone that the false witness is vulnerable and his exposure is feasible.

I think that the most honest comment about collateral facts was made by Irving Younger, who concluded:[15]

> The real question is, when will it be collateral, and when will it not be collateral? The answer is simple: when it is important, it is not collateral. When it is unimportant, it is collateral. Ten thousand cases add up to that.

The role of counsel is to convince the judge of the importance of the evidence sought to be introduced in contradiction.

## 3.    LIMITS ON CROSS-EXAMINATION

It is important to note that the collateral fact rule limits the calling of evidence. The rule is not intended to limit the asking of questions in cross-

---

[13] For a more detailed discussion of collateral facts see D. Paciocco and L. Stuesser, *Essentials of Canadian Law: The Law of Evidence*, 7th ed. (2015) at pp. 475-480.

[14] *Wigmore on Evidence, supra,* note 1, at para.1005.

[15] I. Younger, The Art of Cross-Examination, Proceedings of a speech at the American Bar Association's Annual Meeting in Montreal, Canada, 12th August 1975, American Bar Association (1976), at p. 15.

examination. In fact, the rule contemplates that counsel may cross-examine a witness with respect to collateral matters.

The general rule is that a cross-examiner is given wide latitude in the asking of questions, but this does not mean that counsel have unbridled licence to cast imputations or suggest unproven facts. There are a number of controls on the cross-examiner.

*First*, any question asked must be relevant. No counsel has a right to ask irrelevant questions.

*Second*, questions should not be put whose prejudicial effect outweigh their probative value. This is most likely to arise in criminal prosecutions when an unsavory accused takes the stand and the Crown cross-examines as to character, should that door be opened. For example, in *R. v. W.C.*, the accused was on trial for sexual abuse of a little girl. He took the stand and the Crown in cross-examination suggested that he was a Satanist and that members of that cult practiced child abuse as part of their religion. Such an examination was found to be both improper and highly prejudicial to the accused.[16]

*Third*, counsel are officers of the court and are obliged to conduct their cross-examinations in a professionally responsible manner. It is unprofessional to needlessly abuse, hector or harass a witness.[17]

*Fourth*, the cross-examiner must have a "good faith basis" before putting an allegation or suggestion to a witness. The Supreme Court of Canada in *R. v. Lyttle* explained that:[18]

"A good faith basis" is a function of the information available to the cross-examiner, his or her belief in its likely accuracy, and the purpose for which it is used. Information falling short of admissible evidence may be put to the witness. In fact, the information may be incomplete or uncertain, provided the cross-examiner does not put suggestions to the witness recklessly or that he or she knows to be false.

Does the cross-examiner need to adduce evidence to support the suggestions made? No. In *Lyttle*, the Supreme Court of Canada held that questions may be put to a witness in cross-examination regarding matters that

---

[16] *R. v. W.C.* (1990), 54 C.C.C. (3d) 37 (Ont. C.A.).
[17] See e.g. Law Society of Upper Canada, *Rules of Professional* Conduct (2014), S. 5.1-2.
[18] *R. v. Lyttle* (2004), 180 C.C.C. (3d) 476 (S.C.C.).

need not be proved independently. The Court noted that it is not uncommon for counsel to believe that something is true, without being able to prove that it is so.[19] All that is needed is a "good faith basis" for the question.

Our law, therefore, is in accord with the English practice, where Lord Radcliffe summarized the law as follows:[20]

> An advocate is entitled to use his discretion as to whether to put questions in the course of cross-examination which are based on material which he is not in a position to prove directly. The penalty is that, if he gets a denial or some answer that does not suit him, the answer stands against him for what it is worth.

### 3.1    Limits on Crown Counsel

Justice Cory in *R. v. Logiacco* referred to the "great trust" placed in the Crown prosecutor by the courts and by the public. In Justice Cory's words, the Crown prosecutor "must be a symbol of fairness."[21] In the heat of trial, it can be difficult to temper one's zeal. Professionalism gives way to emotion and Crown excesses lead to reversible error. Restraint is especially required in the cross-examinations and certain lines of questions are simply not permitted.

It is improper to ask the accused about the veracity of Crown witnesses. This line of questioning can take a variety of forms:

*   Why would she lie?

*   What reason would she have to accuse you?

*   What motive does she have to make this up?

"Questions of this nature suggest that there is some onus on an accused to provide a motive for the Crown witness's testimony and, as such, they undermine the presumption of innocence."[22]

It is improper to engage in a personal attack on the accused. This may be done directly or indirectly; neither are proper. It is wrong to directly call

---

[19]  *Ibid.*, at para. 47.
[20]  *Fox v. General Medical Council*, [1960] 1 W.L.R. 1017 at p. 1023 (P.C.).
[21]  See *R. v. Logiacco* (1984), 11 C.C.C. (3d) 374 at 379 (Ont. C.A.).
[22]  *R. v. Rose* (2001), 153 C.C.C. (3d) 225 at para. 27 (Ont. C.A.). See also *R. v. Kusk* (1999), 132 C.C.C. (3d) 559 (Alta. C.A.).

the accused a liar.[23] It is equally inappropriate to use ridicule, sarcasm or derision to challenge the accused.

It is improper to question an accused on inadmissible matters. For example, asking an accused whether they made any explanation to the police violates an accused's right to remain silent.[24] Another common wrong arises when an accused puts his or her character into issue. In response, the Crown may cross-examine the accused on his or her bad character. The objective is to neutralize the accused's evidence of good character – not to "nuke him." Unfortunately, too often Crown counsel go overboard and character attack becomes character assassination. Such is unacceptable.[25]

The bottom line is this: Crown counsel must always take the high road. This does not mean that they cannot be tough and vigorous in cross-examination. What it does mean is that they must respect the trial process and the ingrained concern we have to ensure that the accused receives a fair trial.

## 4.   METHODS OF IMPEACHMENT

Leaving aside an attack on the integrity of the witness in terms of veracity or impartiality, there are three ways of impeaching the *testimony* of a witness:

1)   by contradicting the witness's testimony with the testimony of other witnesses or other evidence

2)   by showing that the witness's assertions are contrary to common experience and

3)   by showing that the witness has made prior inconsistent statements.

### 4.1   Using Other Witnesses: "External Inconsistency"

Counsel are preoccupied with "internal" inconsistencies made by the witness. The witness says one thing in direct examination and has said something else in an earlier statement. But not all witnesses will contradict themselves in any meaningful way. Counsel must look for "external" inconsistencies as well, that is, look for inconsistencies between what the

---

[23]   *R. v. Bouhsass* (2002), 169 C.C.C. (3d) 444 (Ont. C.A.).

[24]   *R. v. Wojcik* (2002), 166 Man. R. (2d) 55 (C.A.).

[25]   See *R. v. M.M.* (1995), 102 Man. R. (2d) 312 (C.A.).

witness says and other evidence. In so doing, you will not need to elicit concessions or contradictions from the witness; rather, the witness's testimony will speak for itself. The witness's assertions, which you will show are contradicted by other evidence, are all that you need.

Use one witness against another. The plaintiff says "X" and you have three witnesses who will say "Y." Let the plaintiff say "X," even let the plaintiff commit to "X," because you have the evidence to contradict, to explain away, the plaintiff's testimony. Better yet, let the plaintiff say "X" and you use one of the plaintiff's *own* witnesses to say "Y."

Let us turn to the cross-examination of Richard Waite, our plaintiff kick victim. In direct examination he comes across as a calm, mild-mannered, mature individual, who was seriously injured by a karate expert. You wish to establish in cross-examination that Waite was anything but "calm and mild-mannered" on the evening of the fight — he was angry. Waite will probably deny that fact:

**Q.** So when you left the ice you were angry?
**A.** No. I was a little shaken, but I was not angry.

You have achieved little, but you do have his assertion, "I was not angry." You also have the police statement made by a witness yet to be called by the plaintiff. In the police statement, the witness stated that she saw Waite leave the ice:

Richard left the game. I went down to see if he was all right. He was really hot. He wanted to talk to the guy who had high-sticked him. I suggested that he just forget it, but Richard was adamant.

You will be given an opportunity to contradict Waite through the testimony of his *own* witness.

Waite goes on in his direct examination to deny slapping or pushing Stewart:

**Q.** You say that you never slapped Mr. Stewart?
**A.** That's right.

**Q.** You say that you never pushed Mr. Stewart?
**A.** That's right.

**Q.** You never did these things?
**A.** No.

Mr. Stewart will testify differently and so too will an "independent" occurrence witness, whom you will call. Waite will be contradicted and your client's version of events will be corroborated. Thus, in closing, you have your ammunition to suggest that the testimony of your client is to be preferred, at least on these material areas, to that of Mr. Waite, and you have also cast a shadow over the credibility of Mr. Waite's entire testimony.

## 4.2    Offending Common Sense

In the above example, I used certain inferences. Parties to an action have an interest in the proceedings; they will tend to perceive facts in a way most favourable to their case. In contrast, an "independent" witness has no interest in a case; there is no reason for this witness to distort the evidence. Therefore, where there is a disagreement between the evidence of the parties, we are inclined to accept "as fact" the evidence confirmed by the "independent" witness. This is common sense.

In some cases, the testimony of the witness will offend our sense of "common experience" without the need for any "internal" or "external" contradiction. The witness is simply asking the court to accept an unacceptable inference. For example, refer to the case of the eyewitness, who, although she could not see what the man was holding in his hand, saw the man's face from a distance of 50 metres, looking across an unlit parking lot in the middle of the night. Given these circumstances, her identification is difficult to accept. The fact that you will call the two people standing right beside her to testify that they could not see the man's face confirms our own suspicions about her testimony.

Another example is taken from *Constitution Ins. Co. of Can. v. Kosmopoulos*, an important insurance law case.[26] Mr. Kosmopoulos owned a leather goods store. The store burned down. Mr. Kosmopoulos filed a claim for loss with his insurer. The insurer denied liability under the insurance policy and also challenged Mr. Kosmopoulos' claim for damage to his stock of leather goods. At trial the insurer called an expert on fire investigation and damage assessment. The expert questioned Mr. Kosmopoulos' claim for smoke and water damage to the leather goods. In cross-examination it was brought out that the expert had never visited the fire scene, had never conducted any tests on the leather goods to determine the extent of the smoke or water damage and had never actually seen the goods. The expert's conclusion was based upon his review of photographs taken of the fire

---

[26] *Constitution Ins. Co. of Can. v. Kosmopoulos* (1987), 34 D.L.R. (4th) 208 (S.C.C.).

scene. The expert told the court, presumably with a straight face, that by looking at the photographs he could determine the extent of smoke and water damage to the leather goods. Obviously, the photographs were no substitute for a physical inspection of the goods. At the end of the day, Mr. Kosmopoulos won his claim for loss of stock.[27]

## 4.3    Prior Inconsistent Statements

What is the value in showing that a witness has made inconsistent statements? Wigmore, in his treatise on evidence, provides this cogent summary:[28]

> The end aimed at by the present sort of impeaching evidence is the same as that of the preceding sort, namely, to show the witness to be in general *capable of making errors* in his testimony; for upon perceiving that the witness has made an erroneous statement upon one point, we are ready to infer that he is capable of making an error upon other points . . . Two important features of this method of proof are to be noticed.

> (1) The general *end attained* is the same indefinite end attained by the preceding method [contradiction by other evidence], i.e., some *undefined capacity to err*; it may be a moral disposition to lie, it may be partisan bias, it may be faulty observation, it may be defective recollection, or any other quality. No specific defect is indicated; but each and all are hinted at . . .

> (2) The *process of using* a self-contradiction to show error is in one respect weaker, in another respect stronger, than the preceding process of using contradiction by other witnesses. It is *weaker*, in that the proof of the specific error can never be as *positive* as is possible by the other mode. For example, if five credible witnesses testify that the assailant had a scar upon his face, contradicting the first witness, a belief in his present error is more readily reached than if a single former contradictory statement of his own is brought forward; in the latter case we are by no means compelled to believe that his statement on the stand is erroneous. On the other hand, in the present mode, the process of discrediting is in its chief aim incomparably *stronger*, because it *always* shows that the witness has made *some sort of a mistake* at some time, and thus demonstrates a capacity to make errors.

Under traditional common law, prior inconsistent statements made by a witness went to credibility only and were not evidence of the truth of the

---

[27] Taken from the transcript of the trial heard before Mr. Justice R.E. Holland on 20th-22nd October 1981. The cross-examination was conducted by W.P. Somers, Q.C.

[28] Wigmore, *supra*, note 1, at para. 1017, pp. 993-994.

facts contained in the statement. The prior inconsistency was used simply to weaken the witness's in-court testimony. Before you could use the out-of-court inconsistent statement for its truth you had to get the witness to adopt or accept the prior statement as true. Note, such adoption was not necessary when a party or an accused was the witness because in these situations the statement was admissible as an admission.

The Supreme Court of Canada, in *R. v. B. (K.G.)* [referred to as *K.G.B.*], reformed the law to allow for the admissibility of prior inconsistent statements for their truth without acceptance or adoption by the witness.[29] The Court, however, imposed rather rigorous criteria before admitting such statements:[30]

- the statement is made under oath or solemn affirmation following a warning as to the existence of sanctions and the significance of the oath or affirmation;

- the statement is videotaped in its entirety; and

- the opposing party has a full opportunity to cross-examine the witness respecting the statement.

The Supreme Court crafted a very narrow exception, but Chief Justice Lamer, writing for the majority, did state that if the requirements could not be met, one could look to other circumstantial guarantees of trustworthiness. As a substitute for videotaping, the example was given of the testimony of an independent third party who observed the making of the statement in its entirety. Thus, there is some room for flexibility.[31]

## 5.   THE PROCEDURE IN USING PRIOR INCONSISTENT STATEMENTS

There are four steps that counsel must become familiar and at ease with in the impeachment of a witness by way of prior inconsistent statements. These four steps are:

1)   *Confirm* the present inconsistent testimony.

---

[29] *R. v. B. (K.G.)* (1993), 19 C.R. (4th) 1 (S.C.C.).
[30] For a detailed discussion of a "*K.G.B.* application," see Chapter 16.
[31] An example of flexibility is found in *R. v. U. (F.J.)* (1995), 101 C.C.C. (3d) 97 (S.C.C.).

2)  *Confront* the witness with the making of a prior statement.

3)  *Contradict* the present testimony with the prior inconsistent statement, and

4)  *Commit* the witness to the prior statement (if you desire that adoption).

## 5.1   Confirm

What you wish to achieve in this step is to have the witness confirm the present testimony, so that what is testified to is *clear*. First, you want to remove ambiguity and close possible avenues of explanation:

**A.** Oh, I didn't mean to say that; *or*

**A.** I didn't understand your question; *or*

**A.** You misunderstood my answer, this is what I said.

Second, you want to highlight any contradiction so that when you read out the contradiction it stands out vividly.

Now impeachment takes tact. You do not want to "red flag" to the witness the contradiction and thereby give warning of the trap. What I recommend first is that you get the witness to confirm the testimony in an innocuous manner. Once the witness has taken the hook, then you set the hook firmly:

**Q.** Mr. Waite, in direct examination you stated that you left the ice after being cut — right?
**A.** Yes.

**Q.** And you also said that at this time you were not angry?
**A.** That is correct.

**Q.** So even after being high-sticked and cut you say that you were not angry?
[*Obviously, the answer to this question cannot hurt you. If the witness retracts his prior statement, you have a valuable admission and if the witness confirms his above statement you have the impeachment set.*]
**A.** I wasn't angry.

When you go on to show that Waite, in an earlier statement, had said he was "angry" the contradiction will be enhanced. True, it can be said that in so doing you are enhancing the in-court testimony by repeating it. But often you must build the testimony up before you can effectively knock it down. Your impeachment will go for nought if the contradiction is not clear to the judge.

It follows that for a contradiction to be important the testimony that is contradicted must also be important. Save your impeachment ammunition. To impeach a witness on trivial points is a waste of court time and has minimal persuasive value. Common experience indicates that people make mistakes. In general, only impeach on minor inconsistencies when they *cumulatively* go to discredit the witness. In the majority of cases you will have far greater impact by revealing a few really serious inconsistencies. An exception to this advice is the category of witnesses whom we expect to be exact and accurate: police officers, investigators and expert witnesses. These witnesses are trained to be thorough and precise and their minor inconsistencies take on increased importance. A careful police officer, investigator or expert would not have made these mistakes.

## 5.2   Confront

At this stage, fairness demands that you put to the witness the circumstances surrounding the making of the prior inconsistent statement. Witnesses must be given an opportunity to address their minds to the time and place of the making of statements. At this stage there is no need to show the witness the statement, unless you so wish, as a part of your description of the circumstances. Further, if you intend to ask the witness to accept the prior statement as true, then you must also turn your mind to enhancing the circumstances surrounding the making of the statement. You may have the witness confirm that:

- At the time of the making of the earlier statement, the events were fresher in the witness's mind.

- At the time of the making of the statement, the witness knew of the importance of the statement, wanting it to be truthful, and accurate.

- At the time of the making of the statement, the witness was under oath.

You are now in a position to contradict the witness with the prior inconsistent statement.

## 5.3   Contradict

The prior inconsistent statement is then put to the witness in verbatim form. Do not give the witness or opposing counsel an opportunity to accuse you of misstating what was said. I recommend that counsel read the prior inconsistent statement. Others disagree and feel that it is more effective to hear the contradiction from the lips of the witness. My view is that by having counsel read the prior inconsistent statement it will be done slowly and clearly, whereas the witness will read without emphasis, quickly and often quietly. I leave the actual approach to you. Just as with steps 1 and 2, think about the most effective way to enhance the contradiction. One suggestion is to ask the very question that was put to the witness in the previous proceeding. The same question was asked and a different answer was given — the contrast is clear.

Should the witness deny or not remember the making of the statement, then you will have to call evidence in your case to prove the making of the statement. Such a course of action is not usually necessary. Simply remind the witness of the futility of such quibbling:

> **Q.** You were asked that question and gave that answer at the examination for discovery?
> **A.** I don't really remember saying that.
>
> **Q.** Let me show you the transcript [*shows witness the transcript*].
> **A.** Well, that's what it says.
>
> **Q.** Do you want me to call the court reporter who made the transcript?
> **A.** No, that's not necessary.
>
> **Q.** So you admit that you made that statement?
> **A.** Yes, I said that.

## 5.4   Commit

As was mentioned earlier, if the witness does not adopt the prior statement, then the prior inconsistency goes to credibility only. Now, if that is your purpose and you do not need the adoption and are only concentrating on showing the witness's self-contradictions, then you need not ask:

> **Q.** And was your answer true?
> **A.** Yes.

For an adoption, for you to argue that what was said earlier is a true statement of the facts so stated, you need to ask this last question.

The impeachment ends here. You need go no further, unless you wish to enhance the contradiction, or the adoption, or decide to proceed to a *K.G.B.* application.

**Q.** So when you told us in court today that you were not *angry*, that statement was not true?
**A.** I was mistaken.

**Q.** You were mistaken.
**A.** Yes.

Do not ask the witness to explain the contradiction. There is no need. You will provide your own explanation in closing. If you ask the witness to explain the contradiction, the real danger is that she will do just that and provide the court with an explanation!

**Q.** You have admitted that in your statement to Officer Meese, which was taken the day after the accident, you said the westbound traffic on Main Street had a *red* light. Correct?
**A.** That is what I told the police officer.

**Q.** Now, in court today you say that the light was *green*?
**A.** Yes.

**Q.** Well, which is it, Mrs. Smith, red or green?
**A.** It was green.

**Q.** So you're telling us that your memory improves with time?
**A.** No.

**Q.** Well could you explain how you are now sure that the light was green, when the day after the accident you were sure it was red?
**A.** Yes, I am not good at directions. I got the "west" and "east" mixed up. I realized this the other day as I was driving down Main Street. What I meant to say to the officer is that the eastbound traffic had a red light. I just got my directions wrong. Therefore, I am certain that the westbound traffic had a green light. It was green.

Counsel got the explanation.

## 6.   PRIOR INCONSISTENT *WRITTEN* STATEMENTS

The procedure for using prior inconsistent written statements is governed by the applicable Evidence Acts.[32] Section 10(1) of the *Canada Evidence Act* reads:

---

[32] *Manitoba Evidence Act*, R.S.M. 1987, c. E150, s. 20; *Ontario Evidence Act*, R.S.O. 1980, c. 145, s. 20; *Canada Evidence Act*, R.S.C. 1985, c. C-5, s. 10.

10. (1) On any trial a witness may be cross-examined as to previous statements that the witness made in writing, or that have been reduced to writing, or recorded on audio tape or video tape or otherwise, relative to the subject-matter of the case, without the writing being shown to the witness or the witness being given the opportunity to listen to the audio tape or view the video tape or otherwise take cognizance of the statements, but, if it is intended to contradict the witness, the witness' attention must, before the contradictory proof can be given, be called to those parts of the statement that are to be used for the purpose of so contradicting the witness, and the judge, at any time during the trial, may require the production of the writing or tape or other medium for inspection, and thereupon make such use of it for the purposes of the trial as the judge thinks fit.

Provided below is an example of the correct procedure to follow:[33]

---

**[*Confirm the present testimony*]:**

**Q.** When my friend asked you what the man who was running down the street was wearing, you told him that he had on a bright red coat and beige pants. Isn't that what you swore?
**A.** Yes.

**Q.** You're sure it was the coat that was bright red, not the pants?
**A.** I'm sure.

**Q.** In other words there's no possibility that the man's pants were bright red and his coat beige?
**A.** Not at all.

**Q.** Are you certain that the coat was bright red rather than some other colour — green, or black or beige?
**A.** I'm sure.

**Q.** And the pants, might they have been black or dark brown or yellow?
**A.** No sir, they were beige.

*(cont'd)*

---

[33] Adapted from A. Cooper, "The Use of Prior Statements," in Advocacy, a symposium presented by the Canadian Bar Association — Ontario in collaboration with the Law Society of Upper Canada (1982), p. 213 at pp. 224-226.

**Q.** Not dark brown?
**A.** No, beige.

**Q.** You are absolutely certain.
**A.** Yes.

---

*At this point the witness' testimony is clearly and unequivocally imprinted both on the transcript and, more importantly, in the mind of the court.*

**[Confront the witness with the making of a prior statement]:**

---

**Q.** I'm going to show you a document. Is that your signature on it? (*pointing out his signature at the bottom of the last page*)
**A.** Yes, it is.

**Q.** Are those your initials at the bottom of each page?
**A.** Yes, sir.

**Q.** The officer interviewed you about this robbery on September 15th, the day after the robbery?
**A.** Yes.

**Q.** The officer wrote down what you said?
**A.** Yes.

**Q.** Then he read it back to you, and you signed and initialled it?
**A.** Yes, I recall I did.

**Q.** And a second officer, Officer Pierce, was also present?
**A.** Yes — I don't remember his name — but I do remember another officer there.

**Q.** Is this the statement that you gave the police on that date?
**A.** It appears to be.

---

**[Contradict the witness with the inconsistent statement]:**

*(cont'd)*

**Q.** In your statement you told the police, "I was looking out the bus window when I saw a man running down the street with a black bag in his hand."

That's what you told the police on September 15th?
**A.** Yes, sir.

**Q.** Was that true?
**A.** Yes, that's what happened.

**Q.** In the next sentence you said, "The man was wearing a beige leather or vinyl jacket that came down to his waist and dark brown or black pants."

That's what you told the police on September 15th?
**A.** Well, it appears to be.

---

**[*Commit the witness to the statement*]:**

---

**Q.** Well, were you trying to tell the police the truth?
**A.** What I said, I said.

**Q.** The man was wearing a beige leather or vinyl jacket. That's what you told the police?
**A.** I said that, but now I recall it was red.

**Q.** So you want to change your statement now?
**A.** Well, it was red.

**Q.** You want to change your statement about the colour of that jacket from beige to bright red?
**A.** I don't know if it is a change.

**Q.** You will agree with me that the jacket can't have been both beige and bright red?
**A.** Yes.

**Q.** It certainly wasn't a reddish beige?
**A.** No, it was red.

*(cont'd)*

> **Q.** So your evidence before the jury about the colour of the coat has changed completely from what you told the police?
> **A.** I guess so.
>
> **Q.** You'll agree that your memory of the robbery was much clearer on September 15th, a day after the robbery took place, than it is today?
> **A.** I'm not sure of that.
>
> **Q.** I'm suggesting to you that the coat might well have been beige?
> **A.** Well, it might have been — that's what I said there.
>
> **Q.** All right, I'll take that answer.

Counsel did not get the witness to adopt the earlier statement, therefore the inconsistency goes to credibility, although admittedly a large shadow has been cast over the witness's in-court testimony.

Does the written statement now have to be tendered as a document? I am of the view that it need not be tendered as an exhibit. You used the document only for the purpose of impeaching the witness on the prior inconsistent statement and presumably you have, in all fairness, put to the witness the relevant portions of the document that go to explain or qualify that statement. There is no further need for the court to examine the document. Some courts, however, have ruled that the document containing the statement be marked as an exhibit. The concluding sentence in s. 10 of the *Canada Evidence Act*, for example, allows the judge to "make such use of it [the writing] for the purposes of the trial as the judge thinks fit." Much will depend upon the extent of the use made of the writing. If the document is used for "one" short impeachment, there seems little reason for the *entire* document to be marked as an exhibit. The converse is also true; if the document is extensively used in impeachment, then for clarification the judge may well wish to have it marked. Should the document be marked as an exhibit, as cross-examining counsel, you should remind the judge that your limited use of the document was for impeachment *only* on the contradictory statement and that you neither accept nor adopt the remaining contents of the document. (Obviously you would only take this position if the remaining contents of the document were damaging to your case.)[34]

---

[34] For a discussion of this issue, see J. Sopinka, *The Trial of an Action* (1981), at pp. 76-77, and A. Bryant, "The Adversary's Witness: Cross-examination And Proof of Prior Inconsistent Statements" (1984), 62 Can. Bar Rev. 43. See also *R.*

## 7.   PRIOR INCONSISTENT *ORAL* STATEMENTS

Once again, the procedure and introduction of prior inconsistent oral statements is governed by the applicable Evidence Acts.[35] Section 11 of the *Canada Evidence Act* reads:

> 11.  Where a witness, on cross-examination as to a former statement made by him relative to the subject-matter of the case and inconsistent with his present testimony, does not distinctly admit that he did make the statement, proof may be given that he did in fact make it, but before that proof can be given the circumstances of the supposed statement, sufficient to designate the particular occasion, shall be mentioned to the witness, and he shall be asked whether or not he made the statement.

---

*[Have the witness confirm the present testimony.]*

**Q.** This morning you said that you thought that the "red" car was going at least 100 km/h. Do I have that correct?
**A.** Yes.

**Q.** So you're saying that the red car could not have been going less than 100 km/h?
**A.** That's right.

**Q.** You are certain of that, Mr. Smith?
**A.** Yes.

*[Confront the witness with the making of a prior statement.]*

**Q.** Now right after the accident you talked to a police officer — an officer Bennett. Do you recall that?
**A.** I recall speaking to a police officer but I don't remember the name.

*(cont'd)*

---

*v. Rowbotham* (1988), 41 C.C.C. (3d) 1, where the Ontario Court of Appeal ruled that the statement cross-examined on should not have been marked as an exhibit and allowed to go to the jury room. A contrary position was taken in *R. v. Newall* (1984), 9 C.C.C. (3d) 519 (B.C.C.A.).

[35] *Manitoba Evidence Act*, s. 21, *Ontario Evidence Act*, s. 21, and the *Canada Evidence Act*, s. 11.

**Q.** And you told the officer about what you observed?
**A.** I did.

**Q.** And the officer took notes of what you said, is that not correct?
**A.** Yes, he did.

**Q.** You knew at this time that a person had died in the accident?
**A.** I knew that.

**Q.** So you knew that it was important for the police to find out what caused the accident?
**A.** Yes.

**Q.** You wanted to be as accurate as you could?
**A.** Yes.

**Q.** Things were fresh in your mind because the accident had just happened — correct?
**A.** Yes.

---

*[Contradict the witness with the inconsistent statement.]*

---

**Q.** Mr. Smith, didn't you tell Officer Bennett that the red car you saw was going "no more than 80 km/h?"
**A.** I don't remember.

**Q.** You don't remember saying that?
**A.** I can't remember.

**Q.** But you do remember speaking to a police officer?
**A.** Yes.

---

*In this example the witness has not admitted to making the statement and there is no adoption possible. You will have to call Officer Bennett as part of your case and have him read the statement. The contradiction will go only to credibility.*

## 8.   PRIOR INCONSISTENT *TESTIMONY*

In a criminal proceeding the primary source for inconsistent testimony will be the preliminary inquiry transcript, while in a civil proceeding the primary sources are the examinations for discovery. That is the reason for you to "question for admissions" in these pre-trial proceedings. By so doing, you elicit admissions, which will be used for impeachment if the witness recants at trial.

One note of caution. The accused in a criminal trial may be immune from impeachment based on his or her earlier testimony given at a prior proceeding. The accused has protection under s. 13 of the *Charter of Rights and Freedoms:*[36]

### Self-crimination

**13.** A witness who testifies in any proceedings has the right not to have any incriminating evidence so given used to incriminate that witness in any other proceedings, except in a prosecution for perjury or for the giving of contradictory evidence.[37]

The procedure for impeachment through the use of prior testimony is the same as for written statements. In a civil context, R. 31.11(2) applies to the use of the examination for discovery at trial for impeachment:

**31.11** (2) The evidence given on an examination for discovery may be used for the purpose of impeaching the testimony of the deponent as a witness in the same manner as any previous inconsistent statement by that witness.

---

[36] *Canadian Charter of Rights and Freedoms*, being Pt. I of the Constitution Act, 1982, s. 13.

[37] The law on Section 13 is outlined in D. Paciocco and L. Stuesser, *Essentials of Canadian Law: The Law of Evidence*, 7th ed. (2015) at pp. 310-324. See also *R. v. Nedelcu*, 2012 SCC 59 (S.C.C.).

Let us turn to the case of *Waite v. Stewart* (Chapter 2). In direct examination Richard Waite testifies that when he left the ice after being high-sticked and cut he was not angry:

---

**[*Have the witness confirm the present testimony*]**

**Q.** Mr. Waite, you were high-sticked?
**A.** Yes.

**Q.** You were cut above the eye?
**A.** Yes.

**Q.** And when you left the ice you testified earlier that you were not angry. Is that correct?
**A.** I was not angry.

**Q.** You did not feel angry?
**A.** No.

**[*Confront the witness with the making of a prior statement.*]**

**Q.** Mr. Waite you were examined for discovery in this action on the 19th of December at my firm's office?
**A.** Yes.

**Q.** I asked you certain questions at that time?
**A.** Yes.

**Q.** And a person was present to record what was said?
**A.** Yes.

**Q.** In fact, that person, the recorder, had you take an oath prior to answering any questions. Correct?
**A.** Yes.

**[*Contradict the witness with the inconsistent statement.*]**

*(cont'd)*

---

**Q.** Mr. Waite I'm going to read to you the following questions and answers from that examination. M'Lord, I refer to the plaintiff's examination for discovery at page 9. [*Wait for the judge to find the spot. I assume that you have already filed the discovery with the court. If not, you would do so at this time. This latter option would be extremely effective if you had a* **major** *inconsistency to put to the witness. The ominous suspense as the examination is filed heightens the expectation, provided, of course, the inconsistency merits such emphasis!*]

**Q.** Question 39: "You left the game after being hurt?"
**A.** Answer: "Yes."

**Q.** Question 40: "And how did you feel at this time?"
**A.** Answer: "I was angry. I had just been high-sticked and cut."

**Q.** Mr. Waite you were asked those questions and gave those answers?
**A.** Yes.

---

[*Commit the witness to the prior statement.*]

---

**Q.** You were under oath at that time just as is the case now. I take it that you told the truth?
**A.** Yes, I told the truth as best I could recall.

**Q.** And the examination for discovery was held six months after the fight. Correct?
**A.** Yes.

**Q.** We are now a year later?
**A.** Yes.

**Q.** Things would have been fresher a year ago?
**A.** I can't deny that.

**Q.** So, Mr. Waite, you were angry when you left the ice?
**A.** Yes, I guess I was.

---

*You have your impeachment and your adoption of the earlier testimony.*

## 9.   IMPEACHMENT BY OMISSION

A final way of using prior writings to impeach a witness is to concentrate upon what is *not* in the prior statement, rather than to confront the witness with what was stated earlier. You are impeaching by way of omission, rather than by way of commission. This technique is useful when cross-examining witnesses whom we expect to be thorough — it is their job.

---

**Q.** Constable, you are with the traffic division, are you not?
**A.** Yes, sir.

**Q.** So part of your daily duties is the investigation of accidents?
**A.** Yes, besides traffic enforcement.

**Q.** How many accidents do you investigate in a given year?
**A.** I couldn't tell you.

**Q.** Well, let's estimate officer. About 200, say one per work day?
**A.** I would think that is about right.

**Q.** And you keep notes for each?
**A.** Yes.

**Q.** You need the notes to help you keep each accident straight in your mind?
**A.** Yes.

**Q.** You record what is important in these notes in order to accurately recall that information if the matter goes to trial, like this one. Is that not correct?
**A.** Yes.

> [*Have the witness confirm the present testimony.*]

**Q.** Officer Brown, you testified earlier that Mr. Hill said, "I was going too fast," when you spoke to him at the scene. Is that your testimony?
**A.** That is correct.

*(cont'd)*

---

**Q.** You are certain that he said that to you?
**A.** I am, sir.

**Q.** The speed that Mr. Hill was driving at the time was important?
**A.** Yes, it was.

> [*Confront the witness with the making of a prior record.*]

**Q.** In this accident investigation involving Mr. Hill you made notes?
**A.** Yes, I did.

**Q.** In fact, prior to court you were reviewing those notes in the waiting room, weren't you?
**A.** Yes, I was.

**Q.** Your notes on this accident cover six pages. Correct?
**A.** Yes.

**Q.** You have a diagram of the scene?
**A.** Yes.

**Q.** You have witness statements?
**A.** Yes.

**Q.** And you have two pages of a statement made by Mr. Hill?
[*Earlier ruled admissible.*]
**A.** Yes.

> [*Contradict the witness by showing the omission.*]

**Q.** Constable, where in this report have you recorded that Mr. Hill said "I was going too fast?"
**A.** [*After reviewing his notes.*] I do not have that recorded.

**Q.** In these six pages that statement is not recorded?
**A.** It is not in the report.

**Q.** No it is not, officer . . .

In all of the examples on impeachment through prior inconsistent statements you have been given illustrations of how to "enhance" each of the steps of impeachment. Of course, it would be poor tactics for you to unduly "enhance" *minor* inconsistencies. As well, you need not repeat the enhancement each time you impeach the witness on the earlier statement. The steps become shorter, nevertheless they remain to be done. The true art of impeachment is to use the four-step procedure to proper effect and with proper tact.

## 10.   PROBLEM — IMPEACHMENT

1.   You are cross-examining RICHARD WAITE. In direct examination he said:

> I just happened to see Stewart in the parking lot as I was loading my car. So I decided to talk to him.

In Richard Waite's examination for discovery taken on 10th October at your firm's board room, Waite said:

**Page 10**

> **Q.** Now after you got cleaned up, you waited for Stewart didn't you?
> **A.** Yes I did. I wanted to talk to him.

Assume that Waite will stick to his direct examination evidence.

Impeach Mr. Waite with his prior testimony.

2.   JAMES STEWART in his direct examination testified:

> **Q.** Mr. Stewart, on March 13th did you have any martial arts training of any kind?
> **A.** Yes, I did.
>
> **Q.** Please tell the court what training you had.
> **A.** I had just started a year, a year and a half before in karate. It was a hobby with me and I only had limited karate skill at that time.

You are cross-examining Mr. Stewart. Refer to Stewart's karate record which is Exhibit 3, tendered by consent, and is Tab C in the document book made available to the judge for reference. (*The karate record is found in Problem 1, (Chapter 12).*)

Impeach Mr. Stewart using the karate record.

# 15

# OBJECTIONS AT TRIAL

- **How Do You Object?**

- **When Do You Object?**

- **To What Do You Object?**

- **Evidentiary Hearings**

- **A *Voir Dire* on Confessions**

- **Arguing a *Charter* Motion**

The making of a *proper* objection at trial is one of the most difficult crafts that a litigator must acquire. A *proper* objection requires that counsel combine a good understanding of the law of evidence along with tactical wisdom, an ear for error and the ability to respond quickly.

The primary reason to object is to exclude improper evidence.[1] The objection brings the impropriety of the evidence to the attention of the judge, who then is asked to enforce the rules of evidence. This is where counsel have significant impact. Many of the rules of evidence are nebulous and much enforcement is left to the discretion of the judge, who must act in relative haste during the course of the trial. The opportunity presents itself for prepared counsel to persuade.

---

[1] R. Keeton, *Trial Tactics and Methods*, 2nd ed. (1973), at p. 166. Professor Keeton (as he then was) provides an excellent chapter on "Objections to Evidence."

Counsel also must look beyond the trial to the appeal and act to protect the trial record. In civil *jury* trials a failure to object is usually fatal.[2] The oft-stated principle is that:[3]

> While the failure of counsel at trial to make an objection to a charge to the jury does not in every case preclude counsel on appeal from raising the objection, it should be made plain once again that the omission of counsel at trial to make an objection to the charge must not be regarded lightly, but, on the contrary, in such a case when counsel seeks to raise the objection as a ground of appeal, a new trial cannot be granted as a matter of right, but only as a matter of discretion. A new trial should not be granted unless the Court is fully satisfied that it is necessary in the interests of justice.

The above rationalia apply to *non-jury* trials as well. But in trials before a judge alone the failure to object is not as fatal. In non-jury trials the rules of evidence are relaxed.[4] Trial judges are accorded the power of disabusing their minds of improper evidence. Similarly in criminal trials, defence counsel's failure to object is "not determinative" on appeal, but "says something about both the overall accuracy of the jury instructions and the seriousness of the alleged misdirection."[5]

Although the failure to object in a non-jury trial is not fatal, it remains an important factor. Mr. Justice Twaddle of the Manitoba Court of Appeal made this telling comment:[6]

> It is regrettable that objection to this evidence, the admission of which is now the principal ground of appeal, was not made by the accused's counsel (not counsel who appeared for him in this court) at the time the evidence was tendered. The absence of objection no doubt influenced Glowacki J. in permitting its reception as it would certainly have influenced me if the decision to admit the evidence were one of discretion rather than of law.

A further reality is that the law of evidence favours inclusion over exclusion. You will often hear a judge rule, "I'll allow the evidence, and

---

[2] *K. (G.) v. K. (D.)*, 1999 CarswellOnt 1615, [1999] O.J. No. 1953 (Ont. C.A.) at para. 15, leave to appeal refused 2001 CarswellOnt 1073 (S.C.C.).

[3] *Arland v. Taylor*, [1955] O.R. 131 (Ont. C.A.) at p. 137 per Laidlaw J.A.; see also *Mazur v. Lucas*, 2010 BCCA 473 (B.C. C.A.).

[4] See 1 Wigmore, *Evidence*, Tillers rev. (1983), para. 4d.1, at p. 212.

[5] *R. v. Araya*, 2015 SCC 11 (S.C.C.) at para. 51.

[6] *R. v. G. (K.A.)* (1988), 40 C.C.C. (3d) 333 at 335 (Man. C.A.), reversed [1988] 1 S.C.R. 228. The Manitoba Court of Appeal decision is included with the Supreme Court of Canada's judgment. The Supreme Court by a majority of 3:2 allowed the Crown appeal, ruled that similar fact evidence was properly admitted and restored the conviction.

accord it the appropriate weight." Chief Justice Dickson provides this apt summary of evidence principles:[7]

> I agree with my colleague La Forest J. that basic principles of the law of evidence embody an inclusionary policy which would permit into evidence everything logically probative of some fact in issue, subject to the recognized rules of exclusion and exceptions thereto. Thereafter the question is one of weight. The evidence may carry much weight, little weight, or no weight at all. If error is to be made, it should be on the side of inclusion rather than exclusion, and our efforts, in my opinion, consistent with the ever-increasing openness of our society, should be toward admissibility unless a very clear ground of policy or law dictates exclusion.

Therefore expect that many of your objections will be *overruled*, but that does not necessarily mean that the objection has been wasted. You have made a point. Problems have been raised with the evidence and the judge is put on notice. You have cast a cloud over the evidence, which may succeed in reducing the weight to be attached to the admitted evidence. In this way an objection can be effective, even if overruled.

This chapter will address three essential questions that need to be answered before counsel can become competent at raising proper objections:

- How do you object?

- When do you object? and

- To what do you object?

It will then examine evidentiary hearings and the conduct of a *voir dire* and *Charter* motion.

## 1.    HOW DO YOU OBJECT?

Edward Greenspan provided this anecdote on how he learned to object at trial:[8]

> One can't be a lawyer without going to law school. However, one can't become a lawyer just by going to law school either. Law schools teach a great

---

[7] *R. v. Corbett* (1988), 64 C.R. (3d) 1 (S.C.C.) at 21-22.
[8] E. Greenspan and G. Jonas, Greenspan, *The Case for the Defence* (1987), at pp. 25-26.

deal about the theory of being a courtroom advocate. They teach much less about the craft, and almost nothing about the art.

Remarkably, they teach next to nothing about the nuts and bolts of courtroom work either. In fairness, perhaps courtroom practice cannot be taught in a classroom. It must be acquired through experience.

For example, far-fetched as it sounds, I didn't know how to express an objection in court to a question or statement by my opponent. I thought that there may be a proper, formal way to do it, but I had no idea what it might be. As Dombie's trial began, a couple of minor matters came up almost immediately to which I would have liked to object. But what should I say? I did not want to interrupt the Crown or address the bench; I thought it might not be the right thing to do.

I stood up, hoping that the judge would recognize me. His Honour glanced at me, but said nothing. The trial continued. I was standing there, feeling exceptionally foolish, and I could see the jurors' eyes beginning to turn toward me. Finally I reached over to the water jug and, as if I had been meaning to do it all along, poured myself a glass of water. I don't do that sort of thing too well, but I managed to get the water into the glass. I drank it, too, though I wasn't the least bit thirsty.

During the first recess I saw in the hallway a seasoned Crown Attorney, Frank Armstrong, whom I happened to know. Needing advice desperately, but too ashamed to admit that I wasn't familiar with such a rudimentary procedure, I said to him: "Frank, I know there are many individual ways of objecting in court, but, as a matter of interest, how do *you* do it?"

Armstrong seemed a bit surprised. "Me?" he asked. "I guess I just say: 'I object! What else?"

What else, indeed. Back in court I had to resist the impulse to test my new-found expertise every five minutes. When the Crown asked the next witness what his occupation was, I felt like saying: "I object!"

Counsel must do more than rise and say, "I object." "I object" is too general a statement. What are you objecting to? The question? The answer? The witness? The opposing counsel? The judge? The entire proceeding? One commentator stated that such an objection represented the "inarticulate mental frustration of a fearful attorney who will probably be disappointed in the ruling and might as well not have made the objection."[9] Moreover, if your "general" objection is overruled, do not complain on appeal. Wigmore

---

[9] M. Ladd, "Objections, Motions and Foundation Testimony" (1958), 43 Cornell L.Q. 543, at p. 545.

wrote, "The cardinal principle (no sooner repeated by the courts than ignored by counsel) is that a general objection, if overruled, cannot avail the objector on appeal."[10] You should have raised and articulated the valid objection at trial. Conversely, if the judge sustains a "general" objection, the party tendering the evidence should request that the objection be specified because appeal courts usually uphold the objection if any valid ground exists.[11]

Thus you are obliged to make your objections specific. The court and opposing counsel have a right to know the basis for the objection.[12] The general rule is that, "No ground for the admission or rejection of evidence can be urged on appeal by the party who lost on that issue, unless that ground was advanced at trial."[13]

Consider the following:

## Problem 1

• Plaintiff seeks to introduce into evidence a document.

• Defendant objects on the ground that the document is hearsay evidence. A wrong objection.

• The objection is *overruled*. The document is admitted.

• The correct objection is that the document should be excluded on the basis of privilege.

• On appeal defendant seeks to argue privilege.

• What result?

## Problem 2

• Same facts as problem 1 except:

---

[10] Wigmore, *supra*, note 4, para. 18, at p. 818. There are some narrow exceptions to this rule, one being where the general objection "should have been obvious to judge and opposing counsel without stating it": see *McCormick on Evidence*, 3rd ed. (1984), by E. Cleary, at p. 129.

[11] See McCormick, *ibid*.

[12] J. Sopinka and S. Lederman, *The Law of Evidence in Civil Cases* (1974), at p. 473.

[13] A. Sheppard, *Evidence* (1988), at p. 199.

- The objection is *sustained*. The document is excluded.

- What result?

In Problem 1, appeal courts are not sympathetic to objecting counsel, who should have articulated the correct ground of objection, thereby giving opposing counsel the opportunity to correct the defect. In Problem 2, the wrong objection has succeeded. On appeal the correct ground should be considered. No point would be served by finding an error and ordering a new trial. At the new trial, counsel would then raise the correct objection to exclude the evidence. There is one proviso. If the correct ground of objection is *curable* then, where warranted, a new trial should be ordered. For example, in our problem, plaintiff counsel could cure the privilege exclusion by calling the appropriate person who may agree to waive the privilege.

The best explanation that I have found to support these rules governing objections to evidence is as follows:[14]

> They are directed to the parties, placing a responsibility on each side to make clear what is being offered and what is being objected to and the grounds of objection so that errors can be corrected, if possible, at the trial level. They are aimed at the trial court. The making of specific objections and adequate offers of proof supported by specific grounds for admitting or excluding are designed to enable the trial judge to rule intelligently and quickly. They are also designed to provide an adequate basis for appeal with enough material in the record so that the appellate court can intelligently decide whether the error, if any, merits reversal. Overall, they should serve the goal of reducing the necessity for retrials which, of course, involve costs for the parties and the administration of justice.

The mechanics of objecting are twofold: notice and grounds.

**Notice**: Rise and, as you are rising, say, "I object," "Your Honour, I object" or "Objection." The court is on notice of your objection. The question or answer is stopped. Pause . . . At this time, if the objection is patently obvious, the judge may agree without further comment . . . If not, you go on.

**Grounds:** Specify your objection:

Counsel is leading the witness.

---

[14] J. Weinstein, J. Mansfield, N. Abrams and M. Berger, *Cases and Materials on Evidence*, 7th ed. (1983), at p. 1197.

The question calls for a conclusion from the witness and the witness is not qualified to give that conclusion.

Be simple when giving your objections.[15] Objections are a matter of law, but that is no reason for you to be legalistic. For example, the best way to explain your hearsay objection is to emphasize to the court the fundamental problem with it, which is that you are precluded from cross-examining the person making the statement:

> Your Honour, counsel is asking for hearsay evidence. The witness is being asked to tell this court what *someone else* has said and I cannot cross-examine that person.

The tone of your objection will also vary depending upon the circumstances that give rise to the objection. Objecting need not be objectionable. Your tone may well be apologetic in interrupting, or helpful in seeking to clarify a matter. Be diplomatic, rather than confrontational, if opposing counsel has, in your view, made an innocent mistake:

> My Lord, objection ... counsel indicated that the witness in direct said the car was in the southbound lane. I believe the witness's evidence was northbound lane.

Be more pointed should counsel misstate the evidence again:

> My Lord, I must object again ... the witness did not say in direct that the car was going 50 km/h. The witness distinctly said the car was going 60 km/h.

Be indignant, if in your view opposing counsel is unfairly questioning your witness:

> My Lord, I object! Counsel is badgering the witness.

> Counsel has made a number of unfounded accusations.

Your objections therefore should be appropriate to the occasion.

## 2. WHEN DO YOU OBJECT?

A trial is not an evidence examination and there is no need to object to every objectionable question or answer.[16] Tactics, along with the law of

---

[15] See Keeton, *supra*, note 1 at pp. 210-215, for excellent examples of common objections.

[16] J. McElhaney, "When to Object" (June 1989), 75 A.B.A.J. 98.

evidence, will dictate when you should or should not object. Pick your objections. One lawyer likened himself to a baseball player:[17]

> When a question is asked in a courtroom, I think of it like a pitch. I may not want to swing even though it is a strike the same way that a batter need not swing at every pitch. Often there are good reasons for not swinging, yet the batter does not have much time to make up his mind.

It is true, you do not have much time to consider your objection and the decision whether to object is not an easy one to make. One tactical concern is that by objecting you emphasize the evidence. The objection stops the trial and all attention is turned to the objectionable evidence. Does the evidence deserve this attention? It may be wise to let the objection pass, provided of course that you are not concerned with safeguarding the record for appeal.

There is also a downside in raising an objection only to be overruled. If you continually raise objections only to be overruled, you lose credibility with the judge. Your frivolous objections are stamping your own ignorance of the law of evidence. Do not object unless your objections *deserve* to be sustained.[18] This is not to say that you must win all objections only that the objections have merit. Objections based on meritorious grounds will rarely damage your case.

A further factor to consider is that once you raise an objection, besides highlighting the evidence, you are providing opposing counsel with an opportunity to explain and focus on the importance of the impugned evidence. That opening can be seized by opposing counsel to devastating effect.

Certain objections are made for tactical rather than legal reasons. They are designed primarily for interruption. These tactical objections include the protecting of a witness from a steamroller type of cross-examination or to raise an objection simply to throw opposing counsel off. For example, you object to opposing counsel asking a leading question. Experienced counsel will simply rephrase it, but inexperienced counsel may get flustered, find it difficult to rephrase and as a result abandon the question and with it the evidence sought. There is nothing wrong with making such tactical objections, provided they are not devoid of legal merit. To rise and simply object in order to interrupt is objectionable. The judge will see through the objection and you can expect to be rebuked. Wait for a valid legal opening

---

[17] J. Curtin, "Objections," in American Bar Association, *The Litigation Manual* (1983), at p. 191.

[18] McElhaney, *supra*, note 16, at p. 99.

on which to found your tactical objection. The opening will arise. Is it a compound question? Is the question confusing? Has the witness been given an opportunity to answer? Once the opening presents itself, rise to interrupt.

Another trial reality is that judges do not like objections. There are two reasons for this. First, an objection interrupts the trial and prolongs the process. Pay careful attention to the judge's reaction to your objections. You do not want to antagonize the judge. Watch for the danger sign of judicial impatience and, if you sense it, then rein in your objections. Second, an objection seeks to exclude evidence and a judge, like any person, is curious. An objection fuels the curiosity. The judge wants to know what counsel is seeking to hide.

Once the decision is made to object, do so in a *timely* fashion. Take this advice:

Sooner is better than later and later is better than never.

Where possible object in advance of the improper evidence. Now it is true that it is not as important in a trial before a judge alone to be quick to your feet. The judge is able to disabuse himself of the improper evidence.[19] However, judges will not tolerate counsel who are tactically tardy in raising objections. As a general proposition, you either object to the question asked or to the answer given. If your objection is directed to the question, you are to object immediately after it is asked. You are not free to sit mute and wait to hear the answer, not objecting if in your favour, but objecting if unfavourable. In many cases, expect to be overruled for your tardiness.

You may end up objecting to both the question and the answer. In fact, let me share a true story where defence counsel actually objected to his own question! Defence counsel was cross-examining a prosecution witness in an assault case and this is what transpired:

**Counsel:**   Mr. Smith, if you were in the other room at the time, how do you know the accused struck the complainant on the head with a bottle?

**Witness:**   Because the accused told me later that is what he did.

**Counsel:**   Your Honour, I object to that answer.

**His Honour:**  You can't object to that answer, you asked the question.

---

[19] See *Edmonton Securities Ltd. v. LePage* (1913), 14 D.L.R. 66 at 70 (Alta. C.A.).

**Counsel**:   Then I object to the question!

The timing of an objection is premised on a sensitive ear. Experienced counsel react to foreshadowing phrases that introduce objectionable evidence. Outlined below are some common foreshadowing phrases:

- *"Is it possible that. . .?"* invariably announces that an opinion is going to be sought from the witness.

- *"Would it be fair to say . . .?"* is asking for an opinion. You should be turning your mind to the question as to whether the witness is qualified to give the opinion.

- *"Did you. . .?"* or *"Were you . . .?"* If counsel in direct examination is in the habit of asking these types of questions, often as not counsel will start to lead the witness in critical areas.

- *"Were you talking to . . ..?"* As soon as a witness begins to mention a conversation, you should be considering hearsay. Whether or not the conversation is hearsay or not is another matter, but you are ready.

Objections to the witness's answer usually occur after the fact. Do you then move to "strike" the evidence? No. That is an American practice. You object to the evidence:

My Lord, I object. The witness is giving hearsay evidence.

If the judge agrees with you, she will caution the witness about hearsay evidence, and it is implicit that the judge will disregard the impugned evidence.

Since objections should be made in advance of the evidence being heard, an obligation is imposed on the counsel introducing the evidence to put into the record the evidence that is lost, should the objection be sustained. This is called an "offer of evidence." Otherwise the trial judge and the appeal court have no idea what evidence was excluded. The offer of evidence can be made prior to, or after, the judge's ruling on admissibility. Have the witness excused. Then inform the court of the anticipated evidence and have it put on the record. This will assist both the judge in determining the issue and the appeal court. Otherwise how can a court of appeal make an informed ruling in the absence of the excluded evidence? How does the appellate court know whether the exclusion of the evidence amounted to harmless error or a substantial error that would bring into question the trial result?[20] It is not open to you at the appeal hearing to offer this evidence. Your time is at trial. You put it on the record as follows:

**Counsel A**: Officer, and then what did you do?

**Officer**: I then opened the door with a passkey provided by the hotel security and I entered the hotel room . . .

**Counsel B**: Objection, My Lord. It is my submission that this is an unauthorized entry into the hotel room and constitutes an unreasonable search and seizure under section 8 of the *Charter of Rights and Freedoms*. And it is my submission that any evidence obtained by the officer while in the hotel room should be ruled inadmissible.

**Judge**: Counsel, I appreciate your objection. But the problem that I have is that before I can make a valid decision on exclusion I do not know what evidence was found. I assume that there is some evidence — that is why you are objecting.

**Counsel A**: My Lord, perhaps at this time the officer could step down and I could make an offer of evidence to inform Your Lordship of the anticipated evidence [or a *voir dire* could be entered into with the officer giving his evidence.]

**Judge**: Yes . . . officer you are excused for the moment. Please wait outside the courtroom.

The evidence is on the record *although it does not become evidence in the cause.*

It is also important for counsel to insist that the judge rule on any objection. In a trial before judge alone the decision may be reserved but it nevertheless must be made. Once again the reason is to protect the record. How can the appeal court be asked to reverse an evidence ruling if it is not clear what the trial judge's ruling was?

## 3.   TO WHAT DO YOU OBJECT?

Possible objections are as numerous as are the rules of evidence. That is why a litigator must be familiar with the law of evidence. Certain objec-

---

[20] For an example of an appellate court facing such a vacuum in the trial record, see *R. v. Collins* (1987), 56 C.R. (3d) 193 (S.C.C.). For an example of an offer of proof see: *United States of America, Re,* 2014 BCSC 1132 (B.C. S.C.).

tions can be identified prior to trial and should be prepared for in advance. These are the critical areas on which you have prepared an evidentiary brief. Other objections are the product of the normal trial process and cannot be anticipated. These objections you simply know. This segment is concerned with common spontaneous objections.

There are two basic types of objections, substantive or form. Substantive questions go to the root principles of admissibility. What is sought to be introduced runs afoul of the rules of evidence. Substantive objections include:

**Opinion**    The witness is not qualified to give that opinion.

**Privilege**    The question invades solicitor-client privilege.

**Hearsay**    The witness is giving hearsay evidence. The evidence he is giving is not based on his personal knowledge. It is based on what he has been told. And the person who told him is not present in court and subject to cross-examination

**Relevancy**    My Lord, I fail to see how this evidence is relevant.

This list of substantive objections is far from exhaustive. What is important for counsel to appreciate is that a substantive error can be fatal. The fate of the evidence is in the balance. For example, if a document is caught by solicitor-client privilege and that privilege is not waived, then the document cannot be used. Other substantive errors may be saved only through major trial surgery. For example, in the case of hearsay, the person making the out-of-court statement will have to be called.

The form objection is easier to correct. For most form objections all that is required is for counsel to rephrase the question. The consequence flowing from a form objection is also usually not fatal. A perfect example is a leading question. Leading questions are easy to rephrase and the testimony elicited remains admissible. The leading only goes to weight. Form objections include:

**Leading**    Counsel is leading the witness in a material area.

**Compound**    Counsel is asking two questions.

**Confusion**    My Lord, the question asked is confusing.

**Argumentative**    The question is argumentative.

Besides identification of objectionable evidence, the next crucial task for counsel is to articulate clearly the objection to the court. Hearsay is one area that is difficult for counsel. James McElhaney breaks it down into two easily, stated parts:[21]

1. An out-of-court statement,

2. Offered to prove its truth.

I would also include the further concern, the loss of opportunity to cross-examine. Once the objection is broken down into such understandable terms, it is easy for counsel to rise and state the objection:

> My Lord, I object. The question asks for a hearsay answer. The witness is being asked to give an out-of-court statement, which is offered for its truth. That is hearsay. And I cannot cross-examine the maker of the statement.

Having raised the hearsay, it is incumbent upon you to expect opposing counsel to raise a hearsay exception. Familiarize yourself with these exceptions, and there are many. The most important are:

**State of mind**   The evidence goes to X's state of mind.

**Admissions**   The statement is an admission by a party.

**Res gestae**   The statement is a spontaneous statement and falls within that hearsay exception.

**Notice**   My Lord, this is not hearsay. We are tendering this statement only to show that it was *made* and that the plaintiff was put on notice. *(This is not a true hearsay exception. You are denying that the statement is hearsay at all. In your view the statement is not being tendered for its truth.)*

A useful tip is for new counsel to make a list of the common objections, along with a simple statement on how to phrase the objections, and have the list readily at hand for quick reference.

At this point it may well be helpful to identify certain "American" objections and practices that have no place in a Canadian courtroom. The

---

[21] J. McElhaney, *Trial Notebook*, 2nd ed. (1987), at p. 136.

list below is for new counsel who have been watching too much American television.

---

## Americanisms to Avoid

### Objections to Avoid

- Move to "strike." [*The evidence is on the record and cannot be removed.*]

- "Asked and answered." [*We allow a measure of repetition.*]

- "Answer yes or no witness." [*Our witnesses are allowed to answer any way they wish.*]

- "Beyond the scope of the direct." [*In some American jurisdictions, cross-examination is confined to areas raised in direct examination. In Canada, the scope of cross-examination is determined by relevancy.*]

- "Objection, narrative." [*Our witnesses may give long answers, although this is not the best way to introduce evidence.*]

### Conduct to Avoid

- Asking permission to approach a witness. [*Usually not required in Canadian courts.*]

- Asking for a "side bar." [*We have evidentiary hearings or* voir dires. *No side bars.*]

- Roaming the courtroom. [*Stay at the podium.*]

- Remaining seated when making an objection. [*Always rise to speak.*]

- At the end of the examination, saying "Your witness." [*We generally say something like, "Thank you, Ms Smith. Those are my questions, Your Honour." or "That concludes my direct examination."*]

---

Certain objections are more likely to arise at certain points in the trial. Therefore, you can anticipate and prepare for these objections. The following table outlines the common objections that are apt to arise at particular times during the trial.

---

## *Anticipating Objections at Trial*

### Opening Statement

[*Note: It will be very rare for you to object during or even after the making of an opening statement. Save an objection for only the most egregious or excessive errors in the presenting of an opening.*]

• Counsel is presenting argument on the law [or facts].

• Counsel has referred to inadmissible evidence.

### Direct Examination

• Counsel is leading the witness on a material point.

   *[Do not object to leading on non-material points.]*

• The question seeks to introduce hearsay evidence.

• Counsel is introducing impermissible character evidence.

• The question calls for an opinion that the witness cannot give.

### Re-Examination

• Counsel is leading the witness.

• Counsel is covering areas already dealt with or that should have been dealt with in direct.

### Cross-Examination

• Counsel is misquoting the evidence.

*(cont'd)*

---

- Counsel is not allowing the witness to answer.

- Counsel is being argumentative.

- Counsel is asking the witness to disclose privileged information.

- Counsel is asking the witness two (or more) questions.

**Exhibit Objections**

- Counsel has not properly authenticated the document.

- The witness cannot authenticate the document.

- If the witness is going to be cross-examined on the statement then in fairness the witness ought to be shown the statement.

**Closing Argument**

[*Note: Objections made during a closing address are very rare. Usually you can raise your "objection" in your submission.*]

- Counsel has misstated the evidence.

- Counsel is expressing her personal opinion.

- Counsel is misstating the law.

- Counsel is arguing a point for which there is no foundation in evidence.

## 4.   EVIDENTIARY HEARINGS

More and more objections to critical pieces of evidence are being dealt with in advance of the trial proper. For example, in the Paul Bernardo murder case, once the jury was selected, they were empanelled and then told to go home for two weeks. During this time the trial judge dealt with a number of pre-trial motions brought by the defence — most involving evidence matters. This meant that when the trial started the Crown and defence knew in advance what evidence was admissible and the trial could proceed in a relatively uninterrupted manner.

How these evidentiary rulings are made varies. Motion hearings may be held where counsel provide written motion factums, or a formal *voir dire* may be held. A *voir* dire is required when at issue is the voluntariness of a confession.[22] Yet *voir dires* may be held concerning a number of evidence issues such as the admissibility of expert testimony, similar fact evidence, or evidence subject to *Charter* challenge. A *voir dire* is a "trial within a trial." For example, if the Crown is seeking to admit a confession then they will have to call the officers involved in the taking of the statement to prove that it was voluntarily made by the accused. The police officers are sworn as witnesses in the *voir dire*. The Crown conducts a direct examination and the defence may cross-examine the officers. The defence may also call evidence on the *voir dire*. Once all the evidence is called, the counsel make closing submissions. The judge then rules on the admissibility of the confession. In a jury trial, the *voir dire* is held in the absence of the jury. If the trial judge rules the confession admissible, then it may be put to the jury. If the confession is ruled inadmissible, the jury will never hear about it.

In judge alone trials, *voir dires* are also held. The judge is asked to enter into a *voir dire*, the witnesses are called and the evidence is presented. Should the judge rule the evidence admissible then usually the evidence presented in the *voir dire* is moved by counsel to be "incorporated" into the trial proper. The agreement of both counsel is needed.[23] This saves the trial judge having to re-hear essentially the same evidence. Should the judge rule against admitting the evidence, then it is accepted that the judge will disregard the evidence presented in the *voir dire*. As can be seen, a *voir dire* is a formal and time-consuming process and it is not necessary in deciding every evidence issue. It is more correct to say that the court may hold a "hearing" rather than a "trial within a trial." The key question is whether witnesses need to be called. If not, then there is no need for a *voir dire*. For example, where the facts are not contested, counsel can proceed by way of agreed facts. There may be a preliminary inquiry transcript or previous trial transcript that provides all the information that the trial judge needs to make a ruling, or a ruling can be based solely on counsel's submissions to the court. Counsel and the courts need to look for the most expeditious means of resolving the evidence issues, which at the same time provides the court with all necessary information. Adhering to the formal *voir dire* procedure may well be a complete waste of valuable court time.

---

[22] *R. v. Piche* (1971), 12 C.R.N.S. 222 (S.C.C.).

[23] For a discussion of *voir dires* see *R. v. Hurry*, 2002 ABQB 420 (Alta. Q.B.), where an admission by an accused in a *voir dire* was not admissible in the trial proper when defence counsel specifically did not agree to that admission being used in the trial proper.

A *voir dire* on the admissibility of a confession and a *Charter* motion on the exclusion of evidence are two of the most common evidentiary hearings that arise in criminal trials. We will examine both in more detail and provide a framework for both Crown and defence counsel.

## 5.   *A VOIR DIRE* ON THE ADMISSIBILITY OF A CONFESSION

A confession is simply a statement by an accused made to a person in authority. If the accused says to a friend, "I robbed the bank," this statement is an admission and the friend may testify as to what he was told by the accused. There is no issue with respect to the admissibility of the accused's statement. However, when an accused says to a police officer, "I robbed the bank," before admitting this confession into evidence, there needs to be a *voir dire* to determine its admissibility. The unfortunate history and experience of the common law is that the power to extract answers may well lead to abuse of that power. Therefore, in the *voir dire*, the Crown will have to prove beyond a reasonable doubt that the confession was voluntary.

The leading case on the confession rule is *R. v. Oickle*.[24] In this case the Supreme Court of Canada outlined a "contextual" approach in determining the admissibility of confessions. Trial judges are to look at all the circumstances in determining whether the statement made was voluntary in the sense that it is a reliable statement by an accused who made a free choice to speak to the authorities. Prior to *Oickle*, there were four distinct ways to find that a statement was not voluntary:

1)   That the statement was induced by way of threats or promises made. Here the emphasis is directly upon what the police said or did.

2)   That the statement was the product of an atmosphere of oppression. Here the police action may well be indirect. The accused was subjected to harsh conditions, which overwhelmed his will, even though direct promises or threats were not made.

3)   That the statement was not the product of an operating mind. Here the emphasis is on the accused and may have nothing to do with what the authorities said or did. Statements made by those suffering from shock or intoxication may not have been freely given.

4)   That the statement was the product of unacceptable police trickery,

---

[24] *R. v. Oickle* (2000), 147 C.C.C. (3d) 321 (S.C.C.).

such as to shock the community. This inquiry is not dependent on a finding that the will of the accused was overborne. Here the focus is on maintaining the integrity of the criminal justice system.

*Oickle* collapses these distinct approaches. The ultimate question being whether, in all the circumstances, the will of the accused has been overborne.[25]

Prior to the trial, Crown counsel should see whether the defence is contesting the admissibility of a statement. Defence counsel may waive the need for a *voir dire* and agree to the admissibility of the statement. Moreover, if the defence is contesting the admissibility of a statement, in some instances much court time can be saved by clarifying the witnesses to be called. The general rule is that the Crown is to call or at least make available all persons in authority who were present during the interview or involved with the accused prior to the taking of the statement. For example, two police officers arrested a suspected robber. These officers, in order to continue their investigation, turned him over to other officers, who arrived at the scene. The "custodial" officers transported the accused to the police detachment, where the accused was signed in by the officer in charge and placed into an interview room. Robbery squad detectives were called and they conducted the actual interview. In this example all of the officers may need to be called: the apprehending officers, custodial officers and interviewing officers.

What then are the mechanics of a *voir dire* on the admissibility of a confession? Provided below is a Crown checklist that outlines the general steps involved in such a *voir dire*. Remember the issue in the *voir dire* is voluntariness. The evidence is directed to the issues of inducements, threats, atmosphere of oppression, operating mind and unfair trickery.

### *Checklist for a Voir Dire on the Admissibility of a Confession*

### 5.1   Crown Counsel Requests a *Voir Dire*

As Crown counsel, you should decide when to make the request. For example, a *voir dire* could be held by way of a pre-trial motion under s. 645(5) of the *Criminal Code*. This may be appropriate where the confession is critical to your case and is fairly self-contained, by that I mean only one or two officers are needed. In most cases, the *voir dire* is held when the particular officer, who took the statement, is on the stand. You decide. Indicate to the trial judge that you are entering into a *voir dire*:

---

[25] For a more detailed analysis of the confession rule, see D. Paciocco and L. Stuesser, *The Law of Evidence*, 7th ed. (2015, Irwin) at pp. 344-361.

> **Crown Counsel**: Your Honour, at this time I would ask that we enter into a *voir dire* on the admissibility of a statement made by the accused to Officer Smith.

You may wish to advise the judge of any other witnesses who will be called on the *voir dire*:

> **Crown Counsel**: I will also be calling Officers Jones and Michaels, who were involved in the arrest of the accused.

The judge will usually indicate for the record that a *voir dire* is being entered into.

## 5.2   Crown Calls Evidence

A *voir dire* is conducted like a trial. The Crown bears the onus of proof and calls evidence. Each witness is subject to cross-examination.

### a)  *APPREHENDING OFFICER*

- Can you identify the accused?

- Where arrested, detained or contacted?

- What time?

- Who was present?

- What was said to the accused?

- Was the Charter right to counsel given to the accused? [*if arrested or detained*]

- Was the police caution regarding right to remain silent given?

- Who gave the caution?

- For the record, what exactly was said as to the charge and caution?

- What did the accused say?

- How did the accused respond?

- How did the accused appear?

- Did he appear to understand the charge and caution?

- In your opinion did the accused appear to be under the influence of any drug or alcohol?

- What did you do with the accused? [*Establish that the accused was turned over to another officer or the apprehending officer remained in control of the accused.*]

*b)  CALL CUSTODIAL OFFICER*

- How did the officer take control of the accused?

- What was done with accused?

- Where was the accused held?

- Who was present?

- What time?

- Describe journey to the police station?

- Was there any conversation? What was said?

- What time did you arrive at the police station?

- Where was the accused placed?

*c)  CALL INTERVIEWING OFFICER*

   *i)  Set the Scene*

- Where did the interview take place?

- Describe the room: its size, the lighting, the furniture.

- Was the door locked?

- Could the accused leave?

- Who was present?

- How were the officers dressed?

- Was the accused clothed?

- Was the accused handcuffed?

### ii) Taking the Statement

- What was the accused told?

- Was the accused re-charged and cautioned?

- What did he say?

- How did he appear?

- Did he appear to understand what he was told?

- How was the statement taken or recorded?

- Who asked the questions?

- Who took the statement?

- Were any promises made to the accused?

- Were any threats made to the accused?

- Did anyone suggest that it would be better for the accused to make a statement?

### iii) Establish a Time Line

- When did the interview start?

- When did it finish?

- Were there breaks? How long? When?

- Was the accused given any food? When?

- When did the taking of the formal statement start?

- When was the taking of the statement completed?

  *iv) Verifying the Record*

- Was the statement audio recorded or video recorded?

- If not electronically recorded, why not?

- Was the statement taken down in writing?

- Who took it down?

- Was the statement in narrative or question and answer form?

- Was the statement taken down simultaneously or written out later?

- Did the accused have an opportunity to read the statement?

- Did he appear to read the statement?

- After reading it over, did the accused make any comment?

- Were any changes requested?

- Did the accused sign the statement? If not, why not?

- Was the statement witnessed? By whom?

*[Usually at this stage counsel asks the police officer to identify the statement and have it marked for identification. Some Crown counsel now invite the judge to read, to listen or to view the confession. It is open to the trial judge to do so, although some judges as a matter of practice do not. Defence may object. Crown counsel should explain*

*why looking at the statement will assist the judge in determining vol-
untariness.*]

## 5.3   The Defence May Call Evidence

The accused may testify in the *voir dire*. In cross-examination the
accused can be asked whether the statement given was true. This supposedly
goes to the accused's credibility.[26] However, any testimony given cannot
be used against the accused in the trial proper unless the defence consents.[27]

## 5.4   Submissions on the Admissibility of the Confession

Once all the evidence is in, counsel make submissions. If the trial judge
rules the statement admissible, then the Crown may move to have the
statement marked as an exhibit in the cause. As a fallback position, defence
counsel should explore whether unfairly prejudicial portions of any statement can be edited out.

In a jury trial, the police officer who took the statement will need to
repeat much of his or her evidence on the taking of the statement. In a judge-
alone trial, the judge has already heard all about the circumstances in which
the statement was taken. There is no need to repeat this evidence. However,
since a *voir dire* is a trial within a trial, the Crown should move that the
evidence heard in the *voir dire* be adopted into the trial proper. The consent
of the defence is needed. Where only the Crown calls evidence in the *voir
dire*, defence counsel usually consent as a matter of course. Little point
would be served in hearing this evidence a second time. However, if the
accused testified, or the defence called other witnesses, defence counsel
may consent to the admissibility of the Crown evidence, but not consent to
the defence evidence being adopted into the trial proper.[28] This preserves
the accused's right to remain silent at trial.

> **Crown Counsel**: Your Honour, at this time I would ask that the statement of
> Roger Fisher, marked as exhibit A, be admitted into the cause as an exhibit.

> **Judge**: Very well, exhibit 7.

> **Crown Counsel**: I would now move that the evidence heard in the *voir dire*
> be adopted into the trial proper.

---

[26]  *R. v. DeClercq*, [1969] 1 C.C.C. 197 (S.C.C.).
[27]  See *R. v. Hurry* (2002), 4 C.R. (6th) 358 (Alta. Q.B.).
[28]  See *R. v. Camara* [1997] B.C.J. No. 2832 (S.C.).

**Defence Counsel**: Your Honour, we do consent to the Crown evidence being adopted into the trial, but we do not consent to Mr. Fisher's evidence being so adopted.

**Judge**: Very well. The Crown's evidence is adopted, but not the evidence of Mr. Fisher.

Should the judge rule the statement inadmissible then we accept that the judge will disabuse his or her mind of the statement – if examined – and any evidence heard in the *voir dire*.

## 6.   ARGUING A CHARTER MOTION

A *Charter* hearing on the admissibility of evidence is different than a *voir dire* on the admissibility of a confession. First, the burden of proof is different. In a *Charter* hearing, the burden is on the accused to establish the necessary elements. In a confession *voir dire,* the burden is on the Crown to prove that the statement was made voluntarily. Second, the standard of proof is different. In a *Charter* motion, the accused must prove his case on a balance of probabilities, whereas the Crown must prove voluntariness beyond a reasonable doubt. Third, the consequences of a breach are different. In a *Charter* hearing, a violation of the *Charter* does not lead to exclusion of the evidence, rather the accused must go on to convince the court that the admission of the evidence under s. 24(2) of the *Charter* could bring the administration of justice into disrepute. With a confession, if the Crown cannot convince the judge of the voluntariness of the confession, it is excluded. Because of these differences it is important for the Crown to have the defence clarify their objection to the evidence. This is particularly the case where at issue is the admissibility of an accused's statement made to the police. Clarify — is the statement sought to be excluded because of a Charter breach, or because it was not voluntary, or both?

In order to exclude evidence under section 24(2) of the *Charter*, the accused must prove that:

1)   The accused's rights under the *Charter* have been infringed;

2)   The evidence sought to be excluded is connected to the breach of the *Charter*; and

3)   The admission of the evidence would bring the administration of justice into disrepute.

The following chart outlines the various issues and structure of a *Charter* argument.[29]

---

### *Exclusion of Evidence Under the Charter*

*\* The Accused Must Prove the Following*
*on a Balance of Probabilities*

**1) Breach of the *Charter***

- The accused must show that his rights have been infringed.

- The "infringement" was by the state or a person acting as an agent of the state.

**2) The Evidence was Obtained in a Manner that Infringed the Accused's Rights**

- The *Charter* infringement either led to the obtaining of the evidence or the breach and discovery were an integral part of the same transaction.

**3) The Admission of the Evidence Would Bring the Administration of Justice Into Disrepute**
In determining this question courts must gauge:

- The seriousness of the *Charter*-infringing state conduct,

- The impact of the *Charter* breach on the *Charter*-protected interests of the accused, and

- Society's interest in the adjudication of the case on its merits.

The evidence on each of these heads is then weighed in the balance by the trial judge to determine whether a reasonable person, fully informed of all the circumstances and values underlying the *Charter*,

*(cont'd)*

---

[29] For a more detailed analysis of section 24(2), see D. Paciocco and L. Stuesser, *supra*, note 25 at pp. 403-430.

would conclude that the admission of the evidence would bring the administration of justice into disrepute.[30] In asking this question, the focus is on the damage that condoning the *Charter* violation would do to the long-term interest in maintaining the integrity and public confidence in the justice system.

## 6.1  Procedural Points

Prior to bringing a *Charter* motion, fairness demands that the defence should give the Crown notice. For a number of years there was uncertainty just as to the form and amount of notice required. Now in certain provinces legislation mandates notice.[31]

Notice simply of a motion is not enough. The courts require particularization of the issues. A general "boilerplate" will not suffice.[32] "The golden rule is that real and meaningful notice be given of the intended *Charter* application and that it be sufficiently detailed to alert the respondent and the court as to the issues that will be involved."[33]

Should there be no notice or insufficient notice, the trial judge still retains a discretion to hear the motion. As Justice Sharpe in *R. v. Blom* noted, "procedural rules are servants, not masters. They are servants to the cause of the just and expeditious resolution of disputes."[34] The crucial factor is prejudice. Is the Crown at an unfair disadvantage because of the lack of notice? Even if such is the case, a less drastic remedy is an adjournment rather than the refusal to hear the motion.

A second matter concerns the calling of evidence. The problem is that the burden rests with the accused to prove the breach and that the evidence ought to be excluded. Some prosecutors, therefore, take the position that the defence must call the police officers to establish their case. Technically this position may be correct, but to deny the accused the opportunity to cross-examine key adverse witnesses is fundamentally unfair. Judge Wyant,

---

[30]  See *R. v. Grant*, 2009 SCC 32 (S.C.C.).

[31]  See: In Ontario, *The Rules of the Ontario Court of Justice in Criminal Proceedings*, SI/ 97-133 and in Alberta, *The Provincial Court Act, Constitutional Notice Regulation*, AR 102/ 99.

[32]  See *R. v. Blom* (2002), 167 C.C.C. (3d) 332 (Ont. C.A.).

[33]  *R. v. Francey* (2002), 6 C.R. (6th) 386 at para. 15 (Ont. Ct. Jus.).

[34]  *R. v. Blom, supra*, note 32 at para. 21.

in a thorough review of *Charter* procedure, provided this helpful summary •
on both notice and the calling of evidence:[35]

1.  That notice should be given by the defence at the earliest oppor-
    tunity, preferably at the time a trial date is set.

2.  That the defence need not disclose the evidence it relies on but
    should be reasonably specific with respect to the nature of the
    breach and the remedy sought. It should also specify, where pos-
    sible, those witnesses it wishes the Crown to subpoena.

3.  That a hearing should take place prior to trial, or at the onset of
    trial, through the mechanism of a *voir dire*.

4.  That the witnesses requested by the accused and subpoenaed by
    the Crown will be produced by the Crown and cross-examined by
    the accused. The accused can then provide other witnesses of its
    own which it may direct examine. The Crown has the right to
    examine and re-examine or cross-examine witnesses called.

5.  The legal and evidentiary onus remains on the defence on a balance
    of probabilities to show [a breach] has taken place.

---

[35] *R. v. Lavender* [2000] M.J. No. 50 (Prov. Ct.).

# 16

# SPECIAL WITNESSES

- **When the Witness Turns: The Adverse Witness**

- **Child Witnesses**

- **Expert Witnesses**

## 1. WHEN THE WITNESS TURNS: THE ADVERSE WITNESS

Most witnesses you call will be co-operative and provide helpful evidence for your cause, but you must be prepared for disappointment. Some witnesses will surprise. You expect them to say one thing and in court they cannot recall the evidence or say something completely different. In many cases the inconsistencies or omissions in their testimony is simply the result of nerves and forgetfulness, but in other cases the witness has chosen not to be truthful with you or with the court. The witness has turned on you — has become a turncoat.

Crown prosecutors in particular must be prepared for the turncoat witness. The reality of a criminal prosecution is that the Crown often needs to rely upon the testimony of reluctant, fearful or unsavory witnesses and it is not unusual for Crown witnesses to be sympathetic to the defence, if not friends or relatives of the accused. Therefore, the focus in this section will be on the applicable law in criminal cases. Fortunately, most of the law is transferable to civil cases.

### 1.1 Your Options

What do you do with the turncoat witness? When you have a witness who does not come up to proof, an escalating process is recommended. This will help to separate the forgetful witness from the turncoat. Start by assisting the witness, if that fails, you increase the pressure until you move to attack the witness on their testimony. Your options are outlined below.

---

### *Your Options:*
### *When the Witness Turns*

- **Do nothing**. Move on to call contrary evidence.

- **Refresh the witness's memory**. Place before the witness a prior statement and see if it helps the witness "correct" his evidence.

- **Move to cross-examine the witness on the prior inconsistent statement under subsection 9(2) of the *Canada Evidence Act*.** Leave of the court is required and a 9(2) hearing is entered into.

- **If need be, move to have a *K.G.B.* application.** In this hearing you seek to have the prior inconsistent statement admitted for its truth.

- **Move to have the witness declared adverse under subsection 9(1) of the *Canada Evidence Act*.** If the witness is found adverse then counsel may cross-examine him at large.

---

The first option — do nothing — is, in many cases, your wisest course of action. Where you have other witnesses who can offset the turncoat's testimony, move on to their evidence. It is open to you to call other witnesses who will contradict what the turncoat witness has said. In other words, you are not bound by a witness's evidence. For example, if you call one eyewitness to a robbery and he testifies that the robber had a beard it is still open to you to call three other eyewitnesses to testify that the robber was clean shaven.

At times, however, you have no other witnesses to call and you need the turncoat witness's evidence. In this situation, the law recognizes that you may move to assist the witness. Proceed to refresh the witness's memory. Should that not work, you may be in a position to attack the witness. Under the common law, this is referred to as having a witness declared hostile. Leave must be sought and obtained from the trial judge.

Under the common law, a witness is "hostile" when "he does not give his evidence fairly and with a desire to tell the truth because of a hostile animus towards the party who called him."[1] Note, "hostility" means far more than mere "disappointment" with the witness's evidence. The common law procedure is now codified in the respective *Evidence Acts*,[2] where the witness must be found "adverse." The word "adverse" is a broader term than "hostile." "It includes the concept of hostility of the mind, but also includes what may be merely opposed in interest or unfavourable in the sense of opposite in position."[3] An opposing party in a civil case is adverse.[4]

Once a witness is found to be adverse, then the counsel calling the witness may cross-examine the witness "at large." This does not mean that counsel has free rein in attacking the "general" credibility of the witness. You are precluded from impeaching the witness "by general evidence of bad character." What you can do is cross-examine and challenge the witness on the particular testimony. For example, you are prohibited from cross-examining the witness on prior convictions or prior discreditable acts, but you can certainly challenge the witness on the circumstances surrounding the present testimony: his ability to perceive the events, his relationship to the particular accused, any bias or interest in the particular case.[5]

Criminal cases are governed by section 9 of the *Canada Evidence Act*, which reads:

> **9.** (1) A party producing a witness shall not be allowed to impeach his credit by general evidence of bad character, but if the witness, in the opinion of the court, proves adverse, the party may contradict him by other evidence, or, by leave of the court, may prove that the witness made at other times a statement inconsistent with his present testimony, but before the last mentioned proof can be given the circumstances of the supposed statement, sufficient to designate the particular occasion, shall be mentioned to the witness, and he shall be asked whether or not he did make the statement.
>
> (2) Where the party producing a witness alleges that the witness made at other times a statement in writing, reduced to writing, or recorded on audio

---

[1]   D. Paciocco and L. Stuesser, *Essentials of Canadian Law: The Law of Evidence*, 7th ed. Irwin, (2015), p. 549.

[2]   See *Manitoba Evidence Act*, R.S.M. 1987, c. E150, s. 19; *Ontario Evidence Act*, R.S.O. 1990, c. E.23, s. 23; *Canada Evidence Act*, R.S.C. 1985, c. C-5, s. 9.

[3]   *Wawanesa Mutual Ins. Co. v. Hanes*, [1961] O.R. 495 (C.A.) at 505, per Porter, C.J.O.

[4]   The Rules of Court in Manitoba and Ontario provide that an adverse party may be cross-examined when called as a witness by the opposite party — without the need for a finding of adversity. See: Manitoba Queen's Bench Rule 53.07(4) and Ontario Rules of Civil Procedure 53.07(3).

[5]   Canadian case law is divided as to the exact scope of the permitted cross-examination. See Paciocco, *supra*, note 1 at 551.

tape or video tape or otherwise, inconsistent with the witness' present testimony, the court may, without proof that the witness is adverse, grant leave to that party to cross-examine the witness as to the statement and the court may consider the cross-examination in determining whether in the opinion of the court the witness is adverse.

The section is not well drafted and is not applied as read. Subsection 9(1) is applied to find a witness adverse and allows for cross-examination of the witness at large, although nowhere in the statute is this expressly stated. Subsection 9(2) deals with cross-examination on prior inconsistent statements made by the witness in writing, reduced to writing or tape recorded. Section 9(2) came about because earlier authority had suggested that in criminal cases prior inconsistent statements could not be used to prove adversity.[6] The respective provincial Evidence Acts do not have an equivalent subsection 9(2); in civil cases the authorities recognized that prior inconsistent statements could be used to prove adversity.

Subsection 9(2) can be used as a precursor to finding a witness adverse, but that next step is not always necessary. In many instances, counsel is content with simply showing that the witness has made a prior inconsistent statement. The inconsistency is established, the witness's in-court testimony is neutralized. There is no need to go any further and have the witness declared adverse so that the witness can be cross-examined at large. At times a showing of inconsistency is not enough, however, counsel need the prior inconsistent statement to be accepted as true. The Supreme Court of Canada's decision in *R. v. B. (K.G.)* [commonly referred to as *K.G.B.*] provides a case on point.[7] The Crown needed the prior inconsistent statements to be introduced for their truth or the Crown had no case. The accused was charged with murder. Three of the accused's companions were interviewed by the police. Each gave a statement implicating the accused. At trial each recanted. Each admitted making the statement, but denied that it was true. Without having these statements admitted for their truth, there was insufficient evidence to establish the accused's identity as the killer. On appeal, the Supreme Court of Canada recognized a new hearsay exception for the admissibility of prior inconsistent statements, provided that the statements were sufficiently reliable. Chief Justice Lamer spoke of the following prerequisites:

- the statement is made under oath or solemn affirmation following a warning as to the existence of sanctions and the significance of the oath or affirmation;

---

[6] See Paciocco, *supra*, note 1 at pp. 417-420.

[7] *R. v. B. (K.G.)* (1993), 19 C.R. (4th) 1 (S.C.C.).

- the statement is videotaped in its entirety; and

- the opposing party has a full opportunity to cross-examine the witness respecting the statement.

The Chief Justice did go on, however, to state that if the requirements could not be strictly met, one could look to other circumstantial guarantees of trustworthiness.[8] A "*K.G.B.*" application usually follows upon a section 9(2) hearing.

## 1.2 The Subsection 9(2) Application Procedure

It is important to remember that subsection 9(2) only applies to statements made in writing, reduced to writing or audio or videotape recorded. If the statement does not meet these requirements, then you need to use subsection 9(1). Keep in mind as well that a successful application only means that you are permitted to cross-examine the witness on the prior inconsistent statement. You are not free to cross-examine the witness at large. The accepted procedure is outlined in the case of *R. v. Milgaard*.[9] That case set out a seven step-process as follows:

1. Counsel should advise the Court that he desires to make an application under s. 9(2) of the *Canada Evidence Act*.

2. When the Court is so advised, the Court should direct the jury to retire.

3. Upon retirement of the jury, counsel should advise the learned trial Judge of the particulars of the application and produce for him the alleged statement in writing, or the writing to which the statement has been reduced.

4. The learned trial Judge should read the statement, or writing, and determine whether, in fact, there is an inconsistency between such statement or writing and the evidence the witness has given in Court. If the learned trial Judge decides that there is no inconsistency, then that ends the matter. If he finds there is an inconsistency, he should call upon counsel to prove the statement or writing.

5. Counsel should then prove the statement, or writing. This may be done by producing the statement or writing to the witness. If the witness

---

[8] For a discussion on *K.G.B.*, see Paciocco, *supra*, note 1 at pp. 103-110.
[9] (1971), 14 C.R.N.S. 34 (Sask. C.A.) at 49-50.

admits the statement, or the statement reduced to writing, such proof would be sufficient. If the witness does not so admit, counsel then could provide the necessary proof by other evidence.

6.  If the witness admits making the statement, counsel for the opposing party should have the right to cross-examine as to the circumstances under which the statement was made. A similar right to cross-examine should be granted if the statement is proved by other witnesses. It may be that he will be able to establish that there were circumstances which would render it improper for the learned trial Judge to permit the cross-examination, notwithstanding the apparent inconsistencies. The opposing counsel, too, should have the right to call evidence as to factors relevant to obtaining the statement, for the purpose of attempting to show that cross-examination should not be permitted.

7.  The learned trial Judge should then decide whether or not he will permit the cross-examination. If so, the jury should be recalled.

## 1.3   The Procedure on a *K.G.B.* Application

A *K.G.B.* application normally follows upon a section 9(2) hearing. Once the trial judge is satisfied that the witness has made a prior inconsistent statement and that cross-examination will be permitted, counsel may seek to have the statement admitted for its truth. The procedure outlined is as follows:

1.  The calling party must state its intention in tendering the statement. If the party gives notice that it will seek to have the statement admitted for its truth, the section 9(2) hearing will continue on that issue.

2.  The calling party bears the burden of proof to establish on a balance of probability the admissibility of the prior inconsistent statement for its truth.

3.  The calling party must establish that the necessary indicia of reliability — warning, oath, solemn affirmation, or solemn declaration, and videotape record, or sufficient substitutes — are present and genuine.

4.  The opposing party has full opportunity to cross-examine the witness at trial respecting the statement.

5.  The calling party must also establish that the statement was made voluntarily, if to a person in authority, and that there are no other factors

that would tend to bring the administration of justice into disrepute if the statement is admitted for its truth.

### 1.4    The Procedure in Having a Witness Declared Adverse

The procedure on a subsection 9(1) application to have a witness declared adverse is similar to the section 9(2) application. The adversity ruling may follow upon a section 9(2) application. A *voir dire* is entered into on the issue of "adversity." The hearing therefore has a broader scope than a section 9(2) *voir dire*. In terms of the evidence to be called, any and all evidence going to adversity is admissible. You can be guided by the following statement:[10]

> Whether a witness is hostile in mind is a question of fact. To determine this collateral issue a trial Judge should hear all and any evidence relevant to that issue. The fact that a witness has made a previous contradictory statement is relevant, admissible and most cogent evidence on that issue and that evidence alone may be accepted by the Judge as sufficient proof of the hostility of the witness irrespective of the demeanour and manner of the witness in the witness-box. (It is also of course, open to the trial Judge to rule that a witness is hostile solely by reason of his manner of giving evidence and demeanour in the witness-box.)

The procedure on the application is as follows:

1.    Advise the court that you wish to have a witness declared adverse under the applicable statute.

2.    The trial judge should then enter into a *voir dire* on the issue of adversity. This might well be a further extension of the hearing flowing from a section 9(2) application.

3.    Once you have received a ruling that the witness is adverse, you may cross-examine the witness at large in the presence of the jury.

4.    Usually there will be a prior inconsistent statement involved and the circumstances surrounding the making of this statement must be put to the witness in the course of your cross-examination.

## 2.    CHILD WITNESSES

More children are testifying in our courts, especially in the criminal courts involving charges of sexual and physical abuse, and this section will

---

[10] Taken from *Wawanesa Mutual Ins. Co. v. Hanes*, *supra*, note 3 at pp. 534-535 *per* MacKay J.A.

concentrate upon the law and approach to child witnesses in criminal cases. The courtroom is an intimidating and stressful place for children. Fortunately, in recent years we have seen a movement towards making the courts more accommodating for children. For example, in abuse cases under the *Criminal Code* the trial judge has the power to exclude the public from the court (s. 486); allow the child to testify with a support person close by (s. 486.1); allow the child to testify from behind a screen or by closed-circuit television so as not to have to face the accused (s. 486.2); prohibit the accused from personally cross-examining the child (s. 486.3).

There has also been a change in attitude by the courts towards the evidence of children. Gone is the view that the testimony of children is generally unreliable. Rather, children are to be assessed like any other witnesses. The general principle is that a witness is taken to be credible — until shown to be otherwise. Madam Justice McLachlin (as she then was) advised that:[11]

> We approach the evidence of children not from the perspective of rigid stereotypes, but on what Wilson J. called a "common sense" basis, taking into account the strengths and weaknesses which characterize the evidence offered in the particular case.

Yet, children are not adults and they cannot be treated in all ways the same. Child witnesses have special needs. First, they need and deserve special preparation. Second, there is a need for a special competency hearing. Third, counsel must be especially careful in examining children.

### 2.1　Preparing the Child Witness to Testify

It is unfair to expect children to testify in a court of law without adequate preparation. It is absolutely essential that counsel informs the child as to what is going to happen in the court, who will be there, and what the child will have to do.[12] A tour of the courtroom, when not in session, is recommended.

It is important that you get to know the child. The better you know the child, the better your relationship, the better will be the child's testimony.

---

[11] *R. v. W. (R.)* (1992), 74 C.C.C. (3d) 134 at 143 (S.C.C.).

[12] A helpful little book that informs a child about the court process is W. Harvey and A. Watson-Russell, *So, You Have To Go To Court!* 3rd ed. (1992).

You will have to interview the child. Outlined below are a number of suggestions.[13]

---

### *Suggestions on Interviewing Children*

- Prior to the interview learn as much as you can about the child.

- Avoid repeated interviews of the child or repeatedly asking the same questions. If persistently asked questions by authority figures, some children may develop false stories which they perceive the interviewers want to hear.

- Get off on the right foot. Respect the child's needs. Remember the child is an involuntary participant — so accommodate the child. Do not take the child away from his or her baseball game. The child would be far happier missing school.

- Do not come on too strong or be unduly friendly. Respect the child, listen to the child, and tell the child in clear terms what you do and why the two of you need to talk.

- Conduct the interview in as neutral a manner as possible.

- Be very careful about asking leading or suggestive questions.

- Do not provide subtle rewards to obtain answers, nor should you make subtle threats or negative comments if the child fails to answer questions.

- Treat the child with honesty, warmth, and respect.

- Develop in the child a sense of trust that you can help the child.

*(cont'd)*

---

[13] See J.P. Schuman, N. Bala and K. Lee, "Developmentally Appropriate Questions for Child Witnesses", (1999), 25 Queen's L.J. 251-304; M. Mian *et al.*, "The Child as Witness", (1991) 4 C.R. (4th) 359; N. Bala, "Annotation to *R. v. S. (T.)*", (1995) 40 C.R. (4th) 4-6.

> • Avoid big words and legalese.
>
> • Avoid asking the child why he or she did or did not take such action. The "why" question implies criticism.
>
> • Be prepared to invest the necessary time. Conduct the interview at the child's pace and not according to your timetable.

### 2.2   Competency of Child Witnesses

Section 16.1 of the *Canada Evidence Act* creates a separate regime to deal with the competency of child witnesses under the age of 14 and does away with much of the formality and abstraction that made the former section 16 difficult to apply to children. For example, the understanding of an oath, solemn affirmation or even of a promise are abstract concepts often difficult to verbalize – even for adults. Yet, under the former section 16, as interpreted by the courts, it was mandatory that before testifying a child witness had to demonstrate just such an understanding.

Section 16.1 sweeps aside many of the abstractions and makes the competency of children comparable to that of adult witnesses. The section 16.1 regime provides that children will be allowed to testify if they are able to "understand and respond to questions" and they "promise to tell the truth." Section 16.1 provides as follows:

• Children are presumed to have the capacity to testify: subsection 16.1(1). A competency hearing is no longer mandatory. This treats children and adults the same.

• The burden is on the challenger to bring into question the competency of the child: subsection 16.1(4).

• Children are not required to take an oath or make a solemn affirmation: subsection 16.1(2).

• The child witness is required "to promise to tell the truth": subsection 16.1(6).

• However, no questions are to be asked of children as to their understanding of the nature of the promise: subsection 16.1(7).

• "For greater certainty" the testimony of a child, if received under a promise, shall have "the same effect as if it were taken under oath": subsection 16.1(8).

The inquiry outlined in section 16.1 is conducted in front of the jury, since matters of competency will also assist the jurors in weighing the witness's evidence. Usually the trial judge conducts the examination of the child, however, it may well be better practice for the counsel calling the witness to do the examination, especially for young children.[14] The child knows the counsel and does not know the judge. It is also open to call other evidence relevant to the child's competency should that be necessary.[15]

Having the child witness "promise to tell the truth" does not require a formal promise; it is enough if the child witness has clearly committed to tell the truth. Consider the following exchange, which was found by the Ontario Court of Appeal to be sufficient:[16]

The Court: . . . Do you know what it is, the difference between the truth and not telling the truth?

Witness: Yep.

The Court: Okay. And it is important to me that you tell me the truth because I have to make decisions. I want to make sure people are telling me the truth. Okay?

Witness: Okay.

## 2.3    Examination of Child Witnesses

The examination of children is difficult and it requires a great deal of care both in terms of the language used and in the tone of voice; this holds true for direct examination and for cross-examination. The direct examination will be all the easier should you have a rapport with the child going into the court. The child will be nervous — if not terrified. Start easy. Begin with simple questions, which will build up the child's confidence. Use a gentle and patient manner. Let the child know that it is okay if he or she cannot answer a question. Keep in mind as well the limited attention spans for young children. They will need breaks after short periods of time. Also

---

[14] The Ontario Court of Appeal has ruled that the inquiry under section 16 does not require the judge to question the witness. See *R. v. Peterson* (1996), 47 C.R. (4th) 161 (Ont. C.A.).

[15] For a discussion on the conduct of a competency hearing see *R. v. I. (D.)*, 2012 SCC 5 (S.C.C.) at para. 76-83. *I. (D.)* is a section 16 case; however, the procedure is similar for s. 16.1 hearings.

[16] *R. v. F. (C.C.)*, 2014 ONCA 327 (Ont. C.A.) at para. 3.

remember this, if the child is having difficulty answering a question, in all likelihood the problem lies with the question and how you have asked it.

Cross-examination requires even more care. What you definitely cannot do for most child witnesses is to come down hard on the child. If you do, everyone in the courtroom will come to the child's defence, turn against you and you can expect a strong rebuke from the trial judge.

Language is the key. Outlined below are a few thoughts on the choice of words in examining a child.

---

### A Few Suggestions for Questioning Children[17]

1. Break long sentences/questions into shorter ones that have one main idea each.

2. Choose easy words over hard ones.

3. Avoid legal jargon, and "frozels" (term for frozen legalisms) like "What if anything," "Did there come a time."

4. Avoid asking children directly about abstract concepts like what constitutes truth or what the difference is between the truth and a lie. In seeking to judge a young (under 9 or 10) child's knowledge of truth and lies, ask simple, concrete questions that make use of a child's experience. *Example*: What did you have for breakfast today? (*Pause*) If you said you had chocolate cake and cherry pie, would you be telling me the truth, or would you be telling me a lie? [Young children equate truth with *fact*, lies with *non-fact*.]

5. Avoid the question of belief entirely. (Do you believe that to be true?)

(cont'd)

---

[17] Summarized from A. Walker, *Handbook on Questioning Children* (1994), at pp. 95-98.

6. Watch your pronouns carefully (including "that.") Be sure they refer either to something you can physically point at, or to something in the very immediate (spoken) past, such as in the same sentence, or in the last few seconds.

7. Avoid tag questions (e.g., "You did it, *didn't you?*") They are confusing for children. Avoid, too, Yes/No questions that are packed with lots of propositions. (Example of a bad simple-sounding question, with propositions numbered: "[1] Do you remember [2] when Mary asked you [3] if you knew [4] what colour Mark's shirt was, and [5] you said, [6] 'Blue'?" What would a "Yes" or "No" answer tell you here?) It does not help the factfinder to rely on an answer if it's not clear what the question was.

8. See that the child stays firmly grounded in the appropriate questioning situation. If you are asking about the past, be sure the child understands that. If you shift to the present, make that clear too.

9. Be alert to the tendency of young children to be very literal and concrete in their language. "Did you have your *clothes* on?" might get a "No" answer; "Did you have your *p.j.'s* on?" might get a "Yes."

10. Don't *expect* children under about age 9 or 10 to give "reliable" estimates of time, speed, distance, size, height, weight, color, or to have mastered any relational concept, including kinship.

## 3.   EXPERT WITNESSES

There are experts available on any conceivable topic. Most provide helpful evidence. Some do not. One of the problems with expert testimony is that under the guise of "expertise" the evidence takes on added credibility, whether deserved or not. For this reason, expert evidence can be extremely dangerous. A classic example to illustrate the power and abuse of expert evidence is the famous Australian "Dingo Case" involving the conviction of Lynne Chamberlain for the murder of her nine-week-old daughter, Azaria.[18] The Chamberlains were camping near Uluru/Ayers Rock in Central

---

[18] *Chamberlain v. R. (No. 2)* (1984), 153 C.L.R. 521 (Aust. H.C.). In 2012 a coroner was asked to reopen the inquest into the death of Azaria and ruled that Azaria

Australia. Mrs. Chamberlain's account of what occurred is that after nursing Azaria, she put her to bed in one of the tents. Mrs. Chamberlain then returned to the barbecue area, where the Chamberlains and another family, the Lowes, were finishing their evening meal. Mrs. Lowe testified that she heard the baby cry. Mrs. Chamberlain's son and husband thought it was Azaria. Mrs. Chamberlain went to check. She saw a dog — a dingo — taking Azaria. The Crown's case was that Mrs. Chamberlain did not put Azaria to bed, but took her to the car and there cut the baby's throat and returned to the barbecue area. The body was left in the car, possibly in a camera bag, and buried later in the night by Mr. or Mrs. Chamberlain. Mr. Chamberlain was charged as an accessory after the fact to murder and Mrs. Chamberlain was charged with murder.

Azaria's body was never found. A week after her disappearance, a tourist found clothing that Azaria had been wearing, some four km from the Chamberlain campsite and not far from two dingo dens. The Chamberlains were convicted at trial largely on the basis of expert testimony. Experts provided two key incriminating pieces of evidence. One Crown expert testified that in her opinion foetal blood was found in the Chamberlain's car. A second Crown expert testified that in his opinion, damage to Azaria's clothing was caused by it being "cut" by scissors — dingoes don't use scissors.

According to Mrs. Chamberlain, Azaria had been wearing a matinee jacket. This would explain why no saliva was found on Azaria's clothing. The jacket was not found until six years later. It confirmed what Mrs. Chamberlain had said at trial. A Royal Commission of Inquiry was called to review the Chamberlain convictions. The Commission concluded that there were serious doubts as to the guilt of Mrs. Chamberlain and given new evidence heard before the Commission a trial judge would have been obliged to direct a jury to acquit Mrs. Chamberlain.[19] The Commission heard new evidence that seriously brought into question the Crown expert testimony presented at the trial. The alleged "foetal blood" found in the car may not have been anything more than rust. As for a dingo using scissors, new testing showed that dingo teeth could cut like scissors.

The "dingo case" presents a fascinating study in expert testimony. First, it shows the power of expert testimony. There is little doubt that the experts convicted Lynne Chamberlain — notwithstanding the conflicting

---

died "as the result of her being attacked and taken by a dingo". See *Inquest into the death of Azaria Chantel Loren Chamberlain*, [2012] NTMC 020 at para. 31.

[19] T.R. Morling, *Royal Commission of Inquiry into Chamberlain Convictions* (1987).

evidence from eyewitnesses, such as Mrs. Lowe, who were standing by Mrs. Chamberlain when they heard Azaria cry. Second, the case shows the fundamental importance of going to the factual basis for any expert's opinion. The lesson is clear, undermine the factual foundation and the opinion falls. Third, in order to defend against an expert you need your own expert to guide you in cross-examination and to present a contrary opinion on the stand. Fourth, it shows that experts are human; they become committed to a position and are very unwilling to admit alternative theories. With these important lessons in mind, let us turn to the admissibility of expert evidence.

## 3.1 The Admissibility of Expert Evidence

Because of cases like *Chamberlain* courts have become more vigilant in admitting expert evidence. Trial judges are called upon to play a "gatekeeper" role in admitting such evidence. Justice Rothstein stated that "Courts must fulfil their gatekeeper role to ensure that unnecessary, irrelevant and potentially distracting expert and survey evidence is not allowed to extend and complicate court proceedings."[20]

The decision of the Supreme Court of Canada in *R. v. Mohan* provides a helpful structure for the admissibility of expert evidence.[21] Mr. Justice Sopinka wrote the judgment of the court and he outlined four criteria for the admissibility of expert evidence:

1) relevance;

2) necessity in assisting the trier of fact;

3) the absence of any exclusionary rule;

4) a properly qualified expert.

These criteria are threshold requirements for admissibility. For example, if the expert evidence is not necessary then it ought to be excluded. In addition, the gatekeeper function requires that even if the thresholds are met the trial judge must globally weigh the potential risks and benefits in receiving the expert evidence.[22]

---

[20] *Masterpiece Inc. v. Alavida Lifestyles Inc.*, 2011 SCC 27 (S.C.C.) at para. 76.

[21] *R. v. Mohan* (1994), 29 C.R. (4th) 243 (S.C.C.).

[22] *White Burgess Langille Inman v. Abbott and Haliburton Co.*, 2015 SCC 23 (S.C.C.) at paras. 23-24.

Mr. Justice Sopinka in *Mohan* spoke of a "cost-benefit analysis" – "whether its value is worth what it costs." He explained:[23]

> Cost in this context is not used in its traditional economic sense but rather in terms of its impact on the trial process. Evidence that is otherwise logically relevant may be excluded on this basis, if its probative value is overborne by its prejudicial effect, if it involves an inordinate amount of time which is not commensurate with its value or if it is misleading in the sense that its effect on the trier of fact, particularly a jury, is out of proportion to its reliability.

The cost-benefit analysis is for the trial judge to consider. Inextricably linked to this analysis is the need to assess the reliability of the science. The science needs to pass some minimal threshold test of reliability, otherwise the danger of misleading the trier of fact is enormous. Mr. Justice Sopinka went on to write:[24]

> The reliability versus effect factor has special significance in assessing the admissibility of expert evidence.

There is a danger that expert evidence will be misused and will distort the fact-finding process. Dressed up in scientific language which the jury does not easily understand and submitted through a witness of impressive antecedents, this evidence is apt to be accepted by the jury as being virtually infallible and as having more weight than it deserves.

## (a) Relevancy

All evidence must be relevant to be admissible. The threshold for relevancy is low: Does the proposed evidence make a fact in issue more or less probable than it would be without the evidence? However, Mr. Justice Sopinka did not use the term "relevancy" in the sense of logical relevancy — minimal probative value. Rather, he was looking to the *admissibility of relevant evidence*, which requires heightened scrutiny.

How is such an assessment undertaken? Mr. Justice Sopinka referred to the decision of Moldaver J. in *R. v. Melaragni*.[25] In that case, Mr. Justice Moldaver ruled on admitting the evidence of an expert on glass fracture analysis. In making his ruling, he considered nine factors. Mr. Justice Sopinka cited two of these in *Mohan*, but the entire list is worthy of note:[26]

---

[23] *R. v. Mohan, supra,* note 21 at 252.
[24] *Ibid.,* at 252.
[25] (1992), 73 C.C.C. (3d) 348 (Ont. Gen. Div.).
[26] *Ibid.,* at 353.

1) Is the evidence likely to assist the jury in its fact-finding mission, or is it likely to confuse and confound the jury? [Cited in *Mohan*.]

2) Is the jury likely to be overwhelmed by the "mystic infallibility" of the evidence, or will the jury be able to keep an open mind and objectively assess the worth of the evidence? [Cited in *Mohan*.]

3) Will the evidence, if accepted, conclusively prove an essential element of the crime which the defence is contesting, or is it simply a piece of evidence to be incorporated into a larger puzzle?

4) What degree of reliability has the proposed scientific technique or body of knowledge achieved?

5) Are there a sufficient number of experts available so that it can be independently tested by the defence?

6) Is the scientific technique or body of knowledge such that it can be independently tested by the defence?

7) Has the scientific technique destroyed the evidence upon which the conclusions have been based, or has the evidence been preserved for the defence analysis if requested?

8) Are there clear policy or legal grounds which would render the evidence inadmissible despite its probative value?

9) Will the evidence cause undue delay or result in the needless presentation of cumulative evidence?

Relevancy determines the "box" for the expert's testimony; it sets the parameters. For example, if an emergency room doctor is called to describe the injuries incurred by the victim of a sexual assault it is acceptable for the doctor, who is familiar with trauma, to discuss the wounds and injuries treated – this information is within "the box." It may well not be "within the box," however, for the doctor to testify as to the indicia sexual assaults and that the injuries are consistent with those of a sexual assault. "Box" the expert.

## (b)    Necessity in Assisting the Trier of Fact

A pre-condition for the admissibility of expert evidence is that it will assist the trier of fact. The information provided by the expert must be "beyond the ken" of the average lay person. If not, then the evidence is

364    An Advocacy Primer

unnecessary; it is superfluous. Mr. Justice Sopinka found the "helpfulness" standard too low. He preferred the word "necessity"; "necessary in the sense that it provide information which is likely to be outside the experience and knowledge of a judge or jury."

Once again, the trial judge determines the necessity. Although Mr. Justice Sopinka advised against deciding necessity by "too strict a standard," it is also true that the trial judge is obliged to be vigilant. For example, in a case involving child abuse, is it necessary to call an expert about why the alleged victim would continue to associate with her father despite being abused?[27] Jurors and judges were once children, they lived in family situations and many now are parents themselves. In other words, they understand why a child would not want to disrupt the family, is dominated by the father and could easily be threatened or coerced to stay and remain silent. We do not need an expert to tell us these things.

### (c)   The Absence of Any Exclusionary Rule

The admissibility of expert evidence must comply with the other rules of evidence. For example, expert evidence will not be admissible if it simply goes to introduce impermissible character evidence.

### (d)   A Properly Qualified Expert

The evidence must be given by a witness who is shown to have acquired special or peculiar knowledge through study or experience in respect of the matters on which he or she undertakes to testify. The threshold needed to be deemed an expert is a modest one. What is required is knowledge "beyond the ken of the lay person."

Knowledge alone is not sufficient. The expert also has a responsibility to provide fair, objective and non-partisan evidence that will assist the court. In the *White Burgess* case Justice Cromwell outlined the responsibility of experts as follows:[28]

> Expert witnesses have a special duty to the court to provide fair, objective and non-partisan assistance. A proposed expert witness who is unable or unwilling to comply with this duty is not qualified to give expert opinion evidence and should not be permitted to do so. Less fundamental concerns about an expert's

---

[27] *R. v. C.* (1993), 70 A. Crim. R. 378 (S.A.C.A.).
[28] *White Burgess Langille Inman v. Abbott and Haliburton Co., supra,* note 22 at para. 2.

independence and impartiality should be taken into account in the broader, overall weighing of the costs and benefits of receiving the evidence.

The burden is on the party opposing the expert's qualification to demonstrate a realistic concern that the expert is unable or unwilling to comply with the duty to assist the court. Once so raised, the burden is on the party presenting the expert to establish on a balance of probabilities the essential qualities of independence and impartiality. Justice Cromwell underscores that bias and partisanship go to both the threshold and to the cost-benefit analysis. He explained:[29]

> Finding that expert evidence meets the basic threshold does not end the inquiry. Consistent with the structure of the analysis developed following *Mohan* which I have discussed earlier, the judge must still take concerns about the expert's independence and impartiality into account in weighing the evidence at the gatekeeping stage.

### 3.2    Preparation of Expert Witnesses

The role of the expert is to educate the judge or jury. The challenge for counsel is how to translate this expert knowledge into common, under-standable terms for the non-expert. It is for this reason that expert witnesses need special preparation. Experts may be experts in their field, but that does not mean that they are good communicators. Think back to your university days and how often you were exposed to professors who could not teach. Enough said. Your task is to see that expert knowledge is communicated effectively. Concentrate on two points: make the evidence *simple* and make the expert *credible*.

In terms of making the evidence simple, it is fundamental that you, as counsel, must first understand what the expert is saying. Rest assured that if you do not understand what the expert is saying, no one else in the courtroom will either. Therefore, the first step in preparing an expert is to prepare yourself. You need to do a quick study. Before meeting with the expert, read leading texts in order to familiarize yourself in general terms with the area of expertise. You are now in a better position to understand how this specific expert can be of assistance.

Ask for explanations. Why is the expert of that opinion? What reasoning and evidence support that opinion? Encourage the expert to diagram or chart findings. What you are looking for are ways to simplify the evidence into understandable lay terms.

---

[29] *Ibid.* at para. 54.

Next, the expert's language must be simplified. Every profession has its jargon. Jargon does not impress, it befuddles. Call upon the expert to translate scientific terms into simple language. In other words, get the expert to speak English.

Similarly, the expert's explanation must be put into simple terms. At this point, you should think about the use of diagrams or charts to explain the expert's opinion. A diagram, chart or photograph can be most effective in bringing to light what it is that the expert is saying. This is where an effective PowerPoint presentation could assist in conveying the necessary explanation.

For example, I was involved in a case where we were calling an expert in blood analysis (before DNA testing). The expert was to testify that blood from the victim was consistent with blood taken from the interior of the accused's van. The expert came to this conclusion based on tests conducted on the respective samples. Three tests were undertaken. Each test showed that the blood samples were from the same blood grouping. The expert then took the statistical percentage of the population for each blood grouping, multiplied them together and concluded that only .06 percent of the population had the blood type.

The difficulty that we had was how to explain this to a jury without having them get lost in blood groupings and statistics. The solution was a chart. We prepared a simple overhead transparency that showed the results of the three tests for the victim's blood (column one) and for the sample from the van (column two). The chart highlighted the match. There is power in the visual aid. The jury had a frame of reference from which to follow the expert's evidence. Rather than abstract concepts, there before them were the real figures. Nowhere in advocacy is the need for imaginative visual aids more necessary than in the area of presenting expert evidence.

When working with an expert, counsel really acts as an editor. Experts get caught up in detail. Counsel must weed out the needless detail and focus on what is crucial to support the expert's opinion. The question that needs to be asked repeatedly is, "What does the judge need to know?" The editing of the expert's evidence takes time, takes numerous consultations and takes understanding on your part as to the strengths and weaknesses of the expert's evidence.

The second hallmark of a good expert witness is one who comes across as being credible. Keep in mind that for every expert you call, the other side will have their expert. Your task is to win the "battle of the experts." You will do so by making your expert the more credible. Beware the absolutely certain expert. Humility is appreciated, over-confidence is not. Heed this advice from Sir David Napley:[30]

> The best expert witness for you to find is often the man who will make concessions to the other side, who will acknowledge that he could be wrong. His view is more likely to be accepted than the view of the man who is dogmatic, assertive and will not give an inch anywhere.

Overconfidence often leads to overstatement. Beware. Overstatement, if exposed, is a fatal flaw for expert witnesses. Do not assume that your expert will get away with overstatement. Overstatement is a trap that can lead experts into absurdity, and with them so goes their evidence. Precision of language is important for experts, who must appear to be careful, prudent persons. For example, in my blood analysis case, the analyst could not say that the blood found in the accused's van was that of the victim. What the analyst could say was that the blood found in the van was "consistent" with the victim's and that only .06 percent of the population had that type of blood. The expert was duly careful on this point in testifying, and by being careful came across as being a fair, objective witness. Let the jury come to the reasonable inference; it was the victim's blood.

The expert's opinion is only as good as the factual foundation for it. Accordingly, it is important early on for counsel to make available to the expert any and all information needed to come to an accurate opinion. Go over the factual foundation with the expert very carefully. This will expose the true strengths and weaknesses of the expert's opinion.

For example, to return to the blood analysis case, there are up to ten different tests possible to type blood. The analyst used only three. Why? The analyst explained that the other seven tests required fresh blood samples. These samples were not fresh. The three tests that were done, however, were the most reliable. We were now prepared to counter this alleged weakness in the analysis.

Another suggestion is for counsel to review leading texts on the area of expertise. Does the opinion of your expert accord with the opinion of the text writer? Did your expert follow the recommended techniques as outlined?

Beyond leading texts in the field, review your expert's own writing on the topic. Credibility suffers greatly when experts are confronted by their

---

[30] Sir David Napley, "Instructing The Expert Witness" in Advocacy, A Symposium presented by the Canadian Bar Association – Ontario, in collaboration with the Law Society of Upper Canada (1982), 27 at 30.

own contrary writings. Imagine the use to be made by cross-examining counsel of such evidence.

A final aspect of credibility is that of the expert's qualifications. You need to highlight the expert's credentials. The jury or judge need to know why they can trust this expert's opinion. Ask for a current resume from the expert. Review it with the expert. Look for areas to enhance in terms of the expert's qualifications as they apply to the opinion being sought in the particular case. Note any special training, experience or research in the exact area under review.

You are now in a position to go through a mock examination-in-chief and cross-examination with the expert. These mock examinations, more than for other witnesses, are absolutely critical as a final preparation for expert witnesses. Expert testimony, in order to be simple and understandable, must be carefully choreographed, and this takes practice.

### 3.3    Qualifying the Expert

The first step in presenting expert evidence is to introduce the expert and outline his or her area of expertise. The witness must be shown to be a person "qualified" to give the opinion sought. In this initial part of the examination, look to cover the following areas:

- Current and previous employment

- Education and training

- Work experience

- Teaching experience

- Memberships in professional organizations

- Licenses, certificates or special courses taken

- Publications

- Court experience

Ideally, these topics should be related to the specific issue on which the witness is going to be asked to express an opinion. For example, if you are going to be asking a doctor to express an opinion regarding the cause of certain burn injuries, then in examination go over the doctor's experience with burn victims.

Credibility is essential. You need to convince the trier of fact that your expert is to be preferred over the expert called by the other side. Plan to highlight features of your expert's background that give extra credibility to the opinion. A good practice is to provide a copy of your expert's resume to the court.

Opposing counsel may concede your witness's expertise, with the suggestion that there is no need to go through the expert's qualifications. Accept the concession but DO NOT dispense with your examination of the expert on his or her credentials. If your witness is so good, make certain that the judge or jury knows it. Only abbreviate your examination if the judge advises you that he or she is very familiar with the expert's qualifications.

At the conclusion of this qualifying phase, you turn to the trial judge and say, "My Lord/Your Honour, that concludes my questioning of Dr. Smith on her qualifications. I propose to ask Dr. Smith to provide an opinion as to the cause of the burns suffered by the complainant." The opposite party will then be given an opportunity to cross-examine the witness on her qualifications or on the admissibility of the opinion sought to be adduced. If the trial judge rules her testimony admissible, then the examination proceeds on to the giving of the opinion. The qualification phase is usually held in the presence of the jury. Qualification is a matter of witness competence and, just as for the competency of children, the evidence is useful to the jury in assessing the weight to give to the witness's testimony should she be allowed to testify. However, if the issues surrounding the admissibility of the evidence are more complicated, for example, there may be a serious question as to the reliability of the science relied upon by the expert, then a *voir dire* should be held in the absence of the jury.[31]

### 3.4    Establishing the Foundation for the Opinion

An opinion is only as good as its foundation of facts, inferences or assumptions. In examining the expert, counsel must bring out the basis for the opinion. Certain experts will be testifying on the basis of personal observation, such as examining doctors or fire inspectors. These witnesses can simply outline what they did as part of their examination or investigation. Other experts may not have conducted any independent investigation,

---

[31] An example is found in *R. v. Mohan, supra*, note 21.

but are asked to provide an opinion based upon applying his or her expertise to the facts of the particular case. Where the facts are contested, it is essential that the judge or jury knows which facts the expert relies upon. The hypothetical question serves this purpose. You put to the witness the facts that you are confident you can prove. Based on these facts, the expert is asked to express an opinion. Remember the expert's opinion will only be as good as its factual underpinnings and one weak fact in your hypothetical could well result in the jury rejecting your expert's opinion. Consider the example below.

---

### The Hypothetical Question

An expert is called to express an opinion as to the cause of an air plane crash. The witness has been duly qualified as an expert in aircraft design and aerodynamics.

Q. Doctor, I am going to ask that you assume the following facts and I will then ask for your opinion based on these facts. Assume the following facts:

1) A Fokker Venger aircraft crashed 800 metres from its take-off point.

2) The air temperature at the time was 0 degrees Celsius.

3) The relative humidity index was at 98%.

4) The aircraft had a passenger load of 42 passengers and a fuel load of 1400 kilograms.

5) The take-off speed of the aircraft was recorded at 250 kph.

6) The aircraft was not de-iced.

. . .

Doctor, based on these facts, do you have an opinion as to what may have caused the Fokker Venger aircraft to crash?

A. I do.

*(cont'd)*

> **Q.** What is that opinion?
> **A.** The cause of the crash is consistent with an ice build-up on its wings.
>
> **Q.** Why do you say that, Doctor?
> **A.** [Explanation given.]

### 3.5    Cross-examination of the Expert Witness

The principles of cross-examination do not change for an expert witness. You either seek to elicit favourable testimony or seek to discredit the testimony. Preparation remains the key. Counsel must become as expert as the expert. Learn about the area through reading texts or being taught by your own expert. The most important document to peruse is the expert's report.[32] Once you understand the area of inquiry, you are in a position to question the expert. Don't look to destroy the expert. Rather, strive for a far more realistic goal — strive to show that you have the better expert.

Consider the following areas for cross-examination:

1)   Are there areas where the expert can give evidence that will support your theory of the case?

2)   Given different facts, would the expert's opinion change? Presumably you seek to support your expert's opinion based on the different facts.

3)   Is the witness's opinion based on personal observation? If so, how thorough was the expert's examination? Were correct procedures followed? How long was the observation period?

4)   If the expert's opinion is based on a hypothetical base, obtain admissions that it is preferred to do tests and examinations first hand.

5)   Narrow the expert's area of expertise. This will reduce the value of any opinion on the periphery of the expertise.

---

[32] Under the Rules of Court, prior to testifying an expert witness must provide a report outlining the substance of his or her proposed testimony. See Manitoba Queen's Bench Rule 53.03(1) and Ontario Rule 53.03(1). See as well s. 657.3 of the *Criminal Code*.

6) Refer to authoritative texts that contradict the expert. Better yet, review all of the expert's writing and find instances where the expert contradicts himself.

7) Have the expert admit that the opinion given is based on probability and is not absolute. In this way the aura of the opinion is removed.

8) Look for bias. Has the expert always testified for certain clients? How much is the expert being paid?

[BEWARE! Your expert may also be vulnerable on this point.]

In cross-examining an expert on a text or article written by others, it is necessary for the witness to first acknowledge that the writing is authoritative. The proper procedure is to begin by asking the witness if she knows the work. If the witness does not know the work or denies its authority, that ends the inquiry on that writing and counsel cannot read from it. If the witness acknowledges the work's authority, then parts of it may be read to the witness. The witness may then agree with the statement read and it becomes evidence in the case. On the other hand, the witness may disagree with the statement. In this instance, the contrary statement goes to the credibility of the witness's testimony.[33]

---

[33] *R. v. Marquard* (1993), 25 C.R. (4th) 1 at 10 (S.C.C.). From database: *R. v. Marquard* (1993) CarswellOnt127, EYB 1993-67538, [1993] S.C.J. No. 119. For a further discussion on the cross-examination of experts on texts and articles refer to Paciocco, *supra*, note 1 at p. 233-234.

# 17

# APPELLATE ADVOCACY

- **The Decision to Appeal**

- **The Notice of Appeal**

- **Writing the Factum**

- **Oral Argument**

- **The Respondent's Position**

- **Preparation of Appeal Materials**

The principles of good advocacy do not change on appeal. It remains fundamental that your arguments be clear and concise. Lengthy and convoluted submissions, whether written or oral, will not impress the learned justices. Increasingly the courts are placing time limits on oral submissions and page limits on written submissions. Your task, as an appellate advocate, is to present argument that is persuasive, not burdensome. Mr. Justice Arnup provided this sage advice:[1]

> The text of this series, therefore, could well be: "Remember the men up *there!*"
> Everything which you can do to make it easier for them is of assistance to
> your case — both what you do in advance, and what you do in Court. This
> approach is designed to create an atmosphere of smooth presentation; it pre-
> vents the court from becoming annoyed with sloppy presentation of the case
> and of the papers which make it up; it gets you off on the right foot.

---

[1] Mr. Justice J. Arnup, "Advocacy On Appeal" in Law Society of Upper Canada Bar Admission Course Materials on Civil Procedure (1972-73), at p. 43.

## 1.    THE DECISION TO APPEAL

An appeal is not a retrial. The appeal must be based upon detached reflection and not upon trial disappointment. Mr. Justice Twaddle of the Manitoba Court of Appeal put it in these terms:[2]

> Why do I belabour the decision to appeal? Because it is the very beginning of good appellate advocacy. An advocate must have something to advocate. If the advocate cannot identify an arguable ground of appeal, how can he persuade a Court of Appeal to change the results? A litigant is entitled to have an arguable ground of appeal determined. He is not entitled to a simple re-hash of the trial.

The appeal court is there to *correct errors made at trial* and preparation for appeal begins at trial. As the trial proceeds, prudent counsel keep alert for any errors and ensure a good trial record in case of an appeal. For example, timely objection ought to be taken to the admissibility of questionable evidence. Your objection may be overruled, but nevertheless it is on the record that you never acquiesced to the admissibility of the "tainted" evidence and any argument on appeal concerning the "disputed" evidence is reinforced.

Once the trial is over, it is incumbent upon counsel, who are contemplating an appeal, to review thoroughly the reasons for judgment and the trial record in search of appealable errors. Look for:

1)    findings of fact not supported by the evidence;

2)    questionable inferences or conclusions taken from the evidence;

3)    errors in evidentiary rulings; and, most importantly,

4)    errors in applying the *correct* law to the facts.

Once potential grounds of appeal are identified, the next task is to assess their merit.

Not all errors are equally arguable on appeal. The appellate court is a court of review and is not to substitute its opinion for that of the trial judge. Therefore *findings of fact* or *findings of credibility* made by the trial judge

---

[2] K. Twaddle, "Appellate Advocacy," in the 1981 Isaac Pitblado Lectures, at p. 35.

will not be lightly overturned.[3] In both these instances the trial judge is in a better position than the appeal court to make the findings. After all, the trial judge saw and heard the evidence. Findings of fact and of credibility, therefore, will only be overturned when it is shown that the trial judge's assessment of the facts or of the witnesses was "palpably" in error.

In contrast, the appeal court judges are in as good a position as the trial judge to make *inferences* from the facts found at trial. Accordingly, the appeal courts are free to overturn "inferences" made by the trial judge, with the caveat that no inference is to be drawn that is inconsistent with a finding of fact that has not been set aside.[4]

The best ground of appeal to press before the court is an error in law. The appeal court is the higher arbiter of the law and no deference is accorded to the learned trial judge's understanding and application of it. Without exception look most carefully for *an error in law*.

An error in law takes on added importance in a criminal appeal in that the *right to appeal* is often limited to questions of law. For example, the Crown can only appeal a verdict of acquittal on a question of law alone.[5]

Counsel must also recognize that the powers of the appeal court are founded by statute and counsel is obliged to become familiar with those statutory powers. In a civil appeal the court has a broad power to:[6]

> . . . give any judgment which ought to have been pronounced, and may make such further or other order as is deemed just.

By comparison, in a criminal appeal, an accused appealing against conviction must frame the grounds of appeal within s. 686(1)(*a*) of the *Criminal Code*:[7]

> . . . the court of appeal

---

[3] For an excellent summary of the powers of an appeal court see the Canadian Encyclopedic Digest under the heading of "Courts"; R.D. Gibbens, "Appellate Review of Findings of Fact" (1992), 123 Adv. Q. 445; T. Woods, "Overturning Findings of Fact on Appeal: A Justifiably Narrow Jurisdiction," 56 The Advocate (January, 1998), p. 61.

[4] See the *Court of Appeal Act*, R.S.M. 1987, c. C240 (also C.C.S.M., c. C240), s. 26(2) and *Courts of Justice Act*, Ontario, s. 134(4)(*a*).

[5] See the *Criminal Code*, R.S.C. 1985, c. C-46, s. 676.

[6] In Manitoba, see the *Court of Appeal Act*, s. 26(1). Comparable wording is found in s. 134(1) of the *Courts of Justice Act*, in Ontario.

[7] The *Criminal Code*, s. 686(1)(*a*).

(*a*) may allow the appeal where it is of the opinion that

    (i) the verdict should be set aside on the ground that it is unreasonable or cannot be supported by the evidence,

    (ii) the judgment of the trial court should be set aside on the ground of a wrong decision on a question of law, or

    (iii) on any ground there was a miscarriage of justice.

As can be seen, the statutory power frames the questions raised on appeal. Prior to commencing an appeal, familiarize yourself with the governing statute law and court rules.

A final factor concerns the tactical wisdom of an appeal. An appeal invites the opposite party to cross-appeal, whereas, if there had been no appeal, the opposing party might well have decided against initiating an appeal. For example, although your client is found liable at trial, the damages awarded are low. Should you appeal, you will encourage the opposite side to move to increase the damage award. Since the matter is going on to appeal, the issue of damages might as well be reconsidered along with the issue of liability. In many cases, it is better to leave well enough alone.

Once arguable grounds of appeal are identified and once your assessment is complete, you are in a position to advise your client. The client makes the final decision, which is only just. It is the client who must shoulder the expense for the appeal; it is the client who must go through the "litigation angst" of a second court proceeding; it is the client who must face the further delay pending the second outcome.

What should you do in the case where your client wants to pursue a hopeless appeal? The Codes of Conduct recommend that counsel is to "discourage" a client from pursuing useless legal proceedings.[8] Mark Orkin, in his book on legal ethics, summarized the lawyer's obligation in this case as follows:[9]

> There is an affirmative duty on the part of a lawyer to check useless litigation. If in the opinion of the lawyer his client has no case, he should tell him so frankly and try to dissuade him from entering litigation . . .

---

[8] See The Law Society of Upper Canada, Rules of Professional Conduct, Rule 3.2-4; The Law Society of Manitoba, Code of Professional Conduct, Rule 3.2-4.

[9] M. Orkin, *Legal Ethics* (1957), at pp. 78-79.

A solicitor, however, is not the judge of his client's case, and if there is a reasonable prospect of success he is justified in proceeding to trial.

In the United States the ethical obligation is placed at a higher level:[10]

### Rule 3.1 Meritorious Claims and Contentions

A lawyer shall not bring or defend a proceeding, or assert or controvert an issue therein, unless there is a basis for doing so that is not frivolous, which includes a good faith argument for an extension, modification or reversal of existing law . . .

Judge Irving R. Kaufman squarely placed responsibility on counsel to keep unworthy appeals out of the courts:[11]

We have reached the point . . . where the lawyers must bear significant responsibility for keeping unworthy cases out of the appellate courts. As officers of the court — and I do not use that as a meaningless phrase — the bar has an obligation not to clutter appellate courts with cases they know are meritless, insignificant or frivolous. Such cases serve as a roadblock to reaching and dealing in depth with cases of substance and are in no small measure responsible for appellate backlogs.

Emphasis is on "meritless." This does not mean that you only appeal if you will win or have a good chance of winning. A lower threshold is required — only that you have an arguable case. However, if you do not have an arguable case, I recommend that you forego the appeal and, if the client insists, let other counsel advance the meritless arguments.

## 2.   THE NOTICE OF APPEAL

The appeal is initiated by the filing of a notice of appeal and the most important thing is to get it filed on time. The purpose of the notice of appeal, like trial pleadings, is to give notice to the parties of the appeal and to frame the issues for appeal (Court of Appeal R. 4). The notice of appeal has three parts:[12]

* information on the decision appealed,

---

[10] American Bar Association, Model Rules of Professional Conduct (1983), R. 3.1.

[11] I. Kaufman, "Appellate Advocacy in the Federal Courts" (1979), 79 F.R.D. 165 at p. 166 as quoted in M. Fontham, *Written and Oral Advocacy* (1985), at p. 8.

[12] The content of the notice of appeal is mandated by the Rules of the Court: Manitoba Court of Appeal, RR. 4-6, and Ontario Rules of Civil Procedure, Form 61A.

- the relief sought on appeal, and

- the grounds of appeal.

The core of the notice of appeal is the grounds of appeal and in drafting these I suggest the following:

1. Rely on a few strong grounds.

2. Organize the grounds.

3. Avoid repetition.

4. Be clear and specific.

## 2.1   A Few Strong Grounds

At this point the structuring of your arguments must begin. Unfortunately, too often the notice of appeal is treated as a dumping ground for any argument regardless of merit. The view of some practitioners is "if in doubt then throw it in." I suggest that this is precisely what not to do.

Mr. Justice Kerr Twaddle (Manitoba Court of Appeal):[13]

In any judgment you are liable to find ten or fifteen potential points to argue on appeal. But I suggest that you can rarely find more than one or two which have any substantial merit. If you are not going to convince the Court on the point which has some merit, you are not likely to convince the Court on all the subsidiary points. You are going to waste the Court's time. Worse than that, if you are raising points which do not appeal to the Court, you will annoy the judges. They are human. If they keep having to listen to points with little merit they are going to get irritated, and if they do, is it likely that they will become convinced by the good argument you make? No. They will see it as being as frivolous as the other arguments they have discarded.

Mr. Justice John Arnup (Ontario Court of Appeal):[14]

Don't argue something you know you can't make stick. This is a common fault. It is far better to throw away a bad point than to try to argue it with might and main in the Court of Appeal. It spoils the taste of the *good* ones.

---

[13] *Supra*, note 2, at p. 36.
[14] *Supra*, note 1, at p. 47.

Strive for focus. Include the "real" grounds of appeal and exclude the frivolous. What if a new ground of appeal arises? Are you precluded from raising it? No. Should a legitimate new ground present itself, leave can be requested to amend the notice of appeal.[15] Further reassurance can be found by including the following "catch all" conclusion to your grounds of appeal:

> And upon such further and other grounds as the court may entertain and counsel may advise.

## 2.2    Organize the Grounds

A fundamental rule of advocacy is to present your strongest argument first. The same holds for the notice of appeal. You should also look to grouping common grounds under one heading. For example, you raise a number of evidentiary errors made by the trial judge:

> The learned trial judge erred in relying upon inadmissible evidence introduced as part of the plaintiff's case in that:
>
> (a)  The learned trial judge admitted the hearsay evidence of A. Smith, and
>
> (b)  the learned trial judge admitted the privileged report prepared by G. Rose.

In this way the isolated grounds which, standing alone, may not be sufficient to overturn the judgment gain added strength because of their "cumulative effect," which is highlighted in the notice of appeal.

## 2.3    Avoid Repetition

What you must avoid is the creation of a "false cumulative effect" through the rephrasing of one ground of appeal. The particular ground of appeal does not improve with repetition. If anything, confusion is created in the mind of the reader, who is searching for a *separate* and *distinct* ground where none exists.

## 2.4    Be Clear and Specific

Look at most notices of appeal and you will find that they are notorious for their ambiguity. Here are some typical boiler plate clauses that are so broad as to be completely meaningless:

---

[15]  K. Twaddle, Q.C. (as he then was), in 1981 wrote "I have never known the Court to refuse to allow counsel to amend the grounds of appeal . . . " *supra*, note 2, at p. 36. See also R. 61.08 of the Ontario Rules of Civil Procedure.

The learned trial judge misdirected himself to the evidence and the law applicable to the evidence.

The said judgment is contrary to law.

The judgment is contrary to the law, the evidence and the weight of evidence.

Mr. Justice Arnup characterized the last boiler plate clause as "a relic from fifty years ago, and it's garbage."[16] Be more specific.

Provided below is a sample notice of appeal and notice of cross-appeal.

## 2.5   Sample Notice of Appeal

---

### IN THE COURT OF APPEAL*

Between:

### RICHARD WAITE

(Plaintiff) Respondent

- and -

### JAMES STEWART

(Defendant) Appellant

### NOTICE OF APPEAL

TAKE NOTICE that a motion will be made on behalf of the defendant** before the Court of Appeal, as soon as the motion can be heard by way of appeal from the judgment of The Honourable Mr. Justice Morton of the Court of Queen's Bench, Winnipeg Centre, pronounced, on the 31st day of March, 20__ and filed on the 2nd day of April, 20__, whereby the learned trial judge awarded judgment in favour of the plaintiff in the sum of $50,000.00 damages, plus costs.

On the appeal, this Court will be asked to set aside the said judgment of the Honourable Mr. Justice Morton and order that the defendant's action be allowed with costs on the following grounds:

*(cont'd)*

---

[16] *Supra*, note 1, at p. 43.

1) The trial judge erred in failing to apply the defence of *ex turpi causa non oritur actio*;

2) The learned trial judge erred in holding that the defendant's actions constituted excessive force;

3) And upon such further and other grounds as the Court may entertain and counsel may advise.

DATED this 17th day of April, 20__.

Per: _____

Solicitor for the Defendant

TO:  The plaintiff.

* For the notice of appeal in Ontario see FORM 61A.

** IN MANITOBA within the body of the appeal documents refer to the parties as they were at trial. See Manitoba Court of Appeal R. 3. IN ONTARIO Form 61A refers to APPELLANT and RESPONDENT in the body of the notice.

## 2.6    Sample Notice of Cross-appeal

IN THE COURT OF APPEAL *

Between:

RICHARD WAITE

(Plaintiff) Respondent

- and -

JAMES STEWART

(Defendant) Appellant

NOTICE OF CROSS-APPEAL

TAKE NOTICE that a motion will be made on behalf of the plaintiff by way of cross-appeal, before the Court of Appeal at the hearing of the appeal herein from the decision of The Honourable Mr. Justice Morton of the Court of Queen's Bench, Winnipeg Centre, pronounced on the 31st day of March, 20__, and filed on the 2nd day of April, 20__, whereby the learned trial judge awarded judgment in favour of the plaintiff in the sum of $50,000.00, plus costs.

At the hearing of the cross-appeal, this court will be asked to increase the assessment of general damages awarded to the Plaintiff, and moved to award punitive damages, on the following grounds:

1) The trial judge's award of general damages is so inordinately low as to be a wholly erroneous assessment of compensation; **

2) The trial judge erred in holding that provocation should reduce the compensatory damages awarded to the plaintiff in that:

a) the trial judge erred in failing to follow the law as set by the case of *Check v. Andrews Hotel Co.* (1975), 56 D.L.R. (3d) 364 (Man. C.A.).

*(cont'd)*

> 3) The trial judge erred in failing to award punitive damages to the plaintiff;
>
> 4) And on such further grounds as the evidence will disclose and counsel may advise and this Honourable Court will allow.
>
> DATED this 20th day of April, 20__ .
>
> 
>
> Per: _____
>
> Solicitor for the Plaintiff
>
> 
>
> TO:  The defendant.

* In Ontario for Notice of Cross-Appeal see FORM 61E.

** The Court of Appeal will not lightly interfere to substitute its opinion for that of the trial judge concerning the assessment of damages. See *Collins v. Hofer* (1983), 21 Man. R. (2d) 243 (C.A.).

## 3.  WRITING THE FACTUM

The factum is your written argument. A well-written factum forms the foundation for a solid appeal. This is truer than ever, as appeal courts move to restrict the time for oral arguments. Remember, first impressions are important and the factum is your first opportunity to put your argument before the court. Make the impression a favourable one. Remember also that the factum stays with the judges. It is a permanent reminder of your argument and will go with the judges into their chambers to be read and reread long after your oral arguments have faded from memory. Remember too that the factum helps to structure your oral argument and, if the factum presents your argument in a clear, concise and convincing manner, then the oral hearing is made all the easier.

The format for the factum varies slightly from jurisdiction to jurisdiction. For example, in Ontario the appellant's factum has five parts (R. 61.11):

Part I    Judgment Appealed From

Part II   Nature of the Appeal [Overview Statement]

Part III  Statement of Facts

Part IV  Issues and Argument

Part V   Order Requested

In Manitoba, the appellant's factum has four parts (Court of Appeal R. 29):

Part I    Introduction [Overview Statement]

Part II   Statement of Facts

Part III  Issues on Appeal

Part IV  Argument

A sample outline of the respective factum formats is provided below.

## 3.1   Sample Factum Format

*Ontario*

---

### COURT OF APPEAL FOR ONTARIO

BETWEEN:                    RICHARD WAITE

Plaintiff (Respondent)

and

JAMES STEWART

Defendant (Appellant)

### APPELLANT'S FACTUM

[Index Page]

### PART I
### JUDGMENT APPEALED

1. This is an appeal by the defendant from the judgment of the Honourable Justice Morton, given on the 31st day of March, 20__, whereby he:

*(cont'd)*

a)  awarded the plaintiff $50,000.00, plus party-and-party costs.

2. The learned trial judge found . . .

## PART II
## NATURE OF THE APPEAL

3.  This case involves a battery and defences to a battery. The plaintiff, Richard Waite, and the defendant, James Stewart, both mature adults, consented to a fight in the parking lot of a recreation complex . . .

## PART III
## STATEMENT OF FACTS

3. On March 13, 2015 the plaintiff and the defendant played on opposite teams in a recreation hockey game. During the game . . .

Transcript, p. 23
Evidence, p. 82
Appeal Book, p. 63
Reasons for judgment, p. 5

## PART IV
## THE ISSUES AND THE LAW

16.  The appellant submits that the issues on appeal are as follows:

1)  The trial judge erred in finding that the defendant used excessive force during a fight with the plaintiff; . . .

THE DEFENDANT'S ACTIONS IN THE FIGHT

17.  The plaintiff sought out the defendant to fight. The plaintiff then instigated the fight . . .

## PART V
## ORDER REQUESTED

34.  It is therefore respectfully submitted that the appeal should be allowed and that:

*(cont'd)*

---

1) the plaintiff's claim should be dismissed with costs.

ALL OF WHICH IS RESPECTFULLY SUBMITTED.

---

Counsel for the Defendant (Appellant)

---

*(a)    Sample Factum Format*

*Manitoba*

---

IN THE COURT OF APPEAL

Between:                      RICHARD WAITE

(Plaintiff) Respondent

- and -

JAMES STEWART

(Defendant) Appellant

APPELLANT'S FACTUM

[Index Page]

PART I
INTRODUCTION

1. This case involves a battery and defences to a battery. The plaintiff, Richard Waite, and the defendant, James Stewart, both mature adults, consented to a fight in the parking lot of a recreation complex . . .

PART II
STATEMENT OF FACTS

5. The plaintiff and the defendant played on opposing teams in a recreation hockey league. During the course of the game on March 13, 2015 . . .

*(cont'd)*

Appeal Book, p. 12.
Evidence, p. 15, line 24 to line 35.
Exhibit number 4, Appeal Book, p. 89.

. . .

## PART III
## ERRORS ALLEGED IN THE JUDGMENT APPEALED FROM

17. The trial judge erred in finding that the defendant used excessive force during a fight with the plaintiff.

18. The trial judge erred . . .

## PART IV
## ARGUMENT

### THE DEFENDANT'S USE OF FORCE

22. The defendant had a right to defend himself. The plaintiff verbally and physically abused the defendant until the defendant was provoked into fighting and the plaintiff was the initial aggressor in the fight. It is within this context that the defendant responded.

23. The law has long recognized the *right* to defend oneself . . .

32. The defendant therefore submits that the appeal should be allowed, the trial judgment set aside, and the plaintiff's action dismissed with costs in the amount fixed by the learned trial judge.

ALL OF WHICH IS RESPECTFULLY SUBMITTED

_____

Counsel for the Defendant

## 3.2  Overview Statement

Under the Ontario Rules, Part I is simply a summary identifying the parties, the court appealed from and the result. Part II is the overview statement. In Manitoba, Part I begins with an overview statement. Justice John Laskin, in an excellent article on factum writing, explains that the overview statement reflects a "fundamental principle of persuasive factum writing: put context before details."[17] The overview statement goes beyond the bare-bones – parties, court below, result – to tell the court why it is you are appealing. Strive to capture in one page what the appeal is all about. This is not just "broad-brush" generalities. For example, in *Waite v. Stewart*, it is too broad to say, "This case is about a wrong-doer seeking compensation for his wrong-doing." This statement really says nothing. You need to provide enough facts to set the scene and provide a context for the statement. In Justice Laskin's view, most counsel do not give enough facts in the overview statement. Remember context before law. David Lepofsky suggests three components for the overview statement:[18]

1)    Summary of facts;

2)    What is under appeal; and

3)    Summary of the legal issues.

Provided below is an example of an overview statement in *Waite v. Stewart*:

---

**PART I**
**INTRODUCTION**

*[Remember the Manitoba Part I usually also includes identification of the parties and judgment appealed from.]*

1.  This case involves a battery and defences to a battery. The plaintiff, Richard Waite, and the defendant, James Stewart, both mature adults, consented to a fight in the parking lot of a recreation complex. Earlier in the evening, the two had been playing hockey on opposite teams. The plaintiff was cut by Mr. Stewart's stick in the game and had to leave the ice. Following the game, the plaintiff confronted Mr. Stewart in the parking lot. Mr. Stewart wanted to leave. The plaintiff would not let him. The plaintiff then provoked and instigated the fight. During the course of the fight, the plaintiff's jaw was broken. He then brought an action in battery to recover for his injury.

*(cont'd)*

---

[17] John Laskin, "Forget the windup and make the pitch: Some suggestions for writing more persuasive factums," The Adv. Soc. J. (August, 1999) at pp. 3-12.

[18] D. Lepofsky, "The unsung art of written advocacy: Strategies, tips, and a call for unorthodoxy", (Summer 2004) 23 Advocates' Soc. J. No. 1, 10 at para. 88-90.

2. The learned Trial Judge found for the plaintiff and awarded damages in the amount of $478.00 in special damages and $50,000.00
in general damages. The total amount of the judgment was then
reduced by 50% because of the plaintiff's actions in provoking the
fight.

3. This appeal really is about a wrong-doer seeking compensation for
his wrong-doing. There are two main issues:

a) Did the defendant use excessive force in defending himself?
The defendant submits that the finding of excessive force is not
supported by the evidence.

b) The defendant submits that, as a matter of law, a wrong-doer,
such as the plaintiff, ought not to benefit from his wrongs and
that the doctrine of *ex turpi causa* bars the plaintiff from any
recovery in this case.

## 3.3   Statement of Facts

Former United States Supreme Court Justice Louis Brandeis stated,
"Let me write the statement of facts, and I care not who writes the law."[19]
Unfortunately, far too often counsel ignore the drafting of the statement of
facts. These counsel forget that the judges also want to see that justice is
done in the particular case. The judges do not pass judgment on the law in
a vacuum. Facts mould the law and the more compelling the facts the more
compelling your argument. The facts put a human face on the law and
provide a context for applying it. Do not ignore the facts. Do not ignore the
equities of the case.

The statement of facts must be fair, accurate and complete. You must
be honest with the court or else you will lose all credibility. Therefore, all
material facts are presented; none are hidden. This does not mean that you
cannot try to persuade the reader as to the justness of your position. Persuasion, however, is not achieved through misstatement or critical omission.
Persuasion is achieved through emphasis. You highlight the favourable and
minimize the unfavourable. Justice Richards described the writing of the
facts as a "high-wire" act where counsel balance tensions between:[20]

---

[19] As quoted in Fontham, *supra*, note 11, at p. 53.
[20] R. Richards, "Writing effective briefs", (Winter 2012), 31 Advocates' J. No. 3,
3 at para. 21.

- being accurate while still putting the best possible face on the case;

- outlining all the relevant facts for the court while still being as concise and pointed as possible;

- in an appellate court, respecting the findings of the trial judge (or other fact finder) while still putting the best evidence forward.

For example, take our assault case, *Waite v. Stewart*. Defendant's counsel concentrate on the preceding provocative acts committed by Waite leading up to the fight. The second "excessive" kick cannot be ignored, however the surrounding facts should be raised to show that the kick was a response to Waite's attack and not deliberately calculated to injure. In this way, attention is diverted from the second kick.

An excellent way of achieving emphasis is by quoting directly from the evidence, rather than using a footnote. Consider this example taken from a factum prepared by counsel for the accused in the case of *R. v. Lavallee*.[21] The accused shot her common law husband in the back and was charged with murder. She raised self-defence and presented evidence that she was a battered woman:

> Constable Popplestone of the City of Winnipeg Police Department testified that on the night in question, he was called to 10 Girdwood Crescent. He testified that after the (Accused) Respondent was advised of the possible charge against her, she began to cry. He testified that she stated he just kept beating me all the time, I just couldn't take it any more, and then she said:
>
> "HE SAID IF I DIDN'T KILL HIM FIRST HE WOULD KILL ME. I HOPE HE LIVES. I REALLY LOVE HIM" (Transcript of Evidence P. 669 — original emphasis).
>
> She also stated:
>
> "I didn't mean to do it. I'm too young to go to jail, and he told me he was going to kill me when everyone left" (Transcript of Evidence P. 669).

The statement of facts is not the place for argument. Do not directly challenge the credibility of the witnesses or the soundness of the inferences made by the trial judge. Be subtle and let the facts raise the arguments for you. Alan Gold, in a superb article on criminal appellate advocacy, advised:[22]

---

[21] *R. v. Lavallee* (1988), 52 Man. R. (2d) 274 (C.A.).

[22] A. Gold, "Criminal Appellate Advocacy," in *Advocacy in Court: A Tribute to Arthur Maloney, Q.C.*, F. Moskoff, ed. (1986), pp. 89-99, at p. 91.

The statement of facts should not contain arguments such as, for example, a statement that a certain prosecution witness was "unbelievable." Rather, matters of fact can be pointed out, such as that the witness admitted testifying in hope of reward. It would be argumentative to set out that the prosecution witness "could not observe" the matters to which he testified . . . but it is proper to relate those circumstances under which the witness made his observations in order to ask the appellate judges to draw such a conclusion.

He went on to point out the importance of language and the "even though" response:

Careful use of language is important, as is true of advocacy generally. Referring to testimony of a witness whose evidence is disputed by the accused by stating the witness so "testified" or "claimed" will make the point, and there can immediately follow a reference to the testimony on behalf of the defence that denied the contradicted prosecution version. Conjunctives such as "although" or "even though" can be used to state the evidence in such a way as to point to the desired conclusion. For example, the facts could be put in this form:

The arresting officer claimed the accused admitted he had robbed the victim in his store immediately upon being confronted by the victim, even though the victim himself and the other officer present at the time and the accused all denied any such admission and even though the arresting officer's note book, written up shortly thereafter, failed to contain any notes of the supposed oral admission.

The point is made.

In contrast, it is worth reinforcing a finding of fact made by the trial judge that is in your favour. Remember, the appeal court is loath to overturn findings of fact.

The equities in the case should be presented in a subtle "factual" way and not through a blatant statement. A fine example of subtle "factual" persuasion comes from the case of *Constitution Ins. Co. of Can. v. Kosmopoulos*.[23] The equities in this case are obvious: wealthy insurance company versus poor insured. Consider how the following opening paragraph taken from Mr. Kosmopoulos' factum crystallizes the equities in the case:

Mr. Kosmopoulos' leather business was carried out in a small store where he sold the leather goods he made in a room at the back of the store. It was a

---

[23] *Constitution Ins. Co. of Can. v. Kosmopoulos* (1987), 34 D.L.R. (4th) 208 (S.C.C.).

small operation. The equipment he used consisted of two sewing machines, two cutting tables, one hand cutting knife and one steam iron. Other than himself, the business had one full time employee, one part time employee and the help of Mr. Kosmopoulos' wife.

The above paragraph is an example of simple language used to convey a powerful message. There is a freshness and strength in being simple. Look to the judgments of Lord Denning. Why do we remember them so well? Because they are simple. He cuts through the convoluted, dull and incomprehensible to tell the reader what the case is about.

Use the same approach in your statement of facts. Do not interrupt your "story" with needless asides that introduce new and confusing facts. Introduce your "characters," set the scene and tell the court what happened. Do so in a concise way including only the material facts. Including only the essentials ensures that you will be brief. Chronological order is best. Should you have a case with various factual issues, then use subheadings to guide the reader from one area to another.

Strive to bring the facts to life. Encourage the justices to *want* to read the brief. Stimulate their interest. Mr. Justice Twaddle wrote:[24]

> The judges sit full days. They do not have that much time to read your material. I know they do in fact read it, but if they have a very long argument, they are going to lose the thread of it. Your job as an advocate is first of all to interest them so that when they come into the hearing they are thinking "Here is an interesting point worth hearing," and not "Oh, not another one of those appeals!" The attitude with which the case is approached both by counsel and the judge is an important aspect of it.

Chief Justice William Holohan of the Arizona Supreme Court echoed that same view:[25]

> The law is dynamic. It is about human conduct. There is nothing dull about it — it is the lawyer who is dull. There is no reason that a brief shouldn't be good literature. When I get a good brief like that, I sit up and take renewed notice and say, "Who is that lawyer? Let's take a look at what he is saying."

The statement of facts is your introduction to the case and to the factum. Make the most of it. Make it simple. Make it interesting.

---

[24] *Supra*, note 2, at p. 37.

[25] M. Rust, "Mistakes to Avoid on Appeal" (September 1988), 74 A.B.A.J. 78, at p. 79.

### 3.4  Issues and Argument

The factum outlines your argument. It provides a framework. In the words of Mr. Justice Twaddle, "The factum is not the argument. It is an indication of what the argument is going to be."[26] It is not a legal treatise on the subject and it is not a legal memorandum. Therefore, the factum is to be *brief* and this is a true challenge for the drafter.[27] It is easy for counsel to take dictaphone in hand and begin rambling. It is far more difficult to pare and hone the argument into a crisp piece of work. But that is good factum writing.

Common sense says it is far better to make the factum brief. Ask yourself this question. Are you more likely to appreciate and thoroughly read a 10-page case than a 100-page case? Appellate court judges have an enormous reading load and they will appreciate a factum that gets to the point quickly and in as few words as possible.

The factum should be concise. Justice Richards provides this sage observation on the meaning of "concise":[28]

> A good brief is concise. It gets to the point and deals with the issues as clearly, succinctly and economically as possible. "Concise" is not the same as "short." Some cases feature complex or multiple issues or rest on involved facts. Judges understand that a short brief will not suffice in those circumstances. Concise does not mean superficial, either. A good brief must be appropriately comprehensive and must deal with the issues at a proper level of depth and sophistication.

### (a)  The Format

This portion of the factum includes, as its title states, the issues and argument. In Manitoba, the issues are listed separately in Part III of the factum. Part IV of a Manitoba factum presents argument on the issues. In Ontario, the issues and argument are dealt with together in Part IV. Some lawyers list the issues at the start of this part and then proceed to outline the argument in a block. Other lawyers, instead of providing a list of all of the

---

[26] *Supra*, note 2, at p. 36.

[27] The Ontario Court of Appeal, in a practice direction, has stipulated that "the factums should be no longer than 10 pages and other than in exceptional cases should not exceed 30 pages." Practice Direction, dated May 1, 1993. Similarly, in Manitoba the Court may reject a factum on the grounds of excessive length [Rule 29(3)].

[28] R. Richards, *supra*, note 20, para. 7.

issues at the beginning of the part, deal with each issue and argument in turn. The choice is yours.

Phrasing the issues is important. We are all aware that the phrasing of a question can suggest the answer. Professor Frank Cooper, in a leading article, "Stating the Issue in Appellate Briefs," suggest six tests for a "good issue":[29]

1) The issue must be stated in terms of the facts of the case.

2) The statement must eliminate all unnecessary detail.

3) It must be readily comprehensible on first reading.

4) It must eschew self-evident propositions.

5) It must be so stated that the opponent has no choice but to accept it as an accurate statement of the question.

6) It should be subtly persuasive.

By way of example, look to the ground of appeal in *Waite v. Stewart* where the defendant refutes the trial judge's finding of excessive force.

**Issue**: The trial judge erred in finding that the defendant used excessive force.

The issue is vague. It does not specifically relate to the facts. Nor does it enhance the defendant's position; if anything it highlights the "excessive force." Let us rephrase:

**Issue**: The trial judge erred in finding that the defendant used excessive force during a fight with the plaintiff.

In the rephrase of the issue, the defendant's use of force is placed in the context of a "fight." Focus is shifted from "excessive force" to a "fight."

However, do not go overboard. Do not be argumentative or rhetorical.

**Issue**: Did the trial judge err in failing to find that the defendant was justified in defending himself against the plaintiff?

---

[29] F. Cooper, "Stating the Issue in Appellate Briefs" (February 1963), 49 A.B.A.J. 180, at p. 181.

The plaintiff will not agree to this statement of the issue and neither will the court. The statement is too vague and is misleading in that the trial judge had found, as a fact, that the first kick had winded Mr. Waite and from that point on he was no longer in a position to carry the fight or to defend himself.

The issues may well form headings for your argument. I strongly encourage you to use headings. These are signposts that direct the reader from one point to another in your argument. They make your argument organized and easier to follow. Look to the judgments written by Chief Justice Dickson, who guides the reader by headings or numbered points.[30] One suggestion is provided below:

---

## PART I

## MAIN HEADING

A. FIRST SUBHEADING

1. SECOND SUBHEADING

(a) Third Subheading

(i) Fourth Subheading

---

The use of headings will also assist you in preparing an index to the factum.

Think in terms of designing your factum. "White space" is important. What you want to avoid is a dense document, which is difficult to read.[31] The rules of court may dictate certain things like page size, font, numbering, but there remains room for you to create a visually pleasing product that is easy to read and helps to focus on points you want highlighted. For example, there is nothing to stop you from providing a diagram, which may be of enormous value in tracing the connection between various individuals or events.

In terms of paragraphs, avoid the long narrative paragraph. Keep to the rule — one idea, one paragraph. The paragraphs should be short, but not too short. One sentence paragraphs should be used for effect and should not be the norm. Otherwise the factum lacks flow and reads choppily.

---

[30] See, e.g., *R. v. Perka* (1984), 14 C.C.C. (3d) 385, 13 D.L.R. (4th) 1 (S.C.C.).
[31] John Laskin, *supra*, note 17, at p. 5.

I recommend the "proposition-authority" format for your paragraphs. The body of the paragraph states your position (proposition) and is not interrupted by citations or footnotes. The authorities are placed below the paragraph:

> 8. The question of constructive murder raises the problem of establishing a balance between the role of courts and legislators in the Charter era. The purpose of the Charter is to provide such a balance without defeating the supremacy of Parliament.
>
> *Canadian Charter of Rights and Freedoms*, Part I of the Constitution Act, 1982, enacted by the Canada Act, 1982 (U.K.)
>
> *R. v. Morgentaler*, [1988] 1 S.C.R. 30 at 46, per Dickson C.J.C.

The paragraphs should also be numbered consecutively.[32] This provides for easy reference during oral argument.

The authorities included in your factum should be selected with care. You will not impress the justices by "dumping" case authority in the factum. Why include ten provincial Court of Appeal decisions when you have a Supreme Court of Canada decision? There is no need to show off the extent of your research. Recognize the key cases. Include those citations in the factum and copies in a book of authorities prepared and tabbed for the court. The justices will read the authorities cited and provided. They will only get irritated if you force them to read needless cases all saying the same thing. You must also consider the weight of the decision that you are including. A Provincial Court or trial decision from another province will carry little weight with the Court of Appeal of your province or with the Supreme Court of Canada.

Finally, the inclusion of numerous parallel citations is, in my view, a waste of paper. There is no need for five or six report citations — two will do. In the body of the factum refer citations and quotes to *one* report (the report which is copied in your book of authorities). The parallel citation is provided only in the list of authorities, which is included at the end of the factum. For certain decisions, such as those of the Supreme Court of Canada,

---

[32] Under the Ontario Rules of Civil Procedure, R. 61.11, the paragraphs are to be "numbered consecutively throughout the factum."

cite the official report series that includes the English and French versions. In terms of the citation, there are a number of citation manuals each espousing different styles.[33] What style you use is not important; what is important is that you be *consistent* and correct.

Write in clear, simple language. Get rid of unnecessary phrasing. Revise "This honourable Court"; to become "this Court."Omit "Learned Trial Judge" and use "Judge" or "Trial Judge" instead.[34] Refer to judges in gender-neutral language: Mr. Justice Smith becomes Justice Smith or Smith J.A. In some factums every paragraph is introduced by "It is respectfully submitted." The phrase is overworked verbiage. Get rid of it. An appeal court can only absorb so much respect. It also makes for poor transition between paragraphs. Link your paragraphs:

*Further . . .*

*It follows . . .*

*As outlined . . .*

*Given the . . .*

Headings also save you the need for a transition, as the heading itself marks the move from one topic to another. Headings should be short and understandable. They are signposts and need to be understandable at first glance. Justice Richards provides this example of a wordy heading that lacks punch:[35]

> Did the learned trial judge err in awarding Ms. Smith retroactive spousal support from September 1, 2008 to July 31, 2010 because she did not apply for support until August 15, 2010?

His reformulation:

> Spousal Support Should Not Have Been Awarded

### (b)  *Organization of Your Argument*

Present your best argument first. "Strike for the jugular vein."[36] Primacy of argument is important. Attention and retention are best achieved

---

[33] See, e.g., *Canadian Guide To Uniform Legal Citation* (1986); Uniform System of Citation (Harvard Law Review).
[34] D. Lepofsky, *supra*, note 18, para. 131.
[35] R. Richards, *supra*, note 20, at para. 7(c).
[36] F. Cooper, *supra*, note 29, at p. 182.

at the start and at the end of a submission, whether written or oral. Further, by starting with a strong argument you stamp your appeal as having merit, whereas striking out on a series of weak grounds loses credibility with the court. Direct the court to the true issues right from the start.

The factum is not a mystery novel. Do not keep the judges in suspense as to your position. Justice Laskin refers to this as "point-first writing."[37] State your point before you develop or discuss it. In the first few paragraphs tell the court where you stand and then go on to support your stated position. This can be achieved by having the heading to the topic state your position. For example, from the *Kosmopoulos* appeal, the opening heading in the argument stated:[38]

THE FACTUAL EXPECTANCY TEST IS THE APPROPRIATE TEST
FOR INSURABLE INTEREST

Compare this heading to a question format:

IS THE FACTUAL EXPECTANCY TEST THE APPROPRIATE TEST
FOR INSURABLE INTEREST?

The latter heading exudes doubt. The asking of the question raises the question. In contrast, the first heading boldly states the position. There is no doubt raised. There is strength and assurance. Here is a lawyer who has conviction enough to say, "This is my position and it should be the law."

Moreover, it is fundamental that you present your argument *before* attacking the other side's position. Using a military analogy, "Secure your beachhead before advancing inland." To do otherwise gives too much credence to the opposing viewpoint. An appeal is like a trial, where most cases are won in direct examination and not in cross-examination. Accordingly, on appeal show how "right" your position is *before* you show how "wrong" your opponent's position is. Once you have the judges on your side, it is far easier to attack the flaws in the other side's case.

### (c)   Writing Style

Eugene Meehan, who specializes in Supreme Court of Canada practice, emphasizes the need for strategic writing aimed at the one goal – to persuade:[39]

---

[37]   John Laskin, *supra*, at p. 4.

[38]   *Kosmopoulos, supra*, note 23.

[39]   Eugene Meehan, "Strategic Legal Writing: preparing Persuasive Documents" a paper presented at the Bora Laskin Faculty of Law March 10, 2015, at para. 18.

You're not writing to entertain, show how smart you are, how many authorities you can cite for one proposition, or even writing to inform. You're writing to **persuade**.

*(i) "Naturally Formal" Writing is Expected* — The factum is a literary work within a legal setting. Both rigid formalism and colloquialism are unacceptable. Rather, strive for a tone of "natural formality," whereby your arguments are presented in an interesting manner with the appropriate measure of respect.

**Colloquialisms**

Police officers are not "cops."

People do not "hold down a job;" they work.

People are not "bombed;" they are drunk or intoxicated.

**Formalism**

"The party of the first part" is Mr. Smith or the plaintiff.

"The said motor vehicle" is Mr. Smith's car.

"A contract of service" is employment. Constantly ask yourself, "What do you want to say?" Once you know what you want to say, move on to say it in a clear and concise way. Be simple. Never drive a judge to a dictionary.

*(ii) Marshal the Facts, the Law and Policy* — Any argument must be approached as a whole. Mould the evidence into the law, both statutory and common law, and tie the case into broader policy concerns. Policy is particularly important if you are asking the appeal court to extend or overturn "accepted" judicial limits of a legal doctrine. The case of *Kosmopoulos* provides a good illustration. A long line of cases held that before an insured could recover on an insurance policy it had to be shown that the insured had a "legal" claim to the property insured. Mr. Kosmopoulos had incorporated his business, therefore he no longer "owned" his leather store and had no legal claim to fire insurance on the property. The issue in *Kosmopoulos* was the validity of this "narrow" interpretation of insurable interest. Counsel for Mr. Kosmopoulos sought to overturn the existing precedent and have the Supreme Court of Canada adopt a broader test. In their factum they first addressed policy concerns:[40]

---

[40] *Kosmopoulos, supra,* note 23.

12. The requirement of insurable interest was developed to remove insurance contracts from the sphere of wagering transactions. This policy consideration can be met without recourse to the rigid test of insurable interest set out in *Macaura* v. *Northern Assurance Company* . . .

13. The decision in *Macaura* has been the subject of severe and frequent criticism. It has been seen to provide the insurer with a technical defence to avoid responding to a policy while going far beyond the interest required to support public policy against wagering. The factual expectancy test supports the anti-wagering policy while at the same time allowing the insurance contract to be enforced according to both parties' reasonable expectations . . .

The case law was then considered within this policy context.

*(iii) Avoid Misstatement* — Never misstate the law or the facts. Never quote out of context. You must treat the court with fairness and candour. If the quote you are including is from the dissent — say so. If the statement was *obiter* — say so. Should you tell the court that "the case stands for the proposition" and you are wrong, then your credibility with the court is brought into question. Mr. Justice Arnup wrote:[41]

> NEVER misstate the facts. I can't put this too strongly. If you do it once, you'll only get a raised eye-brow. If you do it twice, you'll get some speculative (and skeptical looks). If you do it three times, you might as well stick to the trial court, because the Appeal Court will never take your word for it again.

*(iv) Avoid Overstatement* — You must be strong without going to excess. Do not tell the court that it "must" rule in a certain way. Suggest to the court that it "should" so rule. For some counsel, the facts or the law are always "obviously" or "clearly" in their favour. Such is not the case or there would be no need for the lawsuit and continual reference to "obvious" and "clear" points does not, through repetition, make your case any the stronger. In other words, avoid using needless and extravagant adjectives.

*(v) Avoid Personal Attacks* — It is appropriate to attack the legal position of opposing counsel; it is entirely inappropriate to attack opposing counsel personally. Such attacks will brand you as arrogant. No court likes to see a person "beat upon" and the result often is that the justices respond by coming to the aid of the besieged counsel. Therefore, avoid:

**No**: My learned friend would have this court believe . . .

---

[41] *Supra*, note 1, at p. 47.

**Yes**: The respondent's position is . . .

**No**: Where is Mr. Smith's case?

**Yes**: There is no support for the respondent's position.

Nor is there much to be gained from dissecting your opponent's factum, showing every flaw in minute detail. By doing so, your own argument will lose focus. Save your ammunition. Strike only at clear and important flaws. Maintain respect:[42]

> Just as an experienced cross-examiner will approach an attractive witness with courtesy, taking care not to alienate the jury, so will the brief writer approach an opponent's argument. For all he knows the judges or their clerks may find it appealing. Therefore, he will at first describe it in terms that merely imply its weakness: The opponent "attempts" or "suggests" an argument, he "advances" or "urges" or "insists on" a position. There is no suggestion of bad faith; the advocate avoids adjectives like "absurd" or "ridiculous" or "nonsensical." The next step is to point out that the adversary has been "unable" to find facts or law to support his argument, and accordingly "must rely" on inapposite authorities. The implication is that he is doing his competent best, but no such authorities exist.

*(vi)  Be Positive* — You must have conviction or at least show conviction in your cause. Your clients expect you to fight for them. Be strong. Do not show your own inner doubts:

**Weak:**  It would seem . . .

It would appear . . .

One could assume . . .

It is possible to conclude . . .

**Strong:**  It follows . . .

The conclusion from these cases . . .

One way of making your writing stronger is to use the active rather than the passive voice. The structure of a sentence using the active voice is

---

[42]  G. Peck, *Writing Persuasive Briefs* (1984), at p. 86.

simple: subject, active verb and object. The passive voice uses: object, complex verb, subject. Compare these two sentences:

**Active:**  The accused stabbed the victim thirteen times.

**Passive:**  The victim was stabbed thirteen times by the accused.

Remember this rule of thumb: "The subjects, who do the action, come first, and the objects, who have something done to them, come later."[43]

*(vii)  Provide a Context for Cases Relied Upon* — Referring to cases without placing them in context serves little purpose. If you rely upon a case, then provide the context. Briefly relate what the facts were and the legal issue in the case. The reader will then be better able to apply that case to that on appeal.

I do not think that there is a need for you to provide "context" if you cite a case or quote from a case to confirm a broad principle of law. The principle stands or falls on its own. Only when the principle and the case have specific relevance to the case on appeal is there need for context. For example, in applying s. 1 of the *Charter*, the Supreme Court of Canada decision, *R. v. Oakes*, is invariably cited to provide the structured analysis.[44] There is no need to provide the background to *Oakes*. However, if a reverse onus provision is being challenged, as in the case of *R. v. Oakes*, then the similar background becomes relevant.

*(viii)  Use Logic and Not Rhetoric* — A nice turn of phrase is effective. The use of repetition can be effective, but rhetoric is a waste. Instead, sway the judges by logic and reason.

### 3.5  Order Sought

Your factum ends by telling the court what it is you want. In Ontario, a separate Part V contains the order that the court is asked to make. In Manitoba, this "plea for relief" is left to the end of the argument section.

### 3.6  Focus on What is Useful

There are certain required schedules: Schedule A – list of authorities referred to and Schedule B — relevant law.[45] However, there is no rule that

---

[43]  Michele Asprey, *Plain Language for Lawyers* (1996), at p. 127.

[44]  *R. v. Oakes*, [1986 1 S.C.R. 103.

[45]  See the Ontario Rules of Civil Procedure, Rule 61.11.

prohibits additional schedules.[46] Counsel should consider including appendices that would assist the Justices. Consider creating lists, diagrams or charts. A list of witnesses, a chronological timeline and a chart outlining the organization in question may all be helpful. Be creative, and better yet, insert these aids where appropriate in the factum.

## 4.  ORAL ARGUMENT

### 4.1  The Formalities

Just as with a trial, there are certain preliminary matters that must be dealt with before the appeal arguments are heard. Counsel appearances are taken. In Ontario, counsel slips are used to inform the court of counsel. In Manitoba, the appearances traditionally are made at the start of the appeal:

> My Lords, My Lady, my name is Smith. I appear for the plaintiff appellant and I am ready to proceed. Appearing with me is Ms Jones.

[In the Ontario Court of Appeal "Justices" is used, NOT My Lady or My Lord.]

It is important for counsel to familiarize themselves with these little procedural matters because you do not want to let anything throw you off — especially right at the start of the appeal. Familiarize yourself with the mannerisms of the court. Familiarize yourself with where you sit. Counsel for the appellant are generally seated on the left side of the courtroom facing the bench. Such familiarization will assist in putting you at ease and free your mind to concentrate on the appeal at hand.

Following the introductions, counsel for the appellant opens. A traditional opening includes a review of the nature of the appeal, the facts of the case and the legal issues:

### (a)  Nature of the Appeal

> May it please the Court, this is an appeal (and cross-appeal, if applicable) from the judgment of Mr. Justice Morton, who at the trial of this action found for the plaintiff in battery and awarded $50,000 in damages plus costs.

---

[46] See D. Lepofsky, *supra*, note 18, at para. 145.

### (b)    Facts of the Case

> Justices, the facts of this case may be briefly summarized as follows . . .

Or you may anticipate that the justices are familiar with the facts and ask the court:

> Do Your Justices wish me to review the facts of this case?

Please note how much easier it is to use the gender-neutral term "justices." It is hoped that the Ontario practice of using "justice," which is also the practice in the Supreme Court of Canada, will soon become the norm across Canada.

### (c)    Issues on Appeal

> The issues to be resolved on this appeal are three in number. First . . . Second . . . Third . . .

An alternative to the traditional opening is to begin by telling the court in simple terms what the case is all about — capture the essence of the case. In the Supreme Court of the United States, good counsel almost invariably begin by saying, "May it please the Court, this case is about . . ." They cut to the chase and get right to the heart of the appeal. For example, Mr. Justice Sopinka (when a lawyer) opened *Nelles v. A.G. of Canada* [February 29, 1988] with the following:[47]

> My Lords and my Ladies. In this case the Court of Appeal has decided that Crown Attorneys enjoy immunity from civil suits that makes them unique among public servants. The common law has refused to recognize any protection from civil liability for a public servant who has acted maliciously but the Court of Appeal says it made one exception.

Preparation is the key to a good oral submission:[48]

> The next area of preparation is that involved in the oral argument itself. Here the cardinal rule is that counsel must become totally familiar with the facts and law. He must know his case and its record from cover to cover. In addition to fulfilling his professional obligations to the client, exhaustive preparatory work is in counsel's best personal interest because it will allow him maximum professional relaxation for the appeal. Counsel will have a sense of comfort

---

[47] Taken from Eugene Meehan, "Supreme Court of Canada — Process & Advocacy — A Practical Guide for Practitioners" (1996), 75 Can. Bar Rev. 81, at p. 107.

[48] A. Gold, *supra*, note 22 at p. 92.

from the knowledge that everything possible was done to prepare for the appeal that will allow him to do his best. This confidence will go a long way towards overcoming the inevitable jitteriness that is inherent in the intimidating exercise of appellate argument.

Preparation needs to be addressed in two areas: content preparation and presentation preparation.

## 4.2   Content Preparation

You must thoroughly familiarize yourself with the evidence and the law. With respect to the evidence, if you did not handle the trial, read the trial transcript. At this point merely read. Take no notes. Your purpose is to put the evidence and witnesses into context. Once this is done, return to the transcript and prepare an index/summary of the evidence. Record the testimony of each witness on the various "key" issues. In the *Waite v. Stewart* case, the witness evidence could be divided into the issues of: provocation, consent and the fight. The evidence is now at your fingertips to compare, distinguish or reinforce.

You must know the law. You must be completely familiar with the case and the statute authority you rely upon. By being "familiar" I mean that you have the equivalent of a "case brief" in your mind or readily at your disposal. You should know the *ratio* of the case, the facts, the court and the composition of the panel. In particular, it is important to look for what might be called "strong" dissents. Who is the author of the dissent? A dissent written by Mr. Justice Martin of the Ontario Court of Appeal in criminal matters or by former Chief Justice Freedman of the Manitoba Court of Appeal, given the reputation of these justices, takes on added credence.

But it is not good enough that you know your law. You must also know the law relied upon by your opponent. Go through the opposing factum, gather the cases referred to and *read* them. It is only by thoroughly going through the opposing law that you will be able to distinguish, challenge or ultimately destroy the opposing case.

Concentrate upon identifying and attacking the foundation precedents. These are the precedents upon which subsequent cases rely. If the underlying "foundation" for the line of authority is shown to be flawed or erroneous, then the entire case law authority is brought into question.[49]

---

[49] A. Gold provides an excellent example of "undermining the foundation precedent," *supra*, note 22, at p. 93.

### 4.3    Presentation Preparation

An effective oral presentation takes enormous work. The argument must be carefully honed in terms of what is said and how it is said. Do not be afraid to rehearse your submission and do not apologize for so doing. That is precisely what you should do. Go through your submission over and over. Watch yourself in the mirror or on videotape. That is how you "fine tune" your presentation.

The principles of making effective submissions were outlined in Chapter 5. However, on appeal, there are certain specific points that deserve emphasis and these are listed below.

Ultimately, however, you must be true to yourself and it is important that you be you. Allow your oral argument to be stamped by your own personality. Do not try to be flamboyant if that is not you. Do not try to be emotional if that is not you. Do not try to be dramatic if that is not you. Yet, while recognizing that you must be yourself, there are also basic principles of oral advocacy that ought to be followed by *all* advocates.

---

### *Basic Principles of Oral Advocacy on Appeal*

1) **Do Not Read**

2) **Start with Your Strongest Point**

3) **Provide an Organization to Your Argument**

4) **Maintain Interest**

5) **Know When to Concede a Point**

6) **Treat the Court and Counsel with Respect**

7) **Do Not Be Afraid of Questions**

8) **Always Have an Ending**

---

#### (a)    *Do Not Read*

The oral presentation is not a recital of your factum. Certainly the factum should be referred to and used to mould your argument and there is nothing wrong with following the factum's argument sequence. But do not go further and simply read the factum aloud for surely a rebuke from the court will follow:

> Mr. Jones, we have read your factum. Do you have anything else to add?

The judges have neither the time nor the patience to listen to you read a factum that they have already read.

### (b)    Start with Your Strongest Point

Certain panels are very interventionist and you may have only a few minutes of uninterrupted time at the start of your argument to make your points. It is critical that you start the argument on a strong note. By so doing, you impress upon the judges that you have focused your arguments and that the appeal has merit. Mr. Justice Twaddle recounted this experience:[50]

> I remember Lord Goddard, Chief Justice of England, presiding every Monday in the Court of Criminal Appeal in London. There would be some twenty applications for leave routinely before that Court. Counsel had to be quick to get their point across. But sometimes, counsel rambled a little and the Chief Justice would say "Mr. Brown, is that your best point?" If counsel said "No," he would say "Would you please get on to it." If counsel said it was, he said "It is?"

Flowing from this, put your position forward *before* attacking the position put forth by the opposing side.

### (c)    Provide an Organization to Your Argument

Give the court clues as to how you have structured your argument:

> Justices, there are three issues before this court. First . . . Second . . . Third . . .

Then go on to address each issue in turn so that the court has a road map to follow your submissions. I also suggest that for each issue you prepare a self-contained argument having its own introduction, body and conclusion. The reason for this is that, should the court interject and say, "We need not hear you on point number 2," you simply move to your next self-contained issue. If you have inextricably tied the issues to one another, the forced deletion of one issue is fatal to your entire argument and you would have to plough through the hostility of the panel and force the judges to hear your submission on point 2 before moving to point 3. Self-contained issues give

---

[50] *Supra*, note 2, at p. 36.

you greater flexibility. At the conclusion of an issue, advise the court that you are moving on to the next issue:

> Subject to any questions you may have, that concludes my submissions on the issue of provocation. (*Pause*) I will now turn to the second issue.

In terms of dealing with the issues, a common mistake made by counsel is to turn immediately to the law before providing an appropriate context within which to understand the law. For example:

> Justices, I would now like to turn to the issue of provocation. The leading case on provocation is *Landry v. Patterson*, a 1978 decision of the Ontario Court of Appeal cited at 93 D.L.R. (3d) at page 345. In that case Mr. Justice MacKinnon, in giving the judgment of the court, found . . .

The problem with turning immediately to the case law is that it breaks up your argument. Note how providing the case, the date, the citation and the judgment destroyed any flow to your argument. Furthermore, by introducing the case you have diffused the issues before the court. The court's attention will be directed to the case cited and not to the case at bar. New questions are raised. What were the facts in *Landry*? Is the case distinguishable? Was the law fully canvassed in that case? Has *Landry* been overruled? That is why, prior to going to the case law, put the law in context:

1) What is the problem (issue)?

2) What is your position (your solution to the problem)?

3) What facts support your position?

4) What principles and policy support your position? and, finally

5) Tie the facts, principles and policy to the case authority to which you now refer.

### (d)   Maintain Interest

Appeal court judges do not expect to be entertained in oral argument, but it is important that their interest be maintained. One judge observed:[51]

---

[51] Chief Justice William Holohan of the Arizona Supreme Court as quoted, *supra*, note 25 at p. 81.

... the ability of the lawyer to get your attention is the real challenge of oral advocacy. One excellent way to get our attention is simply to begin with "We brought this appeal because," and state the issue. In this court we like a lawyer who can state the issue.

Think of a punchline that will stay with the court. Let us turn to the provocation issue in our case of *Waite v. Stewart*:

> Justices, the issue concerning provocation is whether provocation should go to mitigate compensatory damages. It is our position that where a person *instigates* and *provokes* an assault, provocation *does* go to mitigate *all damages*. The *instigator*, the *provoker*, should not expect to be compensated for injuries he himself provoked. This is in accord with the fundamental principles of tort law . . .

### (e)  Know When to Concede a Point

Before going into the hearing, you should determine what concessions you can make without giving your case away. Wise concessions show that you are being reasonable and that you know where the true issues lie. At one hearing, where the accused appealed from a conviction for criminal negligence causing death, I observed defence counsel steadfastly refuse to concede that her client was in any way negligent in causing the death. The court pursued the point, "Are you saying that your client was not negligent at all?" Counsel refused to budge. One judge persisted, "Not negligent even in a civil sense?" Counsel remained firm. The judges shrugged their shoulders and shook their heads. The admission of civil negligence was not fatal to her case and, given the facts of the case, was really beyond dispute. Criminal negligence refers to negligence of a different kind and degree from civil negligence; it requires a measure of "moral turpitude" to make negligent conduct criminal. Counsel's stubborn stand cost her a large measure of credibility with the court.

### (f)  Treat the Court and Counsel with Respect

Never lose your temper and never let it appear that you have lost your temper. At all times treat the presiding judges with respect and accord that same respect to other judges to whom you refer in argument:

| It Is Not | It Is |
| --- | --- |
| As Dickson said | As Chief Justice Dickson said |
| As Wilson J. wrote | As Justice Wilson wrote |

So, too, treat the opposing counsel with respect, without sarcasm or ridicule.

### (g)  Do Not Be Afraid of Questions

Questions from the bench are not intended as a test of your case preparation. When asking a question, most judges are seeking your help in understanding and resolving the issue before them. Their questions should, in fact, be welcomed in that they indicate the concerns of the court. A silent court leaves counsel in limbo and you will only find out how well or how poorly your arguments fared when the judgment is rendered. Therefore, do not fear questions from the court.

Any fear that you do have can be alleviated by preparing for questions. Have colleagues review the appeal materials and go through mock appeal runs. In this way, questions are anticipated and answers are prepared.

Counsel also make the mistake of not listening to the questions asked. Counsel assume that questions are a challenge to their position and almost by instinct they respond defensively. Yet some questions actually are intended to *help* counsel. For example:

> Mr. Brown, could we look at this issue from this perspective and still find in your favour . . .
>
> No Justice Smith, that is not what I'm saying . . .

Counsel has missed the point. The point is that the judge is providing counsel with an alternative way of resolving the case in his favour.

Counsel need to listen carefully to the question and recognize that there is a variety of types of questions:

### 1. The clarification question

Was there any evidence that the plaintiff was intoxicated?

Are we not bound by the Supreme Court of Canada decision in *R. v. Smith?*

### 2. The authority question

What is your authority for that statement?

Are there any Canadian cases on this point?

### 3. The limit question

If we accept your position, doesn't this mean that we will deny compensation to all claimants who have provoked a wrongful assault and battery upon themselves?

### 4. The policy question

Isn't the fundamental purpose of tort law the compensation of those wronged?

As one can see, most of the questions seek information and if you have prepared your case you will have that information. Remember you are far more familiar with the facts and law of the particular case than the judges. The judges simply want your assistance.

Rarely will you be faced with a directly confrontational question from the bench:

Ms Brown, you surely are not suggesting that provocation goes to mitigate compensatory damages?

How do you wipe away the long line of authority to the contrary in this jurisdiction?

Ms Brown, those are English cases, this is Ontario. You don't have any Ontario cases to support your view, do you?

Should you confront a judge you cannot appease and your argument is bogging down over an issue that you have fully canvassed, then Justice Arnup suggested this response:[52]

When you have said all you can on a point, and one judge keeps on arguing, you have *had* it — with him, at least — you've got to find a way to quit, on that point. I finally adopted the practice of simply saying, "I appreciate what your Lordship is saying, but I don't think I can help you further."

Finally, when asked a question from the bench I recommend that you answer it immediately. Do not postpone your answer. Surely you have sufficient flexibility to leave your prepared text to answer the question. There are exceptions:

---

[52] *Supra*, note 2, at p. 36.

1. The question could be answered immediately but you would like to complete the point you are now arguing. Then say:

> Justice Smith, the short answer to your question is, yes. I do think that we should follow the British Columbia Court authority. If you bear with me, I will explain that point further after I conclude this issue . . . (*Pause*) . . . (*Wait for approval or disapproval from the judge*).

But whatever you do, keep your promise and do refer to the question when the time comes.

2. The question introduces a new issue that would completely sidetrack the argument you are now making. Then say:

> Justice Jones, with respect, that issue is one that goes to self-defence, rather than to provocation, and if I may I would like to address that question when we turn to that issue . . . (*Pause*) . . .

A last piece of advice on questions: if you do not know the answer — say so. Honesty will be appreciated by the court rather than evasion.

### (h)    Always Have an Ending

At the end of your submission you reiterate to the court your "prayer for relief" and what it is that you seek from the appeal court. I recommend that you go further and try to capture in a few sentences or a phrase your position and the reason why the court should rule in your favour:

> Justices, in conclusion, Mr. Waite brought about his own grief. He sought out Mr. Stewart. He provoked Mr. Stewart. He asked for a fight. He got a fight. And now he wants to be compensated because he was injured in the fight he instigated, provoked and willingly participated in. He, and he alone, is responsible for his injuries. Accordingly, we ask that the appeal be allowed and the plaintiffs action be dismissed with costs as set by the learned trial judge. Justices, subject to any questions that you may have, that concludes my submissions.

## 5.    THE RESPONDENT'S POSITION

The general principles of oral and written appellate argument apply equally to the respondent, but in addition there are special concerns that arise in responding to an argument. This section will address:

1) the organization of the respondent's factum,

2) the response argument, and

3) the oral response.

## 5.1   The Organization of the Respondent's Factum

In Manitoba, the format for a respondent's factum mirrors an appellant's factum (Court of Appeal R. 29(1)). In Ontario, the respondent's factum is governed by a separate rule (Rule 61.12), which modifies the four part structure of a factum. The Ontario format for a respondent's factum is as follows:

Part I     Overview Statement [Introduction]

Part II    Statement of Facts

Part III   Issues and Argument

Part IV   Additional Issues

Part V    Order Requested

Sample formats for a Manitoba and Ontario respondent's factum are provided on the following pages.

## (a)   Sample Respondent's Factum

## Ontario

COURT OF APPEAL FOR ONTARIO

BETWEEN:                    RICHARD WAITE

Plaintiff (Respondent)

and

JAMES STEWART

Defendant (Appellant)

RESPONDENT'S FACTUM

[Index Page]

PART I
INTRODUCTION

1. The primary issue on appeal is the right of self-defence . . .

PART II
STATEMENT OF FACTS

4. The Respondent agrees with the facts as set out in the Appellant's factum except as qualified or expanded below.

Or

The Respondent agrees with the facts as set out in paragraphs 1 to 14 inclusive of the Appellant's factum.

*(cont'd)*

5. The Respondent disagrees with the facts set out in paragraphs 15 to 18 inclusive of the Appellant's factum.

ADDITIONAL FACTS RELIED UPON BY THE RESPONDENT

6. On 13th March 2015 the defendant was skilled in Karate . . .

## PART III
## POINTS IN ISSUE AND THE RESPONDENT'S POSITION

ISSUE: THE TRIAL JUDGE CORRECTLY FOUND THAT THE DEFENDANT USED EXCESSIVE FORCE.

17. The second kick to the plaintiff's head was completely unnecessary . . .

## PART IV
## ADDITIONAL ISSUES RAISED BY THE RESPONDENT

35. There are no additional issues raised by the Respondent.

## PART V
## ORDER REQUESTED

46. The Respondent therefore asks that this appeal be dismissed with costs.

ALL OF WHICH IS RESPECTFULLY SUBMITTED.

_____

Counsel for the Plaintiff (Respondent)

*(b)    Sample Respondent's Factum*

*Manitoba*

---

## IN THE COURT OF APPEAL

Between:

### RICHARD WAITE

(Plaintiff) Respondent

- and -

### JAMES STEWART

(Defendant) Appellant

### RESPONDENT'S FACTUM

[Index Page]

### PART I
### INTRODUCTION

1. On appeal the plaintiff raises two new issues . . .

### PART II
### STATEMENT OF FACTS

4. The plaintiff accepts the statement of facts as set out in the defendant's factum, with the addition of the following facts.

2. . . .

Or, if you are not prepared to accept the statement of facts as set out in the appellant's factum, set out your own statement of facts.

6. The plaintiff is a . . .

*(cont'd)*

---

PART III
POINTS IN ISSUE AND THE RESPONDENT'S POSITION

11. *The trial judge erred in finding that the defendant used excessive force during a consensual fight with the plaintiff.*

The plaintiff's position is that it was open for the trial judge to find excessive force and such a finding is entirely consistent with the evidence introduced at trial.

12. . . .

PART IV
ARGUMENT

THE DEFENDANT'S USE OF EXCESSIVE FORCE

15. The second kick to the plaintiff's head was completely unnecessary . . .

33. It is respectfully submitted that the appeal should be dismissed with costs.

ALL OF WHICH IS RESPECTFULLY SUBMITTED

_____

Solicitor for the (Plaintiff) Respondent

---

Under both the Manitoba and Ontario formats, an introduction or overview statement is called for. Counsel should take advantage of this opportunity to state the respondent's position, to provide a context for the respondent's appeal. This is especially important if the respondent has a different view of the case on either the facts or the law.

The "statement of facts" should be shorter than the appellant's fact summary. In fact, if the respondent agrees with the statement of facts as presented by the appellant, say so and move on to the next part of the factum. Normally, however, you will wish to highlight a few additional facts that place your "equities" before the court. If you disagree with much contained in the appellant's facts, then I suggest you start with an entirely new statement of the facts and tell the story of the case as you want. Do not engage in bouncing back and forth from the appellant's factum to yours. Rather strive to prepare a free-standing factum without cross-references to the appellant's factum. For example, references such as, "As to paragraph 13 of the appellant's factum, it is submitted . . ." will only cause the judge to go back and look at the offending paragraph 13.

If you feel compelled to rewrite the facts, tell the court why. Justices are not amused by respondents who provide a second rendition without cause. Explain why a full rendition is necessary. Justice Richards gives the following as one response:[53]

> The [respondent] accepts the broad outline of the summary of facts found in the [appellant's] factum but believes that statement is incomplete in several respects. As a consequence, it is useful to restate the facts this way.

In terms of the "issues and argument" portion of the factum, the respondent should clearly respond to the issues raised by the appellant on appeal. This should be done in short, declarative statements, which are highlighted in the text. In Manitoba, Part III of the respondent's factum lists the issues and the respondent's short response and all argument is left for Part IV of the factum. Under the Ontario format, Part III of the factum contains new issues raised by the respondent and argument on each.

The factum ends with the order sought by the respondent.

## 5.2    The Response Argument

Remember that the appellant, in preparing his factum, deliberately ordered the argument in a sequence that was most advantageous for his position. You are not tied to this agenda. For example, after listing the issues and your position thereto, in the body of the argument you are free to reorganize the argument to suit your wants. You can reorder the arguments under new headings and in an order that places your strongest position at the forefront of the factum.

You are also not bound by the trial judge's reasons for judgment. Obviously, it would be foolish for you to disparage unduly the trial judge's decision since the verdict was in your favour. On the other hand, you can reinforce the trial decision by raising alternative arguments that may be, in

---

[53] R. Richards, *supra*, note 20, at para. 25. David Lepofsky agrees, see *supra*, note 18, at para. 96.

your view, better and stronger reasons for reaching the same result. Correspondingly, if the trial judge is patently in error, concede the mistake (to do otherwise will cost you credibility) and go on to show that, on an alternative basis, the trial judge's conclusion was perfectly correct.

### 5.3   The Oral Response

Respondent's oral argument is *responsive*. You have the advantage of hearing the appellant's argument and of observing the court's reaction. Use this advantage. In your argument respond to the concerns raised by the judges by their questions of the appellant. Seize upon these concerns. Do not present your argument in a void. *Respond* to the argument put forth by the appellant. Do not ignore the appellant's submission. As you proceed through your argument, address the counter-points raised:

> My friend has raised the case of *R. v. Smith* in support of his position. But that case has no application to the case before this court . . .

> Concerning the level of intoxication of the accused, the appellant relied upon the evidence of Constable Black. I invite Your Lordships to consider the evidence of *all* other witnesses present . . .

Therefore, as respondent you need to be flexible enough to adapt to the argument that has gone before and be sensitive to the nuances of the court.

## 6.   PREPARATION OF APPEAL MATERIALS

It is my experience from listening to appellate judges speak on appellate advocacy that without fail they complain about the shoddy materials filed with the court. Obviously this is a source of irritation for the judges, for which there is no excuse. Counsel should take time to ensure that the appeal materials look professional, the materials are proofread and typographical and spelling errors are caught. Think about a typeset and factum format that is pleasing to the eye. Remember that white space on a page is good space.

Familiarize yourself with the rules and practice directions of the court. If in doubt, contact the court.

Packaging counts. Attend to Mr. Justice Arnup's admonition to make it "easier" for the judges. Pay heed to that advice. The appeal book should be thoughtfully prepared. [In Ontario it is an appeal book and compendium. See Rule 61.10.] A *good* index should be provided. The copies of the documents and the cases should be clear and clean. Your book of authorities should be tabbed, indexed and the quotes that you rely upon should be highlighted. The filing of a joint book of authorities is encouraged to avoid needless duplication.

Be considerate. Think back to your days as a student. Were you happy to read assigned cases to which the professor never even referred? Were you happy to read case after case that said the same thing? Were you happy to read a 100-page case when only a narrow point contained on page 75 of the decision was important? Now think of the judges. If you have abandoned certain grounds of appeal, advise the court of that prior to the hearing and prior to their reading of needless cases on the abandoned issue. File your materials on time to afford the court time to read the necessary material. Be selective in the cases that you include in your book of authorities. Otherwise you compel the judges to read cases that have little or no import to the issues before the court. Edit the cases where necessary. Where you are only relying on a part of the case, photocopy that portion along with the headnote and exclude the rest. No judge wants to read 100 pages only to find out that just two pages needed to be read!

These little things do count. Keep in mind that the judges have the final say and the last thing that you want to do as an advocate is antagonize the court. With that in mind, consider the following tips.

---

### *Top Ten List of Court of Appeal Practice Tips*[54]

**10. Limit the grounds of appeal — save for those exceptional cases involving the most complex matters of fact or issues of law, counsel should attempt to restrict the number of grounds pleaded. The "shotgun" approach does not find favour with the Court and may serve to camouflage those grounds that are meritorious.**

*(cont'd)*

---

[54] Presented at a seminar on "The Court of Appeal: New Rules and Effective Appellate Advocacy" February 4, 1994. The seminar included the Chief Justice of Manitoba and these tips seem to be from coming from the bench. Justice Catzman of the Ontario Court of Appeal has also compiled a list of tips on how to lose appeals. His list now is up to 14, but it began with the article, "The Wrong Stuff: How to Lose Appeals in the Court of Appeal," Adv. Soc. J. (August, 2000).

9.  Never underestimate the importance of written argument —
    except in those (hopefully) rare instances where the pressures
    of practice do not allow time to prepare a thorough written
    argument, counsel should use written argument as an oppor-
    tunity to present, briefly and concisely, a full summary of the
    arguments in support of the grounds of appeal.

8.  Apply the "Rule of 30's" to written argument — except in the
    most complex of cases, there should be no need for argument
    to exceed 30 pages in length. Develop all points of argument
    fully, but try to avoid arguments that are prolix, repetitive or
    inadequately focused or edited.

7.  Refer only to the leading case(s) on each issue of law — it is
    not helpful to cite a multiplicity of authorities in support of
    the same proposition. Similarly, lower court authorities ought
    not to be cited if there is a Court of Appeal or Supreme Court
    of Canada decision on point.

6.  Never underestimate the importance of oral argument — the
    Court has purposely chosen to retain oral argument despite
    the move in some jurisdictions to restrict or eliminate that
    right. In a close case, a compelling oral submission can be
    persuasive and determinative. As with written argument, em-
    phasis should be placed upon framing each issue precisely,
    briefly and clearly. Repetition does not add strength to the
    argument and may be counter-productive. And when you
    hear the words "we have your point on that issue," move on
    or sit down!

5.  Argue the strongest points first — there is simply no substitute
    for a strong beginning.

4.  Get to the point — assume that the Court has at least a passing
    familiarity with the legal and factual issues being argued.

*(cont'd)*

3. Do not get bogged down in the transcript — in the factum, refer specifically to areas of the transcript that are relevant. Avoid quoting lengthy excerpts. In oral argument, refer briefly to important areas of the trial evidence by paraphrasing. Assume the panel is conversant with the important portions of the trial evidence.

2. Anticipate the Court's questions and answer them directly.

1. Know the Rules and comply with them — the new Rules are *not* made to be broken. Counsel should consider themselves warned!

# 18

# THE ETHICS OF ADVOCACY

- **Communicating with Witnesses**

- **Entering a Guilty Plea**

- **Withdrawing as Counsel**

- **Counselling Clients**

- **Client Confidentiality**

- **Disclosure of Law**

- **Disclosure of Facts**

- **Disclosure of Information to the Court**

- **Cross-examination Limits**

- **Communicating with Represented Party**

- **Conclusion**

An advocate is subject to competing and conflicting duties. On the one hand, the advocate is expected to fight vigorously for his or her client's cause and the advocate is paid to win. On the other hand, the advocate is not a legal mercenary. The advocate is also an officer of the court and a member of the legal profession. The court and his or her fellow lawyers expect to be treated with fairness, honesty and respect. The advocate therefore serves many masters, each with competing claims, each demanding allegiance. Conflicts arise and nowhere are conflicts of duty more likely to arise than in the heated atmosphere of a trial. For this reason, the trial advocate must be most sensitive to his or her ethical obligations. Lord Birkett put it in these terms:[1]

> The advocate has a duty to his client, a duty to the Court, and a duty to the State; but he has above all a duty to himself that he shall be, as far as lies in his power, a man of integrity. No profession calls for higher standards of honour and uprightness, and no profession, perhaps, offers greater temptations to forsake them . . .

What counsel must not do is to lose perspective. Consider this example, which was raised in a first year criminal law class. We were discussing the role of the defence counsel. A student had been invited to observe a trial the previous day. A senior law student had represented an accused charged with a highway traffic offence. Identification was at issue. The client was present in the courtroom, but was not seated at the counsel table. Another person was seated at the counsel table with the student advocate. No mention of this substitution was made to the court. None of the Crown witnesses identified the "accused," and the client was acquitted. My student asked, "Was this unethical conduct?"

In my view, the student advocate had actively misled the court. Two American cases deal directly with this issue.[2] In each a substitute accused was planted at the counsel table. The counsel involved in each argued that what they had done was simply "zealous advocacy" and each counsel pleaded that he was unaware of any rule preventing such substitution. The counsel in both cases were found in contempt of court.

The student advocate, through a sense of misguided zeal, had blundered into a serious breach of professional conduct by failing to treat the court with "candour, fairness, courtesy and respect."[3] While it is appropriate to test the identification made by a witness, you must not actively deceive or mislead the court. The student should have informed the court of the substitution:[4]

---

[1] H. Montgomery Hyde, *Norman Birkett* (1964), pp. 551-552, as quoted in E. Cherniak, "The Ethics of Advocacy," in F. Moskoff, ed., *Advocacy in Court: A Tribute to Arthur Maloney*, Q.C. (1986), at p. 101.

[2] *U.S. v. Thoreen*, 653 F. 2d 1332 (C.A. 9th Circ., 1981), and *Miskovsky v. Oklahoma*, 586 P. 2d 1104 (Okla. Crim. App., 1978).

[3] The Law Society of Manitoba, Code of Professional Conduct (2010), R. 5.1-1; The Law Society of Upper Canada, Rules of Professional Conduct (2014), R. 5.1-1. Reference throughout this chapter will be to the Manitoba Law Society Code and The Law Society of Upper Canada Rules.

[4] *U.S. v. Thoreen, supra*, note 2, at p. 1342.

The court's ire and this criminal contempt conviction could have been avoided easily and the admirable goal of representing his client zealously preserved if only he had given the court and opposing counsel prior notice and sought the court's consent.

Further, should you conduct such an identification test, *complete* fairness to the court is expected. In the Canadian case of *R. v. Macfarlane*, counsel asked permission to have his client seated in the gallery, but was not entirely candid with the court:[5]

The accused had been permitted by the judge to be seated in the public area of the courtroom during the Crown's case. His counsel had requested this in order to determine whether the police officers who made the arrest would identify the accused as the person they arrested. The accused had come to court clean-shaven and wearing glasses and his counsel did not tell the judge that he wore a beard at the time of the events which led to the charges. Nor did counsel say whether the accused at that time wore glasses. Nor did he tell the judge there was a friend of the accused seated in the public area of approximately the accused's size and age, wearing a beard and no glasses. The friend answered in many respects to the description given by the officers of the man they arrested, a man with a beard and no glasses. The police witnesses both identified the friend as the person they had arrested.

The accused's friend was called by the defence as its sole witness. He testified that he had not been arrested at the time and place described by the officers, nor charged with the offences before the court.

The learned trial judge concluded that the above ploy "smack[ed] almost of trickery" and he declared a mistrial. In reaching this decision, he commented:

Just like I worry about an accused being wrongly convicted, I worry about injustice particularly by people who make a mockery of the system, who can boast in the beer parlour or amongst their friends for the rest of their lives how they've put it over the system, and it brings the whole system into mockery.

On appeal, the trial judge's decision to declare a mistrial was upheld.

In the student example, the mistake was made out of ignorance. However, this is no excuse. Before taking on the conduct of a trial, new counsel have an obligation to acquaint themselves with, and appreciate, their professional responsibilities.

---

[5] *R. v. Macfarlane*, [1987] B.C.J. No. 1304, a decision of Taylor J. of the British Columbia Supreme Court (12th June 1987).

In this chapter, ten common problems are posed for your ethical consideration. They are designed to illustrate competing demands and responsibilities that confront a trial advocate. Following each question, an answer is provided based upon the rules of professional conduct found in Manitoba and Ontario.

## Problem 1 — Communicating with Witnesses

Your client is being cross-examined by opposing counsel. There is a break for lunch. At lunch you discuss with your client anticipated areas yet to be covered on the cross-examination. Is this unethical?

### Answer

Yes.

### Commentary

The Ontario rules clearly prohibit communication between lawyer and client during the cross-examination of the client:

Rule 5.4-2:

(a.2) between completion of examination-in-chief and commencement of cross-examination of the lawyer's own witness, the lawyer ought not to discuss the evidence given in chief or relating to any matter introduced or touched on during the examination-in-chief;

(b) during cross-examination by an opposing legal practitioner, the witness's own lawyer ought not to have any conversation with the witness about the witness's evidence or any issue in the proceeding;

Manitoba is not so clear:

Rule 5.4-2:

(b) during cross-examination of the lawyer's own witness, the lawyer must not discuss with the witness the evidence given in chief or relating to any matter introduced or touched on during the examination-in-chief;

Yet, the Manitoba practice was, and I suggest remains, that of non-communication. The Manitoba Rule includes the following commentary:

[3] The opportunity to conduct a fully ranging and uninterrupted cross-examination is fundamental to the adversarial system. It is counterbalanced by an opposing advocate's ability to ensure clarity of testimony through initial briefing, direct examination and re-examination of that lawyer's witnesses. There is therefore no justification for obstruction of cross-examination by unreasonable interruptions, repeated objection to proper questions, attempts to have the witness change or tailor evidence, or other similar conduct while the examination is ongoing.

The principle behind the non-communication rule is to prevent shaping of testimony by the witnesses, who could be influenced by hearing prior evidence. The specific prohibition on consultation with your witnesses during cross-examination is premised on the truth-finding function accorded to cross-examination and that nothing should be allowed to potentially interfere with that purpose:[6]

> The reason for the rule is one that applies to all witnesses — not just defendants. It is common practice for a judge to instruct a witness not to discuss his or her testimony with third parties until the trial is completed. Such nondiscussion orders are a corollary of the broader rule that witnesses may be sequestered to lessen the danger that their testimony will be influenced by hearing what other witnesses have to say, and to increase the likelihood that they will confine themselves to truthful statements based on their own recollection . . . cross-examination is more likely to elicit truthful responses if it goes forward without allowing the witness an opportunity to consult with third parties, including his or her lawyer.

In Ontario the rules go further to bar communications between a lawyer and witness after cross-examination is concluded and prior to any re-examination:

> 5.4-2(c.1) between completion of cross-examination and commencement of re-examination, the lawyer who is going to re-examine the witness ought not to have any discussion about evidence that will be dealt with on re-examination;

---

[6] *Perry v. Leeke*, 109 S. Ct. 594 at 600-601 (1989), per Stevens J. In *Perry*, the trial judge refused to allow defence counsel to meet with the accused during a 15-minute recess after the accused's direct examination and prior to the start of cross-examination. The accused alleged that his Sixth Amendment right to counsel was violated. Considering that only a short break was involved, the court found no violation of the Sixth Amendment. Mr. Justice Marshall filed a dissenting opinion, in which Justices Brennan and Blackmun joined. Note, in an earlier decision, the Supreme Court of the United States had found that prohibiting counsel from conferring with their client during an overnight recess did violate the Sixth Amendment. See *Geders v. U.S.*, 96 S.Ct. 1330 (1976).

John Sopinka, Q.C. (as he then was), cast some doubt on the scope of this prohibition:[7]

> The guidelines do not, of course, create new rules of evidence but counsel who runs afoul of them may be subjected to disciplinary proceedings. It is submitted with respect that in some respects they may inhibit the discovery of truth and go beyond what was the practice in the High Court.

Mr. Sopinka pointed out that for a witness who is going to be on the stand a long time it is difficult to discuss evidence to be given without discussing the earlier evidence. Also, how does counsel know whether to re-examine his witness on new matters raised on cross-examination without finding out the witness's answers first?

The Manitoba rule allows for consultation:

> 5.4-2(c) upon the conclusion of cross-examination and during any re-examination the lawyer may discuss with the witness any matter.

This is also the practice in British Columbia, where counsel should seek leave to speak with their witnesses after cross-examination and before re-examination and, in most cases, leave will be given readily. The British Columbia approach is premised on the view that consultation "allows counsel to correct honest mistakes, clear up ambiguities, and clarify points left obscure during cross-examination without the risk of unanticipated, and perhaps unresponsive, answers from the witness."[8]

Notwithstanding these concerns, the Court of Appeal of Quebec has ruled, in no uncertain terms, that it is improper for counsel to consult with his witness after cross-examination but before any re-examination.[9] The situation presented to the Court of Appeal provided a classic example. Two accused were charged with first degree murder. The Crown's last witness was a pathologist who testified as to the cause of death. The expert's opinion contradicted the Crown's version of events. The cross-examination of the expert ended early Friday afternoon. The Crown requested an adjournment to Monday. The defence asked that any re-examination be done immediately. The judge adjourned the trial to Monday. On Monday, after discussing

---

[7] J. Sopinka, *The Trial of an Action* (1981), at p. 106.

[8] *R. v. Montgomery* (1998), 126 C.C.C. (3d) 251 (B.C.S.C.) at para. 11. See also The Law Society of British Columbia, The Code of Professional Conduct for BC (2013), Rule 5.4-2(c).

[9] *R. v. Peruta* (1992), 78 C.C.C. (3d) 350 (Que. C.A.), leave to appeal to S.C.C. refused (1993), 81 C.C.C. (3d) vi (note) (S.C.C.).

his evidence with the Crown attorney and the police, the expert in re-examination revised his opinion, performed a "volte-face." Justice Tyndale termed the Crown prosecutor's discussion with the expert "highly improper, if not strictly illegal." Justice Proulx was only slightly less critical:[10]

> ... the Crown prosecutor should know or should have known that it was totally improper and contrary to custom (my brother called it "highly improper") for a counsel to communicate with or meet the witness he has produced before re-examination: this prohibition starts at the time the witness is cross-examined by the adverse party.

What this problem illustrates is that many ethical problems are open to a degree of discussion and interpretation. As a starting point, new counsel should read the respective provincial law society rules dealing with advocacy and, when not certain, ask senior counsel for advice.

---

## Problem 2 — Entering a Guilty Plea

Your client is charged with mischief. He says that he is innocent, but that he wishes to plead guilty. He wants to get the matter over with. He also concludes that if he goes to trial he will lose a day's pay and that that would be more than any fine imposed by the court — not to mention his defence costs. Do you assist him in entering his guilty plea?

### Answer

Unless your client admits his guilt, you cannot assist him in entering a guilty plea. To do otherwise would be to suborn perjury in that the plea of guilty is a lie.

---

### Commentary

Before you can assist the client in pleading guilty, the client must be prepared to admit "the necessary factual and mental elements" of the offence.[11] When confronted with this question, Mr. Arthur Martin (as he then was) replied:[12]

---

[10] *Ibid.*, at p. 372.
[11] Manitoba and Ontario Rule 5.1-8(c).
[12] "Problems In Ethics And Advocacy," a Panel Discussion, in Defending a Criminal Case, Special Lectures of the Law Society of Upper Canada (1969), p. 279, at p. 318.

To permit a client to plead guilty who is innocent and who informs you that he is innocent is really in the nature of a fraud on the administration of justice, and is improper.

Sometimes, however, a client will assert his innocence as a sort of face saving device, although careful investigation, or the evidence adduced at the preliminary hearing makes this position completely untenable, and then he will instruct you that he wishes to plead guilty in order to receive a lighter sentence although he is not guilty. There is a temptation under these circumstances, perhaps, to follow the client's instructions and not take his formal protestations of innocence very seriously.

I think, however, that so long as the client persists in maintaining his innocence after you have confronted him with the evidence against him, and have explained the relevant law, that it is preferable not to represent him for the purpose of entering a plea of guilty.

The key point is that the client continues to maintain his innocence and, as a matter of expediency, is prepared to plead guilty. "The public interest in the proper administration of justice should not be sacrificed in the interest of expediency."[13] In *R. v. K.(S.)* the Ontario Court of Appeal dealt with a situation where a young offender pled guilty to a number of sexual assaults that he claimed he had not committed. His counsel explained to him that criminal courts do not deal with truth but with evidence. The young man then pled guilty. The Ontario Court of Appeal set aside the guilty pleas with the following pointed comment:[14]

I have no hesitation in concluding that the guilty pleas should be set aside. This case presents a graphic example of why it is essential to the plea bargaining process that the accused person is prepared to admit to the facts that support the conviction. The court should not be in the position of convicting and sentencing individuals, who fall short of admitting the facts to support the conviction unless that guilt is proved beyond a reasonable doubt. Nor should sentencing proceed on the false assumption of contrition. That did not happen here, but worse, the sentence became impossible to perform. Plea bargaining is an accepted and integral part of our criminal justice system but must be conducted with sensitivity to its vulnerabilities. A court that is misled, or allows itself to be misled, cannot serve the interests of justice.

---

[13] Commentary 1 to Rule 5.1-8.
[14] *R. v. K. (S.)* (1995), 99 C.C.C. (3d) 376 (Ont. C.A.) at p. 382.

## Problem 3 — Withdrawing as Counsel

Your client is charged with the break and enter of a neighbour's home in which a very valuable computer was stolen. The accused was arrested after he attempted to pawn the computer and the police were alerted. The owner of the computer was an elderly gentleman, who was away at the time. The accused in an interview with you admitted that he stole the computer. You go to trial on the issue of identification. As the trial unfolds, two eyewitnesses testify that they saw the accused leave the house, with what appeared to be a computer. It does not look too good for your client. However, the elderly owner has died. The accused now insists upon taking the stand to say that the disabled man gave him the computer. You are certain that he is lying. Do you withdraw?

### Answer

You "know" that your client is going to commit perjury. You cannot knowingly attempt to deceive or participate in the deception of a tribunal by offering false evidence. In this case you are obliged to withdraw. The difficulty is how to withdraw.

### Commentary

In the above scenario, counsel is obliged to withdraw. The decision to withdraw services is a grave step. "As in marriage, the relationship is not one to be entered into lightly. As such it may not be lightly terminated by the lawyer."[15] Counsel also have a duty to minimize any prejudice to the client.[16]

During the course of a trial, the decision to withdraw becomes even more difficult. Counsel must weigh heavily the prejudice to the client, the increased costs to all sides and the inconvenience to the court.

The Supreme Court of Canada in *R. v. Cunningham* has clarified the law on withdrawal. There was disagreement as to whether the courts had a supervisory role over withdrawal by counsel. The Court in *Cunningham*

---

[15] B. Smith, *Professional Conduct for Canadian Lawyers* (1989), p. 154.
[16] Manitoba and Ontario Rule 3.7-8.

affirmed the power of courts to refuse counsel's motion to withdraw. *Cunningham* was a case that concerned non-payment of fees; however, the Court outlined a supervisory role over all types of withdrawal by counsel. The process outlined is as follows:[17]

- If counsel seeks to withdraw far enough in advance of any scheduled proceedings and an adjournment will not be necessary, then the court should allow the withdrawal. In this situation, there is no need for the court to enquire into counsel's reasons for seeking to withdraw or require counsel to continue to act.

- Assuming that timing is an issue, the court is entitled to enquire further. Counsel may reveal that he or she seeks to withdraw for ethical reasons, non-payment of fees, or another specific reason (e.g. workload of counsel) if solicitor-client privilege is not engaged. Counsel seeking to withdraw for ethical reasons means that an issue has arisen in the solicitor-client relationship where it is now impossible for counsel to continue in good conscience to represent the accused. Counsel may cite "ethical reasons" as the reason for withdrawal if, for example, the accused is requesting that counsel act in violation of his or her professional obligations . . . If the real reason for withdrawal is non-payment of legal fees, then counsel cannot represent to the court that he or she seeks to withdraw for "ethical reasons". However, in either the case of ethical reasons or non-payment of fees, the court must accept counsel's answer at face value and not enquire further so as to avoid trenching on potential issues of solicitor-client privilege.

- If withdrawal is sought for an ethical reason, then the court must grant withdrawal. . . Where an ethical issue has arisen in the relationship, counsel may be required to withdraw in order to comply with his or her professional obligations. It would be inappropriate for a court to require counsel to continue to act when to do so would put him or her in violation of professional responsibilities.

- If withdrawal is sought because of non-payment of legal fees, the court may exercise its discretion to refuse counsel's request. The court's order refusing counsel's request to withdraw may be enforced by the court's contempt power. . . In exercising its discretion on the withdrawal request, the court should consider the following non-exhaustive list of factors:

---

[17] *Cunningham v. Lilles*, 2010 SCC 10 (S.C.C.) at paras. 46-51.

- whether it is feasible for the accused to represent himself or herself; other means of obtaining representation;

- impact on the accused from delay in proceedings, particularly if the accused is in custody;

- conduct of counsel, e.g. if counsel gave reasonable notice to the accused to allow the accused to seek other means of representation, or if counsel sought leave of the court to withdraw at the earliest possible time;

- impact on the Crown and any co-accused;

- impact on complainants, witnesses and jurors;

- fairness to defence counsel, including consideration of the expected length and complexity of the proceedings;

- the history of the proceedings, e.g. if the accused has changed lawyers repeatedly.

- As these factors are all independent of the solicitor-client relationship, there is no risk of violating solicitor-client privilege when engaging in this analysis. On the basis of these factors, the court must determine whether allowing withdrawal would cause serious harm to the administration of justice. If the answer is yes, withdrawal may be refused.

The problem lies in how a lawyer shows good cause without revealing the "cause" and thereby revealing client communications. Two cases illustrate the problem. In *R. v. Gillespie,* counsel sought to withdraw prior to trial.[18] Counsel appeared and made submissions himself. The reasons provided were unconvincing and the trial judge was not satisfied that counsel had given his client reasonable notice. The motion to withdraw was denied. In *R. v. Jenkins,* counsel sought to withdraw near the end of a lengthy murder trial.[19] Senior counsel appeared on behalf of the counsel seeking to withdraw. The senior counsel indicated that the continued representation of the accused raised the potential of misleading the court. Moreover, "substitute" counsel was found. The trial judge granted the motion. In my view, counsel in *Gillespie* said and did too little and in *Jenkins*, if anything, said too much. I suggest a middle course:

---

[18] *R. v. Gillespie* (2000), 146 Man. R. (2d) 279 (Q.B.).
[19] *R. v. Jenkins* (2001), 152 C.C.C. (3d) 426 (Ont. S.C.J.).

1)  As new counsel, judges probably do not know you. Therefore, it is important that you consult senior counsel, preferably a bencher or former bencher of the Law Society.

2)  Advise this counsel of your situation. Your communication with counsel is protected by privilege and your client confidences are protected.

3)  Obtain from counsel an opinion as to whether you have good cause to withdraw.

4)  That counsel may then appear on your behalf, or provide a letter on your behalf, indicating that you have good cause – without revealing *any* of the particulars.

In this way, the court has more than your "inexperienced" opinion that you ought to withdraw and client confidences are fully protected.

---

### *Problem 4 — Counselling Clients*

Consider this problem posed by Professor Monroe Freedman:[20]

Assume that Jurisdictions X and Y are adjacent to each other and that many lawyers practice in both jurisdictions. In Jurisdiction X, there are a large number of workmen's compensation cases in which workers strain themselves while lifting, and recover compensation. In Jurisdiction Y, there is an equivalent number of such cases, but in all of them the workers who strain themselves while lifting also slip or trip on something in the process. That coincidence is fortunate, because in Jurisdiction X it is sufficient for compensation simply that the strain be work-related, while in Jurisdiction Y the applicable law requires that the injury be received in the course of an "accident," such as a slip or a trip. Obviously, the same lawyers whose clients are not slipping or tripping in Jurisdiction X are prompting their clients to recall a slip or trip when the injury is received in Jurisdiction Y.

*(cont'd)*

---

[20]  M. Freedman, "Counseling the Client: Refreshing Recollection or Prompting Perjury?" in *The Litigation Manual*, prepared by the American Bar Association (Litigation Section), p. 76, at p. 79.

> In prompting their clients to recall an "accident," are these law-
> yers acting ethically?
>
> **Answer**
>
> Professor Freedman says, "Yes."

## Commentary

Your obligation, as counsel, is to assist your clients and your witnesses to recount facts and then to communicate those facts to the court. You are not to encourage your witnesses to manufacture or create false evidence. The line is a fine one between valid counselling of facts and invalid counselling of perjury. On the one hand, counsel must not:[21]

> Rule 5.1-2(e) knowingly attempt to deceive a tribunal or influence the course of justice by offering false evidence, misstating facts or law, presenting or relying upon a false or deceptive affidavit, suppressing what ought to be disclosed or otherwise assisting in any fraud, crime or illegal conduct.

On the other hand:

> Manitoba Rule 3.2-2C: A lawyer must obtain the client's instructions and in doing so, provide informed and independent advice.
>
> Commentary [2] A lawyer should clearly specify the facts, circumstances and assumptions upon which an opinion is based. If it is apparent that the client has misunderstood or misconceived the lawyer's advice, matters concerning the position taken or what is really involved in the matter, the lawyer should explain the matter further to the client to a sufficient degree so that the client does understand.
>
> Ontario Rule 3.2-2 Commentary [1.1]:
>
> [1.1] A lawyer has a duty of candour with the client on matters relevant to the retainer. This arises out of the rules and the lawyer's fiduciary obligations to the client. The duty of candour requires a lawyer to inform the client of information known to the lawyer that may affect the interests of the client in the matter.

Professor Freedman termed the above problem a "close case" and resolved it as follows:[22]

---

[21] Manitoba and Ontario Rule 5.1-2(e).
[22] Freedman, *supra*, note 20, at p. 79.

In those cases, there are no issues of intent or of judgment, but only of objective fact. Nevertheless, even if the client's initial narrative of the incident should omit any reference to slipping or tripping, I believe that the lawyer's obligation is to explain to the client in Jurisdiction Y that one of the legal requirements for recovery is an accident, such as a trip or slip. As we have seen in the earlier discussions of experiments by behavioral psychologists, a factual detail of that sort might very well be omitted in a narrative of the incident. Moreover, the narrator's understanding (whether accurate or inaccurate) of his or her own self-interest will affect the remembering-reconstruction of the incident entirely apart from any conscious dishonesty. Thus, the client who incorrectly assumes that tripping or slipping might preclude recovery (perhaps because it might imply carelessness) might unconsciously screen out that fact. Despite the risk, therefore, that a dishonest client might consciously invent a trip or slip to meet the needs of the occasion, the attorney is obliged to prod the client's remembering-reconstruction by explaining the relevance and importance of that factual element.

To sum up, the attorney who is interviewing and preparing a witness must take into account the psychological realities of the situation. That means, at least at the earlier stages of eliciting the witness's story, that the attorney should assume a skeptical attitude, and that the attorney should give the client legal advice that might help in drawing out useful information that the client, consciously or unconsciously, might be withholding. At the same time, there will inevitably come a point at which the lawyer knows, to a moral certainty, that the client's ability to reconstruct in good faith has been fully tapped. It is at that point, I believe, that the attorney who continues to seek the desired testimony crosses the ethical line and enters upon active participation in the creation of perjury.

## Problem 5 — Client Confidentiality

Your client is a hit-and-run driver. He comes to you for advice and asks that you obtain further information on his behalf without revealing his identity. He decides not to go to the authorities. The injured party seeks to have you reveal your client's identity. May you divulge your client's identity?

### Answer

No.

## Commentary

Lawyers are well aware of the sanctity of solicitor-client confidentiality. Certainly confidentiality attaches to communications between the solicitor and client. But Wigmore concluded that, "The identity of the attorney's client or the name of the *real party in interest* will seldom be a matter communicated in confidence because the procedure of litigation ordinarily presupposes a disclosure of these facts."[23] Yet, it is also the case that confidentiality *may* attach to the identity of the client. The rules specifically address this point:[24]

> Rule 3.3-1 Commentary 5:
>
> Generally, unless the nature of the matter requires such disclosure, a lawyer should not disclose having been:
>
> (a) retained by a person about a particular matter; or
>
> (b) consulted by a person about a particular matter, whether or not the lawyer-client relationship has been established between them.

In the problem presented, the reason the client came to you was that you, being a lawyer, could obtain information without disclosing the client's identity. The client expected that his identity would remain confidential. The decision of *Thorson v. Jones* is on point:[25]

> In the matter before me the undisclosed client was a hit-and-run driver whose identity as a hit-and-run driver was concealed; he was in fact hiding his identity as a hit-and-run driver and disclosed his identity to Mr. Heller confidentially, as his solicitor, for the purpose of being advised professionally by his solicitor and has not communicated his identity in this regard to the rest of the world. By virtue of the nature of the matter as to which the client consulted the solicitor, the essence of the confidence was the identity of the person, and this was the crux of the communication between the client and his solicitor, and accordingly the name of the client under the circumstances is a privileged communication and need not be disclosed.

---

[23] 8 Wigmore, *Evidence*, McNaughton rev. (1961), para. 2313, p. 609.

[24] Manitoba and Ontario Rule 3.3-1 Commentary 5.

[25] *Thorson v. Jones* (1973), 38 D.L.R. (3d) 312 at 313 (B.C. S.C.). See also *Baird v. Koerner*, 279 F. 2d 623 (C.A. 9th Circ., 1960).

## Problem 6 — Disclosure of Law

The Supreme Court of Canada recently rendered a decision that is on point to a case in which you are now in trial. The Supreme Court decision undermines your legal position. Your opponent has completed argument without mention of the case. Do you bring the case to the attention of the court?

**Answer**

Yes.

### Commentary

The Manitoba and Ontario rules specifically cover this point:[26]

Rule 5.1-2(i): deliberately refrain from informing a tribunal of any binding authority that the lawyer considers to be directly on point and that has not been mentioned by an opponent.

In this case your obligation to the court prevails over any sense of loyalty to your client. The law is part of the public domain and you are not disclosing any solicitor-client confidence. Your role as counsel places a duty upon you to assist the court with the applicable law. Sir David Napley provided this rationale:[27]

The situation in relation to the law is wholly different from that applicable to the facts. The law is part of the public fund of knowledge. If an advocate discovers or knows of a decision which is adverse to his case, he must not conveniently forget its existence for fear of damaging his client's case. His bounden duty to the court is then to draw the authority to the attention of the court and seek, where possible, to distinguish the facts in the instant case from those of the reported authority or endeavour to show that the authority was wrongly decided, or that, despite the adverse decision, the matter can otherwise be resolved in his client's favour.

Counsel may argue that no case is ever "directly in point," and in this way the rule can be circumvented. Such a position would reduce the rule to

---

[26] Manitoba and Ontario Rule 5.1-2(i).
[27] Sir David Napley, *The Technique of Persuasion* 3rd ed. (1983), at p. 74.

a nullity. In the United States, the following interpretation of "directly" places the word and intent of the rule in proper context:[28]

> Some might argue, therefore, that precedent which can be distinguished is not "directly" adverse and need not be revealed in the first place. This interpretation trivializes the Rule [Model Rule 3.3(a)(3)] and does not adequately protect the court.

> Formal Opinion 280 (1949) sounded the right note on this issue when it suggested that the test should be whether the omitted authorities "would be considered important by the judge sitting on the case," or whether the judge might consider himself "misled" if he remained unaware of them. Although this is a somewhat subjective test, the intent seems clear.

---

## Problem 7 — Disclosure of Facts

You act for a client in a personal injury action. In answer to an advertisement in the local newspaper calling for witnesses to the accident, a Mr. Prim responds. He attends your office and relates seeing the accident in a way that is very damaging to your case. You definitely will not call him as a witness. Do you divulge his existence to the opposing side?

**Answer**

No.

---

### Commentary

A lawyer is under no obligation to produce a witness who can only harm his client's case.[29] Unlike the law, which is in the public domain, facts are within the private domain of counsel. Sir David Napley, in discussing this distinction, wrote:[30]

> The facts which are disclosed to the advocate by the client are not public property as is the case with the law. They are protected by the privilege of the

---

[28] G. Hazard, *The Law of Lawyering: A Handbook on the Model Rules of Professional Conduct* (1989), at p. 353.

[29] M. Orkin, *Legal Ethics, A study of Professional Conduct* (1957), at p. 51.

[30] Napley, *supra*, note 27, at p. 74.

client which he alone can waive. The advocate, therefore, except where it amounts to a positive misleading of the court, is under no duty to bring facts to the notice of the court which may be damaging to his client's case, indeed, by reason of the client's privilege he is precluded from doing so.

However, you must not go further and dissuade or discourage the witness from coming forward to give evidence. To suggest that the witness not talk to the other side would be inappropriate.[31] You simply need not encourage him to do so.

There are two provisos. First, in uncontested or *ex parte* matters, counsel have a higher obligation to assist the court and not to suppress material facts.[32] Similarly, a Crown attorney has a positive duty to inform the defence of all relevant and known facts and witnesses.[33] Second, opposing counsel at the examination for discovery may ask (see R. 31.06(2)):

> Please provide me with the names and addresses of persons who might reasonably be expected to have knowledge of the accident.

If the question is asked, you are duty-bound to disclose. Mr. Justice Borins of the Ontario District Court in *Temoin v. Stanley* had occasion to review R. 31.06(2) and concluded:[34]

> In my view, therefore, it would be contrary to the purposes of modern discovery to permit one party to withhold evidence which may assist the opposite party *in the face of a proper request*. If, for example in the course of its investigation a defendant locates a witness who has evidence which may assist the plaintiff, while the defendant is under no obligation to volunteer his or her identity, r. 31.06(2) requires that the defendant disclose the person's identity *if asked*. [emphasis added]

Mr. Justice Borins went on to justify the rule:[35]

> I am not offended by the prospect that one party may benefit from the preparation for trial of the opposite party. What I do find offensive, however, is the suggestion that a party could be excused from disclosing information which

---

[31]  Manitoba and Ontario Rule 5.1-2(j).

[32]  Orkin, *supra*, note 33, at p. 52. See also Manitoba and Ontario Rule 5.1-1 Commentary 6.

[33]  Manitoba and Ontario Rule 5.1-3 Commentay 1 .

[34]  *Temoin v. Stanley* (1986), 12 C.P.C. (2d) 69 at 72 (Ont. Dist. Ct.), reversed in part on other grounds 7 W.D.C.P. 71 (Ont. H.C.).

[35]  *Ibid.*, at p. 73.

might assist his or her opponent's case, thereby preventing the Court from having before it all of the relevant evidence.

The rules of discovery place an ongoing obligation on disclosure. Therefore, even if the witness comes to light after the discovery, and *the question has been asked as to names of witnesses*, you are duty-bound to disclose (see R. 31.09).

---

## *Problem 8 — Disclosure of Information to the Court*

The accused has a previous assault conviction. He enters a plea of guilty to a charge of assault. The Crown attorney reads a summary of the evidence. The judge asks the Crown, "Has the accused a record?" The Crown answers, "No."

(a) What is the duty of defence counsel in this situation?

(b) Suppose the judge turns to defence counsel and asks, "Does your client have a prior record?"

(c) Should defence counsel refer to the lack of a record in his submissions?

### Answer

Counsel has no duty to inform the court of the prior conviction and, if asked, should decline to answer. However, defence counsel cannot refer to a lack of a record in his submissions.

---

### Commentary

It is the responsibility of the Crown to put the *fact* of a prior record before the court. Disclosure by the defence counsel would breach his client's confidence. But, having said this, it would be inappropriate for defence counsel to seize upon the misrepresentation, which he knows to be false, and suggest in mitigation that his client has no prior record. This would be active misleading of the court. A panel of the Law Society of Upper Canada considered this problem and their conclusion was as follows:[36]

---

[36] *Supra*, note 12, at pp. 326-327.

**Mr. Sedgwick:** . . . Assuming that counsel got his information from his client, what he has been told by the accused is a confidential communication between counsel and client and thus counsel would not have any right, in my opinion, to volunteer the information. However, I do think that as a matter of ethics as he has some knowledge of that kind he should not refer to the absence of previous convictions as being a mitigating circumstance.

**Chief Justice Gale:** Mr. Sedgwick, wouldn't it be most improper for him to do so?

**Mr. Sedgwick:** Oh, I think so. Most improper. I don't think he is bound to tell the provincial judge, but certainly he mustn't tell him lies. It would be telling him lies to say this man has a clean record when he knows that isn't so. No, clearly he should not do that. As to the second part of the question (b). It troubled me considerably . . . Well, in the first instance I don't think a trial judge has any right to ask such a question of defence counsel although I am told it has been done and done not infrequently. And there again we come to the duty of counsel. Clearly he can't lie to the court and it is equally clear, as I have already said, that if the information came to him from his client and only from his client it is a confidential communication and he has no right to disclose it. But he can't just stand there, so what does he do? I worried about it and thought that as a practical matter he might be a little evasive and could say something like this: "Your Honour, the Crown has and I do not have access to police records and thus I cannot give you an authoritative answer." And then he may continue by saying, "The Crown has already answered Your Honour's question which you directed, as is proper, to him." That's the grey area.

The Ethics Committee of the American Bar Association, when confronted with the same problem, came to exactly the same conclusion as Mr. Sedgwick.[37]

---

[37] American Bar Association Ethics Committee, A.B.A. Formal Opinion 287 (27th June 1953).

## *Problem 9 — Cross-examination Limits*

Counsel is cross-examining an eyewitness to a car-pedestrian accident. At the time of the accident, the witness was driving his own car. The witness is a bank employee, married with three children. He testified that he was driving to work. The area where the accident occurred is the city's red light district and is frequented by prostitutes. In cross-examination counsel asks:

**Counsel**: You weren't watching the road, were you?
**Witness**: I was.

**Counsel**: You were trying to pick up a prostitute, weren't you?
**Witness**: No!

**Counsel**: That's something that you do quite regularly before work, isn't it?
**Witness**: I DO NOT!

Counsel has no evidence to support his allegations. Is this appropriate cross-examination?

*Answer*

No.

## Commentary

The cross-examiner must have a good faith basis before asking such a question.[38]

The cross-examiner has enormous power in asking questions. It is a power not to be abused. The rules of professional conduct prohibit the needless abuse, hectoring or harassment of a witness.[39] There is valid social policy behind such a rule, in that witnesses ought to be encouraged to come to court. Unwarranted attacks on the character of a witness will only dissuade that witness and others from coming forward. Tactically such an attack is

---

[38] *R. v. Lyttle* (2004), 180 C.C.C. (3d) 476 (S.C.C.).
[39] Manitoba and Ontario Rule 5.1-2(m).

also unwise. No judge likes to see a witness subjected to unfair character assassination. Sir David Napley provides this well-founded advice:[40]

> He should, moreover, never put questions as to character or credibility unless he believes them to be well founded or true. An advocate in a court, particularly one which is conducted in public, is in a unique position to damage the reputation of those who perhaps cannot answer for themselves and it is right that he should carefully ensure that nothing which he does is directed to causing difficulties for others or damage to their reputation. The power which he has in this regard is one which he must exercise with a due sense of responsibility . . .
>
> In order to put matters in cross-examination, it is not essential that the advocate should be able to prove by affirmative evidence the allegations which he is putting . . . he must satisfy himself that no reason exists for believing that they are intended only to attack the character of the witness, and that there is good reason to believe they are well founded or true. Courtesy should be the handmaiden of good advocacy.

In the problem posed, the witness may suffer serious harm because of the aspersions raised by counsel. He has a responsible position and is a family man. The allegations raised portray a person who is irresponsible and who cheats on his wife. The role of counsel is not to win the case at all costs and the human cost here is too high.

---

## Problem 10 — Communicating with Represented Party

You have had difficulty dealing with an opposing lawyer. He has been most unreasonable. You are confident that if you could talk to the client directly the matter could be resolved quickly. Should you?

**Answer**

No.

---

**Commentary**

Rule 7.2-6 applies:

---

[40] Napley, *supra*, note 27, at pp. 77-78.

Subject to rules 7.2-6A and 7.2-7, if a person is represented by a lawyer in respect of a matter, another lawyer must not, except through or with the consent of the person's lawyer:

(a) approach, communicate or deal with the person on the matter; or

(b) attempt to negotiate or compromise the matter directly with the person.

Counsel are retained to give advice and protection to a party, to advise the party against unwise settlements or concessions and to protect the party against unwise admissions. The non-communication rule prevents a lawyer from nullifying the protection a represented person has achieved by retaining counsel.[41]

## Conclusion

The above problems illustrate various ethical conflicts that may confront a trial lawyer. Some are obvious. Many are not. What is important is that counsel, especially new counsel starting out on their careers, familiarize themselves with their professional responsibilities so that they realize when an ethical conflict or potential ethical conflict arises. Awareness of a conflict, therefore, is the first necessary step to resolving the problem. Many ethical problems are not amenable to easy solution. Seek the counsel and wisdom of senior members of the profession. You have a professional reputation to maintain and, as a lawyer, your reputation is your most important asset.

This book concerns itself with providing new advocates with the tools of litigation. As a professional you are expected to wield these tools responsibly and with wisdom. Understanding the details of court etiquette, court procedure and court conduct, although important, are meaningless unless you have a full appreciation of the moral implications and underlying obligations of being a lawyer. Acting ethically lies at the core of your work, both as a lawyer and as a human being. Build your practice of law on a firm ethical foundation. Treat the court, opposing lawyers and witnesses as you would like to be treated — fairly. Take the advice of Polonius to heart:

> *This above all: to thine own self be true,*
> *And it must follow, as the night the day,*
> *Thou canst not then be false to any man.*

— William Shakespeare, *Hamlet*, Act I, Scene iii.

---

[41] Hazard, *supra*, note 28, at p. 434.

# APPENDIX 1

SAMPLE ANSWER TO PROBLEM ON DRAFTING PLEADINGS

*White v. John*

**Statement of Claim**

THE QUEEN'S BENCH
BIGTOWN CENTRE

BETWEEN:

MARY WHITE,                Plaintiff,

and

WILBER JOHN,

Defendant.

STATEMENT OF CLAIM

(court seal)

TO THE DEFENDANT

A LEGAL PROCEEDING HAS BEEN COMMENCED AGAINST YOU by the plaintiff. The claim made against you is set out in the following pages.

IF YOU WISH TO DEFEND THIS PROCEEDING, you or a Manitoba lawyer acting for you must prepare a statement of defence in Form 18A prescribed by the Queen's Bench Rules, serve it on the plaintiff's lawyer or, where the plaintiff does not have a lawyer, serve it on the plaintiff, and file it in this court office, WITHIN TWENTY DAYS after this statement of claim is served on you, if you are served in Manitoba.

*(cont'd)*

If you are served in another province or territory of Canada or in the United States of America, the period for serving and filing your statement of defence is forty days. If you are served outside Canada and the United States of America, the period is sixty days.

IF YOU FAIL TO DEFEND THIS PROCEEDING, JUDGMENT MAY BE GIVEN AGAINST YOU IN YOUR ABSENCE AND WITHOUT FURTHER NOTICE TO YOU.

13th September 2015                    Issued By _____
                                                              Registrar

TO: WILBER JOHN, 23 Maple Street, Smalltown, Manitoba.

1. The Plaintiff claims:

   (a) General damages;

   (b) An injunction to restrain the Defendant from continuing to publicize information about the Plaintiff's past;

   (c) Punitive damages;

   (d) Costs.

2. The Plaintiff is a homemaker and mother of three children and resides at 22 Wood Street in Smalltown, Manitoba.

3. The Defendant is an automobile salesman and resides at 23 Maple Street in Smalltown, Manitoba.

4. The Plaintiff says that the Defendant wilfully and maliciously orally publicized to the people of Smalltown, Manitoba from on or about 24th May 2015 to the present the private fact that the Plaintiff was a former prostitute in the City of Toronto some sixteen years before.

*(cont'd)*

*Particulars*

(a) On 24th May 2015 at a public dance held in Smalltown, Manitoba the Defendant publicly called the Plaintiff a "Hooker housewife."

(b) The Defendant since May of 2015 has repeatedly told other residents of Smalltown about the Plaintiff's past as a prostitute.

(c) As a consequence of the Defendant's public disclosures the Plaintiff's past is now public knowledge in Smalltown, Manitoba.

5. The Plaintiff's past was not known to her husband, family, friends and neighbours and its wrongful and malicious disclosure by the Defendant has caused the Plaintiff a great deal of distress, annoyance, embarassment, loss of respect and loss of reputation in the community of Smalltown, Manitoba.

6. The Defendant was made aware of the distress that he was causing the Plaintiff but persisted in his public disclosures.

7. As a further consequence of the Defendant's public disclosures, the Plaintiff was forced out of her job as a waitress at Mike's Restaurant in Smalltown, Manitoba.

8. The Plaintiff pleads and relies upon the provisions of *The Privacy Act* (Chapter P125 Consolidated Statutes of Manitoba).

Issued 13th September 2015 by Horace Zilch, c/o Zero, Zilch & Nothing, Barristers and Solicitors, 1900 TD Tower, 100 Portage Avenue, Bigtown, Manitoba (ph. 488-9999).

# COMMENTS ON THE STATEMENT OF CLAIM

## 1. Counselling

As plaintiff counsel, a primary consideration ought to be the "novelty" of the cause of action before you. Although public disclosure of a private fact is a recognized tort in the United States, it has not been raised in Canada. The "novelty" of the cause of action poses two concerns. First, such a claim will undoubtedly spark interest both because of its subject matter and because it is a legal precedent. Interest will lead to increased publicity, which is precisely what your client does not want. Second, because it is a case of first instance, you can expect the defendant to challenge the cause of action by way of a motion to strike the statement of claim for not disclosing a reasonable cause of action.[1] Therefore, you must counsel Mr. and Mrs. White about the publicity danger of going to trial and the uncertainty of success at trial. Let us assume that after so counselling, the Whites advise you to proceed.

## 2.   Where to Commence the Proceedings

You wish to hold the trial in Bigtown and so you file in that judicial centre. This is for your convenience and also gives some hope of anonymity within the larger court docket in Bigtown than proceeding to trial in Smalltown. You rely upon R. 14 of the Queen's Bench Rules and should the defendant seek to transfer the matter to Smalltown he can make a motion to do so under that same rule. In Ontario, the plaintiff names the place of trial in the statement of claim and the defendant, similarly, can move to transfer.[2]

## 3.   Parties to the Action

You named only Mary White. Other family members were possible plaintiffs. The choice of naming only Mary White is legally and tactically correct. Under the American precedents, the action on "privacy" is particular to the person whose privacy is lost. The tactical reason for going with Mary White alone is to keep the "novel" cause of action centred on the truly aggrieved party. The introduction of other family members diffuses the law and creates unnecessary legal hurdles with little to gain. Mr. White can still testify as to the distress caused to his wife without being made a party to the action. With respect to the children, you would never want to include them in such an action dealing with such a subject, as that would leave them open to discovery and require their testifying at trial.

---

[1]   See Manitoba Queen's Bench Rules, R. 25.11.
[2]   Ontario Rules of Civil Procedure, R. 46.

## 4.  Prayer for Relief

The statement of claim includes an injunction, which is available under *The Privacy Act*[3] in Manitoba. The general damages are not specified as to amount, but clearly indicate loss of employment as an indirect loss. The punitive damages are reinforced by the allegation that the defendant was aware of the distress he was causing the plaintiff but knowingly continued to disclose her past to the people of Smalltown. Moreover, under *The Privacy Act*, reference is made to the lack of an apology from the defendant.

## 5.  Cause of Action

The essence of the cause of action is that a "private" fact has been "publicized." The plaintiff alleges as a fact that her past prostitution was "private." "Publicizing" is a problem for her. The defendant did not formally "publicize" the fact in written form. His wrong pertains to his oral statements. One would well anticipate that this will be a defence argument. Second, the defendant may raise the "legitimate public concern" defence. Neither of these "defences" was addressed in the statement of claim — nor should they have been. Particulars of the "publicizing" were provided, partially to ward off a demand for particulars from the defendant and because "publicizing" is a conclusion, which needs a factual foundation. The paragraphs in the statement of claim were short, but were not designed to elicit admissions. Rather the statement of claim was framed to present in a strong fashion the "wrong" suffered to the plaintiff. This will then give counsel a stronger base to defend against any motion to strike the cause of action on the basis that it reveals no valid cause of action.

## 6.  Pleading *The Privacy Act*

No specific provisions in *The Privacy Act* were cited. This is because the Act itself is only eight sections long and any provisions relied upon by the plaintiff are readily identifiable.

## 7.  Malice

Malice was alleged by the plaintiff. Remember that such a state of mind is alleged without further explanation being required.

---

[3] *The Privacy Act*, R.S.M. 1987, c. P125 (also C.C.S.M., c. P125).

## Statement of Defence

---

THE QUEEN'S BENCH
BIGTOWN CENTRE

BETWEEN:

MARY WHITE,                    Plaintiff,

and

WILBER JOHN,                   Defendant.

STATEMENT OF DEFENCE

1. The defendant admits the allegations contained in paragraphs 2 and 3 of the Statement of Claim.

2. In reply to paragraph 4 of the Statement of Claim, the Defendant denies any malice on his part and denies that he publicized in any manner the fact that the Plaintiff was a former prostitute. The Defendant merely passed this information on to acquaintances in private conversation. With respect to the allegation that the Plaintiff being a former prostitute was a "private fact," the Defendant has no knowledge of that fact.

3. In the alternative, if the Plaintiff's former prostitution was a private fact and was publicized by the Defendant, which is not admitted but denied, then the Defendant did so because the matter of the Plaintiff's former prostitution was a matter of legitimate public concern and the Defendant had a right to so publicize the fact.

4. The Defendant has no knowledge of what the other people particularized in paragraph 5 of the Statement of Claim may have known about the Plaintiff's past. Further, the Defendant denies that the Plaintiff suffered any loss or damage as alleged.

*(cont'd)*

---

5. In reply to paragraph 6 of the Statement of Claim, the Defendant admits that he was contacted by the Plaintiff but that he was not made aware of any distress caused to the Plaintiff.

6. The Defendant has no knowledge of the allegations contained in paragraph 7 of the Statement of Claim.

7. The Defendant pleads and relies upon section 5 of *The Privacy Act* (Chapter P125 Consolidated Statutes of Manitoba).

8. The Defendant therefore submits that the Statement of Claim be dismissed with costs.

Filed this 30th day of September 2015 by O. Holmes, Barrister and Solicitor, 1900 Portage Avenue, Bigtown, Manitoba (944-5777).

TO:  Plaintiff's Solicitor

Mr. Horace Zilch,
c/o Zero, Zilch & Nothing,
Barristers and Solicitors,
1900 TD Tower,
100 Portage Avenue,
Bigtown, Manitoba.

## COMMENTS ON STATEMENT OF DEFENCE

### 1.   Prior to Filing the Statement of Defence

Prior to filing any statement of defence, defendant's counsel should consider two matters. First, should a motion to strike be filed and, second, is there a need for particulars. In this case I would recommend a motion to strike, as revealing no "reasonable cause of action." The allegations in the statement of claim really amount to a claim for damages because the defendant "talked about" the plaintiff and the plaintiff goes even further to restrain the defendant from continuing to "talk about" her, even though all that he says is true. A Canadian court may well be loath to find an actionable wrong in such circumstances. Mr. Justice Scollin of the Manitoba Queen's Bench, in a case dealing with the "American tort" of "false light invasion of privacy" stated:[4]

> There is no foundation whatever for claiming that from the primeval mud of the common law in force in Manitoba there has evolved the tort of "false light invasion of privacy": that concept has been fabricated in the markedly different social, constitutional and legal framework of the United States.

## 2.    The Defence

The defendant's defence is grounded in confession and avoidance. He admits to disclosing the plaintiff's past prostitution, but denies the legal wrong in so doing. His defences of (1) no publication and (2) legitimate public concern are clearly before the court. Note that the statement of defence addresses, either through a denial or statement of no knowledge, all of the *factual material* allegations contained in the statement of claim. Also, the defendant specifically relies on the defences available under *The Privacy Act* of Manitoba.

---

[4] *Parasuik v. Cdn. Newspapers Co.* (1988), 53 Man. R. (2d) 78 at 79 (Q.B.).

# APPENDIX 2

## PROBLEM CASE FILE

### *HER MAJESTY THE QUEEN*

#### *- v. -*

### *SHIRLEY MARY MORTON*

This case file involves a criminal prosecution for criminal negligence. Shirley Morton's two-year-old son died in a fire. He was alone at the time in a resort hotel room. Shirley Morton, a single mother, had left him to go and watch the fireworks, which were part of the New Year's Eve celebrations at the resort. The file is designed for two witnesses per side. The Crown must call: Constable Black, the investigating police officer, and L. Frank, a security guard at the resort. The defence must call: the accused, Shirley Morton, and her friend, Joanne Dyck. Counsel can act individually or in pairs. The trial is intended to be completed in a half day. I suggest the following time limits:

### Trial Time Frame

| | |
|---|---|
| 5 minutes | Opening |
| 20 minutes | Direct Examination Witness 1 |
| 15 minutes | Cross-Examination Witness 1 |
| 15 minutes | Direct Examination Witness 2 |
| 15 minutes | Cross-Examination Witness 2 |
| 5 minutes | Opening |
| 20 minutes | Direct Examination Witness 3 |
| 15 minutes | Cross-Examination Witness 3 |
| 15 minutes | Direct Examination Witness 4 |
| 15 minutes | Cross-Examination Witness 4 |
| 20 minutes | Plaintiff/Prosecutor Closing |
| 20 minutes | Defendant/Defence Closing |

** Limit any arguments on the admissibility of evidence. I suggest that you allow only oral submissions on objections and that you not allow any voir dire that requires the calling of witnesses. Do everything by way of oral submission.

** The statements of Shirley Morton made on January 7, 20— and on February 6, 20— have been found voluntary and Charter challenges to the admissibility of these statements have been dismissed.

** Witnesses and counsel, of necessity, must fill in gaps in the facts. However, everyone is to keep within the spirit of the facts provided and facts should not be distorted or created to destroy the situation created.

**NOTE: All years in the problem refer to plus or minus from the current year (—).**

# INDICTMENT

CANADA

PROVINCE

### *HER MAJESTY THE QUEEN*

*against*

### *SHIRLEY MARY MORTON*

1.    SHIRLEY MARY MORTON stands charged

that on or about the 1st day of January, 20— at the Village of Gull Harbour she, being the mother of William Joseph Morton, age two years, did cause the death of William Joseph Morton by criminal negligence, to wit, she failed to provide the necessaries of life to William Joseph Morton, when she was under a duty to do so, thereby showing wanton or reckless disregard for the life or safety of the said William Joseph Morton, contrary to section 220 of the Criminal Code.

Dated this 14th day of June, 20—.

John Smith
Assistant Crown Attorney and Agent for
the Attorney General

# AGREED STATEMENT OF FACTS

1) The deceased, William Joseph Morton, was born on September 7, 20-3. He died at 1:15am on January 1, 20— at Riverton Hospital in the town of Riverton. The cause of death was massive burn injury and burn trauma.

2) The deceased, William Joseph Morton, was the natural son of Shirley Mary Morton and at all material times she was solely responsible for his care and supervision.

3) Geese Harbour Resort is located 140 km north of the City of Champlain and has 150 rooms. On December 31, 20-1 the hotel had full occupancy and there were 315 registered guests.

4) Calls made from the front desk reception telephone and public address system at Geese Harbour Resort are recorded and the transcript of the relevant calls made on January 1, 20— are accepted as accurate and admitted by consent. It is accepted that the public address system was in working order. Any announcement overrides other speakers. Announcements are preceded by a loud siren type whistle, which is followed by a pause and then any announcement.

5) The ambulance arrived at Geese Harbour Resort at 00:25 and parked at the East exit of the North West Wing.

Dated at Champlain this 1st day of September, 20—.

---

Counsel for the accused, Shirley Morton

---

Counsel for the Crown

# WITNESS BACKGROUND

## Constable R. Black

Age: 30
Member of R.C.M.P. Detachment at Riverton
Member of R.C.M.P. since 20-5

## L. Frank

Age: 32
Address: Gull Harbour
Employed at Geese Harbour Resort for the past 3 years as Security Officer
Prior to that 3 years Security Officer with Brinks Ltd.

## Joanne Dyck

Age: 34
Married:
Husband: Fred Dyck
2 children, aged 7 and 11
Address: 19 Morningside Drive, Champlain
Occupation:  part-time salesperson, Walmart, St. Vital Shopping Centre
                    day-time babysitter

## Shirley Morton

Age: 28
Divorced: September, 20-1
One child: William Joseph Morton, Date of Birth: Sept. 7, 20-3
Occupation:  Fabric Assembler Western Fabrics,
                    35 Portage Ave., Champlain
                    Employed with the company for 7 years
Education:  Grade 12
Address:  22 Morningside Drive, Champlain

# POLICE INCIDENT REPORT   # 001-20—

**Incident:  Death of William Joseph Morton**
**Date:      January 1, 20—**
**Officer:   Constable R. Black # 4321**

At approximately 00:20 on January 1, 20— I received a dispatch call for an ambulance and the police to attend Geese Harbour Resort. There was a serious burn injury.

At the time of the call I was on patrol on Hwy. 8 approximately 5 km South of Gull Harbour. I arrived at Geese Harbour Resort at 00:25. I observed an ambulance and went to room 135. There I observed a severely burned infant boy. The ambulance attendants from Gull Harbour were giving the child aid. The child was being prepared for transportation to the Riverton Hospital, which is 25 km distant. The mother of the child, Shirley Morton, was not present. I asked a security officer present, L. Frank, who and where the parents were. Frank advised that there was only the mother and phoned the front desk to page her. Frank further advised me that she was at the New Year's Dance in the Resort Hall. I asked Frank to go there and get her. The mother, Mrs. Morton, arrived back at the room at 00:32 [I noted the time]. She was accompanied by Frank and a friend, Joanne Dyck.

The ambulance attendants had secured the child and were preparing to put him in the ambulance for transport to Riverton Hospital. Mrs. Morton wanted to travel in the ambulance, but the attendants advised against it. I volunteered to transport the mother to the hospital. In my opinion she was in no condition to drive. All persons in the room were asked to leave and I secured the room. The door to the room was locked. I asked Frank to make certain no one entered the room.

I then drove with Mrs. Morton to Riverton Hospital. During the drive to the hospital, Mrs. Morton was crying. My only comment to her was to reassure her that we would be arriving at Riverton as soon as possible.

Mrs. Morton was placed in the back seat of my vehicle. We left Geese Harbour Resort at 00:35 and arrived at Riverton Hospital at 00:55.

While in the police cruiser I did not initiate any conversation with Mrs. Morton. I did hear her say the following:

"Why did I leave him?"
"I knew he was restless."

"It's all my fault."

These comments she repeated over and over.

I observed the following with respect to Mrs. Morton:

- She was wearing a red sleeveless knee-length dress, black shawl and high heel black shoes.

- When she arrived at the room she had no coat. I got her coat from the room closet.

- She had been drinking. I could smell alcohol. Although she was not intoxicated, her eyes were glassy and bloodshot. She seemed somewhat confused.

- When she arrived at the room to find her son burned her reaction was strange. She did not become hysterical. She did not cry. She was very passive, quiet. It was almost like she was trying to figure out what was happening. At times she seemed not to comprehend what had happened.

- I had to repeat a number of times that she was to come with me to the hospital.

At 01:15 I was advised by the doctors that the boy had died. Friends of Mrs. Morton had arrived from the hotel and were comforting her. I was told that they intended to take Mrs. Morton home to Champlain as soon as they could. I advised them that I would like to talk to Mrs. Morton before they left, but that it could wait until she was ready.

At 01:30 I took a statement from Mrs. Joanne Dyck.

At 01:55 I spoke briefly with Mrs. Morton. She was very distraught and I decided to interview her at a later point in time.

At 02:30 I returned to Geese Harbour Resort. L. Frank, who was the security officer at the resort, had already prepared a security report and provided it to me. I followed up with further questions. I then attended to room 135. There I met Constable Stabler, who is an identification officer. Cst. Stabler was responsible for photographing and diagramming the incident scene. I noted the following:

- Room 135 is designated non-smoking. No ashtrays were visible.

- There is a kitchenette in the room with a four burner gas "Smeg" stove top. The burners light by turning the knob counter-clockwise and pressing down at the same time. However, the gas can be turned on for the burners without being ignited. In this case the burners can be ignited by a match or lighter. I tested all of the burners and all were in working order.

- There is also a cover for the stove top, made of the same counter top material. This cover was not on the stove top, but was on the counter to the left [facing] of the stove top.

- There were a number of burnt and unburnt matches on the counter-top. I counted 3 burnt matches and 9 unburnt matches along with a match box, these I collected and placed in an evidence bag.

- To the right of the stove top was a small incense candle, which had been burned.

- I had been advised by Frank that a black lacquer chair with a white cloth seat, which usually would be at the desk/table in the main sitting area, had originally been beside the stove top in the kitchen and had been moved. Frank showed me how the chair was positioned. A photograph was taken of the chair positioned as it was first observed by Frank.

I did not look through any of the personal effects or luggage in the room.

Room 135 is the last unit facing North in the North Wing of the resort. There is an exit door to the parking lot through fire doors immediately to the East of the Unit. To walk to the Hall of the Vikings, where the New Year's Dance was held, one would need to proceed West down the North Wing Corridor, through a connecting hall to the West Wing. One would then need to proceed South down the West Wing. At the end of the West Wing one turns East through a connecting hall into the Lobby, which then has entrances to the restaurant and Hall of the Vikings. I timed my walk from room 135 to the entrance of the Hall of the Vikings at 1 minute 57 seconds. I then retraced my route and timed it at 2 minutes 02 seconds.

After speaking with L. Frank, I had Frank show me where Mrs. Morton and Mrs. Dyck were standing on the balcony outside the Hall of the Vikings. The balcony is a designated smoking area and there was a sand filled ashtray in that area. I moved the ashtray inside and with a screen sifted through the sand. I found what appeared to be a marihuana cigarette butt or "roach." I placed it in a ziploc evidence bag. I was told by Frank that the ashtrays are cleaned daily.

Initial Report completed at 4:30, January 1, 20—

**Supplementary to Report:**

January 2, 20—: Ziploc evidence bag containing burned cigarette butt sent to Central Laboratory of Heath Canada for analysis.

January 7, 20—: Interview with Mrs. Morton.

January 8, 20—: Returned to Geese Harbour Resort and spoke with the manager, M. Hilton. I requested the telephone records for room 135. The in-coming and out-going calls are all recorded for billing purposes. This was provided to me. I also inquired as to records of any alcohol drinks purchased in the Hall of the Vikings on the night of December 31ˢᵗ. I was advised that all room guests use dockets. An order is given to a waiter or bartender. The order is then filled and a docket prepared with the price including GST, PST and a 15% gratuity. The docket is date and time coded in the cash register. When the drink is served, the guest then signs the docket. Mr. Hilton looked through the dockets for the evening of December 31ˢᵗ and the morning of January 1ˢᵗ. There were two dockets made out to room 135, purportedly signed by Shirley Morton. Copies were made and I was provided with the originals.

January 30, 20—: Analysis confirms that substance found in ashtray was burned marihuana. Certificate of analysis provided.

On February 3, 20—: Contacted Mrs. Morton and asked her for the name of her lawyer. Contacted lawyer, E. Greaslie, advised counsel that I would like to meet with Mrs. Morton and counsel. I advised counsel that the purpose of the meeting would be to get Mrs. Morton's consent to provide a DNA sample in order to test against the marihuana cigarette butt found on the balcony of the resort. It was my view that this evidence was pertinent to the investigation. I further advised that if I did not get Mrs. Morton's consent I would then seek to obtain a DNA warrant. It was arranged to meet at the Champlain Police Department on Friday February 6, 20—.

February 6, 20— 10:00 am: Champlain Police Department Interview Room 2, present Mr. E. Greaslie, Shirley Morton and myself. I advised Mrs. Morton and her lawyer of the marihuana cigarette butt that I had found in the ashtray and that given the information that I had received from L. Frank I had reason to believe that Mrs. Morton was smoking marihuana shortly after midnight just prior to her son's death. I further advised that if Mrs. Morton did not consent to provide a DNA sample, then I would be seeking to obtain a warrant. Following a private discussion with her counsel, it was purposed that Mrs. Morton provide a statement concerning the marihuana and that this might alleviate the need for any DNA testing. I agreed to take her statement. The statement was taken in the presence of her counsel at 10:20 and concluded at 10:35. I wrote the statement out and Mrs. Morton then read it over and signed same. The interview ended at 10:40.

File sent for Crown opinion on February 11.

February 13, 20—: Approval to charge for criminal negligence causing death received. Information laid on February 16, 20—.

# SECURITY REPORT

## GEESE HARBOUR RESORT

## DATE: January 1, 20— TIME: 02:00

## INCIDENT: Fire and Injury Room 135

**L. Frank    Security Officer, Geese Harbour Resort**

On December 31, 20-1 I was on duty at the resort. At 00:15 a.m. the fire alarm in room 135 went off. As per hotel procedure, I was immediately notified by the front desk, and I investigated the alarm. At the time I was in the Hall of the Vikings. I ran to room 135, which is the last unit on the East side of the North Wing. When I arrived outside of the room I smelled smoke. I opened the door using a master key and there in the doorway lying on the floor was a badly burned child. The child was burned all over his body. Parts of the clothing had melted onto his skin. Although he was not on fire, there was smoke coming from his person and I covered him with a blanket, which I took from the room closet. There were no other fires. The gas stove top front right burner was on high. I turned it off. There was also a chair from the reading desk moved to in front of the stove.

The boy was unconscious but breathing. Matches were on the counter near the stove. Toys were strewn about the room. I phoned the front desk and advised them to contact an ambulance, the police and to page the hotel for a doctor and the occupants of room 135. I continued to care for the boy. The ambulance arrived at around 00:25. There is an emergency responder Unit in Gull Harbour, just across the bridge to the mainland. A police officer also arrived shortly after the ambulance. The mother of the child, who I knew to be Mrs. Shirley Morton, was not present. She was paged again and I went back to the Hall of the Vikings to get her. I found her there and told her to come with me to her room. She wanted to know why, but I simply told her that she was needed.

The mother of the boy is Shirley Morton. I recognized her. The day before she had left the boy and I had been called to the room and warned her about leaving her son alone. I also observed her on the evening of December 31st dancing and drinking in the Hall of the Vikings. I remained stationed at the doorway to the banquet hall from 9:00 pm until I was contacted at 12:15. Earlier in the evening she had her son with her, but they must have returned to their room. I did not see her leave. There were a lot of people coming and going. At approximately 11:00 am she returned to the dance and she was still there when I was paged at 00:15. I took note because I had that run-in with her the day before and recall thinking about what she had done with her son.

Signed: *L. Frank*    Date: January 1, 20—

# TRANSCRIPT OF AUDIO-RECORDED STATEMENT

**Witness Statement of:**    **L. Frank**
**Address:**    **Gull Harbour**
**Date and Time:**    **January 1, 20— 2:40 a.m.**

This statement is being audio-recorded in the security office of Geese Harbour resort. Present are: Constable Black of the RCMP and security officer L. Frank.

**Q.:**    When did you first see Mrs. Morton return to the dance?
**A.:**    It was at 11:05. It certainly was well before midnight.

**Q.:**    What did Mrs. Morton do when she returned?
**A.:**    She went over to a friend. Did some dancing. I really did not watch her specifically.

**Q.:**    Was she drinking?
**A.:**    The Hotel provided free champagne for those guests who had paid for the banquet, and I did see her with a glass of champagne. She appeared to be drinking it.

**Q.:**    What did you see of Mrs. Morton prior to you leaving the Hall at 12:15?
**A.:**    At midnight there was free champagne and a bonfire was set at West Point, with fireworks over the beach. The fireworks last for about 10 minutes. I noticed that Mrs. Morton and another woman at first were watching the fireworks through the window. A few minutes later they actually went out on the balcony for a smoke. This was somewhat unusual because Mrs. Morton was wearing only a red dress and shawl and it was cold outside – minus 15 degrees. They also were standing on the far north end of the balcony in front of the restaurant. The bonfire and fireworks were to the south. They obviously wanted to be by themselves and were not overly interested in the fireworks.

**Q.:**    How did you know they were smoking?
**A.:**    I saw the embers of the cigarettes, if they were cigarettes, and saw the smoke.

**Q.:**    Where were you at this time?
**A.:**    Actually I had moved out on to the balcony, in front of the Hall of the Vikings. The entrance to the balcony is located on the South side

corner of the Hall. I would estimate that I was about 10-12 metres away from them. I didn't think too much about it. If they were smoking up, it was none of my business.

**Q.:** How long were they there?

**A.:** I can't say. I went back inside and went back to the Hall entrance. I was paged about 5 minutes later.

**Q.:** Anything else?

**A.:** Well, she clearly knew about the babysitting service. I told her the day before and there was big sign in the lobby about the babysitting. She should have stayed with her son. No excuses.

Statement concluded at 02:50 on January 1, 20—.

Taken by Constable Black RCMP Detachment Riverton.

# TRANSCRIPT OF AUDIO-RECORDED STATEMENT

**Witness Statement of:**      **Joanne Dyck**
**Address:**      **19 Morningside Drive**
**Date and Time:**      **January 1, 20— 1:30 a.m.**

This statement is being audio-recorded at the Riverton Hospital in Riverton. Present is Mrs. Joanne Dyck and myself, Constable Black RCMP.

**D:**    Do we have to do this now and here?
**B:**    If you like, we could do this at the detachment office?
**D:**    No, let's get it over with, I'd like to get back to Shirley.

**B:**    Mrs. Dyck, I understand that you are a friend of the accused?
**D:**    Yes, I've known Shirley for I guess 5 years now.

**B:**    Now you went up to Geese Harbour Resort together?
**D:**    No, not really. Our family went up on Dec. 29th. Shirley had to work, so she couldn't come up 'til the 30th of December.

**B:**    Whose idea was it to go to Geese Harbour Resort?
**D:**    It was mine. And I suggested that Shirley come because I didn't think it would be good for her to be alone for New Year's. Another friend of ours had to cancel their reservation and they were going to lose their deposit. They asked if I knew of anyone who would be interested in taking their spot for free. Shirley agreed to go in that she only had to pay for one night's accommodation, the other night already being paid for.

**B:**    Now Mrs. Dyck, you were with Shirley Morton and her son Billy on the evening of Dec. 31st? Is that correct?
**D:**    Yes.

**B:**    Would you please tell me about that evening?
**D:**    Well, Shirley and Billy and my husband and I and my two kids, we had dinner together in the main banquet hall. It was a beautiful buffet dinner, which the kids thoroughly enjoyed because they got to pick what they wanted to eat. Dinner was over about 8:30 p.m. and the hotel wanted to clean up to prepare the room for the dance that followed. We took our children back to their rooms. My husband, Fred, is not a dancer so he was off snowmobiling but was going to return for midnight.

**B:**    When did you return to the banquet hall?

**D:**     I returned at about 11:30 or so.

**B:**     What did you do with your two children?
**D:**     They stayed in the room. I put a movie on for them.

**B:**     Were you aware that babysitting was available through the hotel?
**D:**     Yes I was.

**B:**     How were you made aware?
**D:**     There was a large poster in the front foyer and we were told all about the babysitting service by a security officer the day before.

**B:**     Why did the security guard tell you that?
**D:**     Evidently someone had complained about Billy crying. Billy has tantrums. I babysit him, I know. He wants attention especially since his father left. On Thursday, the 30th, Billy was tired from the trip up from Champlain and he was fussing. Shirley had tried everything. Billy kept crying. So Shirley told Billy she was leaving and she would only come back if he stopped misbehaving. We have done this at home. We live next to each other. So Shirley left her room and came to our room. She was only going to stay for a few minutes and then go back. Well the security guard arrived and got all high and mighty about leaving children. We tried to explain, but the guard would have none of it. Do you know what the guard said to Shirley at the dance? We had heard the announcement and were leaving for the room, when the guard arrived and said, "Come with me." Shirley asked why and the guard said, and I can't believe this, the guard said, "Things happen when you leave your children alone. I warned you, lady." What an ass – pardon my language.

**B:**     Did you talk to Shirley about getting a babysitter for New Years?
**D:**     I don't really recall, I may have. The babysitting was quite expensive.

**B:**     When you left the Hall at 8:30 pm, how did Billy appear to you?
**D:**     Well he was still hyper from all of the activity going on.

**B:**     You've babysat Billy. What type of child was he?
**D:**     He was very active. He also was very agile.

**B:**     What about his sleeping?
**D:**     During the day he wasn't the greatest of sleepers. He rarely would sleep for long periods of time. But at night, once he went to sleep, he usually was gone for the night. I saw him at about 10:30 or so, I went to Shirley's room to see if she was interested in going back to

the dance. Billy was asleep then. Shirley and I talked for a few minutes. Billy never woke. Shirley wasn't sure about coming back to the dance. I then left and went back to my room.

**B**:   Did Billy watch television?

**D**:   Billy loved television.

**B**:   To your knowledge, did he know how to turn the television set on?

**D**:   Well that would depend on the TV. He certainly knew how to turn our TV on. But you always knew when Billy had the TV on because he didn't know how to adjust the volume and it would always be blaring out at us.

**B**:   When you went back to the dance was Mrs. Morton there?

**D**:   No, Shirley didn't come back to the dance until just before midnight.

**B**:   Did you hear the announcement for her to return to room 135.

**D**:   There was an announcement and everyone stopped okay, but no one really listened. People were still talking and all.

**B**:   Did you hear a second announcement for Mrs. Morton to report to room 135? This would have been around 12:30.

**D**:   Yes, Shirley heard that and her face just went white. She said she had to get back to the room and that is when the security guard arrived, just as we were leaving. Look — Shirley should not have left Billy in the room, but it was New Year's and she only came to watch the fireworks and bonfire. Give her a break, she's had a rough time. It has been a tough year for her. First her husband takes off and leaves her with Billy. Then there is the divorce. She deserved a little fun. It was me who suggested she should at least come and watch the fireworks and have a glass of champagne. The Resort provides free champagne, but not free babysitting. Shirley's a good mother and a loving mother. It is just terrible what happened. You aren't going to charge her with anything are you?

**B**:   I'm just investigating the death, that's all. Were you and Shirley drinking?

**D**:   Yes we were.

**B**:   How much did you drink?

**D**:   I had about 2 or 3 drinks.

**B**:   How much did Mrs. Morton drink?

**D**:   Probably the same, she is not a heavy drinker. She had a glass of wine with her meal and then the champagne at midnight. Neither of us were drunk if that is what you are implying.

**B**: I'm not implying anything, just trying to get information. Mrs. Dyck, do you smoke?

**D**: No.

**B**: Does Mrs. Morton smoke?

**D**: No.

**B**: I'd like to turn to what you and Mrs. Morton were doing after midnight. Tell me what you did in as much detail as possible.

**D**: The fireworks were going off and the bonfire. Shirley and I went to the window of the hall that overlooks the beach and watched. We sipped the champagne provided by the resort. We watched the fireworks until they finished. Then we sat down at a table and chatted for a time. Oh yes, we got up together to dance, there was a line-dance and we enjoy that. We went back to our seats and then we heard the announcement.

**B**: Mrs. Dyck, to be honest with you, I smelled marihuana when you and Mrs. Morton came to the hotel room. Were you smoking mari-huana? I'm not looking to charge anyone with any drug offence, but I'd like to know if you were. Were you?

**D**: No. No we weren't. And I don't have anything else to say to you. I'd like to get Shirley back home.

**B**: Well I'd like to speak to her too.

**D**: What?! She has just lost her son. Have you seen her? She is crying her eyes out. She's devastated. You have got to be kidding. Can't you talk to her in Champlain?

**B**: We'll see. Thank you, Mrs. Dyck.

Statement concluded at 1:50.

Constable Black RCMP Detachment Riverton.

# TRANSCRIPT OF AUDIO-RECORDED STATEMENT

**Witness Statement of:**      **Shirley Mary Morton**
**Address:**      **22 Morningside Drive Champlain**
**Date and Time:**      **January 7, 20— 1:45 p.m.**

**Officer Black**: Mrs. Morton, I simply want to put on record that you are aware that this interview is being audio taped?

**Mrs. Morton**: Yes.

**B**:    You consent to having this interview audio taped?
**M**:    I do.

**B**:    Mrs. Morton I want to fully advise you of your rights. You are not under arrest or detained, but I do want to advise you of the following. You are being investigated with respect to the death of your son, William. Criminal charges may be laid against you, including that of manslaughter. But I want to advise you that at this time you are not under charge. You do however have the right to retain and instruct counsel in private without delay. This means that before we proceed with our investigation you may call a lawyer. You may call any lawyer you wish or get free legal advice from duty counsel immediately. If you want to call duty counsel, we will provide you with a telephone and telephone numbers. If you wish to contact any other lawyer, a telephone and a telephone book will be provided. If you are charged with an offence, you may also apply to Legal Aid for assistance. Do you understand?
**M**:    Yes, I understand.

**B**:    Do you wish to contact a lawyer?
**M**:    No, that is not necessary. I'd like to tell you what happened.

**B**:    You are not bound to say anything, but anything you do say may/ will be taken down in writing and may be used as evidence. Do you understand?
**M**:    Yes, I understand.

**B**:    Very well. Mrs. Morton, this will confirm that this interview is taking place at the Champlain police station in interview room 7 and that you were asked to come here and are here voluntarily. Present is myself and Shirley Morton.
**M**:    Yes that is correct.

**B:**    Mrs. Morton, I am truly sorry about the death of your son and know that he was buried just two days ago, but I have to investigate his death. You understand?

**M:**    Yes.

**B:**    Please tell me what you remember about the death of your son.

**M:**    On December 31, 20-1, we were at the Geese Harbour Resort. In the evening we had dinner in one of the ballrooms along with friends. We left at around 9:00 pm and returned to our hotel room.

**B:**    How old was Billy?

**M:**    Billy was 2 years old, born on September 7, 20-3.

**B:**    Go on, what did you do next?

**M:**    I got Billy ready for bed. I put him into his favourite red sleeper and read him a story. We then snuggled. He was excited about the evening but eventually went to sleep. I watched TV. At 11:00, my mother called from Victoria to wish me a happy New Year. Trust her, she got the time changes wrong and thought she was calling me at midnight. We talked for 15 to 20 minutes. Billy slept through it all. Since he was sound asleep, at about 10 to midnight I decided to go back to the banquet hall to watch the fireworks and have a toast of champagne. Everything is such a blur. The next thing I remember is that I heard a page and the resort security guard was telling me to go back to my room.

**B:**    Did you hear an earlier announcement for you to return to your room?

**M:**    No. But Joanne and I went out on to the balcony to watch the fireworks and may have missed any earlier announcements.

**B:**    Do you smoke Mrs. Morton?

**M:**    No.

**B:**    Were you smoking that night?

**M:**    No, I told you I wasn't smoking.

**B:**    Mrs. Morton, I have to tell you that I smelled marihuana that night. Were you smoking marihuana?

**M:**    No, no I wasn't. I don't do drugs.

**B:**    What about Joanne Dyck, was she smoking marihuana? That might explain why I smelled it.

**M:**    I don't want to get Joanne into any trouble.

**B:**  I'm not looking to charge Joanne. I just want to know why I smelled marihuana that night.

**M:**  I'm not going to say.

**B:**  Okay, tell me this. Why didn't you return to the room before 12:30?

**M:**  I wish I had. I only intended to go to the hall, watch the fireworks and the bonfire. The resort was providing a free glass of champagne and I thought it would be nice to sip the champagne and watch the fireworks. I lost track of time.

**B:**  My information is that the fireworks were over at 10 past midnight, but you stayed. Why?

**M:**  I don't know. I was just talking to Joanne.

**B:**  This was outside on the balcony?

**M:**  Yes, for a time.

**B:**  Wasn't it cold? Weren't you cold?

**M:**  It was cold, but it was such a pretty scene with the bonfire and quiet overlooking the lake.

**B:**  Did Billy know how to turn the stove on in the room?

**M:**  No. I had used the stove earlier in the day, but Billy was watching television. He didn't know how.

**B:**  There is a cover for the stove top. Why didn't you put it over the burners?

**M:**  I wish I had, I just didn't think.

**B:**  I found an incense candle by the stove. Did you use it that night?

**M:**  Yes I did. I like the smell, it is soothing.

**B:**  Where would Billy have gotten the matches?

**M:**  They were kept in a cupboard high above the stove top.

**B:**  Could you have left the matches out after lighting the incense candle?

**M:**  I don't think so. I'm sure I would have put them back.

**B:**  How much had you to drink that evening?

**M:**  I only had a glass of wine and the glass of champagne at midnight — that was it.

**B:**  So if I have this right, you had only two drinks from say 7:00 pm to 12:30. Is that right?

**M**:     Yes. . .Look officer, I don't like where this questioning is going and I don't feel very well. Maybe I better speak to a lawyer.

**B**:     Very well, Mrs. Morton. I'll give you a telephone and telephone book. The time is now 2:15 and I'll leave the room.

. . .

**B**:     The time is now 2:45 pm. Did you have an opportunity to talk to a lawyer?

**M**:     Yes, and she advised me not to say anything else unless she was present. So I guess I've got nothing else to say.

**B**:     Very well, this interview is terminated. The time is 2:46 pm. Thank you, Mrs. Morton.

# WITNESS STATEMENT SHEET

**Statement of:  Mrs. Shirley Morton**
**Re:** **Investigation into the Death of Billy Morton on January 1, 20—**

**Date:**     **February 6, 20—**          **Time:  10:20 am**
**Place:**    **Champlain Police Station**

**Q.:**   Mrs. Morton, in the early morning hours of January 1, 20— I recovered a marihuana cigarette butt from the ashtray on the balcony of the Geese Harbour Resort. I have reason to believe that you were smoking that cigarette. Were you?

**A:**   Yes I was.

**Q:**   When would this have been?
**A:**   Shortly after midnight, we were watching the fireworks.

**Q:**   Mrs. Joanne Dyck was with you?
**A:**   Yes.

**Q:**   Was she smoking the marihuana with you?
**A:**   Do I have to answer that?
**Counsel:**  It is okay, answer the question.
**A:**   Yes, Joanne and I were sharing the marihuana cigarette.

**Q:**   How many marihuana cigarettes did you smoke?
**A:**   Only the one. I'm not a drug user. Joanne had the cigarette and offered it to me and it went from there.

**Q:**   Had you smoked any marihuana earlier in the evening?
**A:**   No, definitely not.

**Q:**   So, Mrs. Morton I just want to confirm that as you were watching the fireworks you and Joanne Dyck shared a marihuana cigarette.
**A:**   Yes.

**Q:**   Please read over this statement and confirm that it is correct. If there is anything incorrect please make the change and initial it.

I have read over the above statement, which was taken in the presence of my counsel, and it is accurate and correct.

Signed: *S. Morton*              Date:      February 6, 20—
Witness: *Cst. Black RCMP #4321*

# CERTIFICATE OF ANALYST

I, C.S Eye, being a person on the staff of the Department of Health duly designated prior to May 14, 1997 as an Analyst under the Food and Drugs Act, and thereby also an Analyst within the meaning of and as defined by the Narcotic Control Act, having acted under both of those enactments prior to May 14, 1997, and also duly designated under the Controlled Drugs and Substances Act, do hereby certify:

1.   That at Ottawa in the Province of Ontario on or about the 5th day of January 20— there was submitted to me from Cst. Black #4321 of the Royal Canadian Mounted Police, Riverton detachment a sealed and unopened package which bore, the following identification marks, initials, or numbers: Cst. Black, 4321 – Riverton Detachment RCMP Division 4, investigation number 001-04, death of William Morton.

2.   That I did open the said package and did remove there from a Ziploc plastic bag containing a substance from which I obtained a sample.

3.   That I duly analyzed and examined the said substance and I found it to contain a controlled drug within the meaning of the Controlled Drugs and Substances Act, to wit: cannabis marihuana.

4.   That this certificate is true to the best of my knowledge and skill.

Dated at Ottawa, Ontario this 27th day of January, 20—.

Signed:    C.S. Eye,
           Analyst - Department of Health Canada

# GEESE HARBOUR RESORT

ROOM 135
IN-COMING AND OUT-GOING TELEPHONE CALLS AND CHARGES

| DATE | TIME | TELEPHONE NUMBER | CHARGE |
|------|------|------------------|--------|
| 31/12/-1 | 23:01-23:20 | * 604 889-5655 | 00.00 |

* *Indicates in-coming call*

# GEESE HARBOUR RESORT
# TELEPHONE AND PUBLIC ADDRESS RECORDS

#275 – Security Page:
    00:15/ 01/01/—          Smoke alarm activated room 135 investigate

Room 135:
    00:17/01/01/—          Phone 911 for an ambulance. I have a badly burned child. Page for a doctor to attend room 135. No need for the fire department, there is no fire danger.

# 489-7320 – Front Desk to # 911:
    00:18/01/01/—          **Operator**: Hello, 911
                        **Caller:** Geese Harbour Resort we need an ambulance to attend to room 135. There is a badly burned child.
                        **Operator**: Ambulance is on its way. Estimated arrival in 5 minutes. Will you see that a person is available to direct the ambulance to the room?
                        **Caller**: Will do. I'll do it.
                        **Operator**: Is there any danger with respect to fire?
                        **Caller**: No.

Public Address:
    00:19/01/01/—          Attention: if there is a doctor staying at the resort, would you please attend to room 135 immediately. I repeat: if there is a doctor in the resort, please attend to room 135 in the North Wing immediately. Thank you.

Room 135:
    00:27/01/01/—          Page the guest in room 135 to attend the room immediately. The child is being readied to move to Riverton Hospital.

Public Address:
    00:28/01/01/—          Attention: Would Mrs. Morton please attend to room 135 immediately. I repeat would Mrs. Morton please attend to room 135 immediately.

## GEESE HARBOUR RESORT
## ROOM CHARGE DOCKET

Room 135
Guest: S. Morton

| Item Purchased | Charge |
|---|---|
| Glass of House White Wine | 6.00 |
| GST | .42 |
| PST | .42 |
| Gratuity | .90 |
| Total: | $7.74 |

Date: 31/ Dec / -1
Time: 19:15

Guest Signature: *S. Morton*

## GEESE HARBOUR RESORT
## ROOM CHARGE DOCKET

Room 135
Guest: S. Morton

| Item Purchased | Charge |
|---|---|
| 2 Hot Rum Toddies | 16.00 |
| GST | 1.12 |
| PST | 1.12 |
| Gratuity | 2.40 |
| Total: | 20.64 |

Date: 01/ Jan / —
Time: 00:12

Guest Signature: *S. Morton*

## EXTRACTS FROM TRANSCRIPT OF PRELIMINARY INQUIRY HELD APRIL 19, 20— PROVINCIAL JUDGES COURT, BROADWAY AVENUE, CHAMPLAIN

### HOLMES, P.C.J. presiding

### Direct Examination Constable R. Black

**Q.10:** Constable Black, what were your duties on Dec. 31, 20-1?

**A.:**   I was on general highway patrol duty that evening. And part of my responsibility was to travel down Highway No. 8 between Riverton and Gull Harbour.

. . .

**Q.13:** After receiving the dispatch call what did you do?

**A.:**   I immediately activated my lights and drove to Geese Harbour Resort.

. . . .

**Q.18:** What did you observe when you arrived at room 135?

**A.:**   I observed a badly burned infant. He was wrapped in a blanket. He was being attended to by two ambulance personnel and another individual whom I subsequently found out was L. Frank, a security officer at the resort. The boy was being prepared for transportation to Riverton by ambulance. And I advised that I was prepared to assist with that.

**Q.19:** Who else was in the room?

**A.:**   No one else. I asked where the parents were and Frank advised that the mother had been paged once. I suggested that she be paged again. Mrs. Morton did not arrive until just as the attendants were wheeling her son out of the room. I took note of the time. It was at 12:32.

**Q.20:** Officer, what did you do next?

**A.:**   As soon as the child was prepared for transportation, I checked to see that the room was empty, safe and secure. I asked for the key and locked the door.

**Q.21:** What happened next, officer?

**A.:**   There was no room in the ambulance for the mother and she was obviously intending to go the hospital as well. I had concern, because I could smell alcohol on her breath, and the friend with whom she was with, also had been drinking, and so I volunteered to take Mrs. Morton to Riverton and accompany the ambulance. I also had further concerns.

**Q.22:** Go on, officer, what were these further concerns?

**A.:** I smelled marijuana on both Mrs. Morton and the other woman, who I now know to be Joanne Dyck. I was very close to both women and it was obvious to me that neither was in any condition to drive, both emotionally and physically. I got Mrs. Morton her coat and I placed her in the back seat of the vehicle.

**Q.23:** Why did you do that, officer?

**A.:** It is standard police procedure. No unauthorized persons ride in the front of a police vehicle. That is for both the safety of the officer and the passenger. In this case she would be more secure there. We were going to speed to Riverton and I had concern about her safety. It was also the case that she may well want to be by herself, if you like, on this trip to the hospital. Her son was very badly hurt and from what I saw, it was likely that he was going to be seriously maimed or die.

**Q.24:** How long did it take you to get to the hospital?

**A.:** We arrived at the hospital at approximately 12:55 a.m.

**Q.25:** So the trip between Geese Harbour and Riverton took you some 20 minutes.

**A.:** That is correct.

**Q.26:** How did Mrs. Morton appear to you during this time in the car?

**A.:** I could see her in the rear view mirror. She was distressed, as any mother would be, she was crying. A bit dazed.

**Q.27:** Constable Black, did you come to any conclusion as to her state of sobriety?

**A.:** She certainly had been drinking but did not appear intoxicated. But once again, I detected the smell of marihuana and in my experience she exhibited some symptoms consistent with using marijuana.

**Q.28:** Officer, when you say "in your experience," what experience do you have in drug detection?

**A.:** With our detachment I am often on highway patrol. As part of our training we received instruction on the Drug Recognition Expert Protocol, which provides training to assist in detecting drug impairment. I certainly was not able to do a complete protocol that evening, but her behaviour was consistent with using marihuana.

**Q.29:** What were some of those symptoms?

**A.:** Her speech was slow, deliberate. Her eyes were glassy, partially dilated. She did not seem to respond appropriately to the situation. At times she seemed confused, disoriented.

**Q.30:** In your years of service with the RCMP, how many drug users or offenders have you either arrested or been involved with?

**A.:** Unfortunately I would say hundreds.

. . .

**Q.35:** Constable Black, during the drive to Riverton did you talk to the accused at any time?

**A.:** Yes I did.

**Q.36:** What did you say?

**A.:** I simply tried to reassure her that her son was in good hands and that we were going to the hospital as quickly as we could.

**Q.37:** Constable Black, did Mrs. Morton say anything while in the police cruiser?

**A.:** Yes. She was not talking to me, but was talking to herself. I could not hear all that she was saying, there was road noise and she was talking to herself, but I did hear her say distinctly three things.

. . .

**Cross-Examination from Preliminary Inquiry of Constable R. Black**

. . .

**Q.8:** So Constable, in the police car you never advised Mrs. Morton not to say anything?

**A.:** No, I didn't.

**Q.9:** And why didn't you?

**A.:** To my mind she was not detained, she was not under arrest. I was simply taking her to the hospital to be with her son. If she had wanted she could have left the car at any time.

**Q.**10: Did you at any time tell her that there was going to be an investigation into the death of her son?

**A.**:    No I did not.

**Q.**11: But you certainly intended to investigate, didn't you?

**A.**:    Yes I did.

. . .

**Q.**23: Cst. Black you have provided a telephone record for room 135. Did you obtain a search warrant to obtain that record?

**A.**:    No.

**Q.**24: Why not?

**A.**:    I had the consent of the resort and found no need.

**Q.**25: What about the drink dockets? Did you obtain a search warrant to obtain those?

**A.**:    No.

**Q.**26: What about the room itself? Did you get a search warrant to re-enter the room?

**A.**:    No it was an accident scene. There was no need.

. . .

# EXTRACTS FROM TRANSCRIPT
# PRELIMINARY INQUIRY APRIL 19, 20—

## Direct Examination of L. Frank

*Witness duly sworn.*

. . .

Q.7:   And how long have you worked at the Geese Harbour Resort?
A.:    I've worked there for 3 years.

Q.8:   And what were your duties?
A.:    I was in charge of the hotel's security. I watched for any illegal activity and made certain that the guests did not get too carried away.

Q.9:   And on Dec. 31st, 20-1 were you on duty?
A.:    Yes I was.

Q.11:  When did your shift start and when was it to end?
A.:    My shift started at 6:00 p.m on Dec. 31st and was to end at 2:00 a.m. on the 1st.

. . .

Q.24:  Please describe to the Court what you did on the evening of December 31st.
A.:    As part of our New Year's celebration there was a dinner and dance in the Hall of the Vikings. The dinner went from 6:00 pm to 9:00 pm, a buffet. Then the room was prepared for the dance to follow at 9:00 pm. I did my rounds of the hotel from 6:30 pm to 7:30 pm. I took my supper break at 7:30 - 8:30. From 9:00 pm on I remained at the Hall of the Vikings. Obviously that is where most of our guests would be and where the most drinking would be.

Q.:    Do you recognize Mrs. Morton?
A.:    Yes I do, that's her seated at that table.

**Counsel**: Indicating the accused.

Q.25:  Do you recall seeing Mrs. Morton that evening?
A.:    Yes, I do. Mrs. Morton was at the dance.

**Q.26:** When did you first see her?
**A.:**    That would have been at about 7:00pm. She and her son were eating.

**Q.27:** How long did they stay?
**A.:**    I don't really know. I did not see them during the early part of the dance.

**Q.28:** When did you next see Mrs. Morton?
**A.:**    That was at about 11:15 or so.

**Q.29:** Was her son with her?
**A.:**    No, and I remember thinking about that.

**Q.30:** What was Mrs. Morton doing?
**A.:**    She was at the table with another lady and they each had a glass of champagne.

**Q.31:** From 9:00 pm until you were radioed about the alarm did you leave your station?
**A.:**    I did not. I would circulate around the doorway, foyer of the Hall— that is it.

**Q.32:** Did you ever see Mrs. Morton leave the Hall of the Vikings?
**A.:**    After 11:00 pm? Yes, during the fireworks she and her friend went out on the balcony to have what appeared to be a smoke.

**Q.33:** Where were you at this time?
**A.:**    I was near the balcony doors, about 10-15 metres away from them.

**Q.34:** How do you know they were smoking?
**A.:**    Well, it is fairly obvious. You could see the glow of the cigarettes and smoke. But in all honesty, they were facing for the most part away from me.

**Q.35:** Were other people around them?
**A.:**    No, they were by themselves. It was cold outside and Mrs. Morton must have been freezing because she had on a short dress and it was cold outside, minus 10 at least.

**Q.36:** How long were they outside?
**A.:**    I don't really know. They were still outside when I was paged and left the hall.

. . .

**Q.**45:   Who was playing at the banquet?
**A.:**      Thug and the Dugs.

**Q.**46:   What type of music did they play?
**A.:**      Middle of the road, dance music.

**Q.**47:   How would you describe the sound level in the hall?
**A.:**      It was loud, not only was the band playing, but people were blowing on noise makers. It was a typical New Year's celebration.

**Q.:**      What happens when announcements are made?
**A.:**      Announcements override all other systems. So, for example, the microphones for Thug and the Dugs would go silent and the announcement would then be made. Presumably the band would stop playing.

. . .

**Q.**54:   You mentioned earlier that you recognized Mrs. Morton, why was that?
**A.:**      I had spoken to her the day before. I was summoned to room 135 at about 4:00pm. There was a complaint by the guests in the neighbouring room about a baby crying. They said the baby had been crying for an hour and they had not heard anyone else in the room. I must confess our rooms are not too soundproof. I knocked on the door and no one answered. I opened the door and found the boy by himself. He was standing in the middle of the room crying his head off. Mrs. Morton came to the room right then.

**Q.**55:   Did you have a conversation with Mrs. Morton?
**A.:**      Yes I did.

**Q.**56:   Please tell the Court what was said.
**A.:**      She said that the boy woke up early from his nap. I told her not to leave the child in the room alone. I also suggested that she use our babysitting service. She said, "At $10.00 per hour, no thanks."

**Q.**57:   Did she indicate where she had been?
**A.:**      Yes, she said that she had been just down the hall in room 107 with friends. She said to me, "What's the big deal?"

## Cross-examination of L. Frank

**Q.**19:   This is a busy time of year for the hotel, isn't it?
**A.**:     Yes, that's right.

**Q.**20:   In fact the hotel was completely full, was it not?
**A.**:     Yes, it was.

**Q.**21:   And the hotel has some about 150 rooms, doesn't it?
**A.**:     Yes, it does.

. . .

**Q.**46:   Now you say that you were on duty between 6:00 and 2:00 a.m. on
            Dec. 31st-Jan. 1st, is that right?
**A.**:     Yes.

**Q.**55:   And you said earlier that people would have to pass you to go to
            their rooms, is that correct?
**A.**:     Yes.

**Q.**56:   Now if I understand this diagram correctly, you are just outside of
            the Hall of the Vikings in the lobby area?
**A.**:     Yes, that is correct.

. . .

**Q.**60:   The washrooms, where are they?
**A.**:     They are in the hallway that goes to the West Wing to the North of
            the Restaurant.

**Q.**61:   Just one last question, the lighting in the banquet hall was turned
            down for the dance wasn't it?
**A.**:     Yes it was.

**Counsel**: Thank you, I have no further questions.

**Room 135—Photograph # 1, Kitchenette Stove Top**

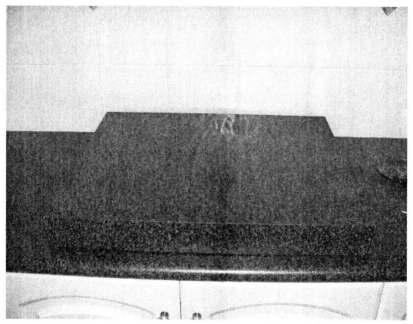

**Room 135 – Photograph # 2, Cover for Stove Top**

**Room 135 — Photograph # 3, Clothing on Floor at Base of Stove Top**

**Room 135 – Photograph # 4**

## DIAGRAM

## ROOM 135

## GEESE HARBOUR RESORT

**Prepared by: Cst. Stabler January 1, 20—**

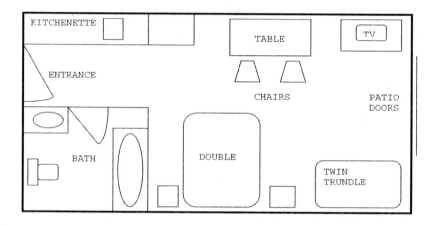

# GEESE HARBOUR RESORT

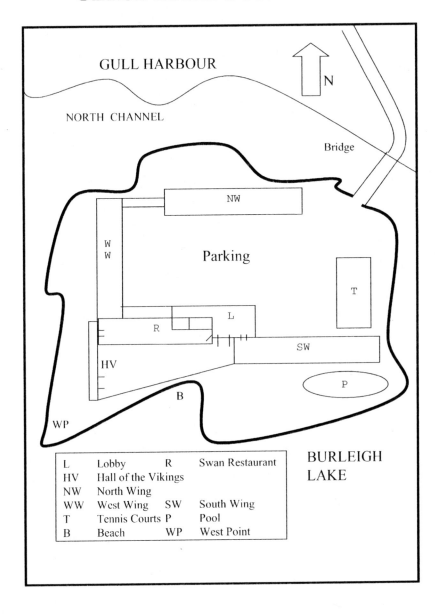

# INDEX